Digital Democracy, Social Media and Disinformation

Kruger Brentt Publishers

Digital Democracy, Social Media and Disinformation

Laura Mabel Sanchez

Kruger Brentt
Publishers
2024

Kruger Brentt Publishers UK. LTD.
Company Number 9728962

Regd. Office: 68 St Margarets Road, Edgware, Middlesex HA8 9UU

ISBN: 978-1-78715-273-1

For information on all our publications visit our website at http://krugerbrentt.com/

Preface

In an era marked by the rapid proliferation of social media platforms and their increasing impact on our daily lives, it has become imperative to scrutinize the intricate relationship between these digital landscapes and the fundamental principles of democracy. The book "Social Media and Democracy - The State of the Field, Prospects for Reform" is an exploration of the intricate interplay between the dynamic world of social media and the bedrock of democratic societies. As we stand at the intersection of technology, communication, and politics, the intention behind this collection of essays is to provide a comprehensive, critical, and timely examination of the challenges and opportunities presented by social media in the context of democracy. It brings together the perspectives of experts from various disciplines, delving into the multifaceted dimensions of this complex relationship.

The book comprises thirteen distinct chapters, each delving into a unique aspect of the intersection between social media and democracy. From understanding the pernicious influences of misinformation, disinformation, and online propaganda to the formation of echo chambers and the deepening of political divisions, the text aims to provide an encompassing overview of the field. Moreover, it investigates the proliferation of online hate speech, the role of computational propaganda and bots, and the landscape of digital political advertising in the United States. As we traverse the digital age, we cannot escape the looming specter of misinformation, and thus, the book scrutinizes the phenomenon and the challenges inherent in its correction. Additionally, it explores the contrasting approaches to media regulation in the United States and Europe, offering a global perspective on the matter. The empirical investigation of internet platforms and content oversight takes center stage in one chapter, revealing the intricate balance between content moderation and free speech. Furthermore, we delve into the contentious debate surrounding Section 230 of the Communications Decency Act, evaluating the arguments for its amendment in managing misinformation on digital platforms. Amidst the evolving landscape of media and democracy, the book also takes a democratic perspective on transparency in the digital platform era, exploring the challenges and opportunities it presents. Finally, it concludes with an overview of the state of social media research and the avenues for further exploration in this dynamic field.

This book provides an extensive overview of the state of research in the field of social media and democracy, making it essential for academics in political science, communications, sociology, and related disciplines. Each chapter offers a deep dive into specific areas, offering a wealth of knowledge for those looking to advance their understanding of these complex issues. Policymakers seeking to understand and address the challenges posed by social media to democratic systems will find this book valuable. It offers insights into areas such as misinformation, online hate speech, and media regulation, helping them make informed decisions and propose reforms. Journalists, media executives, and communication professionals are affected by and influence the dynamics of social media in the news and information dissemination. This book provides a comprehensive understanding of the challenges and opportunities in this evolving media landscape. Professionals in the tech industry, including social media platform developers, content moderators, and data analysts, can gain valuable insights into the societal impact of their work. The chapters on computational propaganda, bots, and content oversight are particularly relevant to this audience. Individuals and organizations dedicated to promoting democratic values and social justice will benefit from the book's exploration of the impact of social media on political divisions, hate speech, and the management of misinformation. It can inform their advocacy efforts and strategies.

It serves as an educational resource for students and educators in courses related to social media, politics, and communication and it is a valuable resource for a broad audience, including policymakers, activists, media professionals, and the general public interested in understanding the implications of social media on democracy. In spite of the best efforts, it is possible that some errors may have occurred into the compilation and editing of the book. Further queries, constructive suggestions and criticisms for the improvement of the book are always welcome and shall be thankfully acknowledged.

Laura Mabel Sanchez

Contents

01 INTRODUCTION TO SOCIAL MEDIA AND DEMOCRACY

INTRODUCTION: AN OVERVIEW

Social media has revolutionized the way we communicate, connect, and engage with information in the 21st century. In this digital age, platforms like Facebook, Twitter, and Instagram have become powerful tools for individuals to express their opinions, share ideas, and mobilize for various causes. While the impact of social media on society is multifaceted, one of its most significant implications lies in its role within the realm of democracy. Social media has the potential to both enhance and challenge democratic processes, shaping the way information is disseminated, political discourse unfolds, and citizen engagement evolves. This introductory paragraph will delve into the complex relationship between social media and democracy, shedding light on how these digital networks have transformed the landscape of modern politics and civic participation.

EFFECTS OF SOCIAL MEDIA ON DEMOCRACY

The effects of social media on democracy are profound and multifaceted. On one hand, these platforms have the potential to enhance democracy by increasing access to information, facilitating political engagement, and giving a voice to marginalized communities. They enable citizens to stay informed about political developments, connect with like-minded individuals, and organize grassroots movements more easily than ever before. Social media also provides a space for political transparency, where public figures and institutions are held accountable by an engaged and watchful online audience. However, on the other hand, the impact of social media on democracy is not without its challenges. The spread of misinformation, the creation of echo chambers, and the rise of algorithmic biases can all contribute to the erosion of trust in institutions and the polarization of public discourse. Social media platforms can be manipulated for disinformation campaigns, amplifying divisive content and undermining the integrity of elections. Moreover, concerns about privacy and data security have arisen, as the collection and use of user data by these platforms have raised ethical and regulatory questions. In sum, the effects of social media on democracy are a double-edged sword, offering both opportunities and risks that demand careful consideration in our rapidly evolving digital age.

Widespread concern about the effects of social media on democracy has led to an explosion in research over the last five years. This research comes from disparate corners of academia: departments of political science, psychology, law, communication, economics, and computer science, alongside new initiatives in data science and even artificial intelligence. A new field is forming, and it is time to take stock of what we know, what we need to know, and how we might find it out. That is the purpose of this book. Of course, research on the impact of technology, in general, and the Internet, in particular, on democracy is not new. The early utopianism of the Internet proffered a theory of "liberation technology" – a mode of unimpeded, transnational communication that would disrupt authoritarian regimes and promote freedom around the world. Similarly, research exists on the impact of this new technology focused on phenomena such as small donor fundraising, online community building, and the subversive use of the Internet in protests and campaigns, in both democratic and nondemocratic regimes. However, early research was scant and far from systematic, as it tended to rely on studies of blogs or individual campaigns. Yet, to the extent the research hinted at some normative argument as to the Internet's potential, it largely pointed in a prodemocratic direction.

The 2016 presidential election in the United States and, to a lesser extent, the Brexit referendum earlier that year in the United Kingdom, changed the received wisdom. Looking for an explanation for those surprising results, many turned to the new technology of political communication. Blame was (and continues to be) cast on bots, foreign election interference, online disinformation, targeted ads, echo chambers, and related phenomena. Indeed, since 2016, analysis of any election, social movement, populist victory, or instance of political violence will almost inevitably include some assessment of the role of new technology in determining winners and losers.

As conventional wisdom concerning the effect of the Internet on democracy abruptly shifted, so too did much of the research. That shift was not uniform; in fact, one might say that two camps have emerged. The first emphasizes the rise of social media echo chambers, fake news, hate speech, "computational propaganda," authoritarian governments' online targeting of opponents, threats to journalism, and foreign election interference. The other school challenges the independent significance of the shift in technology (as opposed to other sociological factors) while also suggesting that the magnitude and prevalence of the alleged technology-related problems are overblown.

The goal of this book is to synthesize the existing research on social media and democracy. We present reviews of the literature on disinformation, polarization, echo chambers, hate speech, bots, political advertising, and new media. In addition, we canvass the literature on reform proposals to address the widely perceived threats to democracy. We seek to examine the current state of knowledge on social media and democracy, to identify the many knowledge gaps and obstacles to research in this area, and to chart a course for future research. We hope to advocate for this new field of study and to suggest that universities, foundations, private firms, and governments should commit to funding and supporting this research.

We have also made a deliberate choice, which might be jarring to some readers, to include both scientific analysis and policy discussion in a single volume. We made this choice consciously because we worry that the policy community and the scientific community are not speaking to one another enough. We are concerned that reliance on untested conventional wisdom based on folk theories of technology's impact on democracy is leading to misguided reform proposals that may even worsen the problems they are attempting to solve. Conversely, we think the academics studying online harms are often uninformed about the legal regime in which the internet platforms operate. Rules relating to content moderation, antitrust, political advertising, and other domains of online speech structure the environment in which the alleged online harms of disinformation, polarization, and hate speech manifest. Social scientists need to appreciate the policy context, and policymakers need to understand the current state of knowledge regarding the harms they seek to manage through legislation and regulation.

We should also emphasize that the development of this field has become even more urgent as the Covid-19 pandemic further transforms the online information ecosystem. We undertook the research for this book in the year before the pandemic hit, but the topic has only grown in significance since then. Concerns about Covid-19–related disinformation, as well as how the platforms and governments have responded, have only increased as a result of the pandemic. Forced to stay at home, the mass public has, if anything, become even more dependent on platforms, such as Facebook, Google, and now Zoom, for information and communication services. As we write this, the platforms appear to be taking extraordinary measures against online speech deemed dangerous to public health and safety, but it remains to be seen whether the Covid-specific responses represent a new normal in regulation of disinformation. Either way, the need for empirically grounded understandings of the changing dynamics of online communication to inform public policy in this arena has become, if anything, even more important.

SUMMARY

This book should be read with the goal in mind of providing an empirical foundation for sound public policy. The first half of the volume contains literature reviews on the central empirical questions surrounding social media and democracy: disinformation, polarization/echo chambers, hate speech, political advertising, bots/computational propaganda, and the changing landscape for journalism and mass media. The second half surveys reform proposals for both the platforms and governments: measures to correct misinformation, reforms of intermediary liability rules for platforms, comparative media regulation, and transparency measures. To be sure, the chapters do not completely cover the landscape of either "the problem" or the potential "solutions," but we hope that the volume provides a good introduction for those interested in understanding this emerging field.

Importance of the research

Despite the limitations to data access all acknowledge, the authors in this volume present certain important insights as to the effect of new communication technologies on democracy. First and foremost, it is now beyond doubt that the way in which citizens consume information about politics – and, consequently, the way in which elites produce information for citizens – has fundamentally changed over the past decade. Moreover, the landscape of political communication is in great flux – so much so that the research presented here will need to be updated in short order as new platforms emerge, existing platforms adopt new policies, and political actors adapt to the dynamics we identify.

Second, we need to update more frequently our substantive understanding of how people are exposed to and process political information. In other words, the questions addressed in the following chapters are important if we want to understand the functioning of politics in the current moment.

Third, we find ourselves in a moment where there has been a radical transformation in the way we can actually study political activity employing both qualitative and, especially, quantitative analysis. The momentous development here has been the emergence of digital trace data – that is, digital records that are left behind from human activity that can subsequently be analyzed. Indeed, it is difficult to think of many aspects of day-to-day life that do not leave behind digital trace data given the ubiquity of smart phones and internet access – to say nothing of electronic locks, credit cards, and digitized transportation records (a feature of modern life that may become all the more important in the "contact tracing" world of Covid-19). For political science, however, the rise of social media may be the most transformative of all. For the first time in human history, we have real time records of millions – if not billions – of people as they discuss politics, share information about politics, and organize politically. Each of these actions simultaneously produces an archived, digitized record. We are also living through a period of time in which great strides have been made in how to extract information from enormous collections of electronic data generally (machine learning) and how to use statistical methods to analyze text (natural language processing and other text-as-data tools). Taken together, these developments have unlocked whole new methods of studying politics and political behaviour. Taking stock of what we can learn, have learned, and should be able to learn from these new methods of analysis is therefore important. Collectively, the research summarized in the ensuing chapters provides a window into these developments insofar as they pertain to social media and politics.

Finally, in the post-2016 US presidential election, post–Cambridge Analytic era, there has been tremendous pressure on policymakers to "do something" about many of the topics discussed in this volume. This pressure, however, presents a serious challenge in view of one of the primary conclusions of this volume: We are only scratching the surface of what we know about many of these phenomena. To present just one example, there is a great desire to design interventions to reduce the spread of fake news. Yet, if we do not know who shares fake news, why they share fake news, or even whether they are sharing fake news because they think it is true or, instead, because they agree with it ideologically and do not care if it is fake, how can we design appropriate policy to reduce its spread? Moreover, if we do not know the effects of exposure to fake news, then we cannot know the "benefits" of reducing exposure to it. Because everyone recognizes the potential harms of empowering companies, such as Facebook and Google, to be "arbiters of truth," the benefits of reducing exposure to fake news must be considerable to justify ceding that kind of power over the speech marketplace to profit-maximizing American companies. Thus, the kind of research that we report throughout this volume has a crucial role to play in informing policy decision-making. We hope that by gathering so much of it in one place, we can make it accessible for policymakers considering reform options. We also hope that by candidly expressing how little we know about the dynamics of social media and democracy in some domains, we issue a note of caution to reformers seeking, hastily and prematurely, "to do something or anything" before we understand the nature of the problems that need solving.

02 UNDERSTANDING OF MISINFORMATION, DISINFORMATION, AND ONLINE PROPAGANDA

INTRODUCTION: AN OVERVIEW

To grasp the significance of misinformation, disinformation, and online propaganda, it is essential to understand their distinct characteristics. Misinformation refers to false or misleading information that is disseminated without an intent to deceive. It can often be the result of honest mistakes, misinterpretation, or the rapid spread of unverified claims. Disinformation, on the other hand, is intentionally false or misleading information created and shared with the purpose of deceiving or manipulating people. It's a deliberate and harmful form of misinformation. Online propaganda involves the systematic spread of information or narratives, often with a biased or political agenda, aiming to influence public opinion, sow discord, or promote a particular ideology. These three phenomena have gained prominence in the digital age, thanks to the rapid dissemination capabilities of the internet and social media, and they pose significant challenges to the integrity of information and public discourse. Understanding these concepts is crucial in navigating the modern information landscape and addressing the associated risks to society.

Not long ago, the rise of social media inspired great optimism about its potential for flattening access to economic and political opportunity, enabling collective action, and facilitating new forms of expression. Its increasingly widespread use ushered in a wave of commentary and scholarship seeking to meld well- established bodies of knowledge on mass media, economics, and social movements with the affordances of this new communication technology. Several political upheavals and an election later, the outlook in both the popular press and scholarly discussions is decidedly less optimistic. Facebook and Twitter are more likely to be discussed as incubators of "fake news" and propaganda than as tools for empowerment and social change. The resulting research focus has changed, too, with scholars looking to earlier literatures on misperceptions and persuasion for insight into the challenges of the present.

The terms "misinformation," "disinformation," and "propaganda" are sometimes used interchangeably, with shifting and overlapping definitions. All three concern false or misleading messages spread under the guise of informative content, whether in the form of elite communication, online messages, advertising, or published articles. For the purposes of this chapter, we define misinformation as constituting a claim that contradicts or distorts common understandings of verifiable facts. This is distinct conceptually from rumours or conspiracy theories, whose definitions do not hinge on the truth value of the claims being made. Instead, rumours are understood as claims whose power arises from social transmission itself (Berinsky 2015). Conspiracy theories have specific characteristics, such as the belief that a hidden group of powerful individuals exerts control over some aspect of society (Sunstein and Vermeule 2009).

This project received funding for Benjamin A. Lyons' time from the European Research Council (ERC) under the European Union's Horizon 2020 research and innovation program (grant agreement No. 682758).

Misinformation, by contrast, is false by definition. Determining what is "false" can, of course, raise thorny epistemological issues: Virtually all our experience of the world beyond our immediate perception is mediated in some way, whether by institutions such as the media or by connections with other individuals, raising concerns about the attainability of objectively verifiable truth in any context outside of the scientific method. Empirical research thus tends to focus by necessity on claims that can be either directly verified (Is Barack Obama an American citizen? Is the election on Wednesday?) or bolstered by a reasonable consensus of appropriate experts or authorities (Did GDP increase last year?). This approach limits but does not eliminate controversy on factual matters. It implies, moreover, that unverifiable claims cannot strictly speaking be classified as misinformation.

Following Tucker et al. (2018), we define disinformation as the subset of misinformation that is deliberately propagated. This is a question of intent: Disinformation is meant to deceive, while misinformation may be inadvertent or unintentional. Proving intent can sometimes be more difficult than proving whether something is true, but, practically speaking, organized attempts to propagate misinformation by political actors – whether domestic or foreign – are typically thought of as disinformation. Another type of disinformation is the false content known as "fake news," or deliberately misleading articles designed to mimic the look of actual articles from established news organizations. Finally, Tucker et al.

(2018) define propaganda as information that can be true but is used to "disparage opposing viewpoints." In this chapter, we will refer to any communications that are intended to persuade people to support one political group over another as propaganda.

The research literature on misinformation, disinformation, and propaganda is vast and sprawling. This chapter will focus on empirical findings that focus on the production, supply, consumption, and dissemination of these materials online. While the spread of various forms of dubious and misleading content is closely related to important phenomena such as political polarization, incivility, hate speech, trolls, and bots, this chapter will not cover them in depth. In addition, research on efforts to correct misinformation and rumorsis covered in Chapter 8 in this volume.

We will focus, instead, on two main types of findings: First, we discuss descriptive research on various types of misinformation and propaganda. This covers the supply and availability of misinformation, patterns of exposure and consumption, and what is known about mechanisms behind its spread through networks. One theme of this chapter is that, while social science research traditionally places a premium on causal identification of effects – appropriately so, given the task of evaluating falsifiable hypotheses – the state of knowledge about social media and misinformation is unsettled enough that assembling basic descriptive data remains a valuable and pressing task. This is true for at least two reasons. First, both the experience of social media and its effects are likely to be highly heterogeneous, raising questions about the generalizability of experimental estimates. Second, the most informative data are often proprietary and unavailable to the public, leaving researchers to make assumptions about the overall landscape about which they are testing counterfactual propositions.

These descriptive findings contextualize and inform the nascent literature on the effects of exposure to online misinformation. Owing to practical and ethical restrictions, such research is necessarily conducted in artificial settings, often with convenience samples, but it provides an opportunity to check intuitions about the hypothetical effects of content such as fake news stories seen on Facebook. Combining estimates of effect size with what is known about the spread and prevalence of similar content during specific time periods, it might be possible to check intuitions about its role in real-world outcomes. In these experiments, the dependent variables that are typically studied relate either to beliefs about the claims made (i.e., misperceptions) or to behaviours ranging from sharing and engagement on social media to voter turnout and vote choice. In the following section, we provide a brief overview of the literature on misinformation in political science and psychology, which provides a basis for understanding the phenomena discussed in this chapter. We then turn to what we know about the production of disinformation and the supply and availability of misinformation more broadly online. We then focus on the consumption side, with a section on exposure and its correlates on the individual level. One important factor determining exposure is how misinformation is spread and disseminated, which we cover next. The penultimate section looks at what we know about the effects of misinformation and how it is studied. We conclude with a discussion of gaps in our knowledge and future directions in research in this area.

MISINFORMATION AND MISPERCEPTIONS

The misinformation literature in political science can be said to begin with the canonical study by Kuklinski et al. (2000). Over two experiments, the authors demonstrated that subjects tend to hold incorrect beliefs about various aspects of welfare policy, such as the portion of the federal budget dedicated to welfare programs and the percentage of recipients who are African American. These beliefs were related to policy views; moreover, the misinformed were more likely to be confident in their beliefs than the correctly informed. This study was among the first to explore the link between misinformation and misperceptions, that is, people with incorrect (rather than nonexistent) factual beliefs.

This strand of research was picked up a few years later as real-world developments suggested the possibility that large portions of the public were misinformed about basic factual matters. When surveys showed that Republicans were substantially more likely to believe that there were weapons of mass destruction in Iraq, even after the administration had abandoned that rationale, scholars took note (Shapiro and Bloch-Elkon 2006; Jacobson 2010).

Similarly, as commentators and conservative websites raised the specter of "death panels" during the debate on health reform, analysts noticed that the belief was hardest to dislodge among those who considered themselves the most knowledgeable (Nyhan 2010). As these two examples illustrated, not only did misperceptions seem to be commonly held but they sometimes seemed to originate from concerted efforts to persuade people of those beliefs. Perhaps as a result of the political nature of those efforts, the misinformed views were not evenly distributed across the population: They were concentrated among partisans and among those with higher levels of knowledge and exposure to political discourse. This pattern has recurred repeatedly, as in the Obama Muslim myth.

These findings should come as no surprise to those familiar with the well-developed literature on partisan bias, which can be traced back to at least The American Voter (Campbell et al. 1960) and explores the extent to which "perceptual screens" color individuals' beliefs about objective facts such as the state of the economy (Achen and Bartels 2017). Today, such phenomena tend to be examined within the framework of motivated reasoning, which views partisan gaps in attitudes and factual beliefs as a function of protective mechanisms such as confirmation bias and selective avoidance (Taber and Lodge 2006; Flynn, Nyhan, and Reifler 2017). What distinguishes much of the later research on misinformation is its focus on misperceptions in factual beliefs and their effect on opinion – rather than the effects of partisan or other commitments on factual beliefs.

This focus on the effects of misinformation, particularly on attitudes and opinions, led to a neglect in basic research on the prevalence, supply, and spread of this content, particularly on social media. As public polls remind us every day, misperceptions are common; but where do they come from? Traditional approaches to mass media imply a broadcast model in which propaganda and disinformation are disseminated from the top down by governments possessing the most powerful megaphone. Today, however, misinformation originating from any number of small outlets can spread organically through existing social networks online. Who is producing it, and why? What kind of misinformation is being published, and what are the processes by which it is shared by individuals?

Production of Disinformation

Because of the nature of disinformation, inquiry into its producers has been limited; those who intend to mislead others also tend to mask their identity.[1] Scholarship addressing producers has focused on a few key groups that have distorted the information ecosystem in recent years. These include Macedonian teenagers publishing pro-Trump fake news during the 2016 election, the Internet Research Agency's Russian "troll farm," and collaborative anonymous networks such as those found on forums like 4chan or 8chan. Research in this area is descriptive and complements the rich work on the sociology of news production by tracking the production of its antithesis. Academic work is complemented by reports from journalists, intelligence agencies, and social media platforms themselves. Key facets revealed in this work include the identities and physical locations of much of the systematic disinformation production in recent years; motives for producing disinformation; and the nature of their organizational practices and methods of dissemination (we cover the latter in greater depth in the section "Spread and Dissemination of Misinformation"). Regardless, we are left with a still-incomplete picture because, as always, disinformation producers are a difficult group of actors to study. Further, as with other questions we discuss – supply, consumption, dissemination – our knowledge is concentrated on Western, and especially US-specific, contexts.

One group of disinformation producers that has received attention in recent years was based in Macedonia. In the town of Veles, roughly 100 pro-Trump fake news sites were registered and operated in the run-up to the 2016 election. These publications used American-sounding domains such as USADailyPolitics.com, WorldPoliticus.com, and DonaldTrumpNews.com. Our knowledge about the Macedonian case is largely drawn from journalistic accounts, such as those published in Wired (Subramanian 2017), BBC News (Kirby 2016), and BuzzFeed News (Silverman and Alexander 2016). Notably, these reports suggest that the motive behind most of the pro-Trump fake news publication in 2016 was profit (Tynan 2016): teenagers producing these stories earned up to $8,000 per month (twenty times the typical wage in Veles during this time period).2 Because these producers were driven by profit rather than ideology, the preponderance of pro-Trump content in 2016 was apparently driven by superior engagement metrics relative to left-leaning fake news (Bakir and McStay 2018).

Another source of disinformation that has received considerable scrutiny is Russia's Internet Research Agency (IRA), a "troll factory" propaganda effort (Bastos and Farkas 2019). The IRA came into the limelight in part due to congressional investigations into Russian meddling in the 2016 US elections. Like the Macedonian case, journalists have contributed significantly to our knowledge of the IRA via interviews with former employees. In addition, academics have conducted several analyses of IRA Twitter activity, which largely corroborate these interviews.

Journalistic accounts show that the IRA operated in an industrialized fashion, with division of labour based on geographic targets and platform Specialization (Volchek and Sindelar 2015). According to interviews, individual operators were responsible for multiple fake accounts and a high volume of expected contributions – ranging from fifty comments daily on news articles, to the maintenance of six Facebook pages with three daily posts, to the maintenance of ten Twitter accounts with at least fifty daily tweets (Dawson and Innes 2019). Workers also were reportedly given daily topics to focus onand Koreneva 2015).

Owing to congressional interest, Twitter has made publicly available datasets of accounts linked to the IRA. According to Twitter, 3,814 accounts were operated by the IRA (Twitter 2018). Analyses of the data corroborate and expand on interviews conducted by news agencies. For instance, accounts of heavy workloads and little personal investment are backed up by data showing significant messaging repetition (Dawson andInnes 2019).3 Likewise, through the analysis of metadata, Boyd et al. (2018) show that "the IRA's operations were largely unsophisticated and 'low-budget' in nature, with no serious attempts at point-of-origin obfuscation being taken" (p. 1). Activity patterns for IRA-linked accounts map directly onto standard Moscow business hours. Boyd et al. (2018) show that IRA Twitter activity displays highly different linguistic patterns than standard English-language tweets, suggesting little attention to masking their foreign origin. Descriptions of the

IRA as an assembly line are supported by studies that show Twitter handles were built into one of several groups and then used interchangeably based on strategic goals (e.g., influencing different demographic targets in the United States) and Twitter bans (Linvill et al.2019). Farkas and Bastos (2018) similarly show that the IRA maintained range of different spoofed account types for various tasks, including "openly pro-Russian profiles, local American and German news sources, pro- Trump conservatives, and Black Lives Matter activists."

Analyses of these Twitter datasets also demonstrate a range of tactics the IRA employed to influence Americans and other targets. A study by Yin et al. (2018) showed that IRA accounts shared significantly more junk news, particularly around the 2016 election, than other users but still only accounted for 6 percent of all links. These accounts also shared local news fifteen times more often than politically interested users and ninety times more than average users in an attempt to take advantage of trust in local news sources. These accounts frequently impersonated American partisans (Yin et al. 2018) but only shared disinformation around 20 percent of the time, spending the rest of the time mimicking interests and values of the social identity being spoofed (Dawson andInnes 2019), making definitive attribution as Russia-based disinformation more difficult for those exposed. Finally, there are also more nebulous groups of producers that are not geographically bound or centrally organized. For instance, Marwick and Lewis (2017) provide qualitative analysis of the communities that foster far- right extremists online, detailing the spaces where these actors convene and tactics they sometimes employ to spread disinformation. The authors argue that participatory media are key to these producers' ability to manipulate mainstream media, allowing those with fringe views to collaborate on the production and dissemination of content. First, those interested in spreading far-right ideologies and the disinformation that supports them often frequent anonymous discussion spaces such as 8chan and 4chan. Many ideological blogs and websites are also important hubs for politically motivated conspiracy theories, ranging from Info wars to The Daily Stormer. These sites constitute a network in that they link to one another and engage with each other's content. Finally, mainstream social media platforms (Twitter, Facebook, YouTube) are used by members of these groups to spread disinformation and conspiracy theories to larger numbers of people and seed topics for journalists. Producers in this broad grouping display a mix of ideological and economic motives, and some may be motivated simply by "the enjoyment they get at the expense of others" (Marwick and Lewis 2017).

Supply of Misinformation

In the academic research literature, there are very few studies that have attempted to estimate quantities related to the supply or availability of misinformation online. This is due in part to the inherent challenge of establishing a "ground truth" standard for what constitutes misinformation or subsets of interest such as fake news; contested judgments about the veracity of a subset of published articles must be used to draw inferences about the production and availability of similar content. Since not all content is shared or consumed equally (or at all), there is additionally a concern about a biased or incomplete search of the set of potential sources of misinformation. As with all research in this area, inferences about the processes behind the consumption of misinformation begin at the end, with observations of the public dissemination of particular dubious content. The challenge is to move backwards through multiple rounds of selection to begin to describe the choice environments people are confronted with in the first place.

With these challenges in mind, one approach to answering these questions is to explore the role of misinformation in the overall media ecosystem. Such studies constitute a common strand in communication research, where media ecology explores the relationship between networked actors and how they influence each other. In a major study on the role of online propaganda and disinformation in the US 2016 presidential election, Benkler, Faris, and Roberts (2018) use articles from online media sources and the links between them to conduct an analysis of the role of partisanship and disinformation in the coverage of the candidates and issues during the campaign. They find, first, that there seems to be a connection between a strong partisan slant and the publishing of dubious content. Moreover, publishers often classified as "hyperpartisan," as well as those known to produce fake content, appear distinct in that their stories are shared much more often on social media. Additional research has verified the existence of a dense "fake news" ecosystem in which automated bots appear to play an important role(Hindman and Barash 2018). These findings confirm the initial reporting of Silverman (2016), whose investigations of fake news generated much of the initial journalistic and scholarly interest in the phenomenon. Beyond the importance of social media as a locus of dissemination, Benkler and colleagues find that looking at sites that were more popular on Facebook than Twitter reveals a list strikingly similar to commonly referenced fake news purveyors such as Ending the Fed, Bipartisan Report, and Western Journalism.

These characteristics of publishers provide some clues about the sources and dynamics of the online misinformation ecosystem. Yet what was the partisan lean of the stories being produced? In a study of fake news consumption behaviour, Guess, Nyhan, and Reifler (2018) estimate the proportion of stories published by fake news domains that were pro-Trump and pro-Clinton during the 2016 campaign. To obtain supply-side data, the authors use a list of "fake news" domains and scrape the text of all articles from those domains still available on the Internet Archive's Wayback Machine. Between June and the election, nearly 500,000 of such articles were published. Then, using supervised learning on a hand-coded set of articles, the authors estimate that 93.5 percent of that supply for which they could gauge slant were pro-Trump in orientation. Of course, these estimates assume that all articles from fake news domains are themselves false or dubious; this is likely not true. Nonetheless, these findings point to a large absolute number of articles being generated by these producers and a highly lopsided slant that tended to favour Donald Trump over Hillary Clinton.

In line with this finding, Benkler et al. (2018) reveal highly asymmetric patterns in the online media ecosystem. The authors argue that partisan conservative media represent a cluster that encompasses far-right, hyperpartisan, and outright fake sites as well as more mainstream conservative outlets that serve to amplify extreme and/or misleading content and fail to check factual excesses. By contrast – and like mainstream media in general – left-wing partisan media tend to be more constrained by journalistic practices and norms than their right-wing counterparts. This creates an asymmetry in the ideological valence of extremist content and misinformation that circulate on social media.

Consumption of Misinformation

Why were these articles being generated? Quite simply, there is and was demand for them. Given an increasingly fragmented media ecosystem and the power of social media gatekeepers to drive traffic, this does not necessarily mean that people are clamouring for a continuous stream of fake news. It potentially means, however, that, within a multifaceted information environment with streams of news and other distractions, misinformation – often designed to be vivid and compelling – can often command people's limited attention (and therefore clicks). That the contours and incentives of social media ranking algorithms can change drastically and without warning is well known, as the once-mighty click bait purveyors Upworthy and Demand Media discovered. Yet, within any given regime, it appears that producers of misinformation, disinformation, and fake news were able to tailor content to maximize engagement and, with it, online advertising revenue.

Both to understand how this targeting process works and to address questions about the prevalence and impact of online misinformation, it is necessary to move beyond macro-level analyses of the availability of content and how it is situated within a larger media ecosystem. To explore these demand-side dynamics more fully, a number of studies have focused on analyzing the consumption of misinformation by individuals. The simplest approach to doing so is simply to ask people in surveys whether they recall having seen, clicked on, or read a particular article, such as a fake news story in 2016. However, relying on self-reported survey measures can lead to biased conclusions due to faulty recall, social desirability concerns, and other sources of misreporting (Prior 2013; Guess 2015). These problems are likely exacerbated when eliciting responses about individual news items rather than exposure to a news source in general. Anticipating this challenge, Allcott and Gentzkow (2017) included "placebo" fake news stories – articles designed to look like "fake news" that had not actually been published – to estimate the baseline level of false recall by respondents. They found that 14 percent of respondents reported seeing the "fake fake" articles and 15 percent reported seeing the "real fake" articles. After correcting for misreporting, their estimate is that the average American adult saw and remembered slightly more than one fake news article in 2016.

Even this clever estimation approach is subject to the limitations of surveys – namely, the ability to ask only about the recall of a relatively small sample of articles. A more direct way of studying consumption patterns is to obtain web visit data, either in aggregated form from analytics firms or from individual- level tracking data. Guess, Nyhan, and Reifler (2018) collected these kinds of tracking data, linked to a national online survey, over five weeks near the end of the 2016 campaign (N = 2,525). Using lists derived from existing research, the authors estimate that approximately 27 percent of Americans were exposed to at least one fake news article – a potentially large number representing more than 65 million people in the United States. However, as a share of a broad category of "hard news" visits, the proportion is small, in the order of 2 percent. Other studies have found comparable results using aggregated traffic data from various sources. Analyzing comScore multiplatform data covering desktop and mobile visits, Nelson and Taneja (2018) find that the ratio of monthly visits to "real" news sites to fake news sites was 40 to 1. The average audience size for a fake news site in a given month was 675,000 – a far cry from the kinds of numbers generated by "engagement" metrics on social media. In another study from Microsoft Research, anonymized web visit data from Internet Explorer 11 and Edge browsers in the United States was checked against a list of fake news domains over a period from July to November 2016 (Fourney et al. 2017). In line with the other estimates, the authors find, for example, that, on a given day,0.34 percent of users sending data visited a fake news site.

How did people encounter this information? In the following section, we explore research findings on the spread and dissemination of misinformation online in general. Given the prominent role of social media in narratives about fake news, we also consider existing evidence on its prevalence on these platforms. Facebook-wide data on the prevalence and availability of misinformation are sparse, but Twitter's open application programming interface (API) allows for estimates of the amount of fake news a typical user may have seen. Grinberg et al. (2019) match Twitter accounts to American voter file data and use follow patterns to estimate how much of people's feeds may have contained fake news in 2016. In line with the other estimates, prevalence is low – 5 percent of political content originated from fake news sources, although due to the lack of exposure measures on Twitter this fraction constitutes potential exposure to online misinformation. Although, as we discuss in the next section, Facebook appears to be much more powerful as a dissemination mechanism for misinformation, these results from Twitter are still striking. While about double the Guess, Nyhan, and Reifler (2018) estimate, it is on the same order of magnitude and much lower than data from shares would imply; and the findings do not appear to be an outlier: According to a study from the Polito scope Project, 4,888 out of 60 million tweets (less than 0.01 percent) during the French presidential election in 2017 contained a link to a story determined by online fact- checkers to be false.

If these empirical findings seem at odds with popular narratives about fake news and online misinformation, it may be because the averages obscure another recurring finding: the highly skewed nature of consumption patterns. This can be illustrated in multiple ways. Looking specifically at fake news articles with a clear pro-Trump slant, Guess, Nyhan and Reifler find in their web consumption data that more than 40 percent of Trump supporters (as determined by the linked survey data) read at least one article, compared to less than 15 percent of Clinton supporters. Even more striking is that, when respondents are grouped according to the overall ideological lean of their news consumption habits, more than65 percent in the most conservative decile visited at least one fake news website. Grinberg and colleagues similarly find that 1 percent of Twitter users in their sample accounted for roughly 80 percent of the potential fake news exposures that they identified. Regardless of the data or approach, it appears that fake news consumption is relatively rare but highly concentrated among key subgroups.

In Europe, it appears that there is a similar story. Evidence so far suggests that the reach of fake news sites was limited: Using analytics data from comScore and CrowdTangle, Fletcher et al. (2018) found that their sample of fake news sites in France and Italy had an average monthly reach of 3.5 percent. (For comparison, that number for the major newspaper Le Figaro was22.3 percent and for La Repubblica it was 50.9 percent.) People also spentless time on these sites than on news sites. Interestingly, they found that, despite these consumption figures, social media engagement metrics for a subset of these fake news sites approached or even exceeded those of "real" news sites. This suggests another explanation for the divergence between consumption figures and perceptions of widespread dissemination: A small fraction of both producers and consumers of fake news can generate the vast bulk of online engagement, even if most people never encounter it. Similarly, in an analysis of junk news during the EU parliamentary elections in 2019, Marchal et al. (n.d.) show that less than 4 percent of EU-related news links circulating on Twitter during this time were from disreputable sources. Notably, though, the Polish Twitter sphere stood out with junk news comprising 21 percent of traffic. Still,just as Fletcher et al. (2018) found, individual stories from these outlets often surpassed traditional news engagement metrics on Facebook. The most "successful" junk news stories were found to center on populist, anti-immigration, and Islamophobic themes.

In sum, the consumption of various forms of online misinformation at the individual level is relatively limited as a share of people's overall information diets, on average. However, this can mask differences between subgroups; people with strongly partisan news consumption habits may be much more likely to encounter and consume pro-attitudinal misinformation. Given the heterogeneity and skew of the prevalence of misinformation online, it is important to be cautious about making generalizations on the basis of highly aggregated data and "engagement" metrics, which can be difficult to interpret and whose magnitudes can be misleading.

THE SPREAD AND CIRCULATION OF FALSE INFORMATION

How does misinformation spread online? Researchers have most often tried to address this question by turning to Twitter and analyzing retweet networks for links to articles from low-credibility sources or for content found by fact- checkers to be false (Shao et al. 2018; Vosoughi et al. 2018). By analyzing these networks, this body of work identifies key actors in online diffusion. Some of these studies have identified an amplifying role for social bots in these online networks (Bessi and Ferrara 2016; Ferrara 2017; Gorwa 2017; Shao et al. 2017). Using the Botometer machine-learning algorithm to detect social bots, for instance, Shao et al. (2017) find that relatively few users – likely bots – account for a great deal of the traffic surrounding pieces of misinformation. These bots work to spread misinformation with specific strategies. First, they amplify false content in the early stages of dissemination, prior to achieving organic spread. Second, bots single out influential accounts, trying to leverage their influence by gaining their attention through replies and mentions. These studies find that people retweet bots just as much as other humans, suggesting the strategies are at least in part effective.

In addition to social bots, Andrews et al. (2016) identify "breaking news" sites as key propagators of misinformation on Twitter. Twitter users attribute trust to these accounts that mimic legitimate news sources and have an air of authority. This allows "breaking news" sites to build large, credulous follower bases, to which they broadcast misinformation in a definitive tone. In other words, a combination of social media users' psychology – how they attribute credibility – and platform affordances can help spread misinformation.

Aside from key actors, then, other mechanisms of diffusion include a mix of biases – cognitive, social, and algorithmic (Shao et al. 2017). Information diffusion tends to be bounded by limited attention resources; information disseminated during an "attention burst" – a period of demand for a given topic – is more likely to gain traction (Ciampaglia, Flammini, and Menczer 2015). Beyond these basic cognitive constraints, social media users are often embedded in homogeneous clusters, mixed findings on echo chambers notwithstanding (Guess, Lyons et al. 2018). These network configurations can encourage exposure to and dissemination of agreeable misinformation (Del Vicario, Bessi, and Zollo 2016; Shin et al. 2017). Likewise, social media users place a great amount of trust in their close friends. When it comes to expressing trust in news shared on Facebook, for example, research suggests the person who shared it matters more than the news organization that produced it (American Press Institute 2017). Users are more likely to think news is accurate and well-balanced when it is shared by someone they trust, which may encourage the spread of misinformation, especially because platforms surface these close friends' posts in the name of engagement. Algorithmic bias, then, arises from the design of most social media platforms that prioritizeengagement, favouring popular content over trustworthy content in users' feeds (Ciampaglia et al. 2018).

Much of the research on dissemination and spread lacks individual-level data, limiting the kinds of conclusions that can be made about the types of people who are more likely to share online misinformation. One recent exception is Guess, Nagler, and Tucker (2019), who examine the individual-level determinants of fake news sharing behaviour on Facebook. By combining anonymized profile data with a representative survey of Americans, they find that the most consistent predictor of sharing a fake news article to one's friends is age: Those in the oldest age groups were much more likely to post links to fake news. As the authors discuss, this observational study is not able to disentangle the mechanisms behind the age effect, but one possibility is that age is a proxy for digital media literacy, which may be related to perceptions of source credibility and therefore the likelihood of believing dubious information posted on social media. Grinberg et al. (2019) similarly find evidence for an association with age. The authors also uncover an important empirical regularity that parallels their findings on exposure: The sharing of fake news on Twitter reflects an extreme power-law pattern in which 0.1 percent of users in their sample shared 80 percent of the content.

As a useful point of comparison, several studies have examined the diffusion of accurate information alongside misinformation, thus examining patterns at a more generalizable level (while also moving beyond examinations of single cases of misinformation, such as the Haitian earthquake of 2010 [Oh, Kwon, and Rao 2010] and the Boston Marathon bombing of 2013 [Starbird et al. 2014]). "Truth and falsity spread differently," Vosoughi, Roy, and Aral (2018) find, and "factors of human judgment explain these differences." These researchers examine comprehensive data on all fact-checked rumours on Twitter from its inception in 2006 through 2017.

Falsehoods traveled farther, faster, deeper, and more broadly on Twitter during this time. Furthermore, misinformation spread virally – not simply through broadcast dynamics but through peer-to-peer processes. Importantly, false political news spread deeper and more broadly, and was more viral, than any other category of

Misinformation

Why does misinformation beat out its competitors? Contrary to expectations, characteristics of individual posters appear to play no role in falsehoods' greater velocity. Users who spread misinformation were more likely to have unverified accounts and more likely to have fewer followers and be less active on the platform (Vosoughi et al. 2018). Instead, novelty seems to be the biggest driver of misinformation's diffusion. Using topic modeling, the researchers find that pieces of misinformation that users decided to pass along offered "significantly higher information uniqueness" than other tweets they had seen in recent weeks, and, accordingly, users expressed greater surprise and disgust when passing along misinformation.

One of the key limitations of studies of diffusion is public availability of data across platforms. Most researchers therefore rely on Twitter data, overlooking how misinformation is spread on the world's largest social media site, Facebook. Del Vicario et al. (2016) fill part of this gap by scraping all posts from sixty-seven public Facebook pages – about half devoted to conspiracy theories and half to science news. Although more limited in scope, these data can serve as a Facebook-based proxy for the explorations of high- and low- quality information diffusion conducted elsewhere. For both science news and conspiracy theory pages, diffusion was primarily driven by selective exposure. In other words, users preferred one or the other, generating something approaching separate echo chambers. However, while science news typically reached a high level of diffusion quickly and tapered off, the opposite was true for conspiracy theory content – this form of misinformation spread slowly but interest increased over its lifetime. This general differential diffusion pattern is found again in the findings of Shin et al. (2018), who conducted time series analysis for seventeen political rumours that circulated on Twitter during the 2012 US election period. They find that true information exhibited a single initial spike of sharing, while false rumours periodically resurfaced, often repackaged by partisan websites as "news," and often became more extreme and exaggerated over time.

An important footnote to these findings on the prevalence of misinformation on social media is that they are based on snapshots in time. A more dynamic perspective shows how engagement with and referrals to fake news – but not other types of content – have markedly declined on Facebook since 2016 (Allcott, Gentzkow, and Yu 2018; Guess et al. 2019). This suggests that internal efforts by

Facebook to reduce the spread of misinformation on its platform may be working and illustrates the challenges of studying a "moving target" whose availability and effects are subject to algorithmic changes (Munger 2018).

In addition to Facebook, a number of venues for online misinformation remain understudied relative to the size of their user base, including Reddit, Pinterest, and, perhaps most critically, YouTube (Song and Gruzd 2017; Donzelli et al. 2018). Meanwhile, examinations of the flow of misinformation across multiple platforms (Thorson and Wells 2015; Bode and Vraga 2018) are essentially nonexistent to date. On the other hand, research on misinformation diffusion presents a number of opportunities for future work. More broadly, research into the behaviour behind sharing (and beyond digital trace data) is needed. Researchers might employ functional neuro-imaging to better understand engagement patterns, for instance, as others have for traditional news content (Scholz et al. 2017). Similarly, research to date has overlooked the potential for two-step flows of misinformation (Druckman, Levendusky, and McLain 2018): How does misinformation make the jump from online to interpersonal discussions, and what happens when it does?

Consequences of Misinformation

If misinformation can spread quickly, aided by human and technological biases, how great of a danger does it ultimately pose? How, and to what extent, does it influence those exposed? While researchers have not yet examined the flow of misinformation from online to offline discussion, they have examined the potential for it to set the agenda of legitimate news providers. By computationally analyzing a dataset of news-like content pulled from onlinesources such as Google News, Vargo, Guo, and Amazeen (2018) show that, while fake news websites are not excessively influential over the media landscape at large, they do at times set the issue agenda for partisan news sources, and partisan media were especially responsive to fake news agenda-setting in the 2016election year. Agenda-setting power matters because it influences which issues capture the public's attention.

That said, actual persuasive effects of online misinformation have been particularly difficult to study. Field experiments, which could provide clear evidence, are infeasible for ethical reasons (Gerber and Green 2012). Some studies have relied on observational data to suggest use of online media sources may drive misperceptions (Garrett 2011), but such designs may be subject to inaccurate reporting, reverse causation, or unobserved confounds. There is some evidence from survey experiments that misinformation seen online is believed (Pereira and Van Bavel 2018), particularly by partisans (however, partisans may be able to identify even agreeable headlines as fake when "blatantly inaccurate" [Pennycook and Rand 2018]), those less prone to analytic reasoning (Pennycook and Rand 2018), and those previously exposed to the misinformation (Pennycook et al. 2018). Yet these experiments require strong assumptions about homogeneous treatment effects in order to generalize to the real world; not everyone is exposed to misinformation, nor do they necessarily pay attention when they are. As an exception to these designs, Kim and Kim (2018) leverage variation in survey timing to estimate the causal effect of misinformation diffusion. They analyze data collected around a surge in the circulation of online misinformation about Obama's supposed Muslim faith, using a difference-in-differences strategy to compare belief changes over time for those responding before and after the rumour circulated. They find the rumour's diffusion increases public belief that Obama is a Muslim by 4 to 8 percentage points, although the case (occurring during the 2008 campaign) predates the rise of social media in today's information environment.

Regardless, the effects of misinformation on candidate preferences themselves and, moreover, the effects on electoral outcomes or other behaviour have yet to be reliably detected (Aral and Eckles 2019). Looking to the literature on campaign effects may be instructive here. Using a meta-analysis of forty field experiments and nine original field experiments, Kalla and Broockman (2018) show that the best estimate for the effect of campaign contact and advertising is zero. This work shows that persuasive effects are only likely to appear in rare cases, such as when a candidate takes an unusually unpopular stance and opposing campaigns invest heavily in finding persuadable cross-pressured voters. This rare exception in ad effects identified by Kalla and Brookman, however, might similarly suggest circumstances under which online misinformation is most likely to be persuasive. A disinformation campaign is most likely to be effective if it attributes especially unacceptable positions, rhetoric, or behaviour to a politician and then works to identify and target the subgroups of voters most vulnerable to persuasion (Zuiderveen Borgesius et al.2018).

In any event, the most important effects of misinformation may extend beyond direct persuasion. Media effects research more broadly suggests that exposure to fake news and other misinformation may do most of its damage in increasing cynicism and apathy while feeding extremism and affective polarization (Garrett et al. 2014; Lau et al. 2017; Tsfati and Nir 2017; Lazer et al. 2018; Suhay et al. 2018). These less obvious effects of misinformation have rarely been examined, but a study by VanDuyn and Collier (2018) shows that even the elite discourse surrounding fake news may reduce trust in the media and worsen the public's ability to accurately identify real news. These sorts of second-order effects of misinformation in the media landscape deserve a great deal more attention from researchers. The contemporary Russian model for propaganda, "the firehose of falsehood," for instance, employs rapid, continuous, and repetitive messaging across a high number of channels, while lacking a commitment to consistency

(Paul and Matthews 2016). This method seeks to confuse and overwhelm audiences; the mental fatigue and cumulative effects will be difficult but important to measure.

A Global Phenomenon

While our review has highlighted the US focus of this research area, the perils of misinformation, disinformation, and online propaganda are truly a global issue. In this section, we briefly review what is known about the dissemination of misinformation in the rest of the world – across Europe, a range of authoritarian countries, and finally democracies in the global South.

In addition to the studies of fake news' reach in Europe (Fletcher et al. 2018;Marchal et al. n.d.), scholars at the Oxford Internet Institute have published reports detailing case studies of "computational propaganda" around the world (including Brazil, Canada, China, Germany, Poland, Taiwan, Russia, Ukraine, and the United States), combining expert interviews with computational analysis of posts on a variety of social media platforms (Woolley and Howard 2017). This set of findings shows that in many political contexts social media platforms are dominated by government-organized disinformation campaigns(e.g., in Russia and Poland). Notably, these case studies find that the disinformation campaigns waged over Ukraine may be the most advanced, with manipulation efforts dating back to the early 2000s. The aggregation of the case studies, with even more cases added in the following year (Bradshaw and Howard 2018), allows comparison across authoritarian and democratic regimes. These authors find that across twenty-eight countries every authoritarian regime has targeted their own population via social media influence campaigns but only a handful targeted public user bases in othercountries. Most democracies, on the other hand, were found to target foreign publics, while their national political parties targeted domestic voters (Bradshaw and Howard 2018).

Finally, the rise of WhatsApp, and its potential to sow misinformation via its closed messaging system, has drawn interest from scholars focusing on the global South, where the messaging app is especially popular. India and Brazil, in particular, are believed to be hotbeds of WhatsApp misinformation. A handful of studies have begun to reveal the dynamics of misinformation on this unique platform and help describe the misinformation landscape in these countries more broadly. Narayanan et al. (n.d.) conducted content analysis of information shared in India in the lead-up to the 2019 election. They find that more than 25 percent of the Facebook content shared by the Bharatiya Janata Party (BJP) and a fifth of the Indian National Congress's content was classified as junk news. In a cross-platform comparison, misinformation on WhatsApp tended to be visual, while on Facebook it was more likely to take the form of links to conspiratorial or extremist news sites. Work conducted in Brazil looking at political WhatsApp group text content during the 2018 presidential campaign found that messages containing misinformation spread more quickly within groups but took longer to cross group boundaries (Resende et al. 2019). Examining attention cascades (i.e., message chains) across 120 Brazilian WhatsApp groups, Caetano et al. (2019) present complementary results: Cascades containing false information "tend to be deeper, reach more users, and last longer in political groups than in non-political groups."

Examinations of misinformation in Africa are conspicuously absent from much of this work, though recent work, for instance, has analyzed Ebola rumors on Twitter in Guinea, Liberia, and Nigeria (Oyeyemi, Gabarron, and Wynn 2014). Beyond geographic regions, however, studies of misinformation effects in the rest of the world are also lacking. In light of reports of murders resulting from false WhatsApp rumors in India (Purohit 2019), Sri Lanka (Fisher 2019), and elsewhere, the potential behavioural effects of political misinformation in these areas are particularly salient.

SUMMARY

Even though it is a relatively new area of study, the research literature on online misinformation has already generated useful evidence and insights. It is clear, for example, that the prevalence of misinformation is limited in comparison to other forms of online content and that it is highly concentrated both in the media ecosystem and among the types of people who consume it. Furthermore, while mechanisms behind the spread of misinformation, disinformation, and fake news are not yet fully understood, there is evidence that sheer novelty – rather than the falsity of the information – may play a role in people's decisions to share or forward content to their friends or followers; and, based on what we currently know, caution should be exercised when claims are made about the effects of misinformation, especially on behaviours such as voting. We suggest a focus on system-level outcomes such as trust and cynicism, which, while more difficult to identify, may be of greater long-term importance for society.

A number of gaps in our understanding remain to be explored by researchers. One is the puzzle that "engagement" metrics on social media are orders of magnitude larger than both aggregate traffic statistics and consumption datawould imply. A possible resolution to this apparent discrepancy is that some share of the already-small fraction of the population that encounters misinformation online engages with it frequently and repeatedly. This would explain the skewed patterns of both consumption and sharing and suggests the existence of a relatively small number of accounts, likely on social media (and possibly not human), that drive a vastly disproportionate share of engagement and dissemination activity (Grinberg et al. 2019). A focus on counts or averages obscures this possible reality; also, since site analytics track raw visits, this activity (perhaps by design) could drive the incentives of online publishers to produce more misinformation.

Of course, online misinformation, disinformation, and propaganda are not unique to the United States. As reflected in this chapter, much of the current evidence is from research conducted by American researchers focusing on the United States. However, there is a growing body of work focusing on the problems of online misinformation in other national contexts. Part of the reason for this imbalance is that American awareness and interest in the topic spiked after postelection narratives focused on the role of "fake news" and Russian disinformation tactics in 2016. This likely interacted with the fact that subsequent responses by US technology companies initially focused on their role in the American campaign.

That said, there is growing concern that misinformation spread via the rapid introduction of social media in developing countries, especially via mobile devices, is causing increasing social divisions and even violence. Rigorous evidence on this question does not yet exist, but understanding the mechanisms and potential interventions for stopping the spread of weaponized online propaganda intended to sow discord in contexts with less-established media institutions should be a major priority for future research. Studies should also take stock of evidence across countries so that we can begin to understand the conditions under which misinformation thrives online. What institutional, social, technological, contextual, and other factors increase the likelihood of greater dissemination of falsehoods online? Relatedly, what determines whether mainstream institutions – including media organizations but also political parties – adapt themselves to such messages or choose instead to push back against them?

Ultimately, such questions may be easier to study with access to better data. Much of the existing research cited in this chapter is designed to overcome barriers to direct observation of online misinformation and the factors correlated with its spread. For example, inferences can be drawn from samples, but, given the high degree of concentration and skew, a better understanding of key subgroups would benefit from observing behavioural data from the entire population of interest. Furthermore, while multiple studies suggest that Facebook played a more important role in driving consumption of fake news than Twitter, our best evidence comes from the open API offered by the latter. Bridging these major gaps in knowledge, potentially via privacy-preserving arrangements between academics and social platforms themselves (King and Persily 2018), will help to develop our understanding of this important and ever-evolving topic.

REFERENCES

Achen, C. H., & Bartels, L. M. (2017). Democracy for Realists: Why Elections Do Not Produce Responsive Government, Vol. 4. Princeton: Princeton University Press.

Allcott, H., & Gentzkow, M. (2017). Social media and fake news in the 2016 election. Journal of Economic Perspectives, 31(2), 211–236.

Allcott, H., Gentzkow, M., & Yu, C. (2018). Trends in the diffusion of misinformation on social media. arXiv.org. https://arxiv.org/abs/1809.05901

American Press Institute. (2017). "Who Shared It?" How Americans Decide What News to Trust on Social Media. American Press Institute report. www.americanpressinstitute.org/publications/reports/survey-research/trust-social-media/

Andrews, C., Fichet, E., Ding, Y., Spiro, E. S., & Starbird, K. (2016). Keeping up with the tweet dashians: The impact of "official" accounts on online rumouring. In Proceedings of the 19th ACM Conference on Computer-Supported Cooperative Work & Social Computing (pp. 452–465).

Aral, S., & Eckles, D. (2019). Protecting elections from social media manipulation. Science, 365(6456), 858–861. https://science.sciencemag.org/content/365/6456/858 Bakir, V., & McStay, A. (2018). Fake news and the economy of emotions: Problems,causes, solutions. Digital Journalism, 6(2), 154–175.

Bastos, M., & Farkas, J. (2019). "Donald Trump is my president!": The internet research agency propaganda machine. Social Media and Society, 5(3). https://doi.org/10.1177/2056305119865466

Benkler, Y., Faris, R., & Roberts, H. (2018). Network Propaganda: Manipulation, Disinformation, and Radicalization in American Politics. Oxford: Oxford University Press. https://books.google.com/books?id=6hhnDwAAQBAJ

Berinsky, A. J. (2015). Rumours and health care reform: Experiments in political misinformation. British Journal of Political Science, 47(2), 241–262. www.cambridge.org/core/journals/british-journal-of-political-science/article/rumors-and- health-care-reform-experiments-in-political-misinformation/8B88568CD057242D2D 97649300215CF2

Bessi, A., & Ferrara, E. (2016). Social bots distort the 2016 US presidential election online discussion. First Monday, 21(11). https://papers.ssrn.com/sol3/papers.cfm? abstract_id=2982233

Bode, L., & Vraga, E. K. (2018). Studying politics across media. Political Communication, 35(1), 1–7.

Boyd, R. L., Spangher, A., Fourney, A. et al. (2018). Characterizing the internet research agency's social media operations during the 2016 US presidential election using linguistic analyses. Working paper. http://test.adamfourney.com/papers/boyd_psyarxiv2018.pdf

Bradshaw, S., & Howard, P. N. (2018). Challenging Truth and Trust: A Global Inventory of Organized Social Media Manipulation. The Computational Propaganda Project report. http://comprop.oii.ox.ac.uk/wp-content/uploads/sites/ 93/2018/07/ct2018.pdf

Caetano, J. A., Magno, G., Gonçalves, M., Almeida, J., Marques-Neto, H. T., & Almeida, V. (2019). Characterizing attention cascades in WhatsApp groups. arXiv.org. arXiv:1905.00825

Campbell, A., Converse, P. E., Miller, W. E., & Stokes, D. E. (1960). The American Voter. Chicago: University of Chicago Press.

Ciampaglia, G. L., Flammini, A., & Menczer, F. (2015). The production of information in the attention economy. Scientific Reports, 5, 9452. https://doi.org/10.1038/srep09452

Ciampaglia, G. L., Nematzadeh, A., Menczer, F., & Flammini, A. (2018). How algorithmic popularity bias hinders or promotes quality. Scientific Reports, 8(1), 15951.

Dawson, A., & Innes, M. (2019). How Russia's Internet Research Agency built its disinformation campaign. The Political Quarterly, 90(2), 245–256.

Del Vicario, M., Bessi, A., & Zollo, F. (2016). The spreading of misinformation online. Proceedings of the National Academy of Sciences, 113(3), 554–559. https://doi.org/10.1073/pnas.1517441113

Donzelli, G., Palomba, G., Federigi, I. et al. (2018). Misinformation on vaccination: A quantitative analysis of YouTube videos. Human Vaccines & Immunotherapeutics, 14(7), 1654–1659.

Druckman, J. N., Levendusky, M. S., & McLain, A. (2018). No need to watch: How the effects of partisan media can spread via interpersonal discussions. American Journal of Political Science, 62(1), 99–112.

Farkas, J., & Bastos, M. (2018). State propaganda in the age of social media: Examining strategies of the internet research agency. In 7th European Communication Conference (ECC).

Ferrara, E. (2017). Disinformation and social bot operations in the run up to the 2017 French presidential election. Working paper. https://arxiv.org/pdf/1707.00086&gt Fisher, M. (2019). Sri Lanka blocks social media, fearing more violence. New York Times, April 21. www.nytimes.com/2019/04/21/world/asia/sri-lanka-social-media.html

Fletcher, R., Cornia, A., Graves, L., & Nielsen, R. K. (2018). Measuring the Reach of "Fake News" and Online Disinformation in Europe. Reuters Institute factsheet. Flynn, D., Nyhan, B., & Reifler, J. (2017). The nature and origins of misperceptions: Understanding false and unsupported beliefs about politics. Political Psychology,38(S1), 127–150. https://doi.org/10.1111/pops.12394

Fourney, A., Racz, M. Z., Ranade, G., Mobius, M., & Horvitz, E. (2017). Geographic and temporal trends in fake news consumption during the 2016 US presidential election. In Proceedings of the 2017 ACM on Conference on Information and Knowledge Management, vol. 17 (pp. 6–10).

Garrett, R. K. (2011). Troubling consequences of online political rumouring. Human Communication Research, 37(2), 255–274.

Garrett, R. K., Gvirsman, S. D., Johnson, B. K., Tsfati, Y., Neo, R., & Dal, A. (2014). Implications of pro-and counter attitudinal information exposure for affective polarization. Human Communication Research, 40(3), 309–332.

Gerber, A. S., & Green, D. P. (2012). Field Experiments: Design, Analysis, and Interpretation. New York: W. W. Norton.

Gorwa, R. (2017). Computational propaganda in Poland: False amplifiers and the digitalpublic sphere. Project on Computational Propaganda Working Paper Series, Oxford.

Grinberg, N., Joseph, K., Friedland, L., Swire-Thompson, B., & Lazer, D. (2019). Fakenews on Twitter during the 2016 US presidential election. Science.

Guess, A. (2015). Measure for measure: An experimental test of online political media exposure. Political Analysis, 23(1), 59–75.

Guess, A., Lyons, B., Montgomery, J., Nyhan, B., & Reifler, J. (2019). Fake News, Facebook Ads, and Misperceptions: Assessing Information Quality in the 2018 U.S. Midterm Election Campaign. Democracy Fund report. www.dartmouth.edu/~nyhan/fake-news-2018.pdf

Guess, A., Lyons, B., Nyhan, B., & Reifler, J. (2018). Avoiding the Echo Chamber about Echo Chambers: Why Selective Exposure to Like-Minded Political News Is Less Prevalent Than You Think. Knight Foundation report, February 12. https://kf-site-production.s3.amazonaws.com/media_elements/files/000/000/133/original/Topos_KF_White-Paper_Nyhan_V1.pdf

Guess, A., Nagler, J., & Tucker, J. (2019). Less than you think: Prevalence and predictors of fake news dissemination on Facebook. Science Advances, 5(1). http://advances.sciencemag.org/content/5/1/eaau4586

Guess, A., Nyhan, B., & Reifler, J. (2018). Fake News Consumption and Behaviour in the2016 US Presidential Election. Unpublished manuscript.

Hindman, M., & Barash, V. (2018). Disinformation, "Fake News" and Influence Campaigns on Twitter. Knight Foundation report, October. https://kf-site- production.s3.amazonaws.com/media_elements/files/000/000/238/original/KF-DisinformationReport-final2.pdf

Jacobson, G. C. (2010). Perception, memory, and partisan polarization on the Iraq war.Political Science Quarterly, 125(1), 31–56.

Kalla, J. L., & Broockman, D. E. (2018). The minimal persuasive effects of campaign contact in general elections: Evidence from 49 field experiments. American Political Science Review, 112(1), 148–166.

Kim, J. W., & Kim, E. (2018). Identifying the effect of online rumoring: Evidence fromcirculation of the "Obama-is-a-Muslim" myth on the Internet. Quarterly Journal of Political Science, 14(3), 293–311.

King, G., & Persily, N. (2018). A new model for industry-academic partnerships.(Current version: GaryKing.org/partnerships)Kirby, E. J. (2016). The city getting rich from fake news. BBC News, 5.

Koreneva, M. (2015). Trolling for Putin: Russia's information war explained. Yahoo. www.yahoo.com/news/trolling-putin-russias-information-war-explained-063716887.html

Kuklinski, J. H., Quirk, P. J., Jerit, J., Schwieder, D., & Rich, R. F. (2000). Misinformation and the currency of democratic citizenship. Journal of Politics, 62 (3), 790–816.

Lau, R. R., Andersen, D. J., Ditonto, T. M., Kleinberg, M. S., & Redlawsk, D. P. (2017). Effect of media environment diversity and advertising tone on information search, selective exposure, and affective polarization. Political Behaviour, 39(1), 231–255.

Lazer, D. M., Baum, M. A., Benkler, Y. et al. (2018). The science of fake news. Science,359(6380), 1094–1096.

Linvill, D. L., Boatwright, B. C., Grant, W. J., & Warren, P. L. (2019). "The Russians are hacking my brain!": Investigating Russia's internet research agency twitter tactics during the 2016 United States presidential campaign. Computers in Human Behaviour. Marchal, N., Kollanyi, B., Neudert, L.-M., & Howard, P. N. (n.d.). Junk news during the EU parliamentary elections: Lessons from a seven-language study of Twitter and Facebook.

Marwick, A., & Lewis, R. (2017). Media Manipulation and Disinformation Online. New York: Data & Society Research Institute.

Munger, K. (2018). Temporal validity in online social science. https://q-aps.princeton.edu/sites/default/files/q-aps/files/temporal_validity_kmunger.pdf Narayanan, V., Kollanyi, B., Hajela, R., Barthwal, A., Marchal, N., & Howard, P. N. (n.d.). News and information over Facebook and WhatsApp during the Indian election campaign.

Nelson, J. L., & Taneja, H. (2018). The small, disloyal fake news audience: The role of audience availability in fake news consumption. https://doi.org/10.1177/1461444818758715

Nyhan, B. (2010). Why the "death panel" myth wouldn't die: Misinformation in the health care reform debate. The Forum, 8(1).

Oh, O., Kwon, K. H., & Rao, H. R. (2010). An exploration of social media in extreme events: Rumor theory and twitter during the Haiti earthquake 2010. In ICIS (Vol. 231).

Oyeyemi, S. O., Gabarron, E., & Wynn, R. (2014). Ebola, Twitter, and misinformation: A dangerous combination? BMJ, 349, g6178.

Paul, C., & Matthews, M. (2016). The Russian "firehose of falsehood" propaganda model. RAND Corporation.

Pennycook, G., Cannon, T., & Rand, D. G. (2018). Prior exposure increases perceived accuracy of fake news. https://papers.ssrn.com/sol3/papers.cfm?abstract_id=2958246

Pennycook, G., & Rand, D. G. (2018). Lazy, not biased: Susceptibility to partisan fake news is better explained by lack of reasoning than by motivated reasoning.

Pereira, A., & Van Bavel, J. (2018). Identity concerns drive belief in fake news. PsyArXiv. https://psyarxiv.com/7vc5d/

Prior, M. (2013). The challenge of measuring media exposure: Reply to Dilliplane, Goldman, and Mutz. Political Communication, 30(4), 620–634.

Purohit, K. (2019). WhatsApp rumours have led to 30 deaths in India: Who's next? South China Morning Post, February 25. www.scmp.com/week-asia/society/article/ 2187612/whatsapp-rumours-have-led-30-deaths-india-social-media

Resende, G., Melo, P., Sousa, H. et al. (2019). (Mis)information dissemination in WhatsApp: Gathering, analyzing and countermeasures. In The World Wide Web Conference (pp. 818–828).

Scholz, C., Baek, E. C., O'Donnell, M. B., Kim, H. S., Cappella, J. N., & Falk, E. B. (2017). A neural model of valuation and information virality. Proceedings of the National Academy of Sciences, 201615259.

Shao, C., Ciampaglia, G. L., Varol, O., Flammini, A., & Menczer, F. (2017). The spread of fake news by social bots. arXiv.org preprint arXiv:1707.07592, 96–104.

Shao, C., Hui, P.-M., Wang, L. et al. (2018). Anatomy of an online misinformation network. PloS ONE, 13(4), e0196087.

Shapiro, R. Y., & Bloch-Elkon, Y. (2006). Political polarization and the rational public. Paper presented at the annual conference of the American Association for Public Opinion Research, Montreal, Canada.

Shin, J., Jian, L., Driscoll, K., & Bar, F. (2017). Political rumouring on Twitter during the 2012 US presidential election: Rumour diffusion and correction. New Media and Society, 19(8), 1214–1235. 32 Andrew M. Guess & Benjamin A. Lyons

Shin, J., Jian, L., Driscoll, K., & Bar, F. (2018). The diffusion of misinformation on social media: Temporal pattern, message, and source. Computers in Human Behaviour, 83, 278–287.

Silverman, C. (2016). This analysis shows how fake election news stories outperformed real news on Facebook, BuzzFeed News, November 16. www.buzzfeed.com/craigsilverman/viral-fake-election-news-outperformed-real-news- on-facebook?utm_term=.ohXvLeDzK#.cwwgb7EX0

Silverman, C., & Alexander, L. (2016). How teens in the Balkans are duping Trump supporters with fake news. BuzzFeed News, 3.

Silverman, C., Feder, J. L., Cvetkovska, S., & Belford, A. (2018). Macedonia's pro-Trump fake news industry had American links, and is under investigation for possible Russia ties. BuzzFeed News, 7. www.buzzfeednews.com/article/craigsilverman/american-conservatives-fake-news-macedonia-paris-wade-libert

Song, M. Y.-J., & Gruzd, A. (2017). Examining sentiments and popularity of pro-andantivaccination videos on YouTube. In Proceedings of the 8th International Conference on Social Media and Society (p. 17).

Starbird, K., Maddock, J., Orand, M., Achterman, P., & Mason, R. M. (2014). Rumors, false flags, and digital vigilantes: Misinformation on Twitter after the 2013BostonMarathon bombing. iConference 2014 Proceedings. www.ideals.illinois.edu/ handle/2142/47257

Subramanian, S. (2017). Inside the Macedonian fake-news complex. Wired, 15.

Suhay, E., Bello-Pardo, E., & Maurer, B. (2018). The polarizing effects of online partisan criticism: Evidence from two experiments. The International Journal of Press/ Politics, 23(1), 95–115.

Sunstein, C. R., & Vermeule, A. (2009). Conspiracy theories: Causes and cures. Journal of Political Philosophy, 17(2), 202–227. https://doi.org/10.1111/j.1467-9760.2008.00325.x

Taber, C. S., & Lodge, M. (2006). Motivated skepticism in the evaluation of political beliefs. American Journal of Political Science, 50(3), 755–769.

Thorson, K., & Wells, C. (2015). Curated flows: A framework for mapping media exposure in the digital age. Communication Theory, 26(3), 309–328.

Tsfati, Y., & Nir, L. (2017). Frames and reasoning: Two pathways from selective exposure to affective polarization. International Journal of Communication, 11, 22. Tucker, J., Guess, A., Barberá, P. et al. (2018). Social Media, Political Polarization, and Political Disinformation: A Review of the Scientific Literature. Hewlett Foundation report, March. https://hewlett.org/wp-content/uploads/2018/03/Social-Media-Political-Polarization-and-Political-Disinformation-Literature-Review.pdf

Twitter. (2018). Update on Twitter's review of the 2016 US election. Twitter [blog post]. Tynan, D. (2016). How Facebook powers money machines for obscure political "news" sites. The Guardian, 24.

Van Duyn, E., & Collier, J. (2018). Priming and fake news: The effects of elite discourse on evaluations of news media. Mass Communication and Society, 1–20.

Vargo, C. J., Guo, L., & Amazeen, M. A. (2018). The agenda-setting power of fake news: A big data analysis of the online media landscape from 2014 to 2016. New Media and Society, 20(5), 2028–2049.

Volchek, D., & Sindelar, D. (2015). One professional Russian troll tells all. Radio Free Europe, March 25. www.rferl.org/a/how-to-guide-russian-trolling-trolls/26919999.html

Vosoughi, S., Roy, D., & Aral, S. (2018). The spread of true and false news online. Science, 359(6380), 1146–1151. https://doi.org/10.1126/science.aap9559

Woolley, S. C., & Howard, P. N. (2017). Computational propaganda worldwide: Executive summary. Computational Propaganda Research Project, 2017–11.

Yin, L., Roscher, F., Bonneau, R., Nagler, J., & Tucker, J. A. (2018). Your Friendly Neighborhood Troll: The Internet Research Agency's Use of Local and Fake News in the 2016 US Presidential Campaign. Social Media and Political Participation Lab (SMaPP), New York University data report.

Zuiderveen Borgesius, F. J., Moller, J., Kruikemeier, S. et al. (2018). Online political micro targeting: Promises and threats for democracy. Utrecht Law Review, 14, 82.

FOOTNOTE

1. In this section, we focus on disinformation rather than misinformation writ large because "production" implies an element of intent inherent in our definition of the former.
2. Subsequent reporting has revealed apparent connections between the Macedonians who built the pro-Trump media ecosystem in Veles and a network of American and British political consultants and writers. These connections, along with alleged ties to the Russian "troll factory," are currently being investigated (Silverman et al. 2018).
3. Dawson and Innes are unique in analyzing IRA propaganda efforts in Europe as opposed to the United States.

03 SOCIAL MEDIA'S ROLE IN THE CREATION OF ECHO CHAMBERS AND THE DEEPENING OF POLITICAL DIVISIONS

INTRODUCTION: AN OVERVIEW

In the contemporary digital age, the influence of social media has become increasingly pronounced, shaping not only the way we communicate and access information but also our perceptions of the world around us. One of the most intriguing and concerning phenomena brought about by this digital revolution is the creation of echo chambers, where individuals are exposed primarily to information that aligns with their existing beliefs and values. This insular digital environment has played a pivotal role in the deepening of political divisions in societies worldwide. In this discourse, we will explore how social media platforms contribute to the formation of echo chambers and the subsequent polarization of political ideologies, shedding light on the complex interplay of technology, human behaviour, and the socio-political landscape.

The unexpected rise of populist parties and candidates across developed democracies and the recent uptick in political violence in countries such as Myanmar, Sri Lanka, and India have given urgency to the debate about the role that digital technologies and social media may be playing in exacerbating polarization and inciting extremist violence. A popular argument that is commonly put forth as an explanation linking digital technologies to political polarization is related to their ability to foster the emergence of echo chazbers where extremist ideas are amplified. Sunstein (2018), a leading proponent of this view, argues that the main characteristic of social networking sites is that they allow politically likeminded individuals to find one another. In this environment, citizens are only exposed to information that reinforces their political views and remain isolated from other individuals with opposing views, in part due to the filtering effects of ranking algorithms that generate filter bubbles (Pariser 2011)and create incentives for publishers to share clickbait and hyper-partisan content (Benkler, Faris, and Roberts 2018). The outcome of this process is a society that is increasingly segregated along partisan lines and where compromise becomes unlikely due to rising mistrust of public officials, media outlets, and ordinary citizens on the other side of the ideological spectrum.

This view is now conventional wisdom not only among academics but also in popular accounts of recent political developments. Just to give an example, former US president Barack Obama referred to this argument in an interview with David Letterman:

> If you are getting all your information off algorithms being sent through your phone and it's just reinforcing whatever biases you have, which is the pattern that develops, at a certain point, you just live in a bubble, and that's part of why our politics is so polarized right now. I think it's a solvable problem, but I think it's one we have to spend a lot of time thinking about. Barack Obama (quoted in Hamedy 2018)

Despite this apparent consensus, empirical studies offer a much more nuanced view of how social media affects political polarization, oftentimes questioning basic premises of this argument. Even if most political exchanges on social media take place among people with similar ideas, cross-cutting interactions are more frequent than commonly believed (Barberá, Jost et al. 2015), exposure to diverse news is higher than through other types of media (Barnidge 2017; Fletcher and Nielsen 2018a; Silver et al. 2019), and ranking algorithms do not have a large impact on theideological balance of news consumption on Facebook or Google (Bakshy, Messing, and Adamic 2015; Haim, Graefe, and Brosius 2018). A potential explanation for this series of findings is that social networking sites increase exposure to information shared by weak ties (Granovetter 1977), such as coworkers, relatives, and acquaintances, who are more likely to share novel information – including ideologically diverse news (Bakshy et al. 2012; Barberá 2015).

Of course, the fact that social media increases exposure to diverse political ideas from weak ties does not necessarily mean it has no effect on political polarization. Past research shows that repeated exposure to cross-cutting information leads to political moderation (Mutz 2006), which could explain why political polarization in the United States has actually increased the least among those citizens who are least likely to use social media (Boxell, Gentzkow, and Shapiro 2017). However, a growing body of work challenges this finding, arguing that it is precisely this increased exposure to cross-cutting views that may be having polarizing effects (Bail et al. 2018; Suhay, Bello-Pardo, and Maurer 2018). In a lucid recent book, Settle (2018) identifies the heightened awareness of political identities in social media as a key factor driving affective polarization (Iyengar, Sood, and Lelkes 2012).

Despite the increased scholarly attention to this topic, much remains unknown. Most studies have focused their attention in the US context and the comparative empirical evidence on this question is scarce, despite the well- known link between polarization and political violence in countries with high levels of ethnic fractionalization (see, e.g., Montalvo and Reynal-Querol 2005),which increases the urgency of research on this area. The lack of a shared definition of polarization makes it difficult to assess the overall impact of social media – the varying results across studies are also likely due to differences in how polarization is conceptualized. We also know little about potential asymmetries in the polarizing effect of social media interactions regarding individuals' levels of political interest or their ideological inclinations. The aim of this chapter is to offer an exhaustive review of the literature exploring the link between social media and political polarization. I highlight the areas where a consensus based on empirical evidence has already emerged but also36 Pablo Barberá identify the questions that remain open, and the type of data and analysis that would help us address them.

POLITICAL ECHO CHAMBERS IN THE AGE OF DIGITAL TECHNOLOGIES

The debate on whether digital technologies help bring politically different people together or create isolated ideological communities is almost as old as the Internet. Possibly the earliest formulation can be attributed to Van Alstyne and Brynjolfsson (1996), who warned that information technologies could lead to cyber balkanization. Technology can "shrink geographic distances and facilitate information exchange" (p. 3) thus creating a global village, but that was only one possible outcome. They hypothesized that an alternative scenario would be one where societies are more fragmented and interactions are balkanized because "the Internet makes it easier to find like-minded individuals," which "can facilitate and strengthen fringe communities that have a common ideology but are dispersed geographically" (p. 5); and "once like-minded individuals locate each other," they conclude, "their subsequent interactions can further polarize their views or even ignite calls-to-action" (p. 5).

This argument was further refined and popularized in Robert Putnam's seminal study of social capital in the United States, Bowling Alone (Putnam 2000). In a remarkably prescient passage, Putnam shares his concern about how "Internet technology" may allow and encourage "white supremacists to narrow their circle to like-minded intimates." While "real-world interactions often force us to deal with diversity," he continues, "the virtual world may be more homogeneous." This process could be accelerated by the use of "new 'filtering' technologies that automate the screening of 'irrelevant' messages" (p. 178).

At the same time, Putnam also leaves room for alternative scenarios by arguing that "tendencies toward community homogeneity long predate the internet" and speculating that "weak ties that bridge among distinct groups might create an interwoven community of communities" (p. 179). Putnam's original formulation of this argument already outlined its three main components: (1) digital technologies facilitate the emergence of communities of like-minded individuals, where (2) they are increasingly isolated from any challenging information, a process that is exacerbated by (3) filtering algorithms. All three components are present in most subsequent studies in this question, often discussed within the context of other political communication theories. The following sections offer a more detailed discussion of each of these components, with an overview of the empirical evidence supporting or refuting them.

Communities of Like-Minded Individuals

Access to the Internet dramatically lowers the costs of exchanging messages and finding information regardless of geographic distance. Not being bound by physical proximity, citizens gain the ability to connect and organize based on shared interests, as niche or rare as they may be. These conversations may be taking place in the open, through open forums or blogs, but also in more private settings, such as closed groups on Facebook or private communities.

As Sunstein (2001) argues in Republic.com and his follow-up book,#Republic (Sunstein 2018), online spaces create opportunities for enclave deliberation, which is the form of deliberation that takes place when conversations only occur among like-minded people. Enclave deliberation is not inherently negative. In fact, it can promote the development of positions that would otherwise be silenced or offer a safe space for people who suffer from discrimination. A recent prominent example is "Pantsuit Nation," a private Facebook group in favour of Hillary Clinton during the 2016 US presidential election campaign, where Clinton supporters – predominantly female – could express their opinions without fear of being harassed during a particularly polarizing election. There are many other cases of communities whose members share the same race or ethnic background, sexual orientation, interest in a particular issue, and so on that may not lead to undesirable outcomes from a normative perspective.

However, Sunstein (2001) argues that, in practice, the modal outcome of enclave deliberation is group polarization, which represents a "breeding ground for extremism" (p. 71) and "may even put social stability at risk" (p. 77). His concern here is that, "through the mechanisms of social influence and persuasive arguments, members will move to positions that lack merit." This could happen either because the homogeneity of the group restricts the size of the argument pool or because individuals will be more likely to voice a popular opinion within the group in order to obtain the approval of as many members as possible. The existence of these two mechanisms has been demonstrated in a number of lab experiments that show that individuals who participate in homogeneous discussion groups tend to adopt more extreme positions after deliberating with their like-minded peers (see, e.g., Myers and Lamm 1976). Incontrast, diverse groups tend to perform better in solving problems even if the average ability of their members is lower (Hong and Page 2004).

Sunstein argues that this mechanism is behind the rise in the number of hate groups and extremist organizations with a strong online presence, such as white supremacists and Holocaust deniers. Other scholars have used this argument as an explanation for the emergence of groups with less nefarious intentions but whose success can be equally polarizing. For example, in their book The Outrage Industry, Berry and Sobieraj (2013, p. 165) document how digital tools were critical to the emergence and organization of the Tea Party movement. They lowered the barriers to entry for those who wanted to get involved and offered a space where political messages could be refined and agreed on.

The literature on social networks has also addressed this question in the context of studies of homophiles; that is, individuals' propensity to cluster based on common traits, such as political ideology (McPherson, Smith-Lovin, and Cook 2001). Adamic and Glance (2005) analyzed the network of hyper links connecting the top 1,000 political blogs active during the 2004 US presidential election, finding that "liberals and conservatives [link] primarily within their separate communities" (p. 43). This applies not only to authors but also to blog readers: Lawrence, Sides, and Farrell (2010) found that blog readers gravitate toward blogs that align with their political orientation and are more likely to be polarized than non–blog readers. While most of the early literature focused on the Internet in general, recent work has found similar patterns on social networking sites. Conover et al. (2012) showed that partisan Twitter users are significantly more likely to spread messages that are congenial to their ideological positions. According to Barberá, Jost et al. (2015), close to 75 percent of retweets on political topics take place between users of similar ideological views. Del Vicario et al. (2016) found that information related to scientific news and conspiracy theories also tends to spread in homogeneous and polarized communities on Facebook. Moving beyond strictly political opinions, Aiello et al. (2012) showed that users with similar interests are more likely to be friends in online communities.

To put this set of results into context, it is important to note that these patterns may not necessarily generalize to all social media users. In fact, it is likely that the widespread perception of polarization on social media is due to a minority of highly active and visible partisan individuals. Barberá and Rivero (2015) offer evidence pointing in this direction: A minority of highly active individuals were responsible for the overwhelming majority of hyper-partisan content being spread on Twitter ahead of the 2012 US presidential election. Similarly, a study of news sharing on Twitter (Shore, Baek, and Dellarocas 2016) found that only a small network core exhibited evidence of group polarization. Furthermore, as I discuss in the following section, the fact that users tend to self-select themselves into homogeneous communities does not necessarily imply that they are never exposed to dissonant political messages.

AVOIDING OPINION CHALLENGES?

The second component in the standard argument connecting digital technologies and political polarization is related to people's ability to filter out all information that may challenge their pre-existing views. As individuals increasingly spend their time in communities of like-minded individuals, they not only become more exposed to pro-attitudinal messages – their exposure to counter-attitudinal information decreases as well. This is what leads to the emergence of echo chambers, where citizens do not see or hear a wide range of topics or ideas, which limits their capacity to reach common ground on political issues.

However, past work on selective exposure has found that reinforcement seeking and challenge avoidance are not intrinsically linked. Using survey data, Garrett (2009b) demonstrated that citizens take advantage of the broader availability of online news to increase exposure to political stories consistent with their views but do not systematically avoid opinion challenges. In a follow-up study using behaviour tracking in a realistic setting, Garrett (2009a) found no evidence that individuals abandon news stories that contain information with which they disagree once they have already started reading those stories.

Studies of individual-level online news consumption also offer scarce evidence that citizens actively avoid counter-attitudinal information. Gentzkow and Shapiro (2011) showed that ideological segregation in the news sites that people regularly visit is low in absolute terms and not becoming higher over time. Similarly, Guess (2016) found high levels of overlap in news consumption: A majority of people mostly rely on centrist websites, and those who visit the most partisan websites are a minority that tends to be active news consumers and thus also visit many other sites.

This distinction between reinforcement seeking and challenge avoidance becomes relevant as we focus on social networking sites, where most of the political news that citizens consume is posted by their friends and family. The process whereby social boundaries weaken in online environments is what Brundidge (2010) refers to as the inadvertency thesis: Somewhat counter intuitively, people are inadvertently exposed to additional political differences online. Furthermore, such exposure is not inconsequential. As Messing and Westwood (2014) demonstrate using a lab experiment that recreates a Facebook news feed, individuals are likely to click through and read news stories they potentially disagree with whenever those stories are recommended by their friends and acquaintances. In other words, friends' news recommendations are powerful social cues that can reduce partisan selective exposure to levels indistinguishable from chance.

Of course, this process of social consumption of information may still lead to echo-chamber environments if citizens' networks are politically homogeneous and thus all the content shared by social ties is pro-attitudinal. There is indeed some evidence that social ties in online networks replicate offline ties in their composition and nature (Jones et al. 2013; Bisbee and Larson 2017). Yet study after study demonstrates that despite citizens' ability to select the news stories they consume from a narrower range of sources thanks to digital technologies, they are nonetheless exposed to a diverse set of views through websites and even more so on social media.

This finding is robust to the use of different sources of data and appears to hold across countries. Flaxman, Goel, and Rao (2016) use behavioural data from web-browsing histories of 50,000 online adults that consume online news and offer probably the best evidence regarding the diverging patterns regarding reinforcement seeking and challenge avoidance. On one hand, news consumption through social media and search engines contributes to the increased ideological segregation of audiences. However, at the individual level, these channels lead to more exposure to opposing perspectives than direct browsing. Similar to what Guess (2016) reports, this apparent paradox between macro- and micro-level patterns can be explained by a minority of partisan individuals who are responsible for the majority of partisan news consumption.

Bakshy, Messing, and Adamic (2015) report similar results on Facebook. Their analysis examines the ideological content of the Facebook news feeds of10.1 million US Facebook users. Unsurprisingly, they find that a majority of friendship links take place between people within the same ideological groups and that users are indeed more likely to engage with congenial content. However, many friendships (20 percent for conservatives and 18 percent for liberals) do cut across ideological groups; and, most importantly, exposure to ideologically diverse news and opinion is also high: on average, around 30 percent of political news stories that users see in their news feed are cross- cutting. This proportion is remarkably similar to what Barberá (2015) reports using Twitter data: 33 percent of the tweets to which a sample of politically interested users were potentially exposed are cross-cutting.

Going beyond online news consumption, Barnidge (2017) offers a useful comparison of how US adults report being exposed to political disagreement in different settings. His study relies on survey data which, at the expense of potential reporting biases, has the advantage of allowing a comparison of offline interactions and offline news consumption (newspapers, TV, etc.) with social media interactions. The results confirm the pattern described throughout this section: Respondents admit being more exposed to political disagreement on social media than in other communication settings.

Although comparative studies of news consumption on social media are still scarce, the evidence presented by Fletcher and Nielsen (2017, 2018b) as part of the yearly Reuters Institute Digital News Report suggests that the US case is not an exception. Using representative surveys conducted in thirty-seven countries, they find that online audiences do not appear to be more politically fragmented than offline audiences, that incidental exposure to news content on social media is a generalized phenomenon, and that in fact people who use social networking sites are exposed to diverse news at a greater rate than those who do not. Similarly, a recent report by the Pew Research Center conducted in eleven nations across four global regions (Silver et al. 2019) found that social media users were more likely to interact regularly with a more diverse network, including people from different political parties, than those who were not active on social media. How can we reconcile the fact that citizens now have a much greater ability to filter out any opinion challenges with the fact they actually do not appear to do so? One explanation, which I already advanced earlier in this section, is that perhaps most people do not actually make an effort to avoid counter-attitudinal information (Garrett 2009b), and in that sense the pattern we observe in an online setting replicates what we would observe offline. An alternative argument, however, is specific to social networking platforms – social media sites increase exposure to diverse views because they connect us to weak ties.

A majority of people with whom we interact in our daily life can be considered "weak ties," either because the frequency with which we communicate is low or because we do not perceive them to be close to us. In contrast, "strong ties" are that minority of people that we see frequently and whom we tend to trust more. Weak ties are generally co-workers, school friends, distant relative, and other acquaintances; whereas strong ties are our partners, close friends, and direct family. This distinction becomes relevant in the context of information diffusion because, as Granovetter (1977) discovered, individuals are exposed to novel information (in his study, information about job opportunities) through weak ties.

When we think about social media sites, undoubtedly the main way in which they impact our daily lives is by making it easy to stay in touch with people we would not see in person regularly. In other words, they entail greater exposure and contact with weak ties than in offline interactions (Gil de Zuniga and Valenzuela 2011). As Gladwell (2010) argued in his popular New Yorker essay, "the platforms of social media are built around weak ties." His mainpoint there is that such weak ties do not "lead to high-risk activism"– they do not generate the motivation that people need to protest. However, weak ties are fundamental if we want to understand the spread of information, because they help connect peripheral parts of online networks (De Meo et al. 2014; Barberá et al. 2015). That applies not only to protest movements but also to news consumption in general.

The other way in which tie strength is important to this argument is related to the fact that homophily tends to be lower among weak ties (McPherson et al. 2001). In other words, because humans exhibit a propensity to preferentially establish links to other people who are similar to them, we should expect our weak ties to be more different from us than strong ties; and that applies also to ideological similarity. It is this heterogeneity that explains why weak ties are responsible for the propagation of novel information on social media (Bakshy et al. 2012).

To sum up, the most likely explanation for why citizens are not able to avoid opinion challenges on social media is the fact that (1) they do not have the ability to choose which content they see because exposure is incidental and presented in the context of powerful social cues and (2) most of that content is shared by weak ties, which tend to be more ideologically diverse than strong ties.

THE FILTER BUBBLE

The previous two sections dealt with two mechanisms at the core of how individuals choose to consume (or not) political information. However, in the current online environment, these are not the only two ingredients that determine citizens' media diet. As the number and heterogeneity of choices increase, citizens become unprepared to deal with the information overload that such wide availability entails. In this context, search engines and social networking sites have turned to rely on real-time, automated, and personalized algorithms to help users navigate their web browsing sessions.

In some cases, the set of heuristics and rules that determine how information is displayed on a website is well-understood. For example, search results on Google were ranked, at least in the early iterations of this website, using the Page Rank algorithm developed by its founders (Page et al. 1999). However, when it comes to social media sites, the algorithms that determine how information is ranked on users' news feed (on Facebook) or timeline (on Twitter) are generally considered a black box. Other than some general principles about how these companies take a series of signals and try to make predictions about the relevancy score for each combination of user and piece of content (Mosseri 2018), social networking sites have released little information about how this process really works. The most likely reason for this opaqueness is that releasing more information could make it easier for publishers that try to game the system. However, this lack of transparency has also raised concerns about the extent to which these algorithms could actually be contributing to exacerbating inequalities and ideological segregation. This concern is reminiscent of probably the earliest discussion of algorithmic curation of news, the "Daily Me" concept, popularized in the mid-1990s by MIT MediaLab founder Nicholas Negroponte (although the idea was conceived in the 1970s). In contrast to information consumed through newspapers and TV newscasts, where journalists act as the gatekeepers that determine which stories are newsworthy, the Daily Me would be tailored to each individual's preferences and interests. This "architecture machine" would "track what you skipped and reread and where you paused, then use those cues to evolve into a composite Daily Me that would carry only the news you cared about most"(Hapgood 1995).

Sunstein (2018) uses this concept to justify his worry about the "age of the algorithm," in which citizens are not in control of the news they consume anymore. Even if people would not voluntarily choose to gravitate toward echo chambers, they may have no option, as social media sites become the arbiters of what people see and what they do not.

The most influential book within this line of thought is Eli Pariser's The Filter Bubble (Pariser 2011). His concern applies to both search engines – which would yield completely different results based on the website's prediction of what the user's intention is – and social networking sites – which would show users only content that they are likely to enjoy. As these online services learn more about the users, their accuracy in predicting what they would prefer to see becomes higher, eventually leading to bubbles where citizens would never be exposed to any type of information that may cause them unpleasantness.

Pariser's worry is twofold. First, he expresses concerns about algorithms increasing inequalities in civic engagement between politically interested people and those who would only prefer to consume entertainment news; and second, for those with clear partisan preferences, he claims that algorithms reduce the extent to which they "hear from the other side," even below the level of what they would voluntarily choose to see. The outcome of this dual process, which echoes similar concerns expressed by Prior (2007) and others about cable news, is a society where the type of shared experiences that are necessary in a well-functioning democracy are simply nonexistent.

Although this review of the existing work focuses on Pariser's influential book, it is important to note that the concept of algorithmic bias has received much broader attention in political communication and computer science. Black-box deep learning methods, which sacrifice interpretability in order to improve their accuracy, have frequently been accused of having implicit biases.

The fact that algorithms are automated does not imply that they do not replicate common human flaws, since the training datasets that they use to replicate human behaviour in many cases also incorporate such biases (see, e.g., Caliskan, Bryson, and Narayanan 2017).

In the specific case of ideological segregation, what do we know about the impact of ranking algorithms? The answer is not much. We lack the type of systematic evidence that would allow us to answer key questions in the field. An explanation for this scarcity of evidence is researchers' inability to access or manipulate search or social ranking algorithms. It is thus not surprising that the most extensive study on this topic was conducted by Facebook researchers Bakshy, Messing, and Adamic (2015). Their results show that Facebook's algorithm induces a significant but small reduction in users' exposure to cross-cutting content. In contrast, "individual choices more than algorithms limit exposure to attitude-challenging content" (p. 1131) on Facebook.

This study is not without limitations, however. As they acknowledge, their sample is only limited to active users who self-report their political affiliation on their profile. While this may lead to underestimating the extent to which users are exposed to cross-cutting views, when it comes to the relative importance of individual choices vs. the algorithm, the opposite may be true. In other words, people who self-report their political views are more likely to be politically interested and thus more likely to be more selective about the political content they consume. Individuals with lower levels of political interest may rely to a greater extent on Facebook's algorithm to decide which political news they are exposed to.

What about search engines, the other problematic source of news identified by Pariser (2011)? Again, the empirical evidence that goes beyond anecdotes is scarce. A more recent study (Haim, Graefe, and Brosius 2018) casts doubts on the concerns about algorithmic filter bubbles. Using a set of different profiles in a realistic search scenario on Google, the authors found null effects on content diversity when experimenting with a set of politically heterogeneous profiles. These findings are consistent with results in Flaxman, Goel, and Rao (2016) and Feuz, Fuller, and Stalder (2011), which also found small effects of Google's search personalization algorithms on the information that users actually see. However, without access to Google's internal data and with search algorithms being a moving target given their constant evolution, it is hard to reach firm conclusions.

THE IMPACT OF SOCIAL MEDIA ON POLITICAL POLARIZATION

The review of the literature on social media and "echo chambers" has shown that, rather counter intuitively, there is convincing empirical evidence demonstrating that social networking sites increase the range of political views to which individuals are exposed. However, that tells us little regarding its subsequent impact on individual attitudes and aggregate-level polarization. As I describe next, there are good reasons to expect an effect in either direction.

Political theorists have long considered shared exposure to dissimilar views to be a necessary condition for the type of healthy political deliberation that takes place in thriving democratic societies (Mill 1859; Habermas 1991). Yet beyond this normative argument, diverse deliberation is also important because it can have a profound impact on citizens' beliefs – and their strength. Cross- cutting interactions increase awareness of rationales for individuals' own viewpoints and oppositional viewpoints (Mutz 2006). Exposure to diverse opinions can also be framed within the "contact hypothesis" literature. Based on Allport's (1954) classic intergroup hypothesis, this argument would imply that exposure to members of different groups (in this case, people who support a different party) should reduce prejudice and promote political tolerance.

If social media use indeed increases citizens' awareness of diverse viewpoints and fosters intergroup contact, it seems reasonable to expect that it may also weaken the strength of people's political beliefs and thus reduce political polarization. Although a review of how these two mechanisms operate in the offline context is beyond the scope of this chapter, there is indeed broad evidence that cross-cutting interactions foster political moderation (Carpini,Cook, and Jacobs 2004), for instance, by increasing support for civil liberties of disliked groups (Mutz 2002), and that intergroup contact reduces prejudice (Pettigrew and Tropp 2006; Paluck, Green, and Green 2018).

However, the empirical studies that examine this question in the social media context are few and offer mixed results. Some studies find a negative link between social media usage and political polarization, as the literature discussed in this section would lead us to expect. Probably the most prominent example is the work by Boxell, Gentzkow, and Shapiro (2017), who find that, even if the level of political polarization has increased for all age cohorts in the United States, the change has been smallest in magnitude among the youngest set of people – those most likely to be active on social media. This result suggests that digital technologies are likely to play a limited role in explaining why polarization is on the rise. One important limitation of this study, however, is that its longitudinal analysis of age cohorts could suffer from ecological inference problems if, for example, their composition in terms of unobserved demographic covariates has changed over time.

Despite any concerns with this particular article, at least three other studies using individual-level data yield results pointing in the same direction. Heatherly, Lu, and Lee (2017) find that individuals who engage in cross-cutting discussion on social media report lower levels of political polarization. Barberá (2015) finds that individuals in ideologically diverse Twitter networks tend to moderate their ideological positions over time. Using survey data from twenty-eight European countries, Ngyuen and Vu (2019) find that citizens who consume political news through social media sites are not more polarized than those who rely on other sources. Other studies, on the other hand, do suggest that exposure to political information through social media could have polarizing effects. Bail et al. (2018) show that cross-cutting exposure to political messages from elites can increase polarization. Using an innovative research design that maximizes internal and external validity, the authors recruited a sample of respondents and then asked them to follow bots that were sharing political messages that were counter-attitudinal with respect to their own views. A longitudinal comparison of the respondents' political opinions showed that Republicans became significantly more conservative. Democrats also became somewhat more liberal, although the change was not statistically significant. These results offer evidence of a backlash effect that could be due to motivated reasoning (Lodge and Taber 2013), perhaps operating in a similar way as the boomerang effects that have been found in some fact-checking interventions to rumours and misinformation (Nyhan and Reifler 2010). Note, however, that the existence of these backlash effects is highly debated, as summarized by Wittenberg and Berinsky (Chapter 8, this volume).

Similarly, two experimental studies conducted by Suhay et al. (2018) also find that exposure to political disagreement in online settings increases political polarization. These disagreements are presented in an uncivil context, which, in their view, is representative of the type of cross-cutting interactions that take place online. It is criticism of partisan identities, and not necessarily online opinions on specific issues, that drives polarization.

One last article that examined the overall polarizing effects of social media is Allcott et al. (2020). The authors used an incentive design to study how leaving Facebook affects a variety of outcomes, including political polarization. The results reveal that deactivation did not significantly move affective polarization or polarization in factual beliefs about current events; but it reduced polarization of views on policy issues, using a scale similar to Bail et al. (2018). However, subjects' knowledge about current events also decreased, which suggests that the depolarizing effects of leaving social media may be explained by a lower level of exposure to political information overall. An additional limitation of this study is that it focused on the effects of stopping using social media, which may not necessarily be symmetrical to how the adoption of these platforms affects individual-level attitudes and behaviour.

In conclusion, we see that the existing literature offers results that appear to be at odds. How can we reconcile these diverging findings? To answer this question, it is important to consider how we define political polarization – do we mean just divergence in political views or issue positions (ideological polarization) or dislike for the partisan out-group (affective polarization)? In addition, it is also plausible that the differences across empirical studies could be due to social media having heterogeneous effects across different groups of people, particularly regarding their political orientation and the strength of their partisan identities.

IDEOLOGICAL DIVERGENCE AND EMOTIONAL SCHISMS

We generally think of information environments where individuals are exposed to multiple viewpoints as spaces that should lead to social consensus (DeGroot 1974). However, this argument assumes that individuals do not experience cognitive biases in how they process the messages they receive and that they are Bayesian learners, updating in the direction of the information they receive. Research on partisan motivated reasoning (Lodge and Taber 2013) shows that, when it comes to political information, that may not be the case. For example, when presented with negative information about a candidate that citizens evaluate positively, support for that candidate may actually increase due to affective biases (Redlawsk 2002).

Biased information processing is a relevant factor driving the perceived increase in polarization among the American public. Even if Democrats and Republicans may agree on some policy positions, they tend to increasingly dislike and distrust one another and to perceive that the social distance between them has expanded (Mason 2018). This alternative conceptualization of polarization is often called "affective polarization" (Iyengar et al. 2012) or "psychological polarization" (Settle 2018) as opposed to "ideological polarization," which would be limited to divergence of political views. This distinction may help us reconcile the mixed empirical results: It is possible that increased exposure to cross-cutting views on social media is moderating citizens' political views while at the same time exacerbating their perceived social distance with respect to the partisan out-group.

Settle (2018) articulates this argument in her recent book, Frenemies: HowSocial Media Polarizes America. She convincingly argues that core features of social media platforms, such as the fusion of social and political content, the ubiquity of social feedback, the ability to easily infer other users' political identity, or the incentives to produce "clickbait-y" and inflammatory content to catch people's attention, have a direct impact on the aggregate level of psychological polarization. The mechanism behind these effects is that these features facilitate the type of psychological processes behind affective polarization: the reinforcement of social and political identities, in combination with citizens' biased information processing. As Settle (2018)shows through a series of survey studies and lab experiments, social media usage (and the type of partisan content that is shared on Facebook) increases the perceived differences between individuals' own position and where they perceive the out-group to be, makes political and social identities more correlated, and contributes to the stereotyping (and negative evaluations) of the out-group.

Drawing on the distinction between ideological and affective polarization helps us reconcile the diverging empirical findings but also allows us to derive useful normative implications. Although ideological polarization is generally considered to be undesirable, its absence could also be counterproductive. It can be a sign that political competition is not clearly structured and that parties do not offer distinct positions, which could depress civic engagement. That was actually the concern behind the 1950 report Towards More Responsible Two-Party System, developed by the American Political Science Association (APSA) Committee on Political Parties, which has received increased attention recently (Wickham-Jones 2018) and which suggested the United States needed more political polarization. In contrast, the normative debate about the pernicious effects of affective polarization is settled: When the perceived distance between partisan groups is large, debates are won based on identities and not on substantive arguments and empirical evidence, which in turn can have negative economic consequences such as increased inequality and unemployment (Enns and McAvoy 2012; Bonica et al. 2013; Mason 2018).

UNBALANCED POLARIZATION

There are well-known differences in how individuals select, consume, and process political information depending on their political orientation, interest in politics, and strength of partisanship (see, e.g., Graber 1988; Zaller 1992; Prior 2007). For that reason, expecting to find that social media usage has a homogeneous (de)polarizing effect for all citizens seems too simplistic; in the same way that not all individuals are equally susceptible to misinformation (see Wittenberg and Berinsky, Chapter 8, this volume). However, citizens' online experiences are shaped in predictable ways by their own political and socio-demographic characteristics. Understanding how different research designs – in particular sampling decisions – capture these factors may also help us explain the diverging results described in the previous sections. Here, I offer an overview of research that suggests that two of them – political interest and ideological orientation – may be playing such a role.

In his classic study on the origins of public opinion, Zaller (1992) argues that politically aware individuals are more receptive to pro-attitudinal messages. Similarly, Taber and Lodge (2006) find that those with highest levels of political sophistication are more likely to uncritically accept supporting arguments and reject counter-attitudinal arguments, leading to attitude polarization; and, just like beliefs in misinformation are more difficult to correct among the most informed citizens (see Wittenberg and Berinsky, Chapter 8, this volume), deactivating polarization among this same subset of the population may require more than just increasing exposure to cross-cutting political views. This pattern could be exacerbated simply by citizens' self-selection into the consumption of news vs. entertainment, based on their pre-existing level of political interest (Prior 2007; Stroud 2010).

These are thus good reasons to expect that social media interactions may lead to polarization among the minority of partisan individuals who are most active in discussions about politics on social media (Barberá and Rivero 2015; Shore et al. 2016; Benkler et al. 2018). This may help explain thc backlash reaction to cross-cutting interactions identified by Bail et al. (2018), whose sample contains only self-identified partisans. It is also consistent with the high degrees of ideological segregation found by Conover et al. (2012) or Halberstam and Knight (2016), whose analyses focus on politically engaged Twitter users. Political ideology – or personality traits that have been found to be correlated with it – is a final factor that can help us understand polarization patterns on social media. Examining consumption of traditional media, some past research has found that conservatives are more likely than liberals to engage in selective exposure, biased information processing, and ideological conformity (Lau and Redlawsk 2006; Garrett 2009b; Nyhan and Reifler 2010; Nam, Jost, and Van Bavel 2013; Guess et al. 2019), although other work has found symmetric patterns regarding these behaviours (Munro et al. 2002; Iyengar and Hahn 2009; Nisbet, Cooper, and Garrett 2015).

When it comes to social media more specifically, Barberá, Jost et al. (2015) showed that these asymmetries extend to ideological segregation in information diffusion on Twitter. Their analysis found that liberals were more likely to engage in cross-ideological interactions than conservatives. This finding is consistent with the results of the field experiment conducted by Bail et al. (2018), which found that the increase in polarization in reaction to counter-attitudinal information was larger for conservatives than for liberalsCarney et al. 2008). For example, Kim, Hsu, and de Zuniga (2013) show that social media usage has a smaller effect on the overall heterogeneity of discussion networks among conservatives than liberals. This finding needs to be understood within the broader media ecosystem in the United States which, as Benkler et al. (2018) show, exhibits a similar asymmetry in terms of audience and production, with political click bait and hyper-partisan content being more prevalent on the right than on the left.

THE WAY AHEAD: WHAT WE DO NOT KNOW

The research summarized in this chapter has greatly advanced our understanding of how the success of social networking platforms is transforming the structure and heterogeneity of political conversations and its subsequent impact on political polarization. As we have seen, in many cases the empirical evidence has challenged the conventional wisdom, while in other cases the theory has moved ahead of the evidence and can help us reconcile seemingly contradictory findings. Although the field is reaching a state of maturity, many questions remain still open. This concluding section offers a detailed list of what we do not know (yet).

Do the results described here generalize to other contexts beyond the United States? Mirroring the state of the literature on political polarization more generally, most of what we know about cyber balkanization is based on data from the United States only. With some notable exceptions (Vaccari et al. 2016; Bechmann and Nielbo 2018; Bright 2018), there is a lack of theory and empirical evidence about how contextual factors mediate the relationship between social media usage and political polarization from a comparative perspective; and, while generally we think about polarization in terms of the gridlock and suboptimal economic outcomes it can generate, in some instances it can lead to much worse outcomes, including political violence. For example, a working paper has linked hate speech spread on social media to anti-refugee attacks in Germany (Muller and Schwarz 2017). Journalistic accounts of religious violence in Sri Lanka and Myanmar have shown how these events appear to be fuelled by rumours spread on Facebook and WhatsApp (Taub and Fisher 2018). These two instances illustrate the urgent need for research on how the spread of extremist ideas on social media could be motivating offline violence.

Is there any longitudinal variation regarding the polarizing effects of social media interactions? Are things getting better or worse? In many ways, the study of how digital technologies affect political behaviour is a moving target (Munger 2019). Internet services are in constant evolution, both in terms of which social media platforms or websites become popular and regarding the features of those platforms. Even if Facebook has now existed for more than ten years, it has significantly evolved over this period. How the platforms are used can also change: Twitter was initially just a website where users would post real-time updates about their everyday activities. In 2018, it has become the go-to place for breaking news. The population that is active on these platforms can also radically change: In 2014, there were 2 million Facebook users in Myanmar; today, that number has skyrocketed to more than 30 million (Roose 2018). It is true that some of the findings in this chapter refer to mechanisms that are a core component of human behaviour – for example, biased information processing or the structure of social networks. However, studying a constantly shifting environment may mean an inability to understand the scope conditions under which those mechanisms hold.

How can we disentangle individuals' self-selection into networks from the impact on their attitudes? Most of the empirical research cited in this chapter relies on cross-sectional evidence from observational studies. One challenge when deriving causally valid conclusions from this evidence is that individuals' media consumption and exposure to political messages on social media are highly endogenous. For example, when we find that individuals in heterogeneous networks are less polarized, an alternative interpretation is that individuals with moderate political positions are more likely to feel comfortable when they are exposed to cross-cutting political views (Kim et al. 2013; Barberá 2015; Vaccari et al. 2016).

Disentangling this reverse causality loop is key in order to make progress within this field. In that sense, Bail et al. (2018) and Allcott et al. (2020) offer a blueprint to imitate: a large-scale field experiment where exposure to social media messages is randomly assigned, which allows the authors to make valid causal claims. Ethical considerations should also be part of this debate, however, particularly as scholars focus their efforts on studying how extremism fueled by social media interactions can lead to offline violence.

What are the unintended consequences of potential interventions to reduce polarization? Concerns about the negative societal consequences of political polarization may lead to regulatory changes or new platform features to deactivate it. For example, Settle (2018: chap. 9) offers a helpful list of suggestions that include increasing information quality on social media profiles, incentivizing moderation by upranking reasonable disagreement, and eliminating highly visible quantification. As we consider the benefits and disadvantages of these options, we should bear in mind the trade-offs that fostering moderation involves. The work by Mutz (2002) is a perfect illustration of these challenges: Exposure to civil, cross-cutting exchanges may lead to political tolerance, but it can also make politics more complex and less interesting, which depresses civic engagement and accentuates political inequality. Studying these complex multi causal relationships is essential in order to address one of the most important questions of our time – how digital technologies affect democratic politics.

REFERENCES

Adamic, L. A., & Glance, N. (2005). The political blogosphere and the 2004 US election: Divided they blog. In Proceedings of the 3rd International Workshop on Link Discovery (pp. 36–43). New York: ACM.

Aiello, L. M., Barrat, A., Schifanella, R., Cattuto, C., Markines, B., & Menczer, F. (2012). Friendship prediction and homophily in social media. ACM Transactions on the Web (TWEB), 6(2), 9.

Allcott, H., Braghieri, L., Eichmeyer, S., & Gentzkow, M. (2020). The welfare effects of social media. American Economic Review, 110(3), 629-676.

Allport, G. W. (1954). The Nature of Prejudice. Reading, MA: Addison-Wesley.

Bail, C. A., Argyle, L. P., Brown, T. W. et al. (2018). Exposure to opposing views on social media can increase political polarization. Proceedings of the National Academy of Sciences, 115(37), 9216–9221.

Bakshy, E., Messing, S., & Adamic, L. A. (2015). Exposure to ideologically diverse news and opinion on Facebook. Science, 348(6239), 1130–1132.

Bakshy, E., Rosenn, I., Marlow, C., & Adamic, L. (2012). The role of social networks in information diffusion. In Proceedings of the 21st International Conference onWorld Wide Web (pp. 519–528). New York: ACM.

Barberá, P. (2015). How social media reduces mass political polarization: Evidence from Germany, Spain, and the US. Paper presented at the 2015 American Political Science Association conference.

Barberá, P., Jost, J. T., Nagler, J., Tucker, J. A., & Bonneau, R. (2015). Tweeting from left to right: Is online political communication more than an echo chamber? Psychological Science, 26(10), 1531–1542.

Barberá, P., & Rivero, G. (2015). Understanding the political representativeness of Twitter users. Social Science Computer Review, 33(6), 712–729.

Barberá, P., Wang, N., Bonneau, R. et al. (2015). The critical periphery in the growth of social protests. PloS ONE, 10(11), e0143611.

Barnidge, M. (2017). Exposure to political disagreement in social media versus face-to- face and anonymous online settings. Political Communication, 34(2), 302–321.

Bechmann, A., & Nielbo, K. L. (2018). Are we exposed to the same news in the newsfeed? An empirical analysis of filter bubbles as information similarity for Danish Facebook users. Digital Journalism, 6(8), 1–13.

Benkler, Y., Faris, R., & Roberts, H. (2018). Network Propaganda: Manipulation, Disinformation, and Radicalization in American Politics. Oxford: Oxford University Press.

Berry, J. M., & Sobieraj, S. (2013). The Outrage Industry: Political Opinion Media and the New Incivility. Oxford: Oxford University Press.

Bisbee, J., & Larson, J. M. (2017). Testing social science network theories with online network data: An evaluation of external validity. American Political Science Review, 111(3), 502–521.

Bonica, A., McCarty, N., Poole, K. T., & Rosenthal, H. (2013). Why hasn't democracy slowed rising inequality? Journal of Economic Perspectives, 27(3), 103–124.

Boxell, L., Gentzkow, M., & Shapiro, J. M. (2017). Greater Internet use is not associated with faster growth in political polarization among US demographic groups. Proceedings of the National Academy of Sciences, 114(40), 10612–10617.

Bright, J. (2018). Explaining the emergence of political fragmentation on social media: The role of ideology and extremism. Journal of Computer-Mediated Communication, 23(1), 17–33.

Brundidge, J. (2010). Encountering difference in the contemporary public sphere: The contribution of the Internet to the heterogeneity of political discussion networks. Journal of Communication, 60(4), 680–700.

Caliskan, A., Bryson, J. J., & Narayanan, A. (2017). Semantics derived automatically from language corpora contain human-like biases. Science, 356(6334), 183–186.

Carney, D. R., Jost, J. T., Gosling, S. D., & Potter, J. (2008). The secret lives of liberals and conservatives: Personality profiles, interaction styles, and the things they leave behind. Political Psychology, 29(6), 807–840.

Carpini, M. X. D., Cook, F. L., & Jacobs, L. R. (2004). Public deliberation, discursive participation, and citizen engagement: A review of the empirical literature. Annual Review of Political Science, 7, 315–344.

Conover, M. D., Goncalves, B., Flammini, A., & Menczer, F. (2012). Partisan asymmetries in online political activity. EPJ Data Science, 1(1), 6.

De Meo, P., Ferrara, E., Fiumara, G., & Provetti, A. (2014). On Facebook, most ties are weak. Communications of the ACM, 57(11), 78–84.

DeGroot, M. H. (1974). Reaching a consensus. Journal of the American Statistical Association, 69(345), 118–121.

Del Vicario, M., Bessi, A., Zollo, F. et al. (2016). The spreading of misinformation online. Proceedings of the National Academy of Sciences, 113(3), 554–559.

Enns, P. K., & McAvoy, G. E. (2012). The role of partisanship in aggregate opinion. Political Behavior, 34(4), 627–651.

Feuz, M., Fuller, M., & Stalder, F. (2011). Personal Web searching in the age of semantic capitalism: Diagnosing the mechanisms of personalisation. First Monday, 16(2).

Flaxman, S., Goel, S., & Rao, J. M. (2016). Filter bubbles, echo chambers, and online news consumption. Public Opinion Quarterly, 80(S1), 298–320.

Fletcher, R., & Nielsen, R. K. (2017). Are news audiences increasingly fragmented? Across-national comparative analysis of cross-platform news audience fragmentation and duplication. Journal of Communication, 67(4), 476–498.

(2018a). Are people incidentally exposed to news on social media? A comparative analysis. New Media and Society, 20(7), 2450–2468.

(2018b). Are people incidentally exposed to news on social media? A comparative analysis. New Media and Society, 20(7), 2450–2468.

Garrett, R. K. (2009a). Echo chambers online? Politically motivated selective exposure among Internet news users. Journal of Computer-Mediated Communication, 14(2), 265–285.

(2009b). Politically motivated reinforcement seeking: Reframing the selective exposure debate. Journal of Communication, 59(4), 676–699.

Gentzkow, M., & Shapiro, J. M. (2011). Ideological segregation online and offline. The Quarterly Journal of Economics, 126(4), 1799–1839.

Gil de Zuniga, H., & Valenzuela, S. (2011). The mediating path to a stronger citizenship: Online and offline networks, weak ties, and civic engagement. Communication Research, 38(3), 397–421.

Gladwell, M. (2010). Small change. The New Yorker, October 4. www.newyorker.com/magazine/2010/10/04/small-change-malcolm-gladwell

Graber, D. A. (1988). Processing the News: How People Tame the Information Tide. Lanham, MD: University Press of America.

Granovetter, M. S. (1977). The strength of weak ties. American Journal of Sociology, 78(6), 1360–1380.

Guess, A. M. (2016). Media Choice and Moderation: Evidence from Online Tracking Data. Unpublished manuscript.

Guess, A. M., Nagler, J., & Tucker, J. (2019). Less than you think: Prevalence and predictors of fake news dissemination on Facebook. Science Advances, 5(1), eaau4586.

Habermas, J. (1991). The Structural Transformation of the Public Sphere: An Inquiry into a Category of Bourgeois Society. Cambridge, MA: MIT Press.

Haim, M., Graefe, A., & Brosius, H.-B. (2018). Burst of the filter bubble? Digital Journalism, 6(3), 330–343.

Halberstam, Y., & Knight, B. (2016). Homophily, group size, and the diffusion of political information in social networks: Evidence from Twitter. Journal of Public Economics, 143, 73–88.

Hamedy, S. (2018). Obama explains "what the Russians exploited" in new interviewwith Letterman. CNN, January 12. www.cnn.com/2018/01/12/politics/david- letterman-barack-obama-netflix-interview-russia

Hapgood, F. (1995). The Media Lab at 10. Wired, January 11. www.wired.com/1995/11/media/TS: Link

Heatherly, K. A., Lu, Y., & Lee, J. K. (2017). Filtering out the other side? Cross-cutting and like-minded discussions on social networking sites. New Media and Society, 19 (8), 1271–1289.

Hong, L., & Page, S. E. (2004). Groups of diverse problem solvers can outperform groups of high-ability problem solvers. Proceedings of the National Academy of Sciences, 101(46), 16385–16389.

Iyengar, S., & Hahn, K. S. (2009). Red media, blue media: Evidence of ideological selectivity in media use. Journal of Communication, 59(1), 19–39.

Iyengar, S., Sood, G., & Lelkes, Y. (2012). Affect, not ideology: A social identity perspective on polarization. Public Opinion Quarterly, 76(3), 405–431.

Jones, J. J., Settle, J. E., Bond, R. M., Fariss, C. J., Marlow C., & Fowler, J. H. (2013). Inferring tie strength from online directed behavior. PloS ONE, 8(1), e52168.

Kim, Y., Hsu, S.-H., & de Zuniga, H. G. (2013). Influence of social media use on discussion network heterogeneity and civic engagement: The moderating role of personality traits. Journal of Communication, 63(3), 498–516.

Lau, R. R., & Redlawsk, D. P. (2006). How Voters Decide: Information Processing in Election Campaigns. Cambridge: Cambridge University Press.

Lawrence, E., Sides, J., & Farrell, H. (2010). Self-segregation or deliberation? Blog readership, participation, and polarization in American politics. Perspectives on Politics, 8(1), 141–157.

Lodge, M., & Taber, C. S. (2013). The Rationalizing Voter. Cambridge: Cambridge University Press.

Mason, L. (2018). Uncivil Agreement: How Politics Became Our Identity. Chicago: University of Chicago Press.

McPherson, M., Smith-Lovin, L., & Cook, J. M. (2001). Birds of a feather: Homophily in social networks. Annual Review of Sociology, 27(1), 415–444.

Messing, S., & Westwood, S. J. (2014). Selective exposure in the age of social media: Endorsements trump partisan source affiliation when selecting news online. Communication Research, 41(8), 1042–1063.

Mill, J. S. (1859). On Liberty, Utilitarianism, and Other Essays. New York: Oxford University Press.

Montalvo, J. G., & Reynal-Querol, M. (2005). Ethnic polarization, potential conflict, and civil wars. American Economic Review, 95(3), 796–816.

Mosseri, A. (2018). News feed ranking in three minutes flat. Facebook Newsroom, May 22. https://newsroom.fb.com/news/2018/05/inside-feed-news-feed-ranking/

Muller, K., & Schwarz, C. (2017). Fanning the flames of hate: Social media and hate crime. SSRN. https://ssrn.com/abstract=3082972

Munger, K. (2019). Knowledge decays: Temporal validity and social science in a changing world. Unpublished manuscript. https://osf.io/4utsk/

Munro, G. D., Ditto, P. H., Lockhart, L. K., Fagerlin, A., Gready, M., & Peterson, E. (2002). Biased assimilation of socio-political arguments: Evaluating the 1996 US presidential debate. Basic and Applied Social Psychology, 24(1), 15–26.

Mutz, D. C. (2002). Cross-cutting social networks: Testing democratic theory in practice. American Political Science Review, 96(1), 111–126.

(2006). Hearing the Other Side: Deliberative versus Participatory Democracy. Cambridge: Cambridge University Press.

Myers, D. G., & Lamm, H. (1976). The group polarization phenomenon. Psychological Bulletin, 83(4), 602.

Nam, H. H., Jost, J. T., & Van Bavel, J. J. (2013). Not for all the tea in China! Political ideology and the avoidance of dissonance-arousing situations. PloS ONE, 8(4), e59837.

Nguyen, A., & Vu, H. T. (2019). Testing popular news discourse on the "echo chamber" effect: Does political polarisation occur among those relying on social media as their primary politics news source? First Monday, 24(5).

Nisbet, E. C., Cooper, K. E., & Garrett, R. K. (2015). The partisan brain: How dissonant science messages lead conservatives and liberals to (dis) trust science. The Annals of the American Academy of Political and Social Science, 658(1), 36–66.

Nyhan, B., & Reifler, J. (2010). When corrections fail: The persistence of political misperceptions. Political Behavior, 32(2), 303–330.

Page, L., Brin, S., Motwani, R., & Winograd, T. (1999). The PageRank Citation Ranking: Bringing Order to the Web. Technical report, Stanford InfoLab.

Paluck, E. L., Green, S. A., & Green, D. P. (2018). The contact hypothesis re-evaluated. Behavioural Public Policy, 3(2), 129–158.

Pariser, E. (2011). The Filter Bubble: What the Internet Is Hiding from You. London: Penguin.

Pettigrew, T. F., & Tropp, L. R. (2006). A meta-analytic test of intergroup contact theory. Journal of Personality and Social Psychology, 90(5), 751.

Prior, M. (2007). Post-Broadcast Democracy: How media Choice Increases Inequality in Political Involvement and Polarizes Elections. Cambridge: Cambridge University Press.

Putnam, R. D. (2000). Bowling Alone: America's Declining Social Capital. New York: Simon & Schuster.

Redlawsk, D. P. (2002). Hot cognition or cool consideration? Testing the effects of motivated reasoning on political decision making. The Journal of Politics, 64(4), 1021–1044.

Roose, K. (2018). Forget Washington: Facebook's problems abroad are far more disturbing. New York Times, October 29. www.nytimes.com/2017/10/29/business/facebook-misinformation-abroad.html

Settle, J. E. (2018). Frenemies: How Social Media Polarizes America. Cambridge: Cambridge University Press.

Shore, J., Baek, J., & Dellarocas, C. (2016). Network structure and patterns of information diversity on Twitter. arXiv.org. https://arxiv.org/pdf/1607.06795.pdf Silver, L., Huang, C., & Taylor, K. (2019). In Emerging Economies, Smartphone and Social Media Users Have Broader Social Networks. Pew Research Center report.

Stroud, N. J. (2010). Polarization and partisan selective exposure. Journal of Communication, 60(3), 556–576.

Suhay, E., Bello-Pardo, E., & Maurer, B. (2018). The polarizing effects of online partisancriticism: Evidence from two experiments. The International Journal of Press/ Politics, 23(1), 95–115.

Sunstein, C. R. (2001). Republic.com. Princeton: Princeton University Press.(2018). #Republic: Divided Democracy in the Age of Social Media. Princeton: Princeton University Press.

Taber, C. S., & Lodge, M. (2006). Motivated skepticism in the evaluation of political beliefs. American Journal of Political Science, 50(3), 755–769.

Taub, A., & Fisher, M. (2018). Where countries are tinderboxes and Facebook is a match. New York Times, April 21.

Vaccari, C., Valeriani, A., Barberá, P., Jost, J. T., Nagler, J., & Tucker, J. A. (2016). Of echo chambers and contrarian clubs: exposure to political disagreement among German and Italian users of Twitter. Social Media and Society, 2(3), 1–24.

Van Alstyne, M., & Brynjolfsson, E. (1996). Electronic communities: Global village or cyber balkans. In Proceedings of the 17th International Conference on Information Systems (pp. 80–98). New York: Wiley.

Wickham-Jones, M. (2018). This 1950 political science report keeps popping up in the news: Here's the story behind it. Washington Post, July 24. www.washingtonpost.com/news/monkey-cage/wp/2018/07/24/this-1950-political-science-report-keeps-popping-up-in-the-news-heres-the-story-behind-it/

Zaller, J. R. (1992). The Nature and Origins of Mass Opinion. Cambridge: Cambridge University Press.

04 INTERNET-BASED (ONLINE) HATE SPEECH

INTRODUCTION: AN OVERVIEW

In the digital age, the internet has become an unparalleled platform for communication, offering a vast expanse of virtual space where people from all walks of life connect, share, and exchange ideas. However, this immense connectivity has also exposed the darker side of online interaction, with the proliferation of Internet-based hate speech. This corrosive phenomenon entails the dissemination of offensive, discriminatory, or inflammatory content, often targeting individuals or groups based on their race, religion, gender, or other characteristics. In this era of unprecedented connectivity, addressing and mitigating the impact of online hate speech has become an increasingly urgent and complex challenge, as it can have far-reaching social, psychological, and even legal consequences. This introductory exploration delves into the intricate facets of Internet-based hate speech, seeking to shed light on the complexities of this pervasive issue and the potential strategies to combat it.

Once relegated to the dark corners of the Internet, online hate speech has become increasingly visible on mainstream social media platforms. From targeted anti- Semitic attacks on Jewish journalists to reports of social media's role in mobilizing ethnic violence in Myanmar and Sri Lanka, the offline consequences of online hate speech appear increasingly dire. Fearing that this harmful rhetoric is inciting violence and driving extremism, governments worldwide are passing regulation and pressuring social media companies to implement policies to stop the spread of online hate speech (Gagliardone et al. 2016).

However, these calls for action have rarely been motivated by comprehensive empirical evidence. Moreover, despite increased attention to online hate speech in the scientific literature, surprisingly little is known about the prevalence, causes, or consequences of different forms of harmful language across diverse platforms. Furthermore, researchers have only recently begun to examine the efficacy of approaches to countering online hate, and our understanding of the collateral costs of these interventions is especially limited.

This chapter examines the state of the literature – including scientific research, legal scholarship, and policy reports – on online hate speech. In particular, it explores ongoing debates and limitations in current approaches to defining and detecting online hate speech; provides an overview of what social media data and surveys can tell us about the producers, targets, and overall prevalence of harmful language; reviews empirical evidence of the offline consequences of online hate speech; and offers quantitative insights into what interventions might be most effective in combating harmful rhetoric online.

DEFINITION OF ONLINE HATE SPEECH

There is no single agreed on definition of hate speech – online or offline – and the topic has been hotly debated by academics, legal experts, and policy makers alike. Most commonly, hate speech is understood to be bias-motivated, hostile, and malicious language targeted at a person or group because of their actual or perceived innate characteristics (Cohen-Almagor 2011; Faris et al. 2016). However, as Sellars (2016) argues, "for all of the extensive literature about the causes, harms, and responses to hate speech, few scholars have endeavoured to systematically define the term."

A wide variety of content might or might not fit a definition of hate speech, depending on the context (Parekh et al. 2012; Sellars 2016). For example, while slurs and insults are easily identifiable, language containing epithets may not necessarily be considered hate speech by the speaker or target recipient (Delgado 1982). Conversely, more subtle language attacking an out-group, which can be harder for casual observers to identify, may have particularly damaging effects on individuals and group relations (Parekh et al. 2012). This is especially true in the online sphere, where speech is rapidly evolving and can be highly specialized (Gagliardone et al. 2015). The use of code words as stand-ins for racial slurs is also common in online communities, further complicating the definition of hate speech (Duarte et al. 2018). For example, among members of the alt-right, journalists have documented the use of the term "googles" to refer to the n-word; "skypes" as an anti-Semitic slur; "yahoos" as a derogatory term for Hispanics; and "skittles" as an anti-Muslim term (Sonnad 2016). Alt-right communities have also used steganography, such as triple brackets, to identify and harass Jews online (Fleishman and Smith 2016). In this way, when defining hate speech – and online hate speech in particular – the well-known "I know it when I see it" classification famously applied to obscene content clearly falls short.

As a result, existing definitions of hate speech can be extremely broad or fairly narrow. At one end of the spectrum are definitions that capture a wide variety of speech that is directed against a specified or easily identifiable individual or group based on arbitrary or normatively irrelevant features (Parekh et al. 2012). At the other end are definitions that require intended harm. The narrowest definitions imply that hate speech must be "dangerous speech"– language that is directly linked to the incitement of mass violence or physical harm against an out-group (Benesch 2013). This tension reflects the difficulty of developing a definition that adequately addresses the range of phenomena that might be considered hate speech, without losing valuable distinctions. Online hate speech can involve disparate instigators, targets, motives, and tactics. Sometimes perpetrators know those they attack, whereas others may galvanize anonymous online followers to target particular individuals. Speech that incites violence is distinct from speech that is "merely" offensive, and the use of harmful language by a single attacker isquite different from coordinated hate campaigns carried out by a digital mob (Sellars 2016). Recent work seeks to develop more comprehensive definitions and coding schemes for identifying hate speech that provide context and account for differences in severity and intent (Gagliardone et al. 2016;Waseem and Hovy 2016; Kennedy et al. 2018; Olteanu et al. 2018). Yet despite these advances, there is still no consensus in the scientific literature on how to define online hate speech.

Legal definitions of hate speech are similarly murky. Governments are increasingly defining hate speech in their criminal codes in an attempt to directly regulate harmful rhetoric both on- and offline (Haraszti 2012). As with academic definitions, these range from the relatively broad, such as Canada's characterization of hate speech as language that "willfully promotes hatred against any identifiable group," to more narrow definitions, like the European Union's framework, which defines hate speech as: "Public incitement to violence or hatred directed against a group of persons or a member of such group defined on the basis of race, [color], descent, religion or belief, or national or ethnic origin" and "publicly condoning, denying or grossly trivializing crimes of genocide, crimes against humanity, and war crimes [as defined in EU law], when the conduct is carried out in a manner likely to incite violence or hatred against such group or a member of such group" (Sellars 2016). In the United Kingdom, it is a criminal offense to incite racial or religious hatred, and variations on this legislation – while unconstitutional in the United States – exist in the majority of developed democracies, including Australia, Denmark, France, Germany, India, South Africa, Sweden, and New Zealand (Howard 2019), and in authoritarian contexts, particularly in the Arab World where laws banning online hate speech are often lumped together with laws countering extremism (Chetty and Alathur 2018). Yet despite the existence of laws explicitly banning hate speech, how these laws should be enforced in practice, particularly in the digital age, is a subject of ongoing debate.

More recently, online platforms themselves have developed definitions of hate speech for the purpose of moderating user-generated content. For example,

YouTube's Community Guidelines "hateful content" section states "we don't support content that promotes or condones violence against individuals or groups based on race or ethnic origin, religion, disability, gender, age, nationality, veteran status, or sexual orientation/gender identity, or whose primary purpose is inciting hatred on the basis of these core characteristics"(YouTube 2018). Similarly, Twitter's terms of service state that the company prohibits "hateful conduct" including "promot[ing] violence against or directly attack[ing] or threaten[ing] other people on the basis of race, ethnicity, national origin, sexual orientation, gender, gender identity, religious affiliation, age, disability or disease." The company also emphasizes that it does not allow accounts whose "primary purpose is inciting harm towards others on the basis of these categories" (Twitter 2018). Facebook's definition of hate speech does not contain the incitement to violence language employed by Twitter and YouTube, instead identifying hate speech as "content that directly attacks people based on their race; ethnicity; national origin; religious affiliation; sexual orientation; sex, gender, or gender identity; or serious disabilities or diseases" (Facebook 2018).

Together, this absence of clear and consistent definitions of hate speech in academic research, legal scholarship, and among actors attempting to govern online spaces has meant that despite extensive research, and well-documented policy interventions, our knowledge of the causes, consequences, and effective means of combating online hate speech remains somewhat clouded by definitional ambiguity.

IDENTIFYING HATE SPEECH ON THE INTERNET

Just as there is no clear consensus on the definition of hate speech, there is no consensus with regard to the most effective way to detect it across diverse platforms. The majority of automated approaches to identifying hate speech begin with a binary classification task in which researchers are concerned with coding a document as "hate speech or not," though multiclass approaches have also been used (Davidson et al. 2017).

Automated hate speech detection tends to rely on natural language processing or text mining strategies (Fortuna and Nunes 2018). The simplest of these approaches are dictionary-based methods, which involve developing a list of words that are searched and counted in a text. Dictionary-based approaches generally use content words – including insults and slurs – to identify hate speech (Dinakar et al. 2011; Dadvar et al. 2012; Liu and Forss 2015; Isbister et al. 2018). These methods can also involve normalizing or taking the total number of words in each text into consideration (Dadvar et al. 2012). Recognizing that online hate speech may obscure offensive words using accidental or intentional misspellings, some researchers have used distance metrics, such as the minimum number of edits necessary to transform one term into another, to augment their dictionary-based methods (Warner and Hirschberg 2012). Furthermore, given that code words may be used to avoid detection of hateful terms, other researchers have included known anti–out- group code words in their dictionaries (Magu et al. 2017).

Beyond pure dictionary-based methods, most state-of-the-art hate speech detection techniques involve supervised text classification tasks. These approaches, such as using Naive Bayes classifiers, linear support vector machines (SVM), decision trees, or random forest models, often rely on "bag- of-words" and "n-gram" techniques. In the bag-of-words method, a corpus is created based on words that appear in a training dataset, instead of a pre-defined dictionary. The frequencies of words appearing in text, which has been manually annotated as "hate speech or not," are then used as features to traina classifier (Greevy and Smeaton 2004; Kwok and Wang 2013; Burnap and Williams 2016). To avoid misclassification, if words are used in differentcon texts or spelled incorrectly, some researchers use n-grams, a similar approach to bag-of-words, which combines sequential words into bigrams, trigrams, or lists of length "n" (Burnap and Williams 2016; Waseem and Hovy 2016; Badjatiya et al. 2017; Davidson et al. 2017). More recent work has leveraged these approaches to improve the accuracy of dictionary-based methods – removing false positives by identifying which tweets containing slurs should indeed be classified as hate speech (Siegel et al. 2020). Rule-based approaches and theme-based grammatical patterns, which incorporate sentence structure, have also been used (Fortuna and Nunes 2018).

Other researchers have identified hate speech using topic modeling, aiming to identify posts belonging to a defined topic such as race or religion (Agarwal and Sureka 2017). Still others have incorporated sentiment into their analysis, with the assumption that hate speech is likely to be negative in tone (Liu and Forss 2014; Gitari et al. 2015; Davidson et al. 2017; Del Vigna et al. 2017). Word embedding or vector representations of text techniques including doc2vec, paragraph2vec, and FastText have also been used (Djuric et al. 2015; Schmidt and Wiegand 2017; Siegel et al. 2020), and deep learning techniques employing neural networks have become more common for both text classification and sentiment analysis related to detecting hate speech (Yuan et al. 2016; Zhang et al. 2018, Al-Makhadmeh and Tolba 2020).

Recognizing that these techniques may not be well-suited to identifying subtle or indirect forms of online hate, researchers have also employed more theoretically motivated approaches. For example, Burnap and Williams (2016) and ElSherief, Kulkarni et al. (2018) incorporate the concept of othering or "us vs. them" language into their measure of hate speech. They find that hate speech often uses third-person pronouns, including expressions like "send them all home." Other studies have incorporated declarations of in- group superiority – in addition to attacks directed at out-groups – into their measures (Warner and Hirschberg 2012). Another approach involves accounting for common anti–out-group stereotypes. For example, anti- Hispanic speech might make reference to border crossing, or anti-Semitic language might refer to banking, money, or the media (Alorainy et al. 2018). Additional work has distinguished between hate speech directed at a group (generalized hate speech) and hate speech directed at individuals (directed hate speech) to capture important nuances in the targets of online hate speech (ElSherief, Kulkarni et al. 2018). Beyond relying on textual features, researchers have also incorporated user characteristics, including network features and friend/follower counts to improve the accuracy of hate speech detection (Unsvåg and Gambäck 2018).

Another more recent set of approaches leverages large pre-classified datasets from online platforms to detect online hate speech. These include the bag-of-communities technique (Chandrasekharan, Samory et al. 2017), which computes the similarity of a post to the language used in nine other known hateful communities from 4chan, Reddit, Voat, and MetaFilter. Similar techniques have been employed by Saleem et al. (2017) and Siegel et al. (2020), using data from well-known hateful subreddits to classify hate speech on Twitter. An advantage of these methods is that they are not hindered by low intercoder reliability that can be found in training datasets or by the fact that rapidly evolving speech patterns online can make it difficult to use the same training data over time (Waseem 2016).

Despite these major advances in the automatic detection of online hate speech, existing methods largely have not been tested across multiple platforms or diverse types of hate speech. Owing to ease of data collection, most existing studies have relied on Twitter data. While other works have incorporated data from Reddit, YouTube, Facebook, Whisper, Tumblr, Myspace, Gab, the comment sections of websites, and blogs, these are relatively rare (Fortuna and Nunes 2018; Mathew, Dutt et al. 2019).

Additionally, the vast majority of studies examine English-language content, though some researchers have developed methods to detect hate speech in other languages. These include empirical examinations of hate speech in Amharic (Mossie and Wang 2018), Arabic (Siegel 2015; De Smedt et al. 2018; Siegel et al. 2018, Albadi et al. 2019, Chowdhury et al. 2019), Dutch (Van Hee et al. 2015), German (Ross et al. 2017), Hindi (Santosh and Aravind 2019), Indonesian (Aulia and Budi 2019), Italian (Lingiardi et al. 2019), Korean (Kang et al. 2018), Polish (Czapla et al. 2019), Romanian (Meza 2016), and Spanish (Basile et al. 2019). Crowd-sourced multilingual dictionaries of online hate speech including Hatebase, the Racial Slur Database, and HateTrack have also been developed, demonstrating promising avenues for future work (ElSherief, Kulkarni et al. 2018, Siapera et al. 2018). Yet approaches to automated hate speech detection that are designed to scale across multiple languages are quite difficult to develop, and more work is needed in this area.

Additionally, the majority of studies of online hate speech seek to detect all types of hate speech at once, or "general hate speech" (Fortuna and Nunes 2018). However, other works have examined specific types of harmful language, including jihadist hate speech (De Smedt et al. 2018), sectarian hate speech (Siegel 2015; Siegel et al. 2018), anti-Muslim hate speech (Olteanu et al. 2018), anti-black hate speech (Kwok and Wang 2013), misogynistic hate speech (Citron 2011), and anti-immigrant hate speech (Ross et al. 2017). Recent work has also explored differences in types of hate speech, comparing hate speech targeting diverse out-groups and distinguishing between more and less severe types of hate speech (Beauchamp et al. 2018; Saha et al. 2019; Siegel et al. 2019).

CREATORS OF HATE SPEECH IN THE DIGITAL REALM

While extensive research has explored organized hate groups' use of online hate speech, less is known about the actors in informal communities dedicated to producing harmful content, or the accounts that produce hate speech on mainstream platforms. Moreover, no empirical work has systematically examined how these actors interact within and across platforms.

Organized hate groups established an online presence shortly after the invention of the Internet (Bowman-Grieve 2009) and have proliferated over time. More than a decade of primarily qualitative research has demonstrated that organized hate groups use the Internet to disseminate hate speech on their official websites (Adams and Roscigno 2005; Chau and Xu 2007; Douglas 2007; Flores-Yeffal et al. 2011; Castle 2012; Parenti 2013). This includes the use of interactive forums (Holtz and Wagner 2009) such as chat boards and video games (Selepak 2010). Hate groups use these channels both to broaden their reach and to target specific audiences. For example, the explicitly racist video games that originate on far-right extremist websites are designed to appeal to ardent supporters and potential members alike, especially youth audiences (Selepak 2010). Along these lines, hate groups have used the Internet to recruit new members and reinforce group identity (Chau and Xu 2007; Parenti 2013; Weaver 2013). Online platforms are also especially well-suited to tailoring messages to specific groups or individuals (Castle 2012). By providing efficient ways to reach new audiences and disseminate hateful language, the Internet enables hate groups to be well represented in the digital realm, fostering a sense of community among their members, and attracting the attention of journalists and everyday citizens alike (Bowman-Grieve 2009; McNamee et al. 2010).

In addition to the official websites of organized hate groups, the number of sites dedicated to producing hateful content operated by informal groups and individuals has also increased over time (Potok 2015). These include explicitly racist, misogynistic, or otherwise discriminatory pages, channels, or communities on mainstream social networking platforms like Facebook, Twitter, and YouTube, as well as forums on Reddit 4chan, and 8chan, list serves, internet chat communities, discussion forums, and blogs designed to disseminate hateful rhetoric (Douglas 2007; Marwick 2017). These range from fake Facebook profiles designed to incite violence against minorities (Farkas and Neumayer 2017) to infamous (now banned) Reddit forums like /CoonTown and /fatpeoplehate (Chandrasekharan, Pavalanathan et al. 2017). Well-known white nationalists and hateful accounts have also operated openly on mainstream social media platforms. For example, Richard Spencer, who organized the "Unite the Right" alt-right Charlottesville rally, has more than 75,000 followers and was verified by Twitter up until November 2017, when he was stripped of his verified status. Twitter accounts such as @SageGang and @WhiteGenocide frequently tweet violent racist and anti-Semitic language (Daniels 2017).

However, such concentrations of hateful content are sometimes banned and removed from particular platforms. As a result, these communities often disappear and resurface in new forms. For example, in 2011, 4chan's founder deleted the news board (/n/) due to racist comments and created /pol/ as a replacement forum for political discussion.

4chan's /pol/ board quickly became a home for particularly hateful speech – even by 4chan standards (Hine et al. 2016). Similarly, banned subreddits like Coontown have moved to Voat, a platform with no regulations with regard to hate speech (Chandrasekharan, Pavalanathan et al. 2017). While survey data and ethnographic work suggests that users of 4chan and Redditt are overwhelmingly young, white, and male (Daniels 2017; Costello and Hawdon 2018), because of the anonymous nature of these sites we do not know very much about the users that produce the most hate speech. In particular, we do not know the degree to which their rhetoric represents their actual beliefs or is simply trolling or attention-seeking behaviour, which is quite common in these communities (Phillips 2015).

Outside of these official and unofficial pages and forums dedicated to hateful content, hate speech is also prevalent in general online discussions across a variety of popular platforms, including Facebook, YouTube, Myspace, Tumblr, Whisper, and Yik Yak (Black et al. 2016; Fortuna and Nunes 2018). While little is known about the specific individuals that produce hate speech on these mainstream platforms, recent work has begun to measure and characterize their behaviour. Examining the trajectory of producers of hate speech over time, Beauchamp et al. (2018) find that producers of misogynistic and racist hate speech on Twitter tend to start out expressing "softer," more indirect hateful language and later graduate to producing more virulent hate. The authors posit that this may be due to gradually decreasing levels of social stigma as these users find themselves in increasingly extreme social networks. ElSherief, Nilizadeh et al. (2018) find on Twitter that accounts that instigate hate speech tend to be new, very active, and express lower emotional awareness and higher anger and immoderation in the content of their tweets, compared to other Twitter users who did not produce such content. Similarly, using a manually annotated dataset of about 5,000 "hateful users," Ribeiro et al. (2018) find that hateful users tweet more frequently, follow more people each day, andtheir accounts are more short-lived and recent. They also find that, although hateful users tend to have fewer followers, they are very densely connected in retweet networks. Hateful users are seventy-one times more likely to retweet other hateful users and suspended users are eleven times more likely to retweet other suspended users, compared to non-hateful users. Comparing users that produce hate speech to those that do not on Gab, Mathew, Duttet al. (2019) also find that hateful users are densely connected to one another.

As a result, they argue, content generated by hateful users tends to spread faster, farther, and reach a much wider audience as compared to the content generated by users that do not produce hate speech.

Such behaviour may contribute to the overall visibility of hate speech on mainstream online platforms. For example, on Twitter, although tweets containing hate speech have lower numbers of replies and likes than non- hateful tweets, they contain a similar number of retweets (Klubicka and Fernandez 2018). The highly networked structure of hateful Twitter users also dovetails with qualitative evidence suggesting that people are mobilized on explicitly hateful subreddits or communities like the /pol/ board on 4chan to engage in coordinated racist or sexist attacks on Twitter (Daniels 2017).

Studying the network structure of users who produce online hate speech, Magdy et al. (2016) find that they can predict the likelihood that Twitter users tweet anti-Muslim messages after the 2015 Paris attacks with high levels of precision and accuracy based on their Twitter networks, even if they have never mentioned Muslims or Islam in their previous tweets. Twitter users who follow conservative media outlets, Republican primary candidates, evangelical Christian preachers, and accounts discussing foreign policy issues were significantly more likely to tweet anti-Muslim content following the Paris attacks than those that did not.

In one of the few existing surveys of social media users exploring the use of hate speech, Costello and Hawdon (2018) find that people who spend more time on Reddit and Tumblr report disseminating more hate speech online. Moreover, individuals who are close to an online community, or spend more time in communities where hate speech is common, are more inclined to produce hate material. Counter to their expectations, they find that spending more time online in general, however, is not associated with the production of hate and there is no association between the use of first-person shooter games and producing hate material online.

As with pages and forums explicitly dedicated to online hate speech, individual producers of online hate speech have increasingly been banned from Twitter and other mainstream platforms. While many of these users simply create new accounts after they have been suspended, others have moved to more specialized platforms where they can produce hate more freely. For example, in August 2016, the social network Gab was created as an alternative to Twitter. The platform stated that it was dedicated to "people and free speech first," courting users banned or suspended from other social networks (Marwick and Lewis 2017). Zannettou et al. (2018) found that Gab is mainly used for the dissemination and discussion of news and world events, and that it predominantly attracts alt-right users, conspiracy theorists, and trolls. The authors find that hate speech is much more common on Gab than Twitter but less common on Gab than on 4chan's /pol/ board. Similarly, Lima et al. (2018) found that Gab generally hosts banned users from other social networks, many of whom were banned due to their use of hate speech and extremist content.

TARGETS OF HATE SPEECH ON THE INTERNET

One of the few areas of consensus in defining hate speech, which separates it from other forms of harmful speech, is that hate speech targets groups or individuals as they relate to a group (Sellars 2016). A small body of literature has explicitly analyzed the targets of online hate speech. Studying the targets of online hate speech on Whisper (an anonymous online platform) and Twitter using a sentence-structure–based algorithm, Silva et al. (2016) find that targeted individuals on both platforms are primarily attacked on the basis of their ethnicity, physical characteristics, sexual orientation, class, or gender. Survey research suggests that victims of online hate speech tend to engage in high levels of online activity (Hawdon et al. 2014), have less online anonymity, and engage in more online antagonism (Costello, Rukus, and Hawdon 2018). Examining the targets of hate speech on Twitter, ElSherief, Nilizadeh et al. (2018) find that those targeted by hate speech were 60 percent more likely to be verified than the accounts of instigators and 40 percent more likely to be verified than general users, respectively. This suggests that more visible Twitter users (with more followers, retweets, and lists) are more likely to become targets of hate.

Along these lines, recent qualitative research suggests that journalists, politicians, artists, bloggers, and other public figures have been disproportionately targeted by hate speech (Isbister et al. 2018). For example, when the all-female reboot of Ghostbusters was released in July 2016, white supremacist Milo Yiannopoulos instigated a Twitter storm following the publication of his negative movie review on Breitbart. White supremacists began to bombard African American actress Leslie Jones's timeline with sexist and racist slurs and hateful memes, including rape and death threats. When the abuse escalated as Yiannopoulos began directly tweeting at Jones and egging on his followers, Jones left Twitter. After public pressure convinced the company to intervene, Yiannopoulos was banned from Twitter and Jones returned (Isaac 2016). Similarly, as the author Mikki Kendall describes, "I was going to leave Twitter at one point. It just wasn't usable for me. I would log on and have 2,500 negative comments. One guy who seemed to have an inexhaustible energy would Photoshop my image on top of lynching pictures and tell me I should be 'raped by dogs,' that kind of thing." Kendall was also doxxed – her address was made public online – and she received a picture of her and her family in a photo that "looked like it had been sighted through a rifle" (Isaac 2016).

In June 2016, several highly visible Jewish journalists began to report a barrage of online hate that involved steganography – triple parentheses placed Fleishman and Smith 2016). As a result, the Anti-Defamation League (ADL) added the triple parentheses to their database of hateful symbols. This "digital equivalent of a yellow star" was intended to identify Jews as targets for harassment online (Gross 2017). For example, Jonathan Weisman of the New York Times left Twitter after being subjected to anti-Semitic harassment beginning with a Twitter account known as @CyberTrump, which escalated to a barrage of hateful Twitter activity, voicemails, and emails containing slurs and violent imagery (Gross 2017).

As these examples suggest, online hate speech may be most visible in coordinated attacks detecting this behaviour (Mariconti et al. 2018). Such attacks draw a great deal of attention both online and through traditional media outlets, making these strategic targets useful for both extremists and trolls seeking to reach a broader audience and elevate their messages. Such coordinated harassment campaigns allow groups of anonymous individuals to work together to bombard particular users with harmful content again and again (Chess and Shaw 2015; Chatzakou et al. 2017). One manifestation of this behaviour is known as raiding, when ad hoc digital mobs organize and orchestrate attacks aimed to disrupt other platforms and undermine users who advocate issues and policies with which they disagree (Hine et al. 2016; Kumar et al. 2018; Mariconti et al. 2018). However, while raiding receives a great deal of media attention, we have little understanding of how common or pervasive these attacks are or on what platforms they most commonly occur.

PREVALENCE OF ONLINE HATE SPEECH

While a great deal of research has been devoted to defining and detecting online hate speech, we know surprisingly little about the popularity of online hate speech on either mainstream or fringe platforms, or how the volume of hate speech shifts in response to events on the ground. Social media platforms have increased the visibility of hate speech, prompting journalists and academics alike to assert that hate speech is on the rise. As a result, there is a tendency to characterize entire mainstream social media platforms as bastions of online hate, without using empirical evidence to evaluate how pervasive the phenomenon truly is. For example, after becoming the target of a hateful online attack, Atlantic editor Jeffrey Goldberg called Twitter "acesspool for anti-Semites, homophobes, and racists" (Lizza 2016). While any online hate speech is of course problematic, suggesting that a platform used by more than a quarter of Americans and millions more around the globe is dominated by such speech is misleading and potentially problematic – particularly in countries where civil and political liberties are already under threat and social media provides a valuable outlet for opposition voices (Gagliardone et al. 2016).

With regard to empirical evidence, a small handful of studies have begun to systematically evaluate the prevalence of hate speech on online platforms, though more work is needed. Analyzing the popularity of hate speech in more than 750 million political tweets and in 400 million tweets sent by a random sample of American Twitter users between June 2015 and June 2017, Siegel et al. (2020) find that, even on the most prolific days, only a fraction of a percentage of tweets in the American Twittersphere contain hate speech. Similarly, studying the popularity of hate speech on Ethiopian Facebook pages, Gagliardone et al. (2016) find that only 0.4 percent of statements in their representative sample were classified as hate speech, and 0.3 percent of tweets were classified as dangerous speech, which directly or indirectly calls for violence against a particular group.

While these studies suggest that online hate speech is a relatively rare phenomenon, cross-national survey research suggests that large numbers of individuals have nonetheless been incidentally exposed to online hate speech.

In a cross-national survey of internet users between the ages of fifteen and thirty, 53 percent of American respondents report being exposed to hate material online, while 48 percent of Finns, 39 percent of Brits, and 31 percent of Germans report exposure. Using online social networks frequently and visiting "dangerous sites" are two of the strongest predictors of such exposure (Hawdon et al. 2017). Perhaps explaining the discrepancy between empirical findings that hate speech is quite rare on mainstream platforms and high rates of self-reported exposure, Kaakinen et al. (2018) find that, while hateful content is rarely produced, it is more visible than other forms of content. Hate speech is also more common in particular online demographic communities than others. For example, Saha et al. (2019) find that hate speech is more prevalent in subreddits associated with particular colleges and universities than popular subreddits that were not associated with colleges or universities.

In addition to exploring the prevalence of online hate speech, recent work has investigated how offline events may drive upticks in the popularity of such rhetoric. One avenue of research explores the impact of violent offline events on various types of hate speech. For example, studying the causal effect of terror attacks in Western countries on the use of hateful language on Reddit andTwitter, Olteanu et al. (2018) find that episodes of extremist violence lead to an increase in online hate speech, particularly messages directly advocating violence, on both platforms. The authors argue that this provides evidence that theoretical arguments regarding the feedback loop between offline violence and online hate speech are – unfortunately – well-founded. This finding supports other research suggesting hate speech and hate crimes tend to increase after "trigger" events, which can be local, national, or international, and often drive negative sentiments toward groups associated with suspected perpetrators of violence (Awan and Zempi 2015).

Similarly, seeking to assess the impact of diverse episodes of sectarian violence on the popularity of anti-Shia hate speech in the Saudi Twitter sphere, Siegel et al. (2018) find that both violent events abroad and domestic terror attacks on Shia mosques produce significant upticks in the popularity of anti-Shia language in the Saudi Twitter sphere. Providing further insight into the mechanisms by which offline violent events lead to increases in the use of online hate speech, the authors demonstrate that, while clerics and other elite actors both instigate and spread derogatory rhetoric in the aftermath of foreign episodes of sectarian violence – producing the largest upticks in anti-Shia language – they are less likely to do so following domestic mosque bombings.

Exploring the effect of political – rather than violent – events on the popularity of online hate speech, Siegel et al. (2020) find, contrary to the popular journalistic narrative, that online hate speech did not increase either over the course of Donald Trump's 2016 campaign or in the aftermath of his unexpected election. Using a dataset of more than 1 billion tweets, their results are robust whether they detect hate speech using a machine- learning–augmented dictionary-based approach or a community-based detection algorithm comparing the similarity of daily Twitter data to the content produced on hateful subreddits over time. Instead, hate speech was "bursty" – spiking in the aftermath of particular events and re-equilibrating shortly afterward. Similarly, Faris et al. (2016) demonstrate spikes in online harmful speech are often linked to political events, whereas Saleem et al.

(2017) find that hate speech rose in the aftermath of events that triggered strong emotional responses like the Baltimore protests and the US Supreme Court decision on same-sex marriage.

Together, these studies demonstrate the importance of examining both the prevalence and the dynamics of online hate speech systematically over time and using large representative samples. More work is needed to better understand how different types of online hate speech gain traction in diverse global contexts and how their relative popularity shifts on both mainstream and specialized social media platforms over time.

OFFICE CONSEQUENCES OF ONLINE HATE SPEECH

Systematically measuring the impact of online hate speech is challenging (Sellars 2016), but a diverse body of research suggests that online hate speech has serious offline consequences both for individuals and for groups. Surveys of internet users indicate that exposure to online hate speech may cause fear (Hinduja and Patchin 2007), particularly in historically marginalized or disadvantaged populations. Other work suggests that such exposure may push people to withdraw from public debate both on- and offline, therefore harming free speech and civic engagement (Henson et al. 2013). Indeed, observational data indicate that exposure to hate speech may have many of the same consequences as being targeted by hate crimes, including psychological trauma and communal fear (Gerstenfeld 2017). Along these lines, human rights groups have argued that failure to monitor and counter hate speech online can reinforce the subordination of targeted minorities, making them vulnerable to attacks, while making majority populations more indifferent to such hatred (Izsak 2015). That being said, recent work demonstrates that interpretations of hate speech – what is considered hateful content as well as ratings of the intensity of content – differ widely by country (Salminen et al. 2019), and men and political conservatives tend to find hate material less disturbing than women, political moderates, and liberals (Costello et al. 2019).

On the individual level, qualitative research suggests that Muslims living in the West who are targeted by online hate speech fear that online threats may materialize offline (Awan and Zempi 2015). Furthermore, surveys of adolescent internet users have found that large numbers of African American respondents have experienced individual or personal discrimination online, and such exposure is associated with depression and anxiety, controlling for measures of offline discrimination (Tynes et al. 2008). In studying the differential effects of exposure to online hate speech, Tynes and Markoe (2010) find from a survey experiment conducted on college-age internet users that African American participants were most bothered by racist content (images) on social networking sites, whereas European Americans – especially those who held "colour-blind" attitudes – were more likely to be "not bothered" by those images. Similarly, individuals exposed to hate speech on university-affiliated subreddits exhibited higher levels of stress than those who were not (Saha et al. 2019). Survey data suggest that youth who have been exposed to online hate speech have weaker attachment to family and report higher levels of unhappiness, though this relationship is not necessarily causal (Hawdon et al. 2014). Exposure to hate speech online is also associated with an avoidance of political talk over time (Barnidge et al. 2019). At the group level, online hate speech has fueled intergroup tensions in a variety of contexts, sometimes leading to violent clashes and undermining social cohesion (Izsak 2015). For example, Facebook has come under fire for its role in mobilizing anti-Muslim mob violence in Sri Lanka and for inciting violence against the Rohingya people in Myanmar (Vindu, Kumar, and Frenkel 2018). Elucidating the mechanisms by which exposure to hate speech drives intergroup tension, survey data and experimental evidence from Poland suggest that frequent and repetitive exposure to hate speech leads to desensitization to hateful content, lower evaluations of populations targeted by hate speech, and greater distancing – resulting in higher levels of anti-out-group prejudice (Soral et al. 2018).

A diverse body of literature suggests that hate speech may foster an environment in which bias-motivated violence is encouraged either subtly or explicitly (Herek et al. 1992; Greenawalt 1996; Calvert 1997; Tsesis 2002; Matsuda 2018). Intergroup conflict is more likely to occur and spread when individuals and groups have the opportunity to publicly express shared grievances and coordinate collective action (Weidmann 2009; Cederman et al. 2010). Digital technology is thought to reduce barriers to collective action among members of the same ethnic or religious group by improving access to information about one another's preferences. This is thought to increase the likelihood of intergroup conflict and accelerate its spread across borders (Pierskalla and Hollenbach 2013; Bailard 2015; Weidmann 2015).

Moreover, while hate speech is just one of many factors that interact to mobilize ethnic conflict, it plays a powerful role in intensifying feelings of mass hate (Vollhardt et al. 2007; Gagliardone et al. 2014). This may be particularly true in the online sphere, where the anonymity of online communication can drive people to express more hateful opinions than they might otherwise (Cohen-Almagor 2017). As individuals come to believe that "normal" rules of social conduct do not apply (Citron 2014; Delgado and Stefancic 2014), intergroup tensions are exacerbated. Along these lines, online hate speech places a physical distance between speaker and audience, emboldening individuals to express themselves without repercussions (Citron 2014). Perhaps more importantly, online social networks create the opportunity for individuals to engage with like-minded others that mightotherwise never connect or be aware of one another's existence (Posner 2001). Recognizing the importance of online hate speech as an early warning sign of ethnic violence, databases of multilingual hate speech are increasingly used by governments, policymakers, and NGOs to detect and predict political instability, violence, and even genocide (Gagliardone et al. 2014; Tuckwood 2014; Gitari et al. 2015).

Many have argued that there is a direct connection between online hate and hate crimes, and perpetrators of offline violence often cite the role online communities have played in driving them to action (Citron 2014; Cohen-Almagor 2017; Gerstenfeld 2017). For example, on June 17, 2015, twenty- one-year-old Dylann Roof entered the Emanuel African Methodist Episcopal Church and murdered nine people. In his manifesto, Roof wrote that he drew his first racist inspiration from the Council of Conservative Citizens (CCC) website (Cohen-Almagor 2018). Similarly, the perpetrator of the 2019 Pittsburgh synagogue attack was allegedly radicalized on Gab, and the perpetrator of the 2019 New Zealand mosque shootings was reportedly radicalized on online platforms and sought to broadcast his attack on YouTube. While it is very difficult to causally examine the link between online hate speech and hate crimes, recent empirical work has attempted to do so. This work builds off of a larger literature exploring how the use of hate speech through traditional media platforms can be used to trigger violent outbursts or ethnic hatred. This includes work exploring the effect of hate radio on levels of violence during the Rwandan genocide (Yanagizawa-Drott 2014), research on how radio propaganda incited anti-Semitic violence in Nazi Germany, (Adena et al. 2015), and a study of how nationalist Serbian radio was used to incite violence in Croatia in the 1990s (DellaVigna et al. 2014).

Examining the effects of online hate, Chan et al. (2015) find that broadband availability increases racial hate crimes in areas with higher levels of segregation and a higher proportion of racially charged Google search terms. Their work suggests that online access is increasing the incidence of racial hate crimes executed by lone wolf perpetrators. Similarly, Stephens-Davidowitz (2017) finds that the search rate on Google for anti-Muslim words and phrases, including violent terms like "kill all Muslims," can be used to predict the incidence of anti-Muslim hate crimes over time. Other studies show an association between hateful speech on Twitter and hate crimes in the US context, but the causal links are not well identified (Williams et al. 2019; Chyzh et al. 2019).

In one of the only existing studies that explicitly examines the causal link between online hate and offline violence, Muller and Schwarz (2017) exploit exogenous variation in major internet and Facebook outages to show that anti-refugee hate crimes increase disproportionately in areas with higher Facebook usage during periods of high anti-refugee sentiment online. They find that this effect is particularly pronounced for violent incidents against refugees, including arson and assault. Similarly, in a second paper, Muller and Schwarz(2019) exploit variation in early adoption of Twitter to show that higher Twitter usage is associated with an increase in anti-Muslim hate crimes since the start of Trump's campaign. Their results provide preliminary evidence that social media can act as a propagation mechanism between online hate speech and offline violent crime. Together, this work suggests that online hate speech may have powerful real-world consequences, ranging from negative psychological effects at the individual level to violent attacks offline.

COMBATING ONLINE HATE SPEECH

Rising concern regarding these real-world effects of online hate speech have prompted researchers, policymakers, and online platforms to develop strategies to combat online hate speech. These approaches have generally taken two forms: content moderation and counter-speech.

One strategy to combat online hate speech has been to moderate content, which involves banning accounts or communities that violate platforms' terms of service or stated rules (Kiesler et al. 2012). On May 31, 2016, the European Commission in conjunction with Facebook, Twitter, YouTube,and Microsoft issued a voluntary Code of Conduct on Countering Illegal Hate Speech Online that required the removal of any hate speech, as defined by the European Union (EU). This was spurred by fears over a rise in intolerant speech against refugees as well as worries that hate speech fuels terror attacks (Aswad 2016). Additionally, beginning in December 2017, facing pressure in the aftermath of the deadly August 2017 "Unite the Right" march in Charlottesville, Virginia, Twitter announced a new policy to ban accounts that affiliate with groups "that use or promote violence against civilians to further their causes" (Twitter 2017). The platform began by suspending several accounts with large followings involved in white nationalism or in organizing the Charlottesville march. In this period, Twitter also suspended a far-right British activist who had been retweeted by President Trump, as well as several other accounts affiliated with her ultranationalist group (Nedig 2017). The company announced that their ban on violent threats would also be extended to include any content that glorifies violence (Twitter 2017). Similarly, in April 2018, Facebook announced its twenty-five-page set of rules dictating what types of content are permitted on Facebook (2018). The section on hate speech states, "We do not allow hate speech on Facebook because it creates an environment of intimidation and exclusion and in some cases may promote real-world violence." The goal of banning hate speech from more mainstream online platforms is to reduce the likelihood that everyday internet users are incidentally exposed to online hate speech.

However, little is known about how these bans are actually implemented in practice or how effective they have been in reducing online hate speech on these platforms or exposure to such speech more broadly. Moreover, the use of automatic hate speech detection has come under fire in the media as the limits of these methods have been highlighted by embarrassing mistakes – like when Facebook's proprietary filters flagged an excerpt from the Declaration of Independence as hate speech (Lapin 2018). While a February 2019 review by the European Commission suggests that social media platforms including Facebook and Google were successfully removing 75 percent of posts flagged by users that violate EU standards within 24 hours, we do not know what portion of hate speech is flagged or how this may be biased against or in favour of certain types of political speech (Laub 2019).

Empirical work on the effectiveness of banning hateful content yields mixed results. Studying the effect of banning the /fatpeoplehate and /CoonTown subreddits on Reddit in 2015, Chandrasekharan, Pavalanathan et al. (2017) find the ban was successful. Analyzing more than 100 million Reddit posts and comments, the authors found that many accounts discontinued using the site after the ban, and those that stayed decreased their hate speech usage by at least 80 percent. Although many of these users migrated to other subreddits, the new subreddits did not experience an increase in hate speech usage, suggesting the ban was successful in limiting online hate speech on Reddit. Also on Reddit, Saleem and Ruths (2019) find that banning a large hateful subreddit (r/ fatpeoplehate) prompted users of this subreddit to stop posting on Reddit. Similarly, other work suggests that banning accounts on Twitter disrupts extremist social networks, as users who are frequently banned suffer major drops in follower counts when they rejoin a particular platform (Berger and Perez 2016).

That being said, although bans may have decreased the overall volume of hate speech on Redditt, and disrupted extremist activity on Twitter, such activity may have simply migrated to other platforms. In response to the 2015 bans, Newell et al. (2016) find that disgruntled users sought out alternative platforms such as Voat, Snapzu, and Empeopled. Users who migrate to these fringe platforms often keep their usernames and attempt to recreate their banned communities in a new, less regulated domain (Chandrasekharan, Pavalanathan et al. 2017). In addition to moving hate speech from one platform to another, other work suggests that producers of harmful content simply become more creative about how to continue to use hate speech on their preferred platforms. For example, seeking to avoid content moderation, as previously described, members of online communities often use code words to circumvent detection (Chancellor et al. 2016; Sonnad 2016).

Additionally, attempts to ban user accounts may sometimes be counterproductive, galvanizing support from those who are sympathetic to hateful communities. When well-known users come under fire, people who hold similar beliefs may be motivated to rally to their defense and/or to express views that are opposed by powerful companies or organizations. For example, empirical studies of extremist behavior online examining pro-ISIS accounts suggest that online extremists view the blocking of their accounts asa badge of honor, and individuals who have been blocked or banned are often able to reactivate their accounts under new names (Vidino and Hughes 2015; Berger and Perez 2016). Moreover, banning users often prompts them to move to more specialized platforms, such as Gab or Voat, which may further radicalize individuals who produce online hate. Indeed, banning hateful users removes them from diverse settings where they may come into contact with moderate or opposing voices, elevating their grievances and feelings of persecution and pushing them into hateful echo chambers where extremism and calls for offline violence are normalized and encouraged (Marwick and Lewis 2017; Lima et al. 2018; Zannettou et al. 2018; Jackson 2019). While this is a compelling theoretical argument against banning users from mainstream platforms, more empirical work is needed to track the extent to which banned users migrate to more extreme platforms, as well as whether they indeed become further radicalized on these platforms (Jackson 2019).

In this way, existing empirical work on the effectiveness of content moderation suggests that, while it may reduce hate speech on particular platforms, as disgruntled users migrate to other corners of the Internet, it is unclear whether such efforts reduce hate speech overall. Moreover, thorny legal, ethical, and technical questions persist with regard to the benefits of banning hate speech on global social media platforms, particularly outside of Western democracies. For example, a recent ProPublica investigation found that Facebook's rules are not transparent and inconsistently applied by tens of thousands of global contractors charged with content moderation. In many countries and disputed territories, such as the Palestinian territories, Kashmir, and Crimea, activists and journalists have been censored for harmful speech as Facebook has responded to government concerns and worked to insulate itself from legal liability. The report concluded that Facebook's hate speech content moderation standards "tend to favour elites and governments over grassroots activists and racial minorities." Along these lines, governments may declare opposition speech to be hateful or extremist in order to manipulate content moderation to silence their critics (Laub 2019). Moreover, automated hate speech detection methods have not been well adapted to local contexts, and very few content moderators are employed that speak local languages – including those that are used to target at-risk minority groups who are often targeted by hate speech. In a famous example, in 2015, despite rising ethnic violence and rampant reports of hate speech on Facebook and other social media platforms targeting Muslims in Myanmar, Facebook allegedly just employed two Burmese-speaking content moderators (Stecklow 2018).

Recognizing that censoring hate speech may come into conflict with legal protections of free speech or may be manipulated by governments to target critics, international agencies such as UNESCO have generally maintained that "the free flow of information should always be the norm." As a result, they often argue that counter-speech is usually preferable to the suppression of hate speech (Gagliardone et al. 2015). Counter-speech is a direct response to hate speech intended to influence discourse and behaviour (Benesch 2014a, 2014b). Counter-speech campaigns have long been used to combat the public expression of hate speech and discrimination through traditional media channels. Examples of this in the US context include the use of anti-KKK billboards in the Deep South (Richards and Calvert 2000), and the dissemination of information about US hate groups by the Southern Poverty Law Center (McMillin 2014). Interventions designed to prevent the incitement of violence have also been deployed, including the use of soap operas to counter intergroup tensions in Rwanda and the use of television comedy in Kenya to discourage the use of hate speech (Staub et al. 2003; Paluck 2009; Kogen 2013). Experimental evaluations of these interventions have found that they may make participants better able to recognize and resist incitement to anti–out-group hatred.

More recent work has explored the use of counter-speech in the online sphere. For example, fearing violence in the lead-up to the 2013 Kenyan elections, international NGOs, celebrities, and local businesses helped to fund "peace propaganda" campaigns to deter the spread of online hate speech – and offline violence – in Kenya. For example, one company offered cash and cell phone time to Kenyans who sent peace messages to each other online, including photos, poems, and stories (Benesch 2014a). Demonstrating that counter- speech occurs organically on online platforms, in the aftermath of the 2015 Paris attacks, Magdy et al. (2016) estimate that the vast majority of tweets posted following the attacks were defending Muslims, while anti-Muslim hate tweets represented a small fraction of content in the Twittersphere. Similarly, examining online hate speech in Nigerian political discussions, Bartlett et al. (2015) find that extreme content is often met with disagreement, derision, and counter-messages.

A nascent strand of literature experimentally evaluates what types of counter-speech messages are most effective in reducing online hate speech. Munger (2017) shows that counter-speech using automated bots can reduce instances of racist speech if instigators are sanctioned by a high-status in-group member – in this case, a white male with a large number of Twitter followers. Similarly, Siegel and Badaan (2020) deployed a sockpuppet account to counter sectarian hate speech in the Arab Twittersphere. They find that simply receiving a sanctioning message reduces the use of hate speech, particularly for users in networks where hate speech is relatively uncommon. Moreover, they show that messages priming a common

Muslim religious identity containing endorsements from elite actors are particularly effective in decreasing users' post treatment level of hate speech. Additional research is needed to further evaluate what types of counter-speech from what sources are most effective in reducing online hate in diverse contexts. Recognizing the potential of counter-speech bots, Leetaru (2017) proposed deploying AI bots en masse to fight online hate speech, though the feasibility and consequences of such an intervention are not well understood. Simulating how much counter-speech might be necessary to "drown out" hate speech on Facebook, Schieb and Preuss (2016) find that counter-speech can have a considerable impact on reducing the visibility of online hate speech, especially when producers of hate speech are in the minority of a particular community. In one of the only studies that explicitly detects naturally occurring counter-speech on social media, (Mathew et al. 2018; Mathew, Saha et al. 2019) find that counter-speech comments receive much more likes and engagement than other comments and may prompt produces of hate speech to apologize or change their behaviour. More empirical work is needed, however, to see how this dynamic plays out more systematically on real-world social media platforms over time.

Explicitly comparing censorship or content monitoring to counter-speech interventions, Alvarez-Benjumea and Winter (2018) test whether decreasing social acceptability of hostile comments in an online forum decreases the use of hate speech. They first designed an online forum and invited participants to join and engage in conversation on current social topics. They then experimentally manipulated the comments participants observed before posting their own comments. They included a censoring treatment in which participants observed no hate comments and a counter-speech treatment in which hate speech comments were uncensored but were presented alongside posts highlighting the fact that hate speech was not considered acceptable on the platform. Comparing the level of hostility of the comments and instances of hate across the treatment conditions, they find that the censoring treatment was the most effective in reducing hostile comments. However, the authors note that the fact that they do not observe a statistically significant effect of the counter-speech treatment may be due to their small sample sizes and inability to monitor repeated interactions over time in their experimental setup. Together, this growing body of literature on the effects of censoring and counter-speech on online hate speech provides some optimism, particularly regarding the impact of content moderation on reducing hate speech on mainstream platforms and the ability of counter-speech campaigns to decrease the reach, visibility, and harm of online hate speech. However, we know very little about the potential collateral damage of these interventions. Future work should not only provide larger scale empirical tests of these types of interventions in diverse contexts but seek to evaluate the longer-term effects of these approaches.

SUMMATION AND DIRECTIONS FOR FUTURE RESEARCH

As online hate speech has become increasingly visible on social media platforms, it has emerged at the centre of academic, legal, and policy agendas. Despite increased attention to online hate speech, as this chapter demonstrates, the debate over how to define online hate speech is far from settled. Partly as a consequence of these definitional challenges, and partly as a result of the highly context-specific and evolving nature of online hate speech, detecting hateful content systematically is an extremely difficult task.

While state-of-the-art techniques employing machine learning, neural networks and incorporating contextual features have improved our ability to measure and monitor online hate speech, most existing empirical work is fairly fragmented – often detecting a single type of hate speech on one platform at one moment of time. Moreover, because of ease of data collection, the vast majority of studies have been conducted using English- language Twitter data and therefore do not necessarily tell us very much about other platforms or cultural contexts. Adding further complications, definitions of hate speech and approaches to detecting it are highly politicized, particularly in authoritarian contexts and conflict settings. Though some research has explored multiple types of hate speech, used several datasets, conducted research on multiple platforms, or examined trends in hate speech over time, these studies are the exception rather than the rule (Fortuna 2017). Drawing on the rich literature of hate speech detection techniques in computer science and social science, future work should attempt more systematic comparative analysis to improve our ability to detect online hate speech in its diverse forms.

Though less developed than the literature on defining and measuring online hate speech, recent work has explored both the producers of online hate speech and their targets. A large body of literature has evaluated how hate groups strategically use the Internet to lure recruits and foster a sense of community among disparate members, using primarily small-scale qualitative analysis of data from hate groups' official websites (Selepak 2010). Other work has conducted large-scale observational studies of the users that produce hate speech on mainstream social media platforms like Twitter and Reddit, including their demographic characteristics and network structures. These users tend to be young, male, very active on social media, and members of tightly networked communities in which producers of hate speech frequently retweet and like each other's posts (Costello and Hawdon 2018; Ribeiro et al. 2018).

With regard to the targets of hate speech, researchers have used both big data empirical analyses and surveys of the users targeted online to demonstrate that targets of hate speech are often prominent social media users with large followings

(ElSherief, Nilizadeh et al. 2018). Additionally, qualitative and quantitative work demonstrates that one targeting strategy on mainstream social media platforms is for well-organized groups of users to launch coordinated hate attacks or "raids" on bloggers, celebrities, journalists, or other prominent actors (Mariconti et al. 2018).

This may be one reason why online hate speech has received so much attention in the mainstream media, despite empirical evidence suggesting that hate speech is actually quite rare on mainstream social media platforms in aggregate. Indeed, quantitative work evaluating the prevalence of online hate speech suggests that it may represent only a fraction of a percentage point of overall posts on sites like Facebook and Twitter (Gagliardone et al. 2016; Siegel et al. 2020). Moreover, studies exploring the dynamics of online hate speech over time on Twitter suggest that it is quite bursty – it increases in response to emotional or violent events and then tends to quickly re-equilibrate (Awan and Zempi 2015; Olteanu et al. 2018; Siegel et al. 2020).Although hate speech may be rare, it can still have severe offline consequences. Survey data suggest that online hate speech negatively impacts the psychological well-being of individuals who are exposed to it and can have detrimental consequences for intergroup relations at the societal level (Tynes et al. 2008). A growing body of empirical evidence also suggests that online hate speech can incite people to violence and that it may be playing a particularly devastating role in fueling attacks on Muslim immigrants and refugees. Recent work exploring the causal effect of online hate speech on offline attitudes and behaviours (Chan et al. 2015; Muller and Schwarz 2017; Muller and Schwarz 2019) should be replicated, expanded, and adapted to enable us to better understand these dynamics in other contexts and over longer periods of time. Scientific studies have also assessed what strategies might be most effective to combat online hate speech. Empirical evidence suggests that banning hateful communities on Reddit, for example, reduced the volume of hate speech on the platform overall (Chandrasekharan, Pavalanathan et al. 2017). However, other work indicates that users who are banned from discussing particular topics on mainstream platforms simply move elsewhere to continue their hateful discourse (Newell et al. 2016).

Additionally, content and account bans could have galvanizing effects for certain extremist actors who view the sanction as a badge of honor (Vidino and Hughes 2015). More optimistically, experimental research using counter-speech to combat online hate speech suggests that receiving sanctioning messages from other Twitter users – particularly fellow in- group members, high-status individuals, or trusted elite actors – discourages users from tweeting hateful content (Munger 2017; Siegel and Badaan 2020). Moreover, large-scale empirical studies suggest that counter- speech is quite common in the online sphere, and the same events that trigger upticks in online hate speech often trigger much larger surges in counter- speech (Magdy et al. 2016; Olteanu et al. 2018). Future work should continue to explore what kinds of counter-speech might be most effective in diverse cultural contexts and on different platforms, as well as how counter-speech can be encouraged among everyday social media users. Given the dangerous offline consequences of online hate speech in diverse global contexts, academics and policymakers should continue to build on this existing literature to improve hate speech detection, gain a more comprehensive understanding of how hate speech arises and spreads, develop further understanding of hate speech's offline consequences, and build better tools to effectively combat it.

REFERENCES

Albadi, N., Kurdi, M., & Mishra, S. (2019). Investigating the effect of combining GRU neural networks with handcrafted features for religious hatred detection on Arabic Twitter space. Social Network Analysis and Mining, 9(41), 1–19.

Al-Makhadmeh, Z., & Tolba, A. (2020). Automatic hate speech detection using killer natural language processing optimizing ensemble deep learning approach. Computing, 102, 501–522. https://doi.org/10.1007/s00607-019-00745-0

Adams, J., & Roscigno, V. J. (2005). White supremacists, oppositional culture and the World Wide Web. Social Forces, 84(2), 759–778.

Adena, M., Enikolopov, R., Petrova, M., Santarosa, V., & Zhuravskaya, E. (2015). Radio and the rise of the Nazis in prewar Germany. The Quarterly Journal of Economics, 130(4), 1885–1939.

Agarwal, S., & Sureka, A. (2017). Characterizing linguistic attributes for automatic classification of intent based racist/radicalized posts on Tumblr microblogging website. arXiv.org. https://arxiv.org/abs/1701.04931

Alorainy, W., Burnap, P., Liu, H., & Williams, M. (2018). Cyber hate classification:"Othering" language and paragraph embedding. arXiv.org. https://arxiv.org/pdf/1801.07495.pdf

Alvarez-Benjumea, A., &Winter, F. (2018). Normative change and culture of hate: An experiment in online environments. European Sociological Review, 34(3), 223–237.

Aswad, E. (2016). The role of US technology companies as enforcers of Europe's new Internet hate speech ban. HRLR Online, 1(1), 1–14.

Aulia, N.,& Budi, I. (2019). Hate speech detection on Indonesian long text documents usingmachine learning approach. In Proceedings of the 2019 5th International Conference on Computing and Artificial Intelligence (pp. 164–169). New York: ACM.

Awan, I., & Zempi, I. (2015). We fear for our lives: Offline and online experiences of anti-Muslim hostility. Tell MAMA, October. www.tellmamauk.org/wp-content/uploads/resources/We%20Fear%20For%20Our%20Lives.pdf

Badjatiya, P., Gupta, S., Gupta, M., & Varma, V. (2017). Deep learning for hate speech detection in tweets. In Proceedings of the 26th International Conference on World Wide Web Companion (pp. 759–760). Geneva: International World Wide WebConferences Steering Committee.

Bailard, C. S. (2015). Ethnic conflict goes mobile: Mobile technology's effect on the opportunities and motivations for violent collective action. Journal of Peace Research, 52(3), 323–337.

Barnidge, M., Kim, B., Sherrill, L. A., Luknar, Ž.,& Zhang, J. (2019). Perceived exposure to and avoidance of hate speech in various communication settings. Telematics and Informatics, 44, 101263.

Bartlett, J., Krasodomski-Jones, A., Daniel, N., Fisher, A., & Jesperson, S. (2015). Social Media for Election Communication and Monitoring in Nigeria. Demos report, London.

Basile, V., Bosco, C., Fersini, E. et al. (2019). Semeval-2019 task 5: Multilingual detection of hate speech against immigrants and women in twitter. In J. May,E. Shutova, A. Herbelot, X. Zhu, M. Apidianaki, & S. M. Mohammad (Eds.), Proceedings of the 13th International Workshop on Semantic Evaluation (pp. 54–63). Minneapolis: Association for Computer Linguistics.

Beauchamp, N., Panaitiu, I., & Piston, S. (2018). Trajectories of hate: Mapping individual racism and misogyny on Twitter. Unpublished working paper.

Benesch, S. (2013). Dangerous speech: A proposal to prevent group violence. VoicesThat Poison: Dangerous Speech Project proposal paper. February 23. https:// dangerousspeech.org/wp-content/uploads/2018/01/Dangerous-Speech-Guidelines-2013.pdf

(2014a). *Countering Dangerous Speech to Prevent Mass Violence During Kenya's 2013 Elections.* United States Institute of Peace final report, February 28. https:// ihub.co.ke/ihubresearch/jb_BeneschCFPReportPeacebuildingInKenyapdf2014-3-25-07-08-41.pdf

(2014b). Defining and diminishing hate speech. In P. Grant (Ed.), *Freedom from Hate: State of the World's Minorities and Indigenous Peoples 2014* (pp. 18–25). London: Minority Rights Group International. https://minorityrights.org/wp-content/uploads/old-site-downloads/mrg-state-of-the-worlds-minorities-2014.pdf

Berger, J. M., & Perez, H. (2016). The Islamic State's diminishing returns on Twitter: How suspensions are limiting the social networks of English-speaking ISIS supporters. Occasional paper. Program on Extremism at George Washington University.

Black, E. W., Mezzina, K., & Thompson, L. A. (2016). Anonymous social media:Understanding the content and context of Yik Yak. Computers in Human Behavior, 57(C), 17–22.

Bowman-Grieve, L. (2009). Exploring Stormfront: A virtual community of the radical right. Studies in Conflict and Terrorism, 32(11), 989–1007.

Burnap, P., & Williams, M. L. (2016). Us and them: Identifying cyber hate on Twitter across multiple protected characteristics. EPJ Data Science, 5(1), 1–15.

Calvert, C. (1997). Hate speech and its harms: A communication theory perspective.Journal of Communication, 47(1), 4–19.

Castle, T. (2012). Morrigan rising: Exploring female-targeted propaganda on hate group websites. European Journal of Cultural Studies, 15(6), 679–694.

Cederman, L.-E., Wimmer, A., & Min, B. (2010). Why do ethnic groups rebel? New data and analysis. World Politics, 62(1), 87–119.

Chan, J., Ghose, A., & Seamans, R. (2015). The Internet and racial hate crime: Offline spillovers from online access. MIS Quarterly, 14(2), 381–403.

Chancellor, S., Pater, J. A., Clear, T., Gilbert, E., & De Choudhury, M. (2016). # thyghgapp: Instagram content moderation and lexical variation in pro-eating disorder communities. In Proceedings of the 19th ACM Conference on Computer-Supported Cooperative Work and Social Computing (pp. 1201–1213). New York: ACM.

Chandrasekharan, E., Samory, M., Srinivasan, A., & Gilbert, E. (2017a). The bag of communities: Identifying abusive behavior online with pre-existing internet data. In Proceedings of the 2017 CHI Conference on Human Factors in Computing Systems (pp. 3175–3187). New York: ACM.

Chandrasekharan, E., Pavalanathan, U., Srinivasan, A., Glynn, A., Eisenstein, J., & Gilbert, E. (2017b). You can't stay here: The efficacy of Reddit's 2015 ban examined through hate speech. In Proceedings of the ACM on Human-Computer Interaction,Vol. 1 (CSCW) (pp. 1–22). New York: Association for Computing Machinery.

Chatzakou, D., Kourtellis, N., Blackburn, J., De Cristofaro, E., Stringhini, G., & Vakali, A. (2017). Mean birds: Detecting aggression and bullying on Twitter. In Proceedings of the 2017 ACM on Web Science Conference (pp. 13–22).

Chau, M., & Xu, J. (2007). Mining communities and their relationships in blogs: A study of online hate groups. International Journal of Human-Computer Studies, 65(1), 57–70.

Chess, S., & Shaw, A. (2015). A conspiracy of fishes, or, how we learned to stop worrying about# GamerGate and embrace hegemonic masculinity. Journal of Broadcasting and Electronic Media, 59(1), 208–220.

Chetty, N., & Alathur, S. (2018). Hate speech review in the context of online socialnetworks. Aggression and Violent Behavior, 40, 108–118.

Chowdhury, A. G., Didolkar, A., Sawhney, R., & Shah, R. (2019). ARHNet: Leveraging community interaction for detection of religious hate speech in Arabic. In F. Alva- Manchego, E. Choi, & D. Khashabi (Eds.), Proceedings of the 57th Conference ofthe Association for Computational Linguistics: Student Research Workshop (pp.273–280). Florence: Association for Computational Linguistics.

Chyzh, O., Nieman, M. D., & Webb, C. (2019). The effects of dog-whistle politics on political violence. Political Science Publications, 1–10. https://lib.dr.iastate.edu/pols_pubs/59/

Citron,D.K.(2011).Misogynisticcyberhatespeech.WrittenTestimonyandStatement of Danielle Keates Citron, Professor of Law, Boston University School of Law hearing on "Fostering a Healthier Internet to Protect Consumers" before the House Committee on Energy and Commerce, October 16, 2019, Washington, DC.

(2014). Hate Crimes in Cyberspace. Cambridge, MA: Harvard University Press. Cohen-Almagor, R. (2011). Fighting hate and bigotry on the Internet. Policy and Internet, 3(3), 1–26.

(2017). Why confronting the Internet's dark side? Philosophia, 45(3), 919–929. (2018). When a ritual murder occurred at Purim: The harm in hate speech. ElProfesional de la Informacion, 27(3), 671–681.

Costello, M., & Hawdon, J. (2018). Who are the online extremists among us? Socio-demographic characteristics, social networking, and online experiences of those who produce online hate materials. Violence and Gender, 5(1), 55–60.

Costello, M., Hawdon, J., Bernatzky, C., & Mendes, K. (2019). Social group identity and perceptions of online hate. Sociological Inquiry, 89(3), 427–452.

Costello, M., Rukus, J., & Hawdon, J. (2018). We don't like your type around here: Regional and residential differences in exposure to online hate material targeting sexuality. Deviant Behavior, 40(3), 1–17.

Czapla, P., Gugger, S., Howard, J., & Kardas, M. (2019). Universal language model fine-tuning for Polish hate speech detection. Paper presented at the Proceedings of the PolEval 2019 Workshop: 149. May 31, Warsaw, Poland.

Dadvar, M., de Jong, F. M. G., Ordelman, R., & Trieschnigg, D. (2012). Improved cyber-bullying detection using gender information. In Proceedings of the Twelfth Dutch-Belgian Information Retrieval Workshop (DIR 2012) (pp. 23–25). Ghent: University of Ghent.

Daniels, J. (2017). Twitter and white supremacy: A love story. Dame Magazine, October 19. www.damemagazine.com/2017/10/19/twitter-and-white-supremacy- love-story/

Davidson, T., Warmsley, D., Macy, M., & Weber, I. (2017). Automated hate speech detection and the problem of offensive language. arXiv.org. https://arxiv.org/pdf/ 1703.04009.pdf

De Smedt, T., De Pauw, G., & Van Ostaeyen, P. (2018). Automatic Detection of Jihadist Online Hate Speech. CLiPS Technical Report No. 7 Computational Linguistics & Psycholinguistics Technical Report Series, Ctrs-007, February. www.uantwerpen.be/clips

Del Vigna, F., Cimino, A., Dell'Orletta, F., Petrocchi, M., & Tesconi. M. (2017). Hate me, hate me not: Hate speech detection on Facebook. In A. Armando, R. Baldoni, &R. Focardi (Eds.), Proceedings of the First Italian Conference on Cyber security (ITASEC17), (pp. 86–95). Venice: CEUR.

Delgado, R. (1982). Words that wound: A tort action for racial insults, epithets, and name calling. Harvard Civil Rights-Civil Liberties Review, 17, 133–181.

Delgado, R., & Stefancic, J. (2014). Hate speech in cyberspace. Wake Forest Law Review, 49, 319. https://ssrn.com/abstract=2517406

DellaVigna, S., Enikolopov, R., Mironova, V., Petrova, M., & Zhuravskaya, E. (2014). Cross-border media and nationalism: Evidence from Serbian radio in Croatia. American Economic Journal: Applied Economics, 6(3), 103–132.

Dinakar, K., Reichart, R., & Lieberman, H. (2011). Modeling the detection of Textual Cyberbullying. The Social Mobile Web, 11(02), 11–17.

Djuric, N., Zhou, J., Morris, R., Grbovic, M., Radosavljevic, V., & Bhamidipati, N. (2015). Hate speech detection with comment embeddings. In A. N. Joinson,K. Y. A. McKenna, T. Postmes, & U.-D. Reips (Eds.), Proceedings of the 24th International Conference on World Wide Web (pp. 29–30). New York: ACM.

Douglas, K. M. (2007). Psychology, discrimination and hate groups online. In The Oxford Handbook of Internet Psychology (pp. 155–163). Oxford: Oxford University Press.

Duarte, N., Llanso, E., & Loup, A. (2018). Mixed messages? The limits of automated social media content analysis. In Proceedings of the 1st Conference on Fairness, Accountability and Transparency, PMLR Vol. 81 (pp. 106). New York: Associationfor Computing Machinery.

ElSherief, M., Kulkarni, V., Nguyen, D., Wang, W. Y., & Belding, E. (2018). Hate lingo: A target-based linguistic analysis of hate speech in social media. arXiv.org. https:// arxiv.org/abs/1804.04257

ElSherief, M., Nilizadeh, S., Nguyen, D., Vigna, G., & Belding, E. (2018). Peer to peer hate: Hate speech instigators and their targets. arXiv.org. https://arxiv.org/abs/ 1804.04649Facebook. (2018). Facebook Community Standards. www.facebook.com/communitystandards/introduction

Faris, R., Ashar, A., Gasser, U., & Joo, D. (2016). Understanding harmful speech online. Berkman Klein Center Research Publication No. 2016-21 https://papers.ssrn.com/sol3/papers.cfm?abstract_id=2882824

Farkas, J., & Neumayer, C. (2017). Stop fake hate profiles on Facebook: Challenges for crowd sourced activism on social media. First Monday, 22(9 http://firstmonday.org/ojs/index.php/fm/article/view/8042

Fleishman, C., & Smith, A. (2016). Exposed: The secret symbol Neo-Nazis use to target Jews online. Mic, June 1. https://mic.com/articles/144228/echoes-exposed-the- secret-symbol-neo-nazis-use-to-target-jews-online

Flores-Yeffal, N. Y., Vidales, G., & Plemons, A. (2011). The Latino cyber-moral panic process in the United States. Information, Communication and Society, 14(4), 568–589.

Fortuna, P. C. T. (2017). Automatic detection of hate speech in text: an overview of the topic and dataset annotation with hierarchical classes. U.Porto. https://repositorio- aberto.up.pt/handle/10216/106028

Fortuna, P., & Nunes, S. (2018). A survey on automatic detection of hate speech in text.ACM Computing Surveys (CSUR), 51(4), 85.

Gagliardone, I., Gal, D., Alves, T., & Martinez, G. (2015). Countering Online Hate Speech. Paris: UNESCO Publishing.

Gagliardone, I., Pohjonen, M., Beyene, Z. et al. (2016). Mechachal: Online debates andelections in Ethiopia: From hate speech to engagement in social media. Working paper. https://eprints.soas.ac.uk/30572/

Gagliardone, I., Patel, A., & Pohjonen, M. (2014). Mapping and analysing hate speechonline: Opportunities and challenges for Ethiopia. University of Oxford Comparative Media, Law & Policy website. https://pcmlp.socleg.ox.ac.uk/

mapping-and-analysing-hate-speech-online-opportunities-and-challenges-for- ethiopia/

Gerstenfeld, P. B. (2017). Hate Crimes: Causes, Controls, and Controversies. London: Sage.

Gitari, N. D., Zuping, Z., Damien, H., & Long, J. (2015). A lexicon-based approach for hate speech detection. International Journal of Multimedia and Ubiquitous Engineering, 10(4), 215–230.

Greenawalt, K. (1996). Fighting Words: Individuals, Communities, and Liberties of Speech. Princeton: Princeton University Press.

Greevy, E., & Smeaton, A. F. (2004). Classifying racist texts using a support vector machine. In Proceedings of the 27th Annual International ACM SIGIR Conference on Research and Development in Information Retrieval (pp. 468–469). New York: ACM.

Gross, T. (2017). Attacked by alt-right trolls: A Jewish journalist links Trump to the rise of hate. NPR: Fresh Air, March 19. www.npr.org/2018/03/19/594894657/attacked-by-alt-right-trolls-ajewish-journalist-links-trump-to-the-rise-of-hate

Haraszti, M. (2012). Foreword: Hate speech and coming death of the international standard before it was born (complaints of a watchdog). In M. Herz & P. Molnar(Eds.), The Content and Context of Hate Speech: Rethinking Regulation and Responses (pp. xiii–xviii). Cambridge: Cambridge University Press. https://doi.org/10.1017/CBO9781139042871.001

Hawdon, J., Oksanen, A., & Rasänen, P. (2014). Victims of online hate groups: American youths exposure to online hate speech. In J. Hawdon, J. Ryan, &M. Lucht (Eds.), The Causes and Consequences of Group Violence: From Bullies to Terrorists (pp. 165–182). Lanham, MD: Lexington Books.

Hawdon, J., Oksanen, A., & Rasänen, P. (2017). Exposure to online hate in four nations: A cross-national consideration. Deviant Behavior, 38(3), 254–266.

Henson, B., Reyns, B. W., & Fisher, B. S. (2013). Fear of crime online? Examining the effect of risk, previous victimization, and exposure on fear of online interpersonal victimization. Journal of Contemporary Criminal Justice, 29(4), 475–497.

Herek, G. M., Berrill, K. T., & Berrill, K. (1992). Hate Crimes: Confronting Violence Against Lesbians and Gay Men. London: Sage.

Hinduja, S., & Patchin, J. W. (2007). Offline consequences of online victimization: School violence and delinquency. Journal of School Violence, 6(3), 89–112.

Hine, G. E., Onaolapo, J., De Cristofaro, E. et al. (2016). Kek, cucks, and god emperor Trump: A measurement study of 4chan's politically incorrect forum and its effects on the web. arXiv.org. https://arxiv.org/abs/1610.03452

Holtz, P., & Wagner, W. (2009). Essentialism and attribution of monstrosity in racist discourse: Right-wing Internet postings about Africans and Jews. Journal of Community and Applied Social Psychology, 19(6), 411–425.

Howard, J. W. (2019). Free speech and hate speech. Annual Review of Political Science,22, 93–109.

Isaac, M. (2016). Twitter bars Milo Yiannopoulos in wake of Leslie Jones's reports of abuse. New York Times, July 20. www.nytimes.com/2016/07/20/technology/twitter-bars-milo-yiannopoulos-in-crackdown-on-abusive-comments.html

Isbister, T., Sahlgren, M., Kaati, L., Obaidi, M., & Akrami, N. (2018). Monitoring targeted hate in online environments. arXiv.org. https://arxiv.org/abs/1803.04757 Izsak, R. (2015). Hate speech and incitement to hatred against minorities in the media. UN Humans Rights Council. arXiv.org. www.ohchr.org/EN/Issues/Minorities/ SRMinorities/Pages/Annual.aspx

Jackson, S. (2019). The double-edged sword of banning extremists from social media. https://osf.io/preprints/socarxiv/2g7yd/

Kaakinen, M., Räsänen, P., Näsi, M., Minkkinen, J., Keipi, T., & Oksanen, A. (2018). Social capital and online hate production: A four country survey. Crime, Law and Social Change, 69(1), 25–39.

Kang,S.,Kim,J.,Park,K.,&Cha,M.(2018).ClassificationofhatefulcommentsinaKorean news portal. www.dbpia.co.kr/journal/articleDetail?nodeId=NODE07503234

Kennedy, B., Kogon, D., Coombs, K. et al. (2018). A typology and coding manual for the study of hate-based rhetoric. arXiv.org. https://psyarxiv.com/hqjxn/

Kiesler, S., Kraut, R., Resnick, P., & Kittur, A. (2012). Regulating behaviour in online communities. In R. E. Kraut & P. Resnick (Eds.), Building Successful Online Communities: Evidence-Based Social Design (pp. 125–177). Cambridge, MA: MIT Press.

Klubicka, F., & Fernandez, R. (2018). Examining a hate speech corpus for hate speech detection and popularity prediction. arXiv.org. https://arxiv.org/abs/1805.04661

Kogen, L. (2013). Testing a media intervention in Kenya: Vioja Mahakamani, dangerous speech, and the Benesch guidelines. University of Pennsylvania Scholarly Commons. https://repository.upenn.edu/cgi/viewcontent.cgi?article=1000&context=africaictresearch

Kumar, S., Hamilton, W. L., Leskovec, J., & Jurafsky, D. (2018). Community interaction and conflict on the web. In Proceedings of the 2018 World Wide Web Conference on World Wide Web (pp. 933–943). Geneva: International World Wide Web Conferences Steering Committee.

Kwok, I., & Wang, Y. (2013). Locate the hate: Detecting Tweets against Blacks. In AAAI'13 Proceedings of the 27th AAAI Conference on Artificial Intelligence (pp. 1621–1622). Bellevue, WA: AAAI Press.

Lapin, T. (2018). Facebook flagged Declaration of Independence as hate speech. New York Post, 5 July. https://nypost.com/2018/07/05/facebook-flagged-declaration-of-independenceas-hate-speech/

Laub, Z. (2019). Hate speech on social media: Global comparisons. Council on Foreign Relations Backgrounder, June 7. www.cfr.org/backgrounder/hate-speech-social- media-global-comparisons

Leetaru, K. (2017). Fighting social media hate speech with AI-powered bots. Forbes, February 4. www.forbes.com/sites/kalevleetaru/2017/02/04/fighting-social- mediahate-speech-with-ai-powered-bots/5a22dfa327b1

Lima, L., Reis, J. C., & Melo, P. (2018). Inside the right-leaning echo chambers: Characterizing gab, an unmoderated social system. In 2018 IEEE/ACM International Conference on Advances in Social Networks Analysis and Mining (ASONAM) (pp. 515–522). IEEE.

Lingiardi, V., Carone, N., Semeraro, G., Musto, C., D'Amico, M., & Brena, S. (2019). Mapping Twitter hate speech towards social and sexual minorities: a lexicon-based approach to semantic content analysis. Behaviour and Information Technology, 1–11.

Liu, S., & Forss, T. (2014). Combining n-gram based similarity analysis with sentiment analysis in web content classification. In Proceedings of the International Joint Conference on Knowledge Discovery, Knowledge Engineering and Knowledge Management, Vol. 1. (pp. 530–537). Setúbal: SciTePress.

(2015). New classification models for detecting Hate and Violence web content. In Proceedings of the 7th International Joint Conference on Knowledge Discovery, Knowledge Engineering and Knowledge Management (IC3K 2015), Vol. 1. (pp. 487–495). Lisbon: IEEE.

Lizza, R. (2016). Twitter's anti-Semitism problem. The New Yorker, October 19. www.newyorker.com/news/news-desk/twitters-anti-semitism-problem

Magdy, W., Darwish, K., Abokhodair, N., Rahimi, A., & Baldwin, T. (2016). # isisisnotislam or # deportallmuslims? Predicting unspoken views. In Proceedings of the 8th ACM Conference on Web Science (pp. 95–106). New York: ACM.

Magu, R., Joshi, K., & Luo, J. (2017). Detecting the hate code on social media. arXiv. org. https://arxiv.org/abs/1703.05443

Mariconti, E., Suarez-Tangil, G. Blackburn, J. et al. (2018). "You know what to do":Proactive detection of YouTube videos targeted by coordinated hate attacks. arXiv. org. https://arxiv.org/abs/1805.08168

Marwick, A. (2017). Are there limits to online free speech? Data & Society Research Institute (blog), January 5. https://points.datasociety.net/are-_there-_limits-_to-_online-_free-_speech-_14dbb7069aec

Marwick, A., & Lewis, R. (2017). Media Manipulation and Disinformation Online.New York: Data & Society Research Institute.

Mathew, B., Kumar, N., Goyal, P., & Mukherjee, A. (2018). Analyzing the hate and counter speech accounts on Twitter. arXiv.org. https://arxiv.org/abs/1812.02712

Mathew, B., Dutt, R., Goyal, P., & Mukherjee, A. (2019). Spread of hate speech in online social media. In Proceedings of the 10th ACM Conference on Web Science (pp. 173–182). New York: ACM.

Mathew, B., Saha, P., & Tharad, H. et al. (2019). Thou shalt not hate: Countering online hate speech. arXiv.org. https://arxiv.org/abs/1808.04409

Matsuda, M. J. (2018). Words That Wound: Critical Race Theory, Assaultive Speech, and the First Amendment. London: Routledge.

McMillin, S. E. (2014). Ironic outing: The power of hate group designations to reframe political challenges to LGBT rights and focus online advocacy efforts. Journal of Policy Practice, 13(2), 85–100.

McNamee, L. G., Peterson, B. L., & Peña, J. (2010). A call to educate, participate, invoke and indict: Understanding the communication of online hate groups. Communication Monographs, 77(2), 257–280.

Meza, R. M. (2016). Hate-speech in the Romanian online media. Journal of Media Research, 9(3), 55.

Mossie, Z., & Wang, J.-H. (2018). Social network hate speech detection for Amhariclanguage. Paper presented at the Fourth International Conference on Natural Language Computing (NATL). April 28–29, Dubai, UAE.

Muller, K., & Schwarz, C. (2017). Fanning the flames of hate: Social media and hate crime. SSRN. https://papers.ssrn.com/sol3/papers.cfm?abstract_id=3082972

Muller, K., & Schwarz, C. (2019). Making America hate again? Twitter and hate crime under Trump. SSRN. https://papers.ssrn.com/sol3/papers.cfm?abstract_id=3149103

Munger, K. (2017). Tweetment effects on the tweeted: Experimentally reducing racist harassment. Political Behavior, 39(3), 629–649.

Nedig, H. (2017). Twitter launches hate speech crackdown. The Hill. December, 18. https://thehill.com/policy/technology/365424-twitter-to-begin-enforcing-new-hate-speech-rules

Newell, E., Jurgens, D., Saleem, H. M. et al. (2016). User migration in online social networks: A case study on Reddit during a period of community unrest. In Proceedings of the Tenth International AAAI Conference on Web and SocialMedia (pp. 279–288). Palo Alto, CA: AAAI Press.

Olteanu, A., Castillo, C., Boy, J., & Varshney, K. R. (2018). The effect of extremist violence on hateful speech online. arXiv.org. https://arxiv.org/abs/1804.05704

Paluck, E. L. (2009). Reducing intergroup prejudice and conflict using the media: A field experiment in Rwanda. Journal of Personality and Social Psychology, 96(3), 574–587.

Parekh, B. (2012). Is there a case for banning hate speech? In M. Herz & P. Molnar (Eds.), The Content and Context of Hate Speech: Rethinking Regulation and Responses (pp. 37–56). Cambridge: Cambridge University Press.

Parenti, M. (2013). Extreme right organizations and online politics: A comparativeanalysis of five Western democracies. In P. Nixon, R. Rawal, & D. Mercea (Eds.), Politics and the Internet in Comparative Context (pp. 155–173). London: Routledge.

Phillips, W. (2015). This Is Why We Can't Have Nice Things: Mapping the Relationship Between Online Trolling and Mainstream Culture. Cambridge, MA: MIT Press.

Pierskalla, J. H., & Hollenbach, F. M. (2013). Technology and collective action: Theeffect of cell phone coverage on political violence in Africa. American Political Science Review, 107(2), 207–224.

Posner, R. A. (2001). The speech market and the legacy of Schenck. In G. R. Stone &L. C. Bollinger (Eds.), Eternally Vigilant: Free Speech in the Modern Era (pp.121–152). Chicago: University of Chicago Press.

Potok, M. (2015). The Year in Hate and Extremism. Southern Poverty Law Center intelligence report. www.splcenter.org/fighting-hate/intelligence-report/2015/year- hate-and-xtremism-0

Ribeiro, M. H., Calais, P. H., Santos, Y. A., Almeida, V. A. F., & Meira, W., Jr. (2018). Characterizing and detecting hateful users on Twitter. arXiv.org. https://arxiv.org/pdf/1803.08977.pdf

Richards, R. D., & Calvert, C. (2000). Counterspeech 2000: A new look at the old remedy for bad speech. BYU Law Review, 2000(2), 553–586.

Ross, B., Rist, M., Carbonell, G., Cabrera, B., Kurowsky, N., & Wojatzki, M. (2017). Measuring the reliability of hate speech annotations: The case of the European refugee crisis. arXiv.org. https://arxiv.org/abs/1701.08118

Saha, K., Chandrasekharan, E., & De Choudhury, M. (2019). Prevalence andpsychological effects of hateful speech in online college communities. In Proceedings of the 11th ACM Conference on Web Science (pp. 255–264). New York: ACM.

Saleem, H. M., Dillon, K. P., Benesch, S., & Ruths, D. (2017). A web of hate: Tackling hateful speech in online social spaces. arXiv.org. https://arxiv.org/abs/1709.10159

Saleem, H. M., & Ruths, D. (2019). The aftermath of disbanding an online hateful community. arXiv.org. https://arxiv.org/pdf/1804.07354.pdf

Salminen, J., Almerekhi, H., Kamel, A. M., Jung, S.-g., & Jansen, B. J. (2019). Online hate ratings vary by extremes: A statistical analysis. In Proceedings of the 2019 Conference on Human Information Interaction and Retrieval (pp. 213–217).

Santosh, T. Y. S. S., & Aravind, K. V. S. (2019). Hate Speech Detection in Hindi-EnglishCode-Mixed Social Media Text. In Proceedings of the ACM India Joint International Conference on Data Science and Management of Data (pp. 310–313). New York: ACM.

Schieb, C., & Preuss, M. (2016). Governing hate speech by means of counterspeech on Facebook. Paper presented at the 66th Annual Conference of the International Communication Association: Communicating with Power, June 9–13, Fukuoka,Japan.

Schmidt, A., & Wiegand, M. (2017). A survey on hate speech detection using natural language processing. In Proceedings of the 5th International Workshop on Natural Language Processing for Social Media (pp. 1–10). Stroudsburg, PA: Association for Computational Linguistics.

Selepak, A. (2010). Skinhead Super Mario Brothers: An examination of racist and violent games on White supremacist web sites. Journal of Criminal Justice and Popular Culture, 17(1), 1–47.

Sellars, A. (2016). Defining hate speech. SSRN. https://papers.ssrn.com/sol3/papers.cfm abstract_id=2882244

Siapera, E., Moreo, E., & Zhou, J. (2018). Hate Track: Tracking and Monitoring Online Racist Speech. Dublin: Irish Human Rights and Equality Commission.

Siegel, A. (2015). Sectarian Twitter Wars: Sunni-Shia Conflict and Cooperation in theDigital Age, Vol. 20. Washington, DC: Carnegie Endowment for International Peace.

Siegel, A., Nitikin, E., & Barberá, P. (2020). Trumping Hate on Twitter: Online Hate Speech in the 2016 Presidential Election Campaign and Its Aftermath. Unpublishedmanuscript.

Siegel, A., Tucker, J., Nagler, J., & Bonneau, R. (2018). Socially Mediated Sectarianism.Unpublished manuscript.

Siegel, A., & Badaan, V. (2020). No2Sectarianism: Experimental Approaches to Reducing Online Hate Speech. Forthcoming in the American Political Science Review.

Silva, L., Mondal, M., Correa, D., Benevenuto, F., & Weber, I. (2016). Analyzing the targets of hate in online social media. arXiv.org. https://arxiv.org/abs/1603.07709v1

Sonnad, N. (2016). Alt-right trolls are using these code words for racial slurs online. Quartz, October 1. https://qz.com/798305/alt-right-trolls-are-using-googles- yahoos-skittles-andskypes-as code-words-for-racial-slurs-on-twitter/

Soral, W., Bilewicz, M., & Winiewski, M. (2018). Exposure to hate speech increases prejudice through desensitization. Aggressive Behavior, 44(2), 136–146.

Staub, E., Pearlman, L. A., & Miller, V. (2003). Healing the roots of genocide in Rwanda. Peace Review, 15(3), 287–294.

Stecklow, S. (2018). Why Facebook Is Losing the War on Hate Speech in Myanmar. Reuters Special Report, August 15. www.reuters.com/investigates/special-report/myanmar-facebook-hate/

Stephens-Davidowitz, S. (2017). Everybody Lies: Big Data, New Data, and What the Internet Can Tell Us About Who We Really Are. New York: HarperCollins.

Tsesis, A. (2002). Destructive Messages: How Hate Speech Paves the Way For Harmful Social Movements, Vol. 778. New York: New York University Press.

Tuckwood,C.(2014).Thestateofthe field:Technologyforatrocityresponse. Genocide Studies and Prevention: An International Journal, 8(3), 81–86.

Twitter. (2017). Twitter Rules and Policies. https://help.twitter.com/en/rules-and-policies/violent-groups(2018). The Twitter Rules. https://support.twitter.com/articles/18311

Tynes, B. M., Giang, M. T., Williams, D. R., & Thompson, G. N. (2008). Online racial discrimination and psychological adjustment among adolescents. Journal of Adolescent Health, 43(6), 565–569.

Tynes, B. M., & Markoe, S. L. (2010). The role of color-blind racial attitudes in reactions to racial discrimination on social network sites. Journal of Diversity in Higher Education, 3(1), 1–13.

Unsvåg, E. F., & Gambäck, B. (2018). The effects of user features on Twitter hate speechdetection. In Proceedings of the 2nd Workshop on Abusive Language Online (ALW2) (pp. 75–85). Stroudsburg, PA: Association for Computational Linguistics.

Van Hee, C., Lefever, E., Verhoeven, B. et al. (2015). Detection and fine-grained classification of cyberbullying events. In International Conference Recent Advances in Natural Language Processing (RANLP) (pp. 672–680). Shumen: INCOMA.

Vidino, L., & Hughes, S. (2015). ISIS in America: From Retweets to Raqqa. Program on Extremism, George Washington University report. https://extremism.gwu.edu/sites/g/files/zaxdzs2191/f/downloads/ISIS%20in%20America%20-%20Full%20Report.pdf

Vindu G., Kumar, H., & Frenkel, S. (2018). In Sri Lanka, Facebook contends with shutdown after mob violence. New York Times, March 8. www.nytimes.com/2018/ 03/08/technology/sri-lanka-facebook-shutdown.html

Vollhardt, J., Coutin, M., Staub, E., Weiss, G., & Deflander, J. (2007). Deconstructing hate speech in the DRC: A psychological media sensitization campaign. Journal of Hate Studies, 5(15), 15–35.

Warner, W., & Hirschberg, J. (2012). Detecting hate speech on the World Wide Web. InS. Owsley Sood, M. Nagarajan, & M. Gamon (Eds.), Proceedings of the Second Workshop on Language in Social Media (pp. 19–26). New York: ACL.

Waseem, Z. (2016). Are you a racist or am I seeing things? Annotator influence on hate speech detection on Twitter. In D. Bamman, A. Seza Dog˘ ruöz, J. Eisenstein et al. (Eds.), Proceedings of the First Workshop on NLP and Computational Social Science (pp. 138–142). Stroudsburg, PA: Association for Computational Linguistics.

Waseem, Z., & Hovy, D. (2016). Hateful symbols or hateful people? Predictive features for hate speech detection on Twitter. In M. Sahlgren & O. Knutsson (Eds.), Proceedings of the NAACL HLT Workshop on Extracting and Using Constructions in Computational Linguistics (pp. 88–93). Stroudsburg, PA: Association for Computational Linguistics.

Weaver, S. (2013). A rhetorical discourse analysis of online anti-Muslim and anti-Semitic jokes. Ethnic and Racial Studies, 36(3), 483–499.

Weidmann, N. B. (2009). Geography as motivation and opportunity: Group concentration and ethnic conflict. Journal of Conflict Resolution, 53(4), 526–543. (2015). Communication networks and the transnational spread of ethnic conflict. Journal of Peace Research, 52(3), 285–296.

Williams, M. L., Burnap, P., Javed, A., Liu, H., & Ozalp, S. (2019). Hate in the machine: Anti-Black and anti-Muslim social media posts as predictors of offline racially and religiously aggravated crime. The British Journal of Criminology, 60(1), 93–117.

Yanagizawa-Drott, D. (2014). Propaganda and conflict: Evidence from the Rwandangenocide. The Quarterly Journal of Economics, 129(4), 1947–1994.

YouTube. (2018). Community Guidelines. www.youtube.com/yt/ policyandsafety/communityguidelines.html

Yuan, S., Xintao W., & Xiang, Y. (2016). A two phase deep learning model foridentifying discrimination from tweets. In EDBT: 19th International Conference on Extending Database Technology (pp. 696–697). OpenProceedings.org.

Zannettou, S., Bradlyn, B., De Cristofaro E. et al. (2018). What is Gab? A bastion of free speech or an alt-right echo chamber? arXiv.org. https://arxiv.org/abs/1802.05287

Zhang, Z., Robinson, D., & Tepper, J. (2018). Detecting hate speech on Twitter using a convolution-GRU based deep neural network. In A. Gangemi, R. Navigli, M.-E. Vidal et al. (Eds.), The Semantic Web: ESWC 2018 (pp. 745–760). Cham: Springer.

05 COMPUTATIONAL PROPAGANDA AND BOTS:

UTILIZING AUTOMATION FOR COMMUNICATION AND MANIPULATION

INTRODUCTION: AN OVERVIEW

In the digital age, the convergence of technology and communication has given rise to a formidable force: computational propaganda and the deployment of bots. This complex interplay between automation and communication has transformed the landscape of information dissemination and manipulation. As we delve into the intricate web of computational propaganda, we begin to understand how these automated agents are harnessed to influence opinions, control narratives, and shape the public discourse. This introduction explores the intriguing world of computational propaganda and the pivotal role that bots play in orchestrating its impact on society.

Public awareness surrounding the threat of political bots, of international fears about armies of automated accounts taking over civic conversations on social media, reached a peak in the spring of 2017. On May 8 of that year, former Acting US Attorney General Sally Yates and former US Director of National Intelligence James R. Clapper Jr. sat before Congress to testify on what they called "the Russian toolbox" used in online efforts to manipulate the 2016 US election (Washington Post Staff 2017). In response to their testimony and a larger US intelligence community (IC) report on the subject Senator Sheldon Whitehouse said, "I went through the list [of tools used by the Russians] .. . it looked like propaganda, fake news, trolls, and bots. We can all agree from the IC report that those were in fact used in the 2016 election" (Washington Post Staff 2017).

Yates and Clapper argued that the Russian government and its commercial proxy – the Internet Research Agency (IRA) – made substantive use of bots to spread disinformation and inflame polarization during the 2016 US presidential election. These comments mirrored concurrent allegations made by other public officials, but also by academic researchers and investigative journalists, around the globe. Eight months earlier, during a speech before her country's parliament German Chancellor Angela Merkel raised concerns that bots would affect the outcome of their upcoming election (Copley 2016). Shortly thereafter, the New York Times described the rise of "a battle among political bots" on Twitter.

Around the same time, research from the University of Southern California's Information Sciences Institute concretized the ways that social media bots were being used to manipulate public opinion:

The presence [of] social bots in online political discussion can create three tangible issues: first, influence can be redistributed across suspicious accounts that may be operated with malicious purposes; second, the political conversation can become further polarized; third, the spreading of misinformation and unverified information can be enhanced. (Bessi and Ferrara 2016).

These findings were backed up by several other prominent studies that both preceded this work and have vindicated it since. Metaxas and Mustafaraj (2012) discussed findings in Science illuminating a similar distribution of influence across suspicious Twitter bot accounts used to defame a Massachusetts Senate candidate in 2010. Kramer, Guillory, and Hancock (2015), in the Proceedings of the National Academy of Sciences of the United States of America (PNAS), found that exposure to Twitter bots with oppositional views increased political polarization among participants in an experimental study. Woolley and Howard (2018), in a book of country-specific case studies entitled Computational Propaganda, argued that bots are often used during events around the world to spread and bolster misinformative and disinformative stories online.

This chapter explores these, and other, core arguments surrounding the political use of bots. It details the brief history of their use online. It accesses the academic literature to highlight key themes on the subject of what some researchers call computational propaganda and others simultaneously call "information operations," "information warfare," "influence operations," "online astroturfing," "cybertufing," and many other terms. Computational propaganda, and each of these other concepts to one degree or another, focuses on the ways in which the use of algorithms, automation (most often in the form of political bots), and human curation are used over social media to purposefully distribute misleading information over social media networks(Woolley and Howard 2016a).

This literature review details empirical work on how the bot as an internet-based tool, and computational propaganda as a political communication strategy, function in relationship to social media and democracy. As Luceri et al. (2019) argue, "the presence of social bots does not show any sign of decline despite the attempts from social network providers to suspend suspected, malicious accounts." With this argument in mind, this chapter discusses the implications of the continued use of political bots and computational propaganda for social media and democracy.

The following discussion is broken into five parts: The first section explores bots in the context of their general use online and then unpacks research that examines their social use. The second looks into their political use and discusses research on how to detect such use. The third details arguments on how bots can and have been deployed over social media as tools used in the interest of democracy. The fourth outlines key arguments and research more broadly focused on computational propaganda, information operations, and the like. The fifth, and final, section illuminates gaps in the literature. It outlines ongoing and new research into how bots and computational propaganda are used over social media to effect democracy and summarizes the core ideas of this piece.

To begin, it is important to examine perspectives on exactly why bots have become a particular topic of concern for scholars who study the online world. How are they used technically? What are their social uses?

BOTS

In part due to the political concerns detailed in the Introduction to this chapter, but also because of broader interest in artificial intelligence (AI) and automation, scholars and publics have begun to shine a light on the automated internet software technology known as the bot. Socially oriented versions of bots, which can be programmed to look and act like real people on sites like Facebook or Twitter, are often key tools for spreading computational propaganda. When this is the case, these programs have been referred to as digital "astroturf content" or as "political bots" (Ratkiewicz et al. 2011; Woolley 2016).

The word "bot" is an umbrella term that encapsulates many different kinds of automated online software programs or scripts. In fact, what counts as a bot is the topic of conjecture and debate within the technology community (Martineau 2018). Leonard (1998) called bots "the webs first indigenous species" and set out to discuss and historicize the wide array of automated online actors that could be considered to exist in the category of "bot." Both bots and social bots (sometimes called chat bots), as the narrower category of front-facing, communication-enabled, online bots are often known, do have a broad array of uses online outside of the political sphere, however (Wagner et al. 2012). They were, and are, crucial applications for automating spam messaging over email (Zhuang et al. 2008). The earliest bots were designed for network maintenance by the computer engineers who faced infrastructural challenges and a need for human coders to take on tasks requiring more critical oversight (Leonard 1998). Researchers, however, were quick to see their potential as "intelligent software" that could help people better navigate, and even communicate, via the Internet (Weld and Etzioni 1995).

In their most simple iteration as online programs that run automated tasks (while not directly interacting with other web users) bots have long been infrastructural tools used for activities relating to early iterations of online indexing and internet search (Middlebrook and Muller 2000; Seymour, Frantsvog, and Kumar 2011). Both simple strings of code intended to back up or update personal computers and socially oriented, automated, imposter accounts on Twitter can be referred to as bots. These automated programs have a seriously large presence online. In fact, in 2015 the cyber security firm Incapsula (now known as Imperva Incapsula) found that bot usage made up around 50 percent of all online traffic (Incapsula 2015). In 2014, as many as 20 million accounts on Twitter were identified as bots (Motti 2014). The number of bots functioning on Facebook and other prominent platforms is less clear, in part due to firms' close hold on user data and metrics. In 2018, however, Facebook self-reported to the US Securities and Exchange Commission (SEC) that an estimated 3–4 percent of, or around 50 million, accounts on the site were "fake" (Facebook 2017). It is clear that a significant amount of bots function online today, but it is also true that social bots have existed on the Internet for several decades.

The use of bots in online social settings dates back to before their integral use over Internet Relay Chat (IRC) – a precursor to contemporary social media (Mutton 2004). Social bots also appeared even earlier, in experiments with what programmers then called "chat bots" on the public web's precursor, the Advanced Research Projects Agency Network (ARPANET) (Garber 2014). The automated, perpetual nature of bots, combined with modern computational power, means that bots, whether social or not, are hugely important in scaling work online (Leonard 1998). Bots can achieve discrete, repetitive tasks in a fraction of the time it would take a human counterpart. Because of this, they have been integral to the endless organizational work central to maintaining sites such as Wikipedia and Reddit (Geiger 2014; Long et al. 2017). As bot technology progresses and social media becomes more ubiquitous worldwide, these automatons continue to become more and more useful as political amplification and suppression tools online (Shao et al. 2018).

Advances in machine learning allow social bots to more readily learn from their environment and to use what they find in their interactions on gaming platforms or in their conversations on social media platforms (Baumgarten, Colton, and Morris 2009; Ferrara et al. 2016). For instance, Tay – now known mostly as Microsoft's failed Twitter chat bot experiment – was first seen as unique because it was built to learn from other users on the platform (Vincent 2016). As Suárez-Gonzalo, Mas-Manchón, and Guerrero-Solé (2019) point out, however, Tay was still a product of its human designers. This is an important distinction because, as they argue, people often see bots as independent actors due to the fact bots work autonomously. Yet, ultimately, the identity and agency of bots are complicated by way of their symbiotic relationship with the people who build and use them (Neff and Nagy 2016).

Because this usage extends to the social – where bots have real-time conversations with humans on sites like Facebook and Twitter – the engineers who build them often view them as more than a tool but less than human, a proxy for the creator (Woolley, Shorey, and Howard 2018). Social bots playa key role in generating content and are often used to mimic real users on Twitter and many other social media sites and online discussion communities (Kumar et al. 2017). Researchers have developed ways, but still face challenges, in detecting whether a given online account is a human, bot, or cyborg (Chu et al. 2010; Gorwa and Guilbeault 2018). Though machine learning capabilities used for social bot development are progressing, it is still true that sophisticated propagandists make use of both human and bot communication and work in order to most effectively manipulate public opinion (Paavola et al. 2016). Even the most sophisticated machine learning or deep learning–enabled social bots have trouble parsing human emotion, humour, and sarcasm and as such can be identified more readily than bot-human hybrids that harness human intelligence (Davis et al. 2016; Chatterjee et al. 2019).

Because bots are useful in scaling communication online – and because they provide an additional layer of anonymity over social media – they have become popular tools for spreading political propaganda over social media (Woolley 2016). The next section details research on the various uses – and ramifications – of political bots. It situates the political bot as a global phenomenon, as tools now used in efforts to manipulate public opinion on numerous websites and social media platforms in a variety of languages and countries.

POLITICAL BOTS

Political bots – sometimes known as fake followers, AstroTurf accounts or sock puppets – are automated social media accounts, often built to look and act like real people, in order to manipulate public opinion (Ratkiewicz et al. 2011; Woolley and Howard 2016b). Political bots can be used to amplify the spread of particularly partisan, or completely false, information. They have, for instance, been used by far-right groups on Twitter to spread content and by anti-vaccine activists to boost false messaging on health communication (Marwick and Lewis 2017; Broniatowski et al. 2018). They can drive up the number of likes, re-messages, or comments associated with a person or idea. Researchers have catalogued political bot use in massively bolstering the social media metrics of politicians and political candidates from Donald Trump to Rodrigo Duterte (Zhang et al. 2018; Uyheng and Carley 2019). They can be used to harass journalists, activists, and political opposition in state-sponsored trolling campaigns (Monaco and Nyss 2018). They are even used in attempts to prioritize, and subsequently harness, online views for particular traditional news sources over others (Sanovich, Stukal, and Tucker 2018).

While events including the 2016 US election and the UK Brexit referendum may have catapulted these ideas to the forefront of the Western zeitgeist, political bots and computational propaganda are global in use and continue to play a role in international political communication at present. Bots have been used over Twitter and other applications to harass journalists and attack dissidents in Mexico, for instance, since at least 2012 (Orcutt 2012; Treré 2016). Automated accounts have been estimated to account for up to 50 percent of traffic among accounts tweeting about Russian politics (Stukal et al. 2017). In Syria, bots have been used to spread messages in favor of Bashir al-Assad and to confuse and attack opposition (Abokhodair, Yoo, and McDonald 2015). So-called spambots have been used in conversations about Italian politics online to generate civic noise (Cresci et al. 2017). Canadian researchers found that "identification, evidence, attribution, and enforcement" were among the chief problems associated with bots "disrupting" that country's democratic process (Dubois and McKelvey 2019). During Chile's 2017 presidential race, bots were deployed to spread Twitter messages related to numerous candidates, including a suspiciously large amount of automated traffic for the eventual third-place progressive candidate Marco Enríquez-Ominami (Castillo et al. 2019).

Though country-specific cases of political bot usage are useful in studying particular ways these tools are used in particular places, the same groups of bots are often used in efforts to manipulate public opinion across borders, during different types of situations and in different languages. Studies have revealed that bot accounts used to spread political communication during one country's election have then been used in another separate country and contest (Ferrara2017). Similarly, researchers have found that the same bot accounts used in one event or crisis in the same country have then been reused in another (Starbird et al. 2014). Still others have found bot networks that switch between multiple languages or written versions of the same language (i.e., simplified versus traditional Mandarin) and argued that this can be both a useful feature in bot detection and indicative of outside efforts to influence digital political conversation in other countries (Monaco 2017; Varol et al. 2017). Owing to the complexity of how networks of political bots operate – with the same collections of accounts switching focus between state borders and across multiple tongues – they are often difficult to detect and manage (Morstatter et al. 2016). This has not, however, stopped governments and technology firms from attempting to curb their use.

There has recently been a spate of policies, both in the United States and elsewhere, attempting to deal with the malicious use of political bots on social media. Many of these policies fall short due to a lack of institutional clarity – in both technology and political circles – about what actually constitutes bot traffic and, indeed, whether all automated traffic is problematic. Researchers have argued "that multiple forms of ambiguity are responsible for much of the complexity underlying contemporary bot-related policy" (Gorwa and Guilbeault 2018). Moreover, Gorwa and Guilbeault suggest that "before successful policy interventions can be formulated, a more comprehensive understanding of bots – especially how they are defined and measured – will be needed." Indeed, recent US policy has been criticized for taking an overly censorial, broad, and technologically unsophisticated approach to combating and regulating the political use of bots during elections and other events (West 2017; Bromwich 2018). Maréchal (2016) has argued for a normative framework for bots across social media sites in response to such ambiguity about how online platforms define automated accounts and how the public understands them. Yet the quest for a normative framework for understanding bots is challenged not least by the sheer difference in the ways that different categories of political bots are used, despite recent authorship of several articles that attempt to define and categorize social bots (Grimme et al.2017; Stieglitz et al. 2017; Gorwa and Guilbeault 2018)In an early discussion of malicious bot software, Holz (2005) discussed "the zoo" of bot types: from those harnessed in distributed denial-of-service(DDoS) attacks to those deployed for mass identity theft. There are a similar range of varieties of political bots. Listener bots can monitor social media sites and databases for key information but also track and communicate what they find (Woolley 2016). Spambots, conversely, are built to generate noise (Cresci et al. 2017). Wiki edits bots can be created to monitor politicians' edits to Wikipedia pages, but they are also often programmed to tweet about alleged changes to Twitter in efforts to name and shame – potentially stymying governmental use of Wikipedia (Ford, Dubois, and Puschmann 2016). Sleeper bots are social media accounts that sit on a site like Twitter all but unused for years, in order to generate a more realistic online presence, and are then activated during key political events (Howard, Kollanyi, and Woolley 2016). Troll bots, built to harass, have been used to demobilize activists trying to organize and communicate on Twitter but can also be used to drive traffic from one cause, product, or idea to another (Llewellyn et al. 2019). Finally, honeypot bots are built to attract particular users or even other bots (Lee, Caverlee, and Webb 2010).

It is clear that the collection of academic research into the rise in usage of political bots – and of broader online tactics relating to the promotion of disinformation and polarizing content – has grown since Metaxas, Mustafaraj, and Gayo-Avellos's (2011) early work on suspicious political campaigns on Twitter. Despite this, social scientific research demonstrating large-scale offline sociopolitical effects related to online bot usage remains slim (Tucker et al. 2018). Though many of the aforementioned researchers have demonstrated that social media bots have an active role in political communication around the world, fewer have had success in relating this automated communication directly to electoral outcomes. There has been more success, however, in drawing connections between the types of human users who spread bot content – or dis-informative or polarizing content – and why.

Badawy, Lerman, and Ferrara (2018) examine users who spread Russian content during the 2016 US election and determine "that political ideology, bot likelihood scores, and some activity-related account meta data are themost predictive features of whether a user spreads trolls' content or not." Woolley and Guilbeault (2017) find that those in positions of power – including politicians, pundits, and journalists – often share Twitter bot- related content when it reflects their own views. The work of Stella, Ferrara, and De Domenico (2018), using data from the 2017 Catalan referendum, builds on this idea. They argue that, in this case, bots – despite often existing on the peripheries of social systems – were successful in exposing influential people to inflammatory and extreme views. Still other studies, however, suggest that digital disinformation, automated or otherwise, has little effect on people's understanding of politics or that social media use has an insignificant correlation to polarization (Allcott and Gentzkow 2017; Castillo et al. 2019).The debate about the influence of political bots, and surrounding the larger effects of computational propaganda, continues. The literature makes it clear, though, that political bots have become an important new tool for political communication online. Importantly, not all political uses of social bots are malicious or focused on control. There are a variety of examples, and a growing body of research, on the democratically positive uses of bots.

BOTS PROMOTING DEMOCRATIC VALUES

Journalists, activists, commentators, and civic society groups have built chatbots aimed at openly engendering general political conversation over sites like Wikipedia and over modern social media precursors since the Net went public (Mutton 2004; Tsvetkova et al. 2017). Recently, there has been a rise in those producing public-facing social bots aimed at engendering conversation on pressing social issues, revealing political malfeasance and calling attention to protests (Sample 2015; Følstad et al. 2018). Bots have even been used to generate stories and to report on pending and real-time natural disasters or public health concerns (Lokot and Diakopoulos 2016; Lemelshtrich 2018). Because bots are able to automatically function at a computationally enhanced rate, they are particularly useful for journalists facing the very real demands of traditional story generation in that they can facilitate connections with readers to both spread and retrieve news (Gonzales and González 2017). Gonzalez and Gonzalez, exploring the case of a service known PolitiBot, which operated during the 2016 Spanish election over

Telegram, write that the true journalistic potential of the program was to share relevant news (with more than 70 percent user satisfaction) with readers through that platform.

Hwang, Pearce, and Nanis (2012) explore the ways that bots can be used as a social prosthesis or scaffolding for connecting networks of people that might not otherwise communicate. They argue, citing natural bot-driven experiments on social media, that bots can be effectively used to parse information on a social network, pay particular attention to what people have in common, and connect users based on these interests. They make the point that bots can be used to mitigate the burden of troublesome conversations online. It is important to note that, while the connective use of bots has certain benefits for democracy, it can also be being harnessed for control (Woolley and Guilbeault 2017).

While some researchers have examined journalism bots' capacities to search for information and communicate with readers, others have used these automated digital tools to problematize the idea that communication necessarily exists between two or more people, arguing instead that tools like bots play a key nonhuman role in news sharing online (Larsson and Hallvard2015). Lokot and Diakopoulos (2016) propose a typology of "news bots" in order to guide intent, utility, and functionality of bots constructed by future designers and reporting teams. They note the limits of robot journalists – especially in the areas of automated commentary, opinion writing, algorithmic transparency, and general accountability.

The analysis of Lokot and Diakopoulos (2016) primarily focuses on design elements of a sample of extant news bots on Twitter. They examine the various journalistic functions of these accounts and make it clear that news bots could change the modern media environment. In particular, their exploration of journalism bot accounts is concerned with their function in generating articles and reporting. They discuss problems associated with the opacity of algorithms that drive news bots but leave room for a larger discussion about the people who construct those algorithms, what cultural values they encode into that software, and the function and of the resultant bots during political crises and elections.

Lokot and Diakopoulous (2016), as well as other researchers, have explored the idea that bots could feasibly replace human journalists in some instances. Indeed, tools like the LA Times's Quake Bot can automatically generate and post stories (Walker 2014). Harvard University's Nieman Journalism Lab has argued that there will be a large-scale shift toward the "botification" of the news in coming years (Barot 2016). Others, with more unease about automated reporting, have suggested that journalism may be the latest industry to be under threat by automation – because of article writing bots – or that algorithms may "kill" journalism (Goichman 2017; Keohane 2017). In a case study of three newsrooms, however, Linden (2017) finds that the use of automated software has actually benefited reporters in that bots do the repetitive tasks journalists would otherwise have to do – thus freeing people up for other work. Latar (2018) provides a balanced view of both perspectives, what he terms the pessimistic and optimistic stances on robot journalists. He explores several case studies, including the LA Times, that exemplify both stances.

Democratically beneficial bots provide hopeful foils to their political bot counterparts. In his 2018 hearings before the US Congress (Harwell 2018), which took place because of political misuse of Facebook in 2016, Facebook CEO Mark Zuckerberg spoke of automation and AI as necessary tools to combat the rise of disinformation and misinformation. He pointed out that the sheer informational scale of social media makes it so that human labour alone cannot address the problems at hand. Some researchers have taken up this logic, suggesting that automation may have a role to play in preventing misuse of bots (Wang 2010). Indeed, many bot-detection systems rely on sophisticated algorithms and machine learning (Ratkiewicz et al. 2011; McKelvey and Menczer 2013; Klyueva 2019).

In order to prevent the political misuse of bots over social media, it is crucial to understand the complex ways in which bots facilitate and amplify the flow of misinformation, disinformation, trolling, and propaganda. The next section provides an overview of literature on computational propaganda – one of the umbrella terms and strains of research from the social sciences that attempts to grapple with the problem of political bots.

COMPUTATIONAL PROPAGANDA: AN OVERVIEW

Computational propaganda is specifically defined as "the assemblage of social media platforms, autonomous agents, and big data tasked with the manipulation of public opinion" (Woolley and Howard 2016a). Research on computational propaganda spans the social sciences and computer sciences. Although the Computational Propaganda Project at the University of Oxford's Oxford Internet Institute defined the term and carried out early social scientific work on the topic, the research from Ferrara et al. (2016), Metaxas and Mustafaraj (2012), Ratkiewicz et al. (2011), and others was foundational in building the preliminary understandings of how social bots effected the informational and computational systems that make social media possible.

Early research on computational propaganda was focused primarily on how powerful political actors leveraged social media bots for control. A great deal of this work looked at how governments, militaries, political campaigns, corporations, and other well-resourced entities launched such offensives online (Murthy et al. 2016). Now, however, it is clear that many types of groups – including regular citizens and activists – use the tools and tactics of computational propaganda to spread their own perspectives and communicate politically (Woolley 2018).

Indeed, computational propaganda has been propelled by a broader scale normalization of social media as a means for control by those focused on digital political communication (Karpf 2012). As Chadwick (2013) points out, "even the most radical changes to communications systems must be channeled through structural constraints in order to impact traditional political outcomes" (p. 10). Many old guard members of the political elite remain the same worldwide, and newly powerful individuals and groups have ascended and now make use of digital tools in efforts to gain and retain power (Howard 2015). As Karpf (2012) points out, these actors have adjusted to, and made use of, the altered state of political communication tools as they exist online. In some ways, digital democracy has not played out as cyber-optimists had hoped. The elite on the Internet are still elite and thus "online speech follows winner- take-all patterns" (Hindman 2008).

Socio-technical innovation has led to ever-changing organizational affordances of the multimedia landscape encompassed by social media, both for the elite and for regular people (Treem and Leonardi 2013). The rise of hybridized technology and "networked society" has not only affected the way political conversations occur; it has also altered the ways campaigns are organized, elections function, and power is exerted (Benkler 2006). New political organizations have been birthed, political systems have changed, and politicians have risen and fallen. Some aspects of political communication, however, remain constant. Computational propaganda is a novel mechanism and strategy for enabling control among well-resourced and powerful groups, though the means to build and launch bots over social media is becoming more widespread – and available to regular citizens everyday (Woolley 2018).

Nimmo and the Digital Forensic Research (DFR) team at the Atlantic Council point out three core features of political bots and computational propaganda, which he claims separate it from traditional propaganda: activity, amplification, and anonymity (Nimmo and DFR Lab 2016). He writes that:

Many of these bot and cyborg accounts do conform to a recognizable pattern: activity, amplification, anonymity. An anonymous account which is inhumanly active and which obsessively amplifies one point of view is likely to be a political bot, rather than a human. Identifying such bots is the first step towards defeating them. (n.p.)In order to "defeat" political bots, or broader manipulations that occur by way of algorithms and automation online, researchers have argued that social media firms must accept greater responsibility for the social and political outcomes of the tools they build and design – the algorithms, but also the very concept of platforms, have politics (Gillespie 2010; Gillespie 2014).

Indeed, prominent scholars of political communication argue that social media platforms such as Twitter and Facebook are now crucial transnational communication mechanisms for political communication (Segerberg and Bennett 2011; Tufekci and Wilson 2012). That is, their use in this regard –at least in most country cases worldwide – is not necessarily restricted by state borders. As such, people from around the globe use them to communicate about political issues with one another. As the research detailed in this chapter reveals, computational propaganda itself is also transnational. It is not confined to only one social media site but stretches across them in a tangled web (Council on Foreign Relations 2018). Revelations from Facebook, Twitter, and Google reveal, for instance, that government- sponsored Russian citizens used multiple social media sites to spread propagandistic content during the US presidential election (Allcott and Gentzkow 2017).

Research from several sources suggests that computational propaganda and political bot usage was at an all-time high during key moments of this particular election (Bessi and Ferrara 2016; Ferrara et al. 2016; Howard et al. 2016). Bessi and Ferrara (2016) found that "about 400,000 bots [were] engaged in the political discussion about the [US] Presidential election, responsible for roughly 3.8 million tweets, about one-fifth of the entire conversation." Kollanyi et al. (2016) found that the thousands of Twitter bots supporting Trump outnumbered those supporting Clinton in the days preceding the election at a rate of five to one. Supporters of both candidates used these social automatons to give voters the impression that the campaigns had large- scale online grassroots support, to plant ideas in the news cycle, and to effect trends on digital platforms. At times during the 2016 US contest, regular people were convinced and even tricked by fringe partisans into using bots,coordinated hashtag bombing and other tools to bolster trending topics that benefited candidates and campaigns (Schreckinger 2016).

The concept of "manufacturing consensus" is a central tactic of those who use computational propaganda (Woolley 2018). It occurs not only when bots boost social media metrics but also when the media reinforces illusory notions of candidate popularity because of this same automated inflation of the numbers. The concept of manufacturing consensus is drawn not just from the ways bots and computational propaganda were used during the 2016 US election but also from a range of parallel uses in multiple countries dating back as early as 2007 (Robb 2007; Gorwa 2017, p. 38). In the Americas, political actors in Mexico (Verkamp and Gupta 2013), Ecuador (Woolley 2015), Venezuela (Forelle et al. 2015), and Brazil (Arnaudo 2017) have pioneered the deployment of related techniques in attempts to boost the credibility of candidates and campaigns through increased metrics: follows, likes, retweets, shares, comments, and so on.

State-sponsored trolling, another novel online political manipulation strategy, is specifically concerned with governmentally driven computational propaganda campaigns aimed at attacking political opposition over social media (Monaco and Nyss 2018; Zannettou et al. 2019). Analysis from Monaco and Nyss on this phenomenon notes that the now global trend of "disinformation is often only one element of a broader politically motivated attack on the credibility and courage of dissenting voices: journalists, opposition politicians and activists" (Monaco and Nyss 2018, p. 4). According to their study, informed by more than two years of research and interviews and fieldwork spanning more than eight countries, the use of computational propaganda and astroturf political communication is not only propagated by organizations tangentially associated with governments, such as the IRA in Russia. Politically motivated trolling teams, in some cases outfitted with armies of political bots, are housed within the official governmental infrastructure of some countries. A recent report on cyber-troops by Bradshaw and Howard (2017) corroborates these findings and details the ways in which multiple governments now use the tools of computational propaganda.

Increasingly, computational propaganda and the tactic of using political bots to influence online conversation are moving from the political sphere to other topical areas. In healthcare, Twitter bots have been used to amplify anti-vaccine content (Shao et al. 2017; Allem and Ferrara 2018). In fact, coordinated Russian bots and human trolls have been used to manipulate the vaccine debate online (Broniatowski et al. 2018). Social media bots, alongside groups of people, have also played a role in distributing information and, worryingly, misinformation and rumors during natural disasters and terrorist attacks (Gupta et al. 2013; Starbird et al. 2014; Khaund et al. 2018; Vosoughi et al. 2018). Twitter bots are also used to create a significant amount of tweets linking to scientific articles, creating serious implications for using raw counts of such messages for the evaluation or assessment of the reach or successful uptake of research over that platform (Haustein et al. 2016).

Computational propaganda shows no signs of abating, and there is a great deal of research to be done in order to build thorough understandings of the topic. The next section identifies gaps in the current research and suggestions for future work.

AT A GLANCE AND GAPS

Computational propaganda is still propaganda. What has changed about this new form of an old strategy of control and coercion is that it now happens at scale. This new political communication strategy is scaled not just in terms of the number of people in places around the world that can and do access computational propaganda but also by the computational power and constantly advancing software – including political bots but also data analytics technology including machine learning and sentiment analysis – that facilitate it.

Several areas are at the forefront of innovation, and future problems, associated with political bot and computational propaganda usage. The first, both in the United States and globally, is policy and the law. How will these political domains be affected by the rise in political manipulation over social media? What laws are needed to regulate firms where disinformation is spread? The academy must aid policymakers by undertaking more empirical research to inform policy recommendations to be delivered to key US politicians, policy experts, civil society groups, and journalists. Campaign finance, election law, voting rights, privacy, and several other areas of the law are currently being affected in both unforeseen and complex ways by the spread of political disinformation over social media. Solid research into the ways computational propaganda contravenes the law is a crucial step in addressing the policy gap at the intersection of information dissemination, automation, social media, and politics.

We need better software, informed by both social and computer science research, to help researchers, journalists, and activists keep up with the challenges posed by the modern disinformation threat. Tools could include high-powered data intelligence platforms, that make use of bots in parsing large sets of relevant data, usable by these groups worldwide. They ought to exploit recent advances in graph databases and machine learning and cheap, massive computation to dramatically accelerate investigations. The target should be to accelerate civil society in identifying patterns of activity that would help to root out entities backing disinformation campaigns, in addition to uncovering a great deal about when and where these campaigns are occurring.

Longitudinal work can help establish more solid metrics for tracking information flows – but also effects – related to the use of political bots, computational propaganda, and, correspondingly, disinformation and online polarization. Quantitative insight into the roles of automation, network structure, temporal markers, and message semantics over social media can allow experienced researchers to effectively create ways of measuring the flow of political manipulation over social media over sustained periods. The results of longitudinal research on this phenomenon will be crucial to building evolving long-term public and governmental understandings of computational propaganda.

There is potential for the continued use of bots as technologies for democratic engagement. There are also ongoing efforts in the academy to develop software to detect malicious bots and disinformation. Research- grounded tools to detect bots on social media, led by the team at Indiana University that developed Botometer (previously BotOrNot), are on the rise and are becoming more effective (Varol et al. 2018). Other groups aredeveloping tools to study how disinformation, or fake news, is spread and whether or not a tweet is credible (Gupta et al. 2014; Shao et al. 2016). Start- ups including RoBhat Labs are simultaneously creating browser plug-ins and apps that track both bots and propaganda (Smiley 2017). As Varol and Uluturk (2018) aptly point out, however, "we should also be aware of the limitations of human-mediated systems as well as algorithmic approaches and employ them wisely and appropriately to tackle weaknesses of existing communication systems." Software solutions, no matter how sophisticated the technology, can only mitigate a portion of the problems intrinsic to computational propaganda. Social solutions must be implemented as well.

REFERENCES

Abokhodair, N., Yoo, D., & McDonald, D. W. (2015). Dissecting a social botnet: Growth, content and influence in Twitter. In Proceedings of the 18th ACM Conference on Computer Supported Cooperative Work & Social Computing (pp.839–851). Vancouver: ACM. https://doi.org/10.1145/2675133.2675208

Allcott, H., & Gentzkow, M. (2017). Social media and fake news in the 2016 election. NBER Working Paper No. 23089. https://doi.org/10.3386/w23089

Allem, J.-P., & Ferrara, E. (2018). Could social bots pose a threat to public health?

American Journal of Public Health, 108(8), 1005–1006. https://doi.org/10.2105/AJPH.2018.304512

Arnaudo, D. (2017). Computational propaganda in Brazil: Social bots during elections. Computational Propaganda Research Project Working Paper Series. Oxford: Oxford Internet Institute.

Badawy, A., Lerman, K., & Ferrara, E. (2018). Who falls for online political manipulation? arXiv.org. http://arxiv.org/abs/1808.03281

Barot, T. (2016). The botification of news. Nieman Lab, December. www.niemanlab.org/2015/12/the-botification-of-news/

Baumgarten, R., Colton, C., & Morris, M. (2009). Combining AI methods for learning bots in a real-time strategy game. International Journal of Computer Games Technology. www.hindawi.com/journals/ijcgt/2009/129075/abs/

Benkler, Y. (2006). The Wealth of Networks: How Social Production Transforms Markets and Freedom. New Haven, CT: Yale University Press.

Bessi, A., & Ferrara, E. (2016). Social bots distort the 2016 U.S. presidential election online discussion. First Monday, 21(11). https://doi.org/10.5210/fm.v21i11.7090

Boxell, L., Gentzkow, M., & Shapiro, J. M. (2017). Is the Internet causing political polarization? Evidence from demographics. NBER Working Paper No. 23258. https://doi.org/10.3386/w23258

Bradshaw, S., & Howard, P. (2017). Troops, trolls and troublemakers: A global Inventory of organized social media. Computational Propaganda Research Project Working Paper Series. Oxford: Oxford Internet Institute.

Bromwich, J. E. (2018). Bots of the Internet, reveal yourselves! New York Times, July 18. www.nytimes.com/2018/07/16/style/how-to-regulate-bots.html

Broniatowski, D. A., Jamison, A. M., Qi, S. et al. (2018). Weaponized health communication: Twitter bots and Russian trolls amplify the vaccine debate. American Journal of Public Health, 108(10), 1378–1384. https://doi.org/10.2105/AJPH.2018.304567

Castillo, S., Allende-Cid, H., Palma, W. et al. (2019). Detection of bots and cyborgs in Twitter: A study on the Chilean presidential election in 2017. In G. Meiselwitz (Ed.), Social Computing and Social Media: Design, Human Behavior and Analytics (pp.311–323). Basel: Springer International Publishing.

Chadwick, A. (2013). The Hybrid Media System: Politics and Power. Oxford: Oxford University Press.

Chatterjee, A., Gupta, U., Chinnakotla, M. K., Srikanth, R., Galley, M., & Agrawal, P. (2019). Understanding emotions in text using deep learning and big data. Computers in Human Behavior, 93, 309–317. https://doi.org/10.1016/j.chb.2018.12.029

Chu, Z., Gianvecchio, S., Wang, H., & Jajodia, S. (2010). Who is tweeting on Twitter: Human, bot, or cyborg? In Proceedings of the 26th Annual Computer Security Applications Conference (pp. 21–30). Austin, TX: ACM. http://dl.acm.org/citation.cfm?id=1920265

Copley, C. (2016). Merkel fears social bots may manipulate German election. Reuters, November 24. https://uk.reuters.com/article/uk-germany-merkel-socialbots-idUKKBN13J1V2

Council on Foreign Relations. (2018). Political disruptions: Combating disinformationand fake news. Council on Foreign Relations website. www.cfr.org/event/political- disruptions-combating-disinformation-and-fake-news

Cresci, S., Di Pietro, R., Petrocchi, M., Spognardi, A., & Tesconi, M. (2017). The paradigm-shift of social spambots: Evidence, theories, and tools for the arms race. In Proceedings of the 26th International Conference on World Wide Web Companion (pp. 963–972). Perth: ACM. https://doi.org/10.1145/3041021.3055135

Davis, C. A., Varol, O., Ferrara, E., Flammini, A., & Menczer, F. (2016). BotOrNot: A system to evaluate social bots. In Proceedings of the 25th International Conference Companion on World Wide Web (pp. 273–274). Geneva: ACM.https://doi.org/10.1145/2872518.2889302

Dubois, E., & McKelvey, F. R. (2019). Political bots: Disrupting Canada's democracy. Canadian Journal of Communication, 44(2). https://doi.org/10.22230/cjc.2019v44n2a3511

Facebook. (2017). Facebook, Inc. Quarterly Report September 20, 2017 (10-Q No. 001–35551). Securities and Exchange Commission. www.sec.gov/Archives/edgar/ data/1326801/000132680117000053/fb-09302017x10q.htm

Ferrara, E. (2017). Disinformation and social bot operations in the run up to the 2017French presidential election. SSRN Scholarly Paper No. ID 2995809. https://papers.ssrn.com/abstract=2995809

Ferrara, E., Varol, O., Davis, C., Menczer, F., & Flammini, A. (2016). The rise of social bots. Communications of the ACM, 59(7), 96–104. https://doi.org/10.1145/2818717

Følstad, A., Brandtzaeg, P. B., Feltwell, T., Law, E. L. C., Tscheligi, M., & Luger, E. (2018). Chatbots for social good. Extended Abstracts of the 2018 CHI Conference on Human Factors in Computing Systems. Paper No. SIG06.

Ford, H., Dubois, E., & Puschmann, C. (2016). Keeping Ottawa honest – one tweet at a time? Politicians, journalists, wikipedians, and their twitter bots. International Journal of Communication, 10, 4891–4914.

Forelle, M. C., Howard, P. N., Monroy-Hernandez, A., & Savage, S. (2015). Political bots and the manipulation of public opinion in Venezuela. SSRN Scholarly Paper No. ID 2635800. https://papers.ssrn.com/abstract=2635800

Garber, M. (2014). When PARRY met ELIZA: A ridiculous chatbot conversation from 1972. The Atlantic, June 9. www.theatlantic.com/technology/archive/2014/06/ when-parry-met-eliza-a-ridiculous-chatbot-conversation-from-1972/372428/

Geiger, R. S. (2014). Bots, bespoke code, and the materiality of software platforms. Information, Communication & Society, 17(3), 342–356.

Gillespie, T. (2010). The politics of "platforms." New Media & Society, 12(3), 347–364. https://doi.org/10.1177/1461444809342738

(2014). The relevance of algorithms. In T. Gillespie, P. J. Boczkowski, & K. A. Foot(Eds.), Media Technologies: Essays on Communication, Materiality, and Society(pp. 167–193). Cambridge, MA: MIT Press.

Goichman, R. (2017). Written by a robot: Will algorithms kill journalism? Haaretz, February 15. www.haaretz.com/israel-news/business/1.771758

Gonzales, H. M. S., & González, M. S. (2017). Bots as a news service and its emotional connection with audiences: The case of Politibot. Doxa Comunicación. Revista Interdisciplinar de Estudios de Comunicación y Ciencias Sociales, 0(25), 63–84.

Gorwa, R. (2017). Computational propaganda in Poland: False amplifiers and the digitalpublic sphere. Computational Propaganda Research Project Working Paper Series. Oxford: Oxford Internet Institute.

Gorwa, R., & Guilbeault, D. (2018). Unpacking the social media bot: A typology toguide research and policy. Policy & Internet. https://doi.org/10.1002/poi3.184

Grimme, C., Preuss, M., Adam, L., & Trautmann, H. (2017). Social bots: Human-like by means of human control? Big Data, 5(4), 279–293. https://doi.org/10.1089/big.2017.0044

Gupta, A., Kumaraguru, P., Castillo, C., & Meier, P. (2014). TweetCred: Real-time credibility assessment of content on Twitter. In L. M. Aiello & D. McFarland (Eds.), Proceedings of Social Informatics (SocInfo): 6th International Conference (pp.228–243). Barcelona: SocInfo. https://doi.org/10.1007/978-3-319-13734-6_16

Gupta, A., Lamba, H., Kumaraguru, P., & Joshi, A. (2013). Faking Sandy: Characterizing and identifying fake images on Twitter during Hurricane Sandy. Proceedings of the 22nd International Conference on the World Wide Web 2013(pp. 729–736). Rio de Janeiro: ACM.

Harwell, D. (2018). AI will solve Facebook's most vexing problems, Mark Zuckerberg says. Just don't ask when or how. Washington Post, April 11. www.washingtonpost.com/news/the-switch/wp/2018/04/11/ai-will-solve-facebooks-most- vexing-problems-mark-zuckerberg-says-just-dont-ask-when-or-how/

Haustein, S., Bowman, T. D., Holmberg, K., Tsou, A., Sugimoto, C. R., & Larivière, V. (2016). Tweets as impact indicators: Examining the implications of automated "bot" accounts on Twitter. Journal of the Association for Information Science and Technology, 67(1), 232–238. https://doi.org/doi:10.1002/asi.23456

Hindman, M. (2008). The Myth of Digital Democracy. Princeton: Princeton University Press.Holz, T. (2005). A short visit to the bot zoo [malicious bots software]. IEEE Security Privacy, 3(3), 76–79. https://doi.org/10.1109/MSP.2005.58

Howard, P. N. (2015). Pax Technica: The Impact of Automation on Public Opinion. New York: Yale University Press.

Howard, P. N., Kollanyi, B., & Woolley, S. C. (2016). Bots and automation over Twitter during the US election. Computational Propaganda Research Project Working Paper Series. Oxford: Oxford Internet Institute.

Hwang, T., Pearce, I., & Nanis, M. (2012). Socialbots: Voices from the fronts.Interactions, 19(2), 38–45.

Incapsula. (2015). 2015 Bot Traffic Report. www.incapsula.com/blog/bot-traffic-report-2015.html

Karpf, D. (2012). The MoveOn effect: The Unexpected Transformation of American Political Advocacy. Oxford: Oxford University Press.

Keohane, J. (2017). A robot may have written this story. Wired, February 16. www.wired.com/2017/02/robots-wrote-this-story/

Khaund, T., Al-Khateeb, S., Tokdemir, S., & Agarwal, N. (2018). Analyzing social bots and their coordination during natural disasters. In R. Thomson, C. Dancy, Hyder, & H. Bisgin (Eds.), Social, Cultural, and Behavioural Modelling (pp.207–212). Basel: Springer International Publishing.

Klyueva, A. (2019). Trolls, bots, and whatnots: Deceptive content, deception detection, and deception suppression. In I. Chiluwa & S. Samoilenko (Eds.), Handbook of Research on Deception, Fake News, and Misinformation Online (pp. 18–32). Hershey, PA: IGI Global. https://doi.org/10.4018/978-1-5225-8535-0.ch002

Kollanyi, B., Howard, P. N., & Woolley, S. C. (2016). Bots and automation over Twitter during the U.S. election. Computational Propaganda Research Project Working Paper Series. Oxford: Oxford Internet Institute.

Kramer, A., Guillory, J., & Hancock, J. (2015). Experimental evidence of massive-scaleemotional contagion through social networks. PNAS, 111(24), 8788–8790. https:// doi.org/10.1073/pnas.1320040111

Kumar, S., Cheng, J., Leskovec, J., & Subrahmanian, V. S. (2017). An army of me: Sockpuppets in online discussion communities. In Proceedings of the 26th International Conference on World Wide Web (pp. 857–866). Perth: ACM.https://doi.org/10.1145/3038912.3052677

Larsson, A. O., & Hallvard, M. (2015). Bots or journalists? News sharing on Twitter.Communications, 40(3), 361–370. https://doi.org/10.1515/commun-2015-0014

Latar, N. L. (2018). Robot Journalism: Can Human Journalism Survive? Singapore: World Scientific.

Lee, K., Caverlee, J., & Webb, S. (2010). The social honeypot project: Protecting online communities from spammers. In Proceedings of the 19th International Conference on World Wide Web (pp. 1139–1140). Raleigh, NC: ACM. https://doi.org/10.1145/1772690.1772843

Lemelshtrich, L. N. (2018). Robot Journalism: Can Human Journalism Survive? Singapore: World Scientific.

Leonard, A. (1998). Bots: The Origin of a New Species. New York: Penguin Books. Linden, T. C.-G. (2017). Algorithms for journalism. The Journal of Media Innovations,4(1), 60–76. https://doi.org/10.5617/jmi.v4i1.2420

Llewellyn, C., Cram, L., Hill, R. L., & Favero, A. (2019). For whom the bell trolls: Shifting troll behaviour in the Twitter Brexit debate. JCMS: Journal of Common Market Studies. https://doi.org/10.1111/jcms.12882

Lokot, T., & Diakopoulos, N. (2016). News bots: Automating news and information dissemination on Twitter. Digital Journalism, 4(6), 682–699. https://doi.org/10.1080/21670811.2015.1081822

Long, K., Vines, J., Sutton, S. et al. (2017). "Could you define that in bot terms"?: Requesting, creating and using bots on Reddit. In Proceedings of the 2017 CHI Conference on Human Factors in Computing Systems (pp. 3488–3500). Denver:ACM. https://doi.org/10.1145/3025453.3025830

Luceri, L., Deb, A., Badawy, A., & Ferrara, E. (2019). Red bots do it better: Comparative analysis of social bot partisan behavior. In WWW '19: Companion Proceedings of The 2019 World Wide Web Conference (pp. 1007–1012). San Francisco: ACM.https://doi.org/10.1145/3308560.3316735

Maréchal, N. (2016). Automation, algorithms, and politics| When bots tweet: Toward a normative framework for bots on social networking sites (Feature). International Journal of Communication, 10, 5022–5031.

Martineau, P. (2018). What is a Bot? Wired, November 16. www.wired.com/story/the-know-it-alls-what-is-a-bot/

Marwick, A., & Lewis, B. (2017). Media Manipulation and Disinformation Online. New York: Data & Society Research Institute.

McKelvey, K. R., & Menczer, F. (2013). Truthy: Enabling the study of online social networks. In Proceedings of the 2013 Conference on Computer Supported Cooperative Work Companion (pp. 23–26). San Antonio: ACM. http://dl.acm.org/citation.cfm?id=2441962

Metaxas, P. T., & Mustafaraj, E. (2012). Social media and the elections. Science, 338(6106), 472–473.

Metaxas, P. T., Mustafaraj, E., & Gayo-Avello, D. (2011). How (not) to predict elections. In Privacy, Security, Risk and Trust (PASSAT), 2011 IEEE Third International Conference on and 2011 IEEE Third International Conference on Social Computing (SocialCom) (pp. 165–171). Boston: IEEE. http://ieeexplore.ieee.org/xpls/abs_all.jsp?arnumber=6113109

Middlebrook, S. T., & Muller, J. (2000). Thoughts on bots: The emerging law of electronic agents. Business Lawyer, 56, 341.

Monaco, N. (2017). Computational propaganda in Taiwan: Where digital democracy meets automated autocracy. Computational Propaganda Research Project Working Paper Series. Oxford: Oxford Internet Institute.

Monaco, N., & Nyss, C. (2018). State sponsored trolling: How governments are deploying fake news as part of broader harassment campaigns. Institute for the Future Working Research Papers.

Morstatter, F., Wu, L., Nazer, T. H., Carley, K. M., & Liu, H. (2016). A new approach to bot detection: Striking the balance between precision and recall. In 2016 IEEE/ ACM International Conference on Advances in Social Networks Analysis and Mining (ASONAM) (pp. 533–540). Davis, CA: IEEE/ACM. https://doi.org/10.1109/ASONAM.2016.7752287

Motti, J. (2014). Twitter acknowledges 23 million active users are actually bots. Tech Times, August 12. www.techtimes.com/articles/12840/20140812/twitter-acknowledges-14- percent-users-bots-5-percent-spam-bots.htm

Murthy, D., Powell, A., Tinati, R. et al. (2016). Can bots influence a political discussion? Social capital, technical skill, and conversations about public affairs. International Journal of Communication, 10(Special Issue), 20.

Mutton, P. (2004). Inferring and visualizing social networks on Internet relay chat. In Proceedings of the Eighth International Conference on Information Visualisation, 2004 (pp. 35–43). London: IEEE. https://doi.org/10.1109/IV.2004.1320122

Neff, G., & Nagy, P. (2016). Automation, algorithms, and politics| talking to Bots: Symbiotic agency and the case of Tay. International Journal of Communication, 10, 4915–4931.

Nimmo, B., & DFR Lab. (2016). Human, bot or cyborg? Medium, December 23. https://medium.com/@DFRLab/human-bot-or-cyborg-41273cdb1e17

Orcutt, M. (2012). Twitter mischief plagues Mexico's election. MIT Technology Review, June 21. www.technologyreview.com/news/428286/twitter-mischief- plagues-mexicos-election/

Paavola, J., Helo, T., Jalonen, H., Sartonen, M., & Huhtinen, A.-M. (2016). Understanding the trolling phenomenon: The automated detection of bots and cyborgs in the social media. Journal of Information Warfare, 15(4), 100–111.

Ratkiewicz, J., Conover, M., Meiss, M., Goncalves, B., Flammini, A., & Menczer, F. (2011). Detecting and tracking political abuse in social media. In Proceedings of the Fifth International AAAI Conference on Weblogs and Social Media (ICWSM). Barcelona: AAAI Press. www.aaai.org/ocs/index.php/ICWSM/ICWSM11/paper/ viewFile/2850/3274

Ratkiewicz, J., Conover, M., Meiss, M. et al. (2011). Truthy: Mapping the spread of astroturf in microblog streams. In Proceedings of the 20th International Conference Companion on World Wide Web (pp. 249–252). Hyderabad: ACM. http://dl.acm.org/citation.cfm?id=1963301

Robb, J. (2007). When bots attack. Wired, August 23. www.wired.com/2007/08/ff-estonia-bots/

Sample, M. (2015). Protest bots. In A. Karhio, L. Ramada Prieto, & S. Rettberg (Eds.),The Ends of Electronic Literature (p. 58). Bergen: Electronic Literature Organization and University of Bergen.

Sanovich, S., Stukal, D., & Tucker, J. A. (2018). Turning the virtual tables: Government strategies for addressing online opposition with an application to Russia. Comparative Politics, 50(3), 435–482. https://doi.org/info:doi/10.5129/001041518822704890

Schreckinger, B. (2016). Inside Trump's "cyborg" Twitter army. Politico, September 30. http://politi.co/2dyhCD0

Segerberg, A., & Bennett, W. L. (2011). Social media and the organization of collective action: Using Twitter to explore the ecologies of two climate change protests. The Communication Review, 14(3), 197–215. https://doi.org/10.1080/10714421.2011.597250

Seymour,T.,Frantsvog,D.,&Kumar,S.(2011).Historyofsearchengines. International Journal of Management & Information Systems (IJMIS), 15(4), 47–58. https://doi.org/10.19030/ijmis.v15i4.5799

Shao, C., Ciampaglia, G. L., Flammini, A., & Menczer, F. (2016). Hoaxy: A platform for tracking online misinformation. arXiv.org. https://doi.org/10.1145/2872518.2890098

Shao, C., Ciampaglia, G. L., Varol, O., Flammini, A., & Menczer, F. (2017). The spread of low-credibility content by social bots. ArXiv. https://arxiv.org/abs/1707.07592

Shao, C., Ciampaglia, G. L., Varol, O., Yang, K.-C., Flammini, A., & Menczer, F. (2018). The spread of low-credibility content by social bots. Nature Communications, 9(1), 1–9. https://doi.org/10.1038/s41467-018-06930-7

Smiley, L. (2017). The college kids doing what Twitter won't | Backchannel. Wired, November 1. *www.wired.com/story/the-college-kids-doing-what-twitter-wont/*

Starbird, K., Maddock, J., Orand, M., Achterman, P., & Mason, R. M. (2014). Rumors, false flags, and digital vigilantes: Misinformation on Twitter after the 2013 Boston Marathon bombing. In Proceedings of iConference 2014. Berlin: iSchools Inc. https://doi.org/10.9776/14308

Stella, M., Ferrara, E., & De Domenico, M. (2018). Bots increase exposure to negative and inflammatory content in online social systems. Proceedings of the National Academy of Sciences, 115(49), 12435–12440. https://doi.org/10.1073/pnas.1803470115

Stieglitz, S., Brachten, F., Ross, B., & Jung, A.-K. (2017). Do social bots dream of electric sheep? A categorisation of social media bot accounts. ArXiv. http://arxiv.org/abs/ 1710.04044

Stukal, D., Sanovich, S., Bonneau, R., & Tucker, J. A. (2017). Detecting bots on Russian political Twitter. Big Data, 5(4), 310–324. https://doi.org/10.1089/big.2017.0038

Suárez-Gonzalo, S., Mas-Manchón, L., & Guerrero-Solé, F. (2019). Tay is you: The attribution of responsibility in the algorithmic culture. Observatorio (OBS*), 13(2).https://doi.org/10.15847/obsOBS13220191432

Treem, J. W., & Leonardi, P. M. (2013). Social media use in organizations: Exploring the affordances of visibility, editability, persistence, and association. Annals of the International Communication Association, 36(1), 143–189. https://doi.org/10.1080/23808985.2013.11679130

Treré, E. (2016). The dark side of digital politics: Understanding the algorithmic manufacturing of consent and the hindering of online dissidence. IDS Bulletin, 47 (1). https://doi.org/10.19088/1968-2016.111

Tsvetkova, M., García-Gavilanes, R., Floridi, L., & Yasseri, T. (2017). Even good botsfight: The case of Wikipedia. PLoS ONE, 12(2), e0171774. https://doi.org/10.1371/journal.pone.0171774

Tucker, J. A., Guess, A., Barberá, P. et al. (2018). Social Media, Political Polarization, and Political Disinformation: A Review of the Scientific Literature. Hewlett Foundation report. https://hewlett.org/library/social-media-political-polarization- political-disinformation-review-scientific-literature/

Tufekci, Z., & Wilson, C. (2012). Social media and the decision to participate in political protest: observations from Tahrir Square. Journal of Communication, 62(2), 363–379. https://doi.org/10.1111/j.1460-2466.2012.01629.x

Uyheng, J., & Carley, K. M. (2019). Characterizing bot networks on Twitter: An empirical analysis of contentious issues in the Asia-Pacific. In R. Thomson,H. Bisgin, C. Dancy, & A. Hyder (Eds.), Social, Cultural, and Behavioural Modelling (pp. 153–162). Basel: Springer International Publishing.

Varol, O., Davis, C., Menczer, F., & Flammini, A. (2018). Feature engineering for socialbot detection. In G. Dong & H. Liu (Eds.), CRC Press: Feature Engineering for Machine Learning and Data Analytics (pp. 331–334). Boca Raton, FL: Taylor & Francis.

Varol, O., Ferrara, E., Davis, C. A., Menczer, F., & Flammini, A. (2017). Online human-bot interactions: Detection, estimation, and characterization. In Proceedings of the Eleventh International AAAI Conference on Web and Social Media (ICWSM). Montreal: AAAI Press. www.aaai.org/ocs/index.php/ICWSM/ICWSM17/paper/ view/15587

Varol, O., & Uluturk, I. (2018). Deception strategies and threats for online discussions. First Monday, 23(5). www.firstmonday.dk/ojs/index.php/fm/article/view/7883

Verkamp, J. P., & Gupta, M. (2013). Five incidents, one theme: Twitter spam as a weapon to drown voices of protest. Paper Presented at the USENIX Workshop on Free and Open Communications on the Internet (FOCI), August 13, Washington, DC.

Vincent, J. (2016). Twitter taught Microsoft's friendly AI chatbot to be a racist asshole in less than a day. The Verge, March 24. www.theverge.com/2016/3/24/11297050/ tay-microsoft-chatbot-racist

Vosoughi, S., Roy, D., & Aral, S. (2018). The spread of true and false news online. Science, 359(6380), 1146–1151. https://doi.org/10.1126/science.aap9559

Wagner, C., Mitter, S., Körner, C., & Strohmaier, M. (2012). When social bots attack: Modeling susceptibility of users in online social networks. In Proceedings of the WWW, 12. http://www2012.org/proceedings/nocompanion/MSM2012_paper_11.pdf

Walker, A. (2014). Quakebot: An algorithm that writes the news about earthquakes. Gizmodo, March 19. https://gizmodo.com/quakebot-an-algorithm-that-writes-the- news-about-earth-1547182732

Wang, A. H. (2010). Detecting spam bots in online social networking sites: A machine learning approach. In S. Foresti & S. Jajodia (Eds.), Data and Applications Security and Privacy XXIV (pp. 335–342). Berlin: Springer.

Washington Post Staff. (2017). Full transcript: Sally Yates and James Clapper testify on Russian election interference. Washington Post, May 8. www.washingtonpost.com/news/post-politics/wp/2017/05/08/full-transcript-sally-yates-and-james-clapper-testify-on-russian-election-interference/

Weld, D. S., & Etzioni, O. (1995). Intelligent agents on the Internet: Fact, fiction, and forecast. IEEE Intelligent Systems, 10(4), 44–49.

West, D. M. (2017). How to combat fake news and disinformation. Brookings,December 18. www.brookings.edu/research/how-to-combat-fake-news-and- disinformation/

Woolley, S. (2015). #HackingTeam leaks: Ecuador is spending millions on malware, pro-government trolls. Global Voices Advocacy, August 4. https://advox.globalvoices.org/2015/08/04/hackingteam-leaks-ecuador-is-spending-millions-on- malware-pro-government-trolls/

Woolley, S. (2016). Automating power: Social bot interference in global politics. First Monday, 21(4). http://firstmonday.org/ojs/index.php/fm/article/view/6161

(2018). Manufacturing consensus: Computational propaganda and the 2016 United States presidential election. Ph.D. dissertation, University of Washington.

Woolley, S., & Guilbeault, D. (2017). Computational propaganda in the United States of America: Manufacturing consensus online. Computational Propaganda ProjectWorking Paper Series. Oxford: Oxford Internet Institute.

Woolley, S., & Howard, P. N. (2016a). Automation, algorithms, and politics| Political communication, computational propaganda, and autonomous agents – Introduction. International Journal of Communication, 10(2019), 4882–4890.

(2016b). Social media, revolution, and the rise of the political bot. In P. Robinson, P. Seib, & R. Frohlich (Eds.), Routledge Handbook of Media, Conflict, and Security(pp. 282–292). London: Taylor & Francis.

(2018). Computational Propaganda: Political Parties, Politicians, and Political Manipulation on Social Media. Oxford: Oxford University Press.

Woolley, S., Shorey, S., & Howard, P. (2018). The bot proxy: Designing automated selfexpression. In Z. Papacharissi (Ed.), A Networked Self and Platforms, Stories, Connections (pp. 59–76). London: Routledge.

Zannettou, S., Caulfield, T., Setzer, W., Sirivianos, M., Stringhini, G., & Blackburn, J. (2019). Who let the trolls out? Towards understanding state-sponsored trolls. In Proceedings of the 10th ACM Conference on Web Science (pp. 353–362). Amsterdam: ACM. https://doi.org/10.1145/3292522.3326016

Zhang, Y., Wells, C., Wang, S., & Rohe, K. (2018). Attention and amplification in the hybrid media system: The composition and activity of Donald Trump's Twitter following during the 2016 presidential election. New Media & Society, 20(9), 3161–3182. https://doi.org/10.1177/1461444817744390

Zhuang, L., Dunagan, J., Simon, D. R., Wang, H. J., Osipkov, I., & Tygar, J. D. (2008). Characterizing botnets from email spam records. LEET, 8(1), 1–9.

06 DIGITAL POLITICAL ADVERTISING IN THE UNITED STATES

INTRODUCTION: AN OVERVIEW

The landscape of political advertising in the United States has undergone a remarkable transformation with the advent of the digital age. Digital political advertising, encompassing a diverse array of online platforms and strategies, has emerged as a powerful tool in shaping public opinion, mobilizing voters, and influencing electoral outcomes. This introduction sets the stage to delve into the intricate world of digital political advertising, highlighting its significance, evolution, and impact within the American political arena. From social media campaigns to targeted online messaging, we explore how this dynamic field has become an essential component of modern political communication.

Digital political advertising comes in many forms, appears in a myriad of places, and can be targeted in many more ways than traditional television advertising. At its most basic, digital political advertising is interactive content placed for a fee. It includes display advertising (images, audio, or video) and search advertising (based on keyword search behaviour); the goal may be to build supporter distribution lists, to fundraise for a candidate, party, or specific political cause, to persuade, or to increase name recognition and distribute information. Paid political ads can appear as banners (across the top of the page), as page takeovers, on the side of a webpage or news feed, in mobile apps, or in social media feeds where viewers can interact, like, or share them, further disseminating paid content organically. Some online ads feature call-to-action buttons and some auto-play as pre-roll advertising, appearing before consumers can continue their online activity. Some can be skipped and others will not allow further action until the ad finishes playing.

According to Borrell Associates, digital advertising made up a small fraction (less than 1 percent, $71 million) of political ad spending in the United States in 2014 but was projected to comprise a fifth of spending (20.1 percent,$1.8 billion) in 2018 (Borrell Associates 2018). Although digital advertising in campaigns has been around for a while and has been a growth market for several cycles now, it has long been overlooked by scholars, especially in comparison to traditional television advertising, for which there is a long and robust literature (see Fowler, Franz, and Ridout 2016), and even organic social media content, for which there is burgeoning research (Borah 2016; Bode et al. 2016). The lack of research on paid online advertising stems, in large part, from the difficulty in tracking the placement of and spending on online ads on websites, in apps, and on social media. Unlike television, where commercial tracking data has been available for two decades, systematic commercial tracking of digital advertising is very new, and until the aftermath of the 2016election, the prospects of obtaining data through the large platforms like Google and Facebook seemed dim. In the face of mounting evidence of Russia's involvement in the 2016 elections, and political pressure to do something about it, the large platforms chose to make public libraries of their paid political content starting in the summer of 2018. As should become abundantly clear throughout this review, which was updated in late 2019, the landscape of what we know about digital advertising is at a pivotal moment. In this chapter, we will review the data that scholars have started to assemble on the volume, content, targeting, and effect of paid online advertising in the United States. We will discuss how online advertising is regulated through formal rules and shaped informally by content negotiations between advertisers and platforms. We will also explain how the decentralized methods of purchasing digital ads make systematic research challenging. That said, this review (at best) provides tentative conclusions, which will be tested in earnest over the next few years. In many ways, then, we are at a precipice awaiting the flood of more systematic analyses yet to come as scholars dig into the newly available data. With that in mind, we will review what is known at the end of 2019 and evaluate the information that is available through the platform libraries.

CAMPAIGN FINANCE RULES

In general, online political advertising in the United States is regulated in two different ways. The first is through reporting requirements, which speak to the circumstances under which ad expenditures must be reported to state or federal regulators. The second pertains to rules surrounding the inclusion of disclaimers ("paid for by" lines) in the ads themselves. Within-ad disclaimers have occupied the bulk of regulatory energy in recent years, but the reach of reporting mandates has also been very controversial. Of course, there are also differences in the rules between the federal and state level – and there is variation across states. We discuss all of these issues in the next few sections.

REPORTING REQUIREMENTS

From a practical standpoint, reporting mandates for federal candidates, political parties, and registered political committees (i.e., PACs) are not especially problematic.[1] This is because all expenditures by these committees(those that exceed $200 to a vendor) are reported to the Federal Election Commission (FEC) (see 11 CFR 104.9). Whether for television advertising, radio ads, direct mail, or online/digital ads, these political actors must itemize their expenditures to any vendor, listing the purpose of the expenditure. (Purpose is defined as "a brief statement or description of why the disbursement was made." See 11 CFR 104.3(b)(3)(i)(A).)

The challenge in this area of federal regulations, however, is the absence of any clear reporting standard in the itemization. There is no mandate that political committees uniformly report expenditures for online advertising. For example, if a candidate pays a consulting firm to design and place ads online (or to place ads on TV or radio or to design a print flyer), the itemized expenditure might simply list the firm as recipient and the purpose of the expenditure as "advertising." This makes it incredibly hard for citizens, journalists, and academics to catalog the expenditures of registered political committees for online political advertising. It is also impossible to see the list of purchased creatives (i.e., ads) attached to the expenditures; and so, while the dollars allocated to online political advertising are embedded in reports to the FEC, they are of limited help in tracking these efforts across campaigns and election cycles.

Reporting requirements for other political actors, however, are sometimes even less clear. One gap in existing campaign finance laws became apparent in the aftermath of the enactment of the Bipartisan Campaign Reform Act (BCRA) in 2002. That landmark legislation was the first major campaign finance law since 1974, when Congress passed significant amendments to the 1971 Federal Election Campaign Act. BCRA did not include any specific coverage of online political activity in its campaign finance changes. Two issues became apparent as a result.

First, although BCRA was not intended to address online political activity, it left the reach of campaign finance laws and regulations unclear for individuals participating online in politics.2 The FEC responded to this issue with new regulations in 2006. For the most part, the agency resolved the ambiguity about volunteer efforts online (e.g., whether such efforts were in-kind contributions to campaigns) by exempting almost all pro- or anti-candidate action online from the definition of expenditures and contributions (see 11 CFR 100.94 and 100.155). Individuals or groups, as a result, can use computer equipment and internet services – without regulations – to participate by making websites, sending emails (for emails, see also 11 CFR 110.11(a)),3 and designing or participating on a blog, so long as such efforts are not compensated.4

The one explicit exception was for "communications placed for a fee on another person's Web site" (11 CFR 100.26). Ads placed for a fee were included into the definition of "public communications" and these were as such designated as reportable expenditures to the FEC by registered committees.5 In the online realm at the time, these were generally banner ads placed on websites. As noted, all such expenditures are embedded in the reporting by candidates, parties, and PACs, but they remain incredibly challenging to pull out and isolate in comparison to other categories of spending.

Despite the FEC's rule-making in 2006, the second issue that emerged in the aftermath of BCRA concerned the classification of political ads. The issue was not so much a gray area as it was – in many eyes – an omission. BCRA was motivated in part by an explosion of political advertising on television in the late 1990s by parties and outside groups that purported to be about issue education and not elections (Franz 2008). Parties used so-called unregulated "soft money" to sponsor these ads; and many outside groups who sponsored such "issue ads" (perhaps as their only election-related spending) considered them outside the scope of elections, thereby making it unnecessary, in their view, to register as a PAC with the FEC.

Reformersconsideredthese,incontrast,tobe "loopholes" thatleftmanypolitical ads unregulated. These ads often contained negative or positive statements about candidates but stopped short of explicitly telling viewer show to vote.6 Congress responded in BCRA by banning party soft money and classifying as campaign ads those ads that aired close to an election and that featured a candidate for federal office (by picture or in the text). More specifically, ads that aired within sixty days of the general election or thirty days of a primary were deemed "electioneering communications" that needed to be reported to the FEC. The omission concerned the reach of this reclassification. It covered only ads that aired on television or radio. In practice, this meant that online ads – "communications placed for a fee on another person's Web site" – were only reportable under the pre-BCRA standard: if the ad explicitly asked people to vote for or against a federal candidate. Ads that merely featured a candidate – one famous example from a Russian source in electoral support for or opposition to the candidate, were not considered reportable, whether posted online weeks before the election or merely one day before. (In reality, the expenditures for such ads would be reportable if they came from registered FEC committees, like traditional PACs, but online political ads that do not contain express advocacy are often sponsored by outside groups not registered with the FEC, such as non profit groups funded with large donations; see Kim et al. 2018.)7

To summarize, as of the presidential election of 2016, most online political activity remained exempt from campaign finance laws (i.e., blogging, sharing content on social media, organizing friends and families to vote); only online ads that explicitly urged the election or defeat of a candidate were reportable tothe FEC. Online ads from outside groups that featured candidates in a positive or negative light could be funded by any source, and there was no requirement that these efforts be reported to the FEC.8 Table 6.1 reviews existing laws and regulations as outlined in this section. As is clear, the major reporting "gap" is for outside groups placing "issue ads" online.

DISCLAIMER REQUIREMENTS

To this point, the discussion has considered only the coverage of the law on the reporting of online political advertising expenditures. As noted, however, there has been considerable discussion of the rules for disclaimers in online political ads, that is, requirements that ads list the sponsor and other information directly in the content of the ad. Consider, by way of example, disclaimer requirements for television and radio ads - or more broadly for all "public communications" as defined in 11 CFR 100.26. The regulations pertain not only to ads that expressly advocate for a candidate but also to ads that solicit contributions.

Table 6.1 Reporting requirements for online electioneering

Source	Online activity	Reported to federal regulators?
Private citizens	Blog posts, use of personal computers to advocate in elections	No
	Pay to place express advocacy ad online	Yes, as in-kind contribution (if coordinated with candidate, subject to the contribution limit) or independent expenditure (if uncoordinated, unlimited
	Pay to place "issue advocacy" online	No
Federal candidates	All online ads	Yes, but not well itemized in existing FEC reports
Federal parties	Express advocacy ads	Yes, and classified as either an "independent expenditure" (if uncoordinated with the candidate, unlimited) or as a "coordinated expenditure" (subject to limits in amount spent)
	"Issue advocacy" ads	Yes, but not well itemized in existing FEC reports; must use federal funds for such ads
FEC-registered PACs (incl. "super" PACs)	Express advocacy ads	Yes, and classified as an "independent expenditure." "Super" PACs have no limits on the source of funding for these ads
	"Issue advocacy" ads	Yes, but not well itemized in existing FEC reports
Nonregistered groups	Express advocacy ads	Yes, and classified as an "independent expenditure." Similar to "Super" PACs, there are no regulations on the source of funds used to pay for these ads
	"Issue advocacy" ads	No

* Issue advocacy is defined here as either (1) ads about public policy issues but that do not feature candidates or (2) ads about public policy issues that also feature or depict federal candidates in a negative or positive light.

For ads sponsored by candidates, for example, the disclaimer in the ad must state that the candidate's committee authorized it. For television ads specifically, there must also be a clearly readable written statement that appears legibly on the screen for at least four seconds. Candidates in television and radio ads must also appear in their ads and make an "I endorse this message" statement. For ads sponsored by registered PACs and political parties, uncoordinated messages must contain a disclaimer statement that tells viewers that the ad is not authorized by any candidate or candidate's committee, along with the "full name and permanent street address, telephone number, orWorld Wide Web address of the person who paid for the communication" (11 CFR 110.11(b)(3)).

The regulations in 11 CFR 110.11 lay out the disclaimer requirements for all "public communications," including certain requirements on size and readability (disclaimers "must be presented in a clear and conspicuous manner," for example). Notably, some advertisements are exempt, such as bumper stickers, pins, buttons, pens, and "similar small items" – for reasons of convenience – as well as skywriting, water towers, wearing apparel, "or other means of displaying an advertisement of such a nature that the inclusion of a disclaimer would be impracticable." Inconvenience and impracticability, then, constitute reasons for exempting the inclusion of a disclaimer.

The requirement for disclaimers in online ads is not as clearly established in federal regulations. The regulations are clear concerning certain emails (when the number sent is more than 500 and when they are substantially similar in content) and concerning the web pages of candidates, parties, and PACs registered with the FEC – these must all contain a disclaimer. Yet whether ads purchased online need a disclaimer, or whether they are inconvenient or impractical in that setting is a matter of considerable debate. As has been noted by practitioners during these debates, online banner ads are often small, for example, making the inclusion of a disclaimer possibly inconvenient.

Indeed, the FEC has not provided any formal regulatory clarity on this question but has instead used the advisory opinion process to respond to questions from digital ad sellers and buyers about the possible need for disclaimers.9 The FEC first considered disclaimers in digital ads in advisory opinion 2002-09, where Target Wireless asked the Commission if it must require disclaimers on ads sent via text message to cell phones.10 Given technological requirements at the time – including character limits on text messages – the FEC applied the "small items" exemptions to those political "ads." Similar questions were put to the FEC by Google (AO 2010-

19), Facebook (2011-09), and by a digital firm, Revolution Messaging (2013-18), who asked about disclaimers on mobile banner ads.11 In the Google case, the Commission allowed ad sponsors who purchased character-limited online ads to link to the committee's website, which contained the full disclaimer for the group. They did not justify this under the "small items" exemption, though, and they limited the application of the linking option to FEC-registered committees. In the Facebook and Revolution Messaging cases, however, the FEC could not reach a consensus on how to apply disclaimer requirements in those cases. (For a longer treatment of the circumstances and issues involved in the Google, Facebook, and Revolution Messaging opinions, see Haenschen and Wolf 2019.)

The FEC considered Facebook ads again in 2017 in a request from the group Take Back Action Fund (see AO 2017-12). Here too the FEC had trouble in reaching consensus – two draft opinions split the commissioners – though there was agreement that the group (which was not a registered FEC committee) must include all disclaimers on its proposed image and video ads on Facebook. The commissioners noted that technological advancements since its earlier opinions (spanning the Target Wireless opinion in 2002 and this one in 2017) no longer limited the video length or included text. As such, the application of the "small items" exemption seemed nonsensical in this case.12 Indeed, the Commission noted in its deliberation that Facebook has expanded its ad formats, allowing for unlimited text above and below images as well as posted videos of up to 240 minutes long. (A complication noted by Take Back Action is that Facebook also notes that text can be truncated past certain characters, and some forms of text that overlay with video can result in reduced delivery of the ad; Facebook2018.)

Despite such considerable discussion of this issue and agreement that there should be disclaimers, there are still no formal regulations that make clear when a sponsor must use and when a sponsor is exempt from providing a disclaimer in the various types of online political advertising. Ad buyers on Facebook, for example, interpreted the deadlocked FEC decision in 2011 to mean that disclaimers on Facebook ads were not required. The FEC's 2017 advisory opinion did not provide sufficient clarity either, despite the seeming agreement about disclaimers among the commissioners. ProPublica examined a sample of political ads purchased on Facebook in early 2018 – after the Take Back Action opinion – and noted that the vast majority did not contain sufficient disclaimers in line with the outcome of that case (Valentino-DeVries 2018). Still, by mid-2018, Facebook was requiring that ad buyers include disclaimers, which was part of a round of revisions the company made in response to public pressure in the wake of the 2016 election. These included a formal verification that ad buyers have US-based residences. We discuss Facebook's efforts in more detail in the section on the platform's response to the 2016 election.

Despite Facebook's stated intention to make their political database more transparent, there remains a gap in existing regulatory guidelines. Because of this confusion, the FEC in 2018 opened a rule-making process on this issue.13

The agency held hearings in June 2018 to consider two proposed sets of regulations for online ad disclaimers. The first set of regulations, dubbed Proposal A, would treat all but a subset of paid political ads online as in the same category of radio, television, and print ads, ones that need the full set of clearly legible or audible disclaimers. The one exemption would be for a small category of text or graphic online ads where a disclaimer would take up too much space to be practical. It would allow in this case for an abbreviated disclaimer and/or a "linking" option to full disclaimers (similar to the one authorized in Google's advisory opinion request in 2010).

In contrast, Proposal B would be far more flexible, applying "adapted disclaimers" in many more cases, "depending on the amount of space or time necessary for a clear and conspicuous disclaimer as a percentage of the overall advertisement" (FEC 2018, p. 20). For example, some online ads could bedisplayed as "billboard ads" in the background of city landscapes in online games. Should such ads, viewed perhaps quickly by gamers, contain the full set of print disclaimers as a Facebook sponsored post? Or would the legibility requirement in such a case make the disclaimer too large, obstructing the ad content specifically? Indeed, the FEC noted the challenge at hand in the announcement of its rule-making:

Since the Commission's 2006 internet rule-making, the focus of Internet activity has shifted from blogging, websites, and listservs to social media networks (Facebook, Twitter, and LinkedIn), media sharing networks (YouTube, Instagram, and Snapchat), streaming applications (Netflix, Hulu), and mobile devices and applications. Other significant developments include augmented and virtual reality and the "Internet of things": wearable devices (smart watches, smart glasses), home devices (AmazonEcho), virtual assistants (Siri, Alexa), smart TVs and other smart home appliances. (FEC 2018, p. 16)

Proposal B would codify a general disclaimer requirement for online ads into federal regulations, but it would leave open the possibility for many variations. As might be expected, the FEC's open hearings on the competing proposals featured vigorous defenses and criticisms of both proposals. The held two days of hearings, on June 27 and June 28, 2018, receiving written and oral testimony from nearly twenty scholars, practitioners, and activists.14 As of late 2019, the FEC had yet to decide on a new set of regulations, but the likelihood that the Commission will formally choose between Proposal A and B is slim given its partisan divides (Franz 2018).

The importance of establishing regulatory clarity for online political ads was on display in 2016 when Russian-backed interests purchased political ads on Facebook. The social media giant admitted in fall 2017 that about 3,000 paid ads – costing about $100,000 – that were linked to fake accounts associated with the Internet Research Agency, a pro-Kremlin organization, appeared in users' news feeds. Most of these were "issue" ads, not express advocacy ones, and so they went unreported to the FEC. Given the ban on foreign money in US elections, these ads were additionally concerning, as they were targeted to battleground states important to the outcome of the Electoral College (Kim et al. 2018). As Facebook admitted, the ads appeared to be intended to "amplify divisive social and political messages" (Stamos 2017). With no clarity on disclaimer rules for online ads, along with noted gaps in disclosure requirements for some online political ads (see Table 6.1) and little oversight from Facebook on the purchase and placement of such ads (discussed more in the section on the platform's efforts since 2016), the 2016 presidential campaign exposed real weaknesses and gaps in existing laws and regulations.15

STATE LAWS

To this point the discussion has focused only on federal laws, but there are regulations of online advertising at the state level as well. It is beyond the scope of this review to lay out a comprehensive list of state laws as they relate to digital political advertising. Still, some consideration of state efforts to regulate campaign finance and electioneering online is illustrative.[16] Indeed, there is often not as much clarity in many state laws on the regulation of online advertising and spending. For example, Ohio campaign finance law excludes anything explicit to online ads in its statutory definition of "public political advertising" (for more discussion of Ohio, see Grandjean 2017). To the extent

that online ads are regulated depends on the reach of a catchall phrase in the definition: "other similar types of general public political advertising." By contrast, Maine lists "publicly accessible sites on the Internet" as part of its list of covered communication mediums. Notably, the "top 3 funder" provision in Maine – which requires ads sponsored by outside groups to list the top three founders of the group directly in the disclaimer of the ad – only applies to "Internet audio programming" and therefore not to banner ads or sponsored social media posts that appear only as visuals and/or text.

New York State has been more aggressive in its response to the growth of online electioneering. The "New York State Democracy Protection Act," signed into law by the governor in April 2018, expands the disclosure and disclaimer122 *Erika Franklin Fowler, Michael M. Franz, & Travis N. Ridout* provisions in place for radio and television ads to online political ads, and it requires the State Board of Elections to create an archive of political ads placed online. This includes not only a searchable archive of spending by sponsors but also the ads themselves, to make them open to fact checks by journalists and citizens. The state took as its lead the debate at the federal level over new legislation in response to the Russian efforts with Facebook ads in the 2016 election.

All told, scholars need a more complete accounting of the variations in state laws on the regulation of online political activity. Some states leave online efforts merely implied in their laws, while other states have explicitly included online advertising, with some being more explicit than othes.

CONGRESSIONAL PROPOSALS AND THE PLATFORMS' RESPONSE

The FEC is not alone at the federal level in considering new rules for online advertising. After the 2016 election, Congress considered new legislation to regulate political ads online. In fact, New York's legislation was primarily inspired by drafts of the proposed Honest Ads Act, sponsored by Senators Amy Klobuchar (D-MN), Mark Warner (D-VA), and John McCain (R-AZ) in October 2017 (and introduced simultaneously in the House by Democrat Derek Kilmer of Washington state).17 The bill (when first introduced in the 115th Congress) had twenty-seven additional cosponsors in the Senate, all Democrats plus Independent Angus King of Maine.18

The provisions of the proposed legislation are similar to those in New York's "Democracy Protection Act." More specifically, the legislation expands the definition of reportable electioneering messages to include ads placed online. Recall that the expanded definition of reportable campaign ad spending passed under BCRA omitted online ads. That is, "issue ads" from outside groups that feature a candidate and are purchased close to an election are not reportable to the FEC if they appear online (as opposed to on television or radio). The Honest Ads Act would include such ads, reportable to the FEC as an "electioneering communication." This proposal would at least allow citizens and journalists to track comprehensively the expenditures for all online political ads that mention or depict a federal candidate in the weeks before a primary or general election. The act also proposed to expand the disclaimer requirements to online political ads, in a manner that follows more closely in the spirit of the FEC's Proposal A. In addition, the proposed legislation would mandate the creation of an archive of purchased political ads online. The archive, to be maintained by the FEC, was to contain a digital copy of the ad, a description of the audience targeted, the number of views/impressions, and the rate charged for the ad buy. The bill went nowhere in 2017 and 2018, but it was reintroduced in 2019. Lindsey Graham, a Republican from South Carolina, joined as cosponsor on the Senate bill, but as of this writing there has been no legislative movement on the bill and there is almost no likelihood of passage before the 2020 presidential election.

The response of Facebook, Google, and Twitter to this possible legislation was to increase their transparency in the political ads purchased on their platforms. In a sense, all three companies tried to get out in front of any possible congressional mandates. In late 2017 and at various times in 2018, representatives from Facebook, Google, and Twitter testified before Congress – including Facebook CEO Mark Zuckerberg in April 2018 – about Russian efforts online in 2016 as well as the spread and dissemination of misinformation through social media. Facebook announced new rules in May 2018, such that ads with "political content" (meant to include not just electioneering but all ads related to public policy issues) would now require disclaimers that "accurately represent the name of the entity or person responsible for the ad" and that ad buyers would need to be officially authorized by entering a designated identification code mailed to the buyers of Facebook ads. This was intended to guarantee that ad buyers had a physical US address. Moreover, Google, Facebook, and Twitter separately rolled out in mid-2018 versions of the ad archive proposal from Klobuchar and Warner's legislation. Facebook created a searchable library for all political ads purchased after May 2018 and has stated that all ads will stay online for at least seven years.19 Users can search by keywords and select ads from specific sponsors to see rough approximations of impressions (ad views) by gender, age, and state. (We will further discuss the Facebook library and its limitations in the "Measuring Digital Spending" section.) Twitter, which stopped selling political ads in late 2019, and Google allow users to see just election-related ads (and not public policy-focused ads), but like Facebook they also show some statistics on audience demographics. These are important first steps in providing citizens, journalists, and scholars access to a wide range of data on digital advertising, but initial reviews of the libraries pointed to a host of limitations and challenges, including the ability to see the specific targeting goals of ad buyers (Singer 2018a; Mozilla 2019; Rosenberg 2019).

BEYOND FORMAL REGULATION: THE PROCESS OF DISCUSSING AND ESTABLISHING ADVERTISING POLICIES ON DIGITAL PLATFORMS

In the vacuum created by the lack of governmental regulations on online advertising, technology firms have created their own rules for political ad content on their platforms. These evolving sets of rules range from requirements to disclose the sponsor and to provide content that meets "community standards" (giving firms the capacity to take down offensive or hateful political commentary), but these rules are not always clearly explained, and firms often make changes in how they interpret these rules with little noticeor clear explanation (Kreiss and McGregor 2018). Moreover, some have large consequences for democratic discourse. For instance, some advertising by news media organizations promoting their political content was initially tagged as violating the rules (Brandom 2018).

Drawing on extensive interviews with campaign staffers, digital political consultants, former platform employees from Google and Facebook, and email exchanges between Facebook staffers and two campaigns, Kreiss and McGregor (2019) show that, while firms now actively vet political ad content through AIand human moderation, there is often an additional layer of content negotiation that occurs between campaign staffers and the platforms that sometimes results in changes. For example, Kreiss and McGregor (2019) detail a protracted exchange between campaign staffers and Facebook representatives centering on the accuracy of an opponent's campaign ads which used an edited (and therefore misleading) Washington Post headline. After a long back-and-forth,

> the company took down the posts without explanation at the time, but when the edited headline resurfaced in video form, the back-and-forth discussion started up again with the Facebook representative suggesting that videos differed from link shares and therefore on procedural (and not substantive content) grounds the new policy prohibiting editing headlines did not apply to videos.

In addition, Kreiss and McGregor's (2019) research suggests that internal negotiations over ad policies within the firms are also important. For example, sales team representatives within a firm like Facebook may advocate for their political clients with their colleagues on the policy team, helping ad sponsors by shaping the interpretation of particular policies (Kreiss and McGregor 2019).

HOW DIGITAL ADVERTISING IS PURCHASED AND WHY IT MATTERS FOR RESEARCH

In addition to the regulatory challenges of tracking and analyzing digital advertising, the decentralized way in which advertising is purchased online represents an enormous hurdle to understanding the universe of online and social media advertising. Some digital advertising is purchased directly from the source on which it will appear (e.g., a local mayoral campaign in Denver may go directly to the Denver Post to purchase advertising on its website just as a national political organization might buy a banner ad directly from Politico or a candidate might go to Facebook), but much of the online inventory on the web is purchased through intermediary ad networks, which allow buyers to purchase advertising space through a broker of multiple sites and similarly allow suppliers to aggregate the inventory they have available to sell. In addition, the development of programmatic purchasing, also referred to as ad exchanges, provides advertisers the ability to bid for advertising space in real time. In short, the path that any given digital ad can take before it is served to a user can vary widely, sometimes passing through multiple networks or exchanges before reaching the viewer.

Because different ads take multiple and varied paths, there is no central clearinghouse for information on digital ad inventory. Therefore, in spite of recent efforts by the major digital platforms to make data on advertising available for researchers, there are still gaps in our knowledge of the broader universe of digital advertising, and there are issues of comparability. Because each of the newly available libraries was designed and built individually by each social media company, making comparisons across platforms is difficult at best. At its most basic, it is impossible to compare all paid political advertising from the platform libraries because only Facebook makes more than just election- related advertising available. The universe of what should be included in the broader set of political advertising, however, is a challenging definitional issue that would not be guaranteed to be identical across libraries even if Google were to make such ads available. In addition, even election-related content is not comparable across sources as Google only makes election-related advertising available for federal and state wide races, and Facebook data lack programmatic access to FEC and employer identification number (EIN) identifiers for ad sponsors that would help researchers more easily match up the federal election-related content for comparison with other sources.20

In addition, there are additional technical challenges researchers face in making comparisons. For example, Google's political ad library currently includes "ads purchased through Google Ads and Google Marketing Platform," but the documentation in August 2018 stated that the initial launch did not include advertising that is available through approved third- party vendors who also serve ads on Google; and, in 2019, the content of third- party ads was often unavailable, inhibiting content comparisons. As of late 2019, Facebook's library and researcher API still did not allow searching for particular time windows, meaning that, to access 2018 election content, one may have to page through thousands of ads placed in 2019 to access the desired advertising. More problematic is that researcher calls to the API are rate limited and often buggy, and Facebook fixes to reported bugs can take weeks or in some cases months (Rosenberg 2019).

Both Facebook's and Google's libraries included both actively running ads and inactive ads, but Twitter's searchable archive contained only ads currently running (Singer 2018a). Google has easy-to-use congressional district information not yet available from Facebook but currently only makes data available by week whereas Facebook added daily data in mid- 2019. Although Google and Facebook both make aggregate information available, the content of both reports depends on when a researcher pulls the information, which creates inherent problems for researcher replication. As should be obvious, having multiple libraries, all with differing features and no central clearinghouse, makes describing the universe and comparing across sources challenging. Moreover, even if we were able to merge identical datasets from Facebook, Google, and Twitter's libraries, we would still miss direct purchase advertising and advertising sold on the web or in-apps outside of Google.

THE CHANGING FUNCTION OF PLATFORMS AS ADVISORS IN THE MEDIA INDUSTRY

Developments in the online deployment of advertising made targeting and testing different versions of creatives very easy; and, because online behaviour is easily tracked, ad sponsors can assess which version of an ad encourages more user responsiveness. As digital advertising grew, the big social media firms built more options on their programmatic purchasing dashboards to aid self-serve purchasing and testing. The platforms also offered additional help to demonstrate the product and showcase optimization methods. In 2016, they even made themselves available as real-time "quasi-digital" consultants to the presidential campaigns, acting as both inventory suppliers and direct consultant/collaborators in both finding key audiences and optimizing engagement of those audiences with the advertising (Kreiss and McGregor 2018). Facebook has since announced that it will no longer provide campaign "embeds" and has stopped commission-based compensation for political ad sales (Glazer and Horwitz 2019).

With the attention to digital campaigning increasing following the 2016 election, additional ad purchasing methods are rolling out on Facebook, which in both scope and description appear designed to lure traditional television buyers. Documentation from June 2018 on how to purchase ads described two specialty purchasing options to "empower advertisers who are used to purchasing brand awareness and television media" (Facebook n.d.). These include "reach and frequency" campaigns, which are designed to reach more than 200,000 people at a fixed price and "target rating points," which can be purchased up to six months in advance and are booked directly with Facebook.

TARGETING

One of the biggest benefits of online advertising is the more specific targeting it enables. Campaigns can choose audiences based on key features (e.g., demographics, interests, locations, or behaviours), based on their own lists, or based on lookalike audiences (those who share similar features to any given set of individuals). It is this last category where the role of the platforms as consultants again asserts itself in providing a subsidy to campaigns in tailoring and expanding their audience (Kreiss and McGregor 2018).

Although targeting is frequently described in news coverage, research assessing the reach and effect of targeting is much more limited given obvious constraints in data availability. Analyzing the paid Facebook advertising donated from 9,519 participants from the last six weeks of the 2016 election, Kim et al. (2018) found clear geographic targeting focused on battleground areas and some evidence of issue-based targeting based on income and race. Although Facebook's dashboard does not have "race" as a targeting category, campaigns can provide Facebook with custom audiences to target – people chosen by the campaign on the basis of their race. In an additional report covered in the New York Times, Kim suggests that "Russian groups appeared to identify and target non white voters months before the election with benign messages promoting racial identity" and "later appeared to interfere in the elections with voter suppression messages" (Kim cited in Singer 2018b).

Another study of Facebook advertisements from the United Kingdom, however, found little evidence of segmentation; the "targeted" Facebook ads contained messages similar to the messages being disseminated by the campaign nationally (Anstead et al. 2018). This finding, however, may not generalize to the United States, with its weaker parties and decentralized political system.

The new libraries released by each of the platforms will enable additional research on targeting. However, there are limits to what researchers will be able to say, stemming from the fact that the firms are independently creating their own libraries rather than responding to or complying with specific regulations or requirements. For example, Google's library provides targeting information on age, gender, and location but not information on who (by age and gender buckets) actually saw the ads. By contrast, the Facebook archive provides the reverse: who actually saw the ad, not necessarily who was intended to be targeted. Data are aggregated by each instance of an ad buy, and duplicate creatives frequently appear in the archive signifying that the advertiser changed something regarding cost or targeting with respect to the purchase, but what specifically was changed may be challenging to infer. Further, impressions and cost of each ad buy are provided as ranges – for example, an ad may list between10k and 100k impressions – but obviously the difference between the lower and upper range are nontrivial, especially when aggregated over numerous ad buys. It is also notable what is not available, namely partisanship or ideological lean of targets or views and other demographic categories beyond age and gender.

European regulations would prevent this information from being used to target their citizens,21 but there is nothing preventing the platforms from allowing targeting by ideology for the United States. In short, although a lot more information is now available, the lack of consistency across platforms, the level of aggregation of the information, and the information that is excluded altogether will continue to present challenges to researchers attempting to better understand online targeting.

QUANTIFYING EXPENDITURES IN THE DIGITAL REALM

How much is spent on digital political advertising in the United States each year? It is difficult to pinpoint an agreed-on figure, though all agree that the amount is rising with each election cycle. In September 2018, Borrell and Associates, a firm that tracks media, estimated that $1.8 billion would be spent on digital advertising in the 2018 election cycle (Borrell Associates 2018),$400 million more than the $1.4 billion spent in the 2016 cycle – a year that featured a presidential campaign. Both figures represent a massive increase from the $159 million spent on digital in the 2012 election cycle (Borrell Associates 2017). The company defines digital advertising as video ads, mobile ads, email, social media, and search.

The $1.8 billion in digital spending in 2018 represents just over 20 percent of total political ad spending (Borrell Associates 2018), up from the 14 percent share that digital had in the 2016 election cycle (Borrell Associates 2017). In 2012, digital's share of total political ad spending was just 1.4 percent.

Although these numbers are useful in providing the big picture of digital ad spending, they do not allow us to get a sense of how much individual candidates or other ad sponsors are spending on online advertising and social media. There are at least three ways to track digital ad spending at a more fine-grained level, though each has its disadvantages.

One is to use campaign committee filings with the FEC. In reporting their spending, campaign committees must identify a purpose for each expenditure. Unfortunately, campaigns are not required to use consistent categories, and so it can be a herculean (and potentially error-prone) task to sort through and identify whether each expenditure was for digital advertising. Nonetheless, Williams and Gulati (2018a) used this approach to try to quantify digital media spending by various campaigns in the 2012 and 2016 election cycles by identifying words such as "digital, Internet or email" in the purpose field of the campaign's report filed with the FEC. Using this technique, they identified$77 million in digital media spending by the Obama and Romney campaigns in the general election of 2012 – and $104 million by the Clinton and Trump campaigns in the general election of 2016. One of their most striking findings was that Trump vastly outspent Clinton on digital, which comprised only 8 percent of her campaign's media expenditures compared to 47 percent of the Trump campaign's media expenditures.

In a follow-up study, Williams and Gulati (2018b) focused on the spending of outside groups on digital advertising in the 2012 and 2016 presidential election races. They chart a rise in digital spending by independent groups from $89 million in 2012 to $219 million in 2016, an increase of almost 250 percent. The authors find that, in general, established outside groups focused relatively more spending on traditional media, while the largest single- candidate groups placed more of their efforts on digital advertising.

The examination of FEC filings, as demonstrated by the research of Williams and Gulati (2018a, 2018b), is one important source of information about digital ad spending in the political realm, but it does have some drawbacks. For one, the approach relies on the campaigns' classifications of expenditures, which may vary from campaign to campaign; there are no standard categories provided by the FEC. Second, not all groups must report their political spending to the FEC (see again Table 6.1). Non profit groups, in particular, must report political spending to the FEC only when they explicitly electioneer for a candidate; many groups stop just short of that in their political ads. Third, the information from the FEC on digital ad spending is dated by the time it is released, as committees must disclose their spending on a monthly or even quarterly basis, depending on the entity and type of race.

A second approach to tracking spending on digital media in campaigns is to rely on data collected by platform-independent media tracking firms. A typical approach employed by these companies is to send web crawlers to the top trafficked websites each day, capturing the volume of advertising from various sponsors and estimating the sponsor's spending, based on the number of ads identified. Ridout et al. (2017, 2018) used data from a firm called Pathmatics to report on spending in the 2016 presidential race – and to identify when various sponsors deployed advertisements online. Pathmatics estimated at least $58 million in spending on digital in the 2016 presidential campaign, but this is admittedly a severe underestimate because the firm at the time did not track spending on social media and, most importantly, on Facebook. On average, candidates in Senate races spent 11.4 percent of their ad budgets on Google and Facebook, while candidates in competitive House races spent 8.0 percent of their ad budgets on those two platforms (Fowler, Franz, and Ridout 2020), though there was much variation across campaigns. Still, these data allow one to examine the relative emphasis that various campaigns placed on online advertising vs. television advertising, and because these data were collected on a daily basis, one can track the ebb and flow of online ad spending as election day approaches. For instance, Ridout et al. (2018) found that the amount of online ad spending each day was much less predictable than the amount of television ad spending each day; online spending seemed much more responsive to the news of the day and campaign events.

Although the use of platform-independent data from media tracking firms seems promising – and some are now beginning to track social media spending based on online panels of individuals who provide their advertising data – there are still some drawbacks. One is that the numbers they report are only as good as the quality of their estimates, which are difficult to verify. Second, the firms that use web crawlers (as opposed to panels) typically track only the most- visited websites, and thus they may miss out on advertising in down-ballot races. For example, instead of making ad purchases from a big company like Google, a candidate for a congressional race may purchase advertising directly from a small local newspaper to be placed on its website. Because the newspaper's website has relatively low traffic, it will likely not be visited by the tracking firm's web crawlers. Finally, media tracking firms generally do not provide important information on who is being targeted, that is, how much spending is aimed at young people vs. older people or women vs. men. Panel methods do provide targeting information because they track the advertising seen by individuals, but their findings depend heavily on the representativeness of the panel, which is hard to verify.

A third and very recent source of data on digital spending is the technology firms that sell ad space online themselves: the platform libraries. In the wake of intense criticism over Facebook's selling of ads to Russian actors during the 2016 presidential campaign, Facebook agreed to provide more transparency about its political advertisers. As noted, in May 2018 Facebook launched a web library that allows anyone to search for a particular candidate or advertiser; the library provides an image of each of the ads that was purchased by that advertiser – along with any ads that mention the candidate. However, there were some difficulties in figuring out spending by sponsor, as Edelson et al. (2019) outline. One problem is that, like impressions, spending on each ad is only given in broad categories (e.g., less than $100, $1,000–$4,999), a decision that makes it difficult to calculate exact spending by sponsor. Second, one can only search ads purchased as of May 2018, so the many ads shown during the primary election season, not to mention the 2016 election cycle, are not available.

Finally, Facebook's interface in 2018 allowed pages to change their names without changing the associated numeric identifier and collects the funding information (of which a page can have many) in string format only without a numeric identifier (in 2019, Facebook began standardizing funding entity entries). These decisions create huge logistical headaches for researchers trying to report on spending by different types of entities. In our own investigation of the November 10, 2018, aggregated report published by Facebook following the 2018 midterm elections, we discovered that our team had three different versions of the report (indicating that the report was likely updated and, depending on when we pulled it down, we got different information).22 In collaboration with the Center for Responsive Politics(CRP), we attempted to identify and classify all of the entities in the report. Table 6.2 reports the identification status of all of the 91,651 non duplicate page name and funding entity records in the aggregate report by those for whom we were able to find a match in CRP's databases ("identified sponsor subtotal") and those for whom we were unable to do so ("unidentified sponsor"). Because the aggregate report contains at least one row for every page name/funding entity (or disclaimer) combination, there are multiple possibilities for sponsor identification (i.e., through the page name or through the disclaimer information). For example, Priorities USA Action, a major outside group supporting Democrats, funded a variety of Facebook ads through different Facebook pages (e.g., Working for Us, It's Our America, Missouri's Voice, Keep Them Accountable as well as a through a page called Priorities USA Action); some of these ads were jointly sponsored with other Democratic groups, Senate Majority PAC or House Majority PAC. Each of these instances appears as a separate row of the aggregate report, and the funding entity sometimes appeared in the page name but more often appeared in the disclaimer line, which read something like "Priorities USA Action. (302) 469- 3772. Not authorized by any candidate or candidate's committee." In general, we assume that the disclaimer information – although messy due to its string format as typos or missing periods result in additional rows – may be the better information source because, unlike the page name, which can be more generic, the funding information often contains the legal name of the funder along with a phone number (as in the Priorities USA Action example), an address, or treasurer's name, which can aid the classification process.

Table 6.2 Spending, ad volume, and entries from the November 10, 2018, Facebook aggregate report by identification status

Spending (millions)		% of spend	Number of ads	% of ads	Number of entries	% of entries
Identified sponsor subtotal	288.9	70%	1,252,008	57%	20,315	22%
By funding entity (PFB match)	259.4	63%	1,121,679	51%	11,553	13%
No funding entity listed (page match no PFB line)	12.6	3%	58,642	3%	7,362	8%
	16.8	4%	71,767	3%	1,400	2%
By page match only (page match no PFB match)	123.8		935,937	43%	71,336	78%
	412.7	30%	2,188,025	100%	91,651	
Unidentified sponsor (unmatched)						100%
TOTAL		100%				

Note. PFB = paid for by.

Source. *Wesleyan Media Project and Center for Responsive Politics (CRP) investigation and classification of the Facebook aggregate report from November 10, 2018.*

As shown in Table 6.2, we were able to identify 70 percent of the spending and 57 percent of the ads from the November 10, 2018, aggregated report, but only 22 percent of the total entries as 20,315 page name/disclaimer combinations were responsible for that activity. Most of the identified matches were made through the funding entity information, but 7,362 of those records were ads that ran without disclaimer information, so the classification in those cases had to be done based on page name. For the remaining 1,400 matches, we relied solely on the page name, which may be less accurate. The large number of unidentified records (71,336 in total representing $123.8 million in spending and 935,937 ads) attests to the challenge of identifying and reporting on digital advertising activity. Many of these entities are likely to be state and local organizations who simply do not appear in CRP's extensive but federally focused databases, but they may also include obscure or unregulated entities funding digital advertising.

In sum, our review of digital ad spending suggests that it is rising in volume over time – and rising as a share of total media spending. It also underscores the very real challenges involved in assessing even high-profile, federal election-related activity. Even more difficult is assessing digital spending in down-ballot races, during particular days or weeks of the campaign, or on particular platforms (e.g., on Facebook or in online display ads).

DIGITAL AD CONTENT

Our knowledge of the content of digital political advertising is thin. When researchers examine digital campaign content, they typically examine free content such as posts on a campaign's Facebook page (e.g., Borah 2016), tweets made by a candidate (e.g., Conway, Kenski, and Wang 2015), or campaign videos posted on YouTube (e.g., Ridout et al. 2015). We are aware of only one published study (Ballard, Hillygus, and Konitzer 2016) that focuses on the content of paid online advertising, but this research does reveal something important: The goals of digital ads are much more varied than the goals of televised political advertising.

The Ballard, Hillygus, and Konitzer (2016) study examined 840 online display ads from the 2012 presidential campaign that were compiled by a company called Moat Ad Search. The company's computers scoured the web on a daily basis and catalogued each unique ad. The researchers examined 737 Obama ads and 103 Romney ads and then coded each ad on a variety of factors. One of their most important findings was that online ads pursue a variety of goals. Only 37 percent of the ads they coded were aimed at persuasion, while 25 percent requested a donation, 20 percent tried to recruit viewers to do something for the campaign, and 18 percent encouraged people to turn out to vote. Arguably, 100 percent of campaign ads on television have persuasion as their chief goal. A working paper found a similar distribution of goals in online display ads in the 2016 presidential campaign (Ridout et al. 2017), with 52 percent of ads designed to gather information about the viewer,37 percent designed to persuade, 15 percent asking for a donation, and 14 percent encouraging campaign involvement (percentages are higher than 100 percent because ads could have more than one goal). Consistent with the varied focus of online advertising, many contain little policy information; just under a quarter of online ads in the Ridout et al. (2017) study contained discussion of policy compared to more than 70 percent of television ads from the same campaigns. Another paper (Franz et al. 2020) confirmed this finding of more issue discussion on television than online but found considerable consistency in the issue agendas across the two media; moreover, the predictions of mentioning an issue were similar across the two media.

Ballard, Hillygus, and Konitzer (2016) also found evidence of group targeting online, with 30 percent of the Obama campaign's ads directed at a specific group, such as women or African Americans, though only 10 percent of Romney's ads were similarly targeted. Their research found some evidence of issue ownership, that is, Obama focusing on issues that people believed the Democratic Party was better at handling and Romney focusing on issues that people believed the Republican Party was better at handling. Yet issue convergence – competing candidates talking about the same issues – was relatively low and much lower than found in campaigns' television advertisements.

How negative is digital advertising? The Ridout et al. (2017) study found low levels of negativity in online ads during the 2016 presidential campaign in the United States, with just 10 percent being pure attack ads and another 5 percent contrast ads. Candidate-sponsored ads were even less negative. This low level of negativity, however, contrasts with the findings of Roberts (2013) who found more attacks online than on television in the 2004 and 2008 presidential campaigns. Importantly, though, Roberts examined web-only videos posted by campaigns, and it is unclear if the ads were paid for or posted for free on websites like YouTube. It also contrasts with work done on the 2017 general election in the United Kingdom, where more than half of the Facebook ads placed by the major parties mentioned another party (which, in the authors' conceptualization, makes them negative; Anstead et al. 2018). The percentage of ads that were negative ranged from 56 percent for the Conservatives to64 percent for the Labour Party. The authors, note, however, that these percentages are only slightly higher than what one sees with party election broadcasts.

There are some additional studies that look at the content of unpaid communications to voters. One study of the 2009 European parliament elections made comparisons between paid ads and those posted on YouTube, finding that YouTube ads were longer and employed more emotional language(Vesnic-Alujevic and Bauwel 2014). Another study made comparisons among candidates' tweets, their Facebook pages, and their websites (Kelly 2011). The study found that candidates were most likely to attack on their websites but used social media to try to earn support from and mobilize followers.

In the most comprehensive content analysis that we are aware of to date, Fowler, Franz, Martin et al. (2019) examined all Facebook and television advertising by candidates for US Congress, statewide, and state legislative offices from May 2018 through Election Day. Relying on human content coding of all TV ads (5,569 creatives) and a random sample of 9,073 Facebook ads, they used a supervised learning approach to train a model predicting the tone and issue content of all ads, including the uncoded Facebook creatives. The results suggest (similar to prior work) that candidate advertising on Facebook is less negative than on television and contains less issue content and less issue diversity than television creatives but is also more partisan.

DISCUSSION

As online advertising continues to evolve – as well as spread to more electoral contexts, especially down the ballot – a number of important questions demand answers. For example, what is the impact of online spending? There was significant concern among many policymakers and among the general public that Russian efforts on social media in 2016 may have helped Donald Trump win the election. The Special Counsel's report on the matter of Russian interference in the election, and specifically the Trump campaign's knowledge of such efforts, implies there is deep concern in the United States about the ability of foreign interests to influence election outcomes and/or voter decision- making. Although Robert Mueller and his team did not issue a verdict on whether Russian efforts changed voters' minds, the broader question is paramount: Do digital ads work?

On this question, we still do not know. More generally, political scientists are skeptical that any advertising is effective (Kalla and Broockman 2018), though studies that focus on online advertising effects specifically are still small in number (Broockman and Green 2014). It could be that online ads are about as persuasive as traditional advertising, which would suggest small and fleeting effects only; but, because online ads are finely targeted to specific audiences, and tailored specifically for those audiences, their effects could be much greater thanfor television advertising.

Work by Shaw, Blunt, and Seaborn (2018) begins to speak to the question. The authors, working with a gubernatorial campaign in Texas, randomizedthe placement of internet ads, pre-roll ads, and Facebook ads by zip code. They find that the internet ads had a positive impact on people's favourability toward the sponsoring candidate and turnout in the primary election, but the pre-roll ads had no impact, and the impact of Facebook ads was border line negative. Although the impact of internet ads was smaller than for television, when one considers cost, the return on investment was just as high. More research like this is needed to get a full assessment of the impact of digital advertising, but other studies have found no impact. One experiment targeted legislators' constituents with Facebook ads but found no difference in people's evaluations or recognition of the candidate shown in the ad between those who saw the ad repeatedly and those who never saw it (Broockman and Green 2014). Another experiment found no impact of exposure to a week's worth of online display ads on people's views toward the Black Lives Matter movement (Coppock and Broockman 2015). One study did reveal a small impact of exposure to banner and pre-roll ads on voter turnout in a municipal election – but only when the race was competitive (Haenschen and Jennings 2019).

Almost certainly, campaigns will devote more of their resources to paid digital advertising in the future – and digital advertising is more likely to be a "difference maker" in future campaigns. Thus, it is imperative that more scholarship picks up the topic; but that will not be easy until access to data becomes easier – either through the efforts of large internet and social media companies or through government regulation.

REFERENCES

Anstead, N., Magalhães, J. C., Stupart, R., & Tambini, D. (2018). Political advertising on Facebook: The case of the 2017 United Kingdom general election. Paper presented at the Annual Meeting of the American Political Science Association. August 30 to September 2, Boston, MA.

Ballard, A. O., Hillygus, D. S., & Konitzer, T. (2016). Campaigning online: Web display ads in the 2012 presidential campaign. PS: Political Science & Politics, 49(3), 414–419. https://doi.org/10.1017/S1049096516000780

Bode, L., Lassen, D. S., Kim, Y. M. et al. (2016). Coherent campaigns? Campaign broadcast and social messaging. Online Information Review, 40(5), 580–594.

Borah, P. (2016). Political Facebook use: Campaign strategies used in 2008 and 2012 presidential elections. Journal of Information Technology & Politics, 13(4), 326–338. https://doi.org/10.1080/19331681.2016.1163519

Borrell Associates. (2017). The Final Analysis: What Happened to Political Advertising in 2016 (and Forever). Borrell Associates report. www.borrellassociates.com/shop/ the-final-analysis-political-advertising-in-2016-detail

(2018). Political Advertising Overload. April Update. Borrell Associates report. www.borrellassociates.com/industry-papers/papers/april-update-new-forecast-for-2018- political-advertising-report-detail

Brandom, R. (2018). Facebook's ad rules are forcing news outlets to Register as Political Advertisers. The Verge, June 1. www.theverge.com/2018/6/1/17416710/facebook-political-ad-rules-news-promotion-blocked

Broockman, D. E., & Green, D. P. (2014). Do online advertisements increase political candidates' name recognition or favorability? Evidence from randomized field experiments. Political Behavior, 36(2), 263–289. https://doi.org/10.1007/s11109-013-9239-z

Conway, B. A., Kenski, K., & Wang, D. (2015). The rise of Twitter in the political campaign: Searching for intermedia agenda-setting effects in the presidential primary. Journal of Computer-Mediated Communication, 20(4), 363–380. https://doi.org/10.1111/jcc4.12124

Coppock, A., & Broockman, D. (2015). Summary Report: The Effectiveness of Online Ads: A Field Experiment. https://alexandercoppock.com/papers/CB_blacklivesmatter.pdf

Edelson, L., Sakhuja, S., Dey, R., & McCoy, D. (2019). An analysis of United States online political advertising transparency. arXiv.org. preprint:1902.04385

Facebook (2018). About text in ad images. Facebook for Business. www.facebook.com/business/help/980593475366490

(n.d.). How much do Facebook ads cost? Facebook for Business. www.facebook.com/business/learn/how-much-facebook-ads-cost

FEC (Federal Election Commission). (2018). Internet communication disclaimers and definition of "Public Communication." Agenda Document No. 18-12-A, March. www.fec.gov/resources/cms-content/documents/mtgdoc_18-12-a.pdf

Fowler, E. F., Franz, M., King, G., Mukerjee, Z., & Persily, N. (2019). Facebook Ad Library. Harvard Dataverse, V1. https://doi.org/10.7910/DVN/9OAMBW

Fowler, E. F., Franz, M. M., Martin, G. J., Peskowitz, Z., & Ridout, T. N. (2019). Political advertising online and offline. Paper presented at the Annual Meeting of theAmerican Political Science Association Conference, August 29 to September 1, Washington, DC.

Fowler, E. F., Franz, M. M., & Ridout, T. N. (2016). Political Advertising in the UnitedStates. New York: Routledge.

Fowler, E. F., Franz, M. M., & Ridout, T. N. (2020). The blue wave: Assessing political advertising trends and democratic advantages in 2018. PS: Political Science & Politics, 43(1), 57–63.

Franz, M. M. (2008). Interest Groups in the Electoral Process. Philadelphia, PA: TempleUniversity Press.

(2018). FEC divided: Ideological polarization in commission votes since 1990. Paper presented at the Annual Meeting of the American Political Science Association, August 30 to September 2, Boston.

Franz, M. M., Fowler, E. F., Ridout, T. N., & Wang, M. Y. (2020). The issue focus of online and television advertising in the 2016 presidential campaign. American Politics Research, 48(1), 175–196.

Glazer, E., & Horwitz, J. (2019). Facebook curbs incentives to sell political ads ahead of 2020 election. Wall Street Journal, May 23. www.wsj.com/articles/facebook-ends- commissions-for-political-ad-sales-11558603803

Grandjean, A. M. (2017). As technology advances, laws governing online political advertising remain the same. Bricker & Eckler website, July 7. www.bricker.com/industries-practices/government-relations/insights-resources/publications/ as-technology-advances-laws-governing-online-political-advertising-remain-the-same

Haenschen,K.,&Jennings,J.(2019).Mobilizingmillennialvoterswithtargetedinternet advertisements: A field experiment. Political Communication, 36(3):357–375.

Haenschen, K., & Wolf, J. (2019). Disclaiming responsibility: How platforms deadlocked the Federal Election Commission's efforts to regulate digital political advertising. Telecommunications Policy, 43(8).

Kalla, J. L., & Broockman, D. E. (2018). The minimal persuasive effects of campaign contact in general elections: Evidence from 49 field experiments. American Political Science Review, 112(1), 148–166. https://doi.org/10.1017/S0003055417000363

Kelly, A. G. (2011). Internet Campaign Strategies in the 2010 Massachusetts Gubernatorial Election. Worcester Polytechnic Institute. https://web.wpi.edu/Pubs/E-project/Available/E-project-030811-171405/

Kim, Y. M., Hsu, J., Neiman, D. et al. (2018). The stealth media? Groups and targets behind divisive issue campaigns on Facebook. Political Communication, 35(4), 515–541. https://doi.org/10.1080/10584609.2018.1476425

Kreiss, D., & McGregor, S. C. (2018). Technology firms shape political communication: The work of Microsoft, Facebook, Twitter, and Google with campaigns during the 2016 U.S. presidential cycle. Political Communication, 35(2), 155–177. https://doi.org/10.1080/10584609.2017.1364814

(2019). The "arbiters of what our voters see": Facebook and Google's struggle with policy, process, and enforcement around political advertising. Political Communication, 36(4): 499–522. https://doi.org/10.1080/10584609.2019.1619639

Mozilla (2019). Facebook and Google: This is what an effective ad archive API looks like.

Mozilla (blog), March 27. https://blog.mozilla.org/blog/2019/03/27/facebook-and-google-this-is-what-an-effective-ad-archive-api-looks-like/

Ridout, T. N., Fowler, E. F., Branstetter, J., & Borah, P. (2015). Politics as usual? When and why traditional actors often dominate YouTube campaigning. Journal of Information Technology & Politics, 12(3), 237–251.

Ridout, T. N., Fowler, E. F., Franz, M. M., & Wang, M. Y. (2017). Comparing digital and television advertising strategy in the 2016 presidential campaign. Paper presented at the American Political Science Association Political Communication Pre-Conference, August 30, San Francisco.

(2018). All in good time: Comparing the responsiveness of online and television advertising in the 2016 presidential campaign. Paper presented at the Annual Meeting of the International Communication Association, May 24–28, Prague.

Roberts, C. (2013). A functional analysis comparison of Web-only advertisements and traditional television advertisements from the 2004 and 2008 presidential campaigns. Journalism and Mass Communication Quarterly, 90(1), 23–38.

Rosenberg, M. (2019). Ad tool Facebook built to fight disinformation doesn't work as advertised. New York Times, July 25. www.nytimes.com/2019/07/25/technology/facebook-ad-library.html

Shaw, D. R., Blunt, C., & Seaborn, B. (2018). Testing overall and synergistic campaign effects in a partisan statewide election. Political Research Quarterly, 71(2), 361–379.

Singer, N. (2018a). Taking a spin through data behind ads for candidates. New York Times, September 3. www.nytimes.com/2018/09/02/technology/03adarchive.html Singer, N. (2018b). "Weaponized ad technology": Facebook's money-maker gets a critical eye. New York Times, August 16. www.nytimes.com/2018/08/16/technology/facebook-microtargeting-advertising.html

Stamos, A. (2017). An update on information operations on Facebook. Facebook Newsroom, September 6. https://newsroom.fb.com/news/2017/09/information- operations-update/

Valentino-DeVries, J. (2018). I approved this Facebook message – but you don't know that. ProPublica, February 13. www.propublica.org/article/i-approved-this- facebook-message-but-you-dont-know-thatVesnic-Alujevic, L., & Van Bauwel, S. (2014). YouTube: A political advertising tool? A case study of the use of YouTube in the campaign for the European Parliament elections. Journal of Political Marketing, 13(3), 195–212. https://doi.org/10.1080/15377857.2014.929886

Williams, Christine B., & Gulati, G. J. (2018a). Digital advertising expenditures in the 2016 presidential election. Social Science Computer Review, 36(4), 406–421. https://doi.org/10.1177/0894439317726751

(2018b). Digital ad expenditures by outside groups in the 2016 presidential election. In J. Baumgartner & T. Towner (Eds.), The Internet and the 2016 Presidential Campaign (pp. 127–147). New York: Lexington Books.

Zuiderveen Borgesius, F., Moeller, J., Kruikemeier, S. et al. (2018). Online political micro-targeting: Promises and threats for democracy. Utrecht Law Review, 14(1),82–96.

FOOTNOTE:

1. This discussion refers to all committees that report to the Federal Election Commission (FEC). All federal candidates and political parties must maintain campaign committees that track and report contributions and expenditures. Outside groups that register as Political Action Committees (PACs) also report to the FEC. Most PACs are organized by corporations or labor unions and are defined as "separate segregated funds" under 52 U.S.C. 30118(b)(2)(C). They are also some- times called "traditional" PACs. These groups are allowed to collect and distribute contributions to federal candidates, as well as make uncoordinated expenditures on behalf of candidates during an election. Some PACs are colloquially referred to as "super" PACs because they do not make contributions to candidates but are allowed to collect unlimited contributions from any American and use those for ads that attack or promote federal candidates. One of the major controversies of campaign finance law in recent decades, however, has concerned the reach of reporting requirements for outside groups who do not believe they meet the regulatory definition of a PAC as described in this note. These groups are considered later in this section.
2. This was important because the law went into effect in 2003, just as online political activity was constitute something "of value" that needed to be reported as an in-kind contribution? Citizens, after all, spend their own money to get access online or to update and replace computer software. It is conceivable to consider these efforts reportable contributions to a campaign.
3. If an email distribution consists of "more than 500 substantially similar" emails, the message must contain a disclaimer listing who sponsored the message. Disclaimers for online ads and messages are considered more in the next section.
4. It is important to note, though, that if an individual or group pays to buy or rent an email list, used subsequently to distribute pro- or anti-candidate messages, that is a reportable expenditure.
5. The full definition of "public communication" in 11 CFR 100.26 is: "a communication by means of any broadcast, cable, or satellite communication, newspaper, magazine, outdoor advertising facility, mass mailing, or telephone bank to the general public, or any other form of general public political advertising. The

term general public political advertising shall not include communications over the Internet, except for communications placed for a fee on another person's Web site."

6. 11 CFR 100.22 defines the relevant phrases regarding an exhortation to vote to include "vote for the President," "re-elect your Congressman," "support the Democratic nominee," "cast your expanding rapidly. For example, Howard Dean would make aggressive use of online volunteer coordination in 2003. Facebook would launch in 2004 and rapidly expand through 2005 and 2006. Twitter was launched in 2006. Federal regulations require registered committees to report any contribution from an individual or other political committee. Contributions are defined as "A gift, subscription, loan ... advance, or deposit of money or anything of value made by any person for the purpose of influencing any election for Federal office" (11 CFR 100.52). Did online political activity – such as using one's computer to organize volunteers, or for making payments to support a pro-candidate blog, or by organizing and distributing campaign materials online – ballot for the Republican challenger for U.S. Senate in Georgia," "Smith for Congress," "Bill McKay in '94."
7. Prior to Citizens United v. Federal Election Commission 558 U.S. 310 (2010), express advocacy messages as outlined in this section (on television, in print, on radio, online, and so on, regardless of format) were banned for certain sponsors, such as corporations and labour unions (unless sponsored by their regulated PACs). In light of the court's decision, however, express advocacy became permissible by any domestic sponsor, including online with banner ads.
8. Federal law outlaws the expenditure of money by foreign nationals and corporations in US elections, which applies also to online political advertising. However, without effective disclosure and disclaimer requirements in place, it is often impossible to know if foreign interests are investing in elections (Kim et al. 2018).Issue advocacy is defined here as either (1) ads about public policy issues but that do not feature candidates or (2) ads about public policy issues that also feature or depict federal candidates in a negative or positive light.
9. The FEC issues "advisory opinions" as part of its statutory responsibility (see 11 CFR 112). These are formal statements from the Commission, approved by at least four commissioners and that answer a specific question about the reach and scope of the law. The issued opinions provide guidance to political actors about the legality of specific proposed campaign financing activity, and they do not take the place of the FEC's charge to write official regulations that provide more general clarity on the law. (In truth, other political actors look to resolved advisory opinions for some idea of what the Commission might think about a political action, but the outcome of these opinions is not actual regulatory policy.)
10. All completed advisory opinions are accessible at www.fec.gov/data/legal/advisory-opinions/.The FEC first considered the issue of disclaimers in internet communications in two advisory opinions in 1995, both about soliciting campaign contributions via the Internet. See AO 1995-09 and 1995-35.

11. The Club for Growth in 2007 asked the FEC if it could truncate disclaimers on short (ten- or fifteen-second) television ads. The FEC did not approve of that request because the choice of the group to air such ads was a political decision, not one driven by technological limitations (AO 2007-33).
12. Republican commissioners, however, were hesitant to exclude the application of the exemption to all online ads, if only because the group in the advisory opinion did not formally ask for the exemption to apply. As Take Back Action Fund noted, while Facebook does not apply rigid character limits to paid advertising posts, there is a strong recommendation from Facebook that text be limited. As such, there are instances where ad sponsors might still want the Commission to consider whether an exemption is appropriate.
13. The other area of interest in the 2018 rule-making process concerns the phrase "communications placed for a fee on another person's Web site" in 11 CFR 100.26. Because of the explosion of smart phones and "apps" (applications) on these phones, the FEC proposed to expand the regulatory reach to include ads accessed through an "internet-enabled device or application." For example, paying to place an ad in someone's Facebook newsfeed is conceivably not technically a "Web site" when it's viewed through someone's Facebook iPhone app.
14. Written comments and a transcript of the hearings are available at: www.fec.gov/updates/june-27-28-2018-public-hearing/.
15. This last point is a contestable one, to be sure. Some have argued, as the June 2018 debate at the FEC made clear, that expanded disclaimer mandates for online ads could be burdensome and that online electioneering should be left unregulated. Some also argue that a ban on foreign investments in elections is already in place, as is the regulatory infrastructure to provide oversight around violations of the law. Moreover, many of the Russian-backed Facebook ads did not mention or picture federal candidates, and many argue that such ads are rightly unregulated as protected speech under the First Amendment. For an example of this argument, see the October 2017 testimony before Congress of Randall Rothenberg, President and CEO of the Interactive Advertising Bureau: www.iab.com/news/read-the-testimony-from-randall-rothenberg-president-and-ceo-iab/.
16. The Campaign Finance Institute, a division of the National Institute on Money in Politics, maintains a searchable database of state laws on campaign finance. It is accessible at: http://cfinst.org/State/Laws Database. aspx. In some cases, state campaign finance laws could be seen as more restrictive than federal laws. Ten states, for example, limit individual contributions to state legislative candidates to $1,000 or less, in comparison to the federal limit of $2,700 to congressional and presidential candidates. Twenty-five states impose restrictions on state candidates from accepting contributions or holding fundraising events during a legislative session. There is no such limit at the federal level. Five states provide candidates with state subsidies to fund electioneering efforts, for which there is no federal equivalent. In contrast, twelve states have no limit on contributions

from individuals to state candidates. Eight states allow unlimited contributions from corporate treasury funds to candidates for state office. Twenty-one additional states put limits on corporate contributions – which are banned to federal candidates – but nonetheless allow them. Indeed, there is considerable variation across states in the regulation of campaign finance and electioneering. For television and radio ads, some states have imposed requirements that go further than the disclaimer mandates at the federal level. For example, Maine state law (as approved by voters in a 2015 citizen initiative) requires ads sponsored by outside groups to list the top three founders of the group directly in the disclaimer of the ad. (See Maine Revised Statues, Title 21-A, chapter 13, subchapter 1, Section 1014(2-B).) Similar provisions are in place in Alaska, California, Massachusetts, and Washington.

17. The full text of the proposed legislation is available at: **www.congress.gov/bill/115th-congress**/senate-bill/1989/text.
18. Notably, in 2017–2018, the bill had twenty-three cosponsors in the House, about half of whom were Republicans. In the 116th Congress, the bill was reintroduced in the House with thirty- three cosponsors, about half being Republicans.
19. In practice, we have found evidence of instability and instances where ads that were previously retrieved from keyword searches become unavailable. See especially the discussion on missing ads in the links to "known issues" available in the Social Science One API codebook (Fowler, Franz, King et al. 2019).
20. Up until June 2019, the Facebook aggregate reports lacked numeric identifier information, hindering efforts to connect the reported aggregated spend by page name and funding entity and the information retrieved from the library API.
21. Moreover, scholars argue that micro targeting is likely to be used less often in Europe compared to the United States (Zuiderveen Borgesius et al. 2018).
22. This report no longer seems to be accessible from the Facebook library website.

07

DEMOCRATIC CREATIVE DESTRUCTION?

THE IMPACT OF AN EVOLVING MEDIA ENVIRONMENT ON DEMOCRATIC SYSTEMS

INTRODUCTION: AN OVERVIEW

In an age marked by relentless technological advancements and shifting societal norms, the intersection of democracy and media has become an intriguing landscape for examination. The phrase "Democratic Creative Destruction" encapsulates the notion that within the realm of democratic governance, the traditional structures and processes are continually challenged and redefined by the dynamic forces of an ever-evolving media environment. This interplay between democracy and media not only reflects the changing dynamics of information dissemination but also raises profound questions about how these transformations influence the very foundations of democratic systems worldwide. This exploration delves into the multifaceted impact of a rapidly changing media landscape on democracy, shedding light on both its constructive potential and the challenges it poses to the ideals of an informed and engaged citizenry.

The move to a more digital, more mobile, and more platform-dominated media environment represents a change to the institutions and infrastructures of free expression and a form of "democratic creative destruction" that challenges incumbent institutions, creates new ones, and in many ways empower individual citizens, even as this change also leaves both individuals and institutions increasingly dependent on a few large US-based technology companies and subjects many historically disadvantaged groups to more abuse and harassment online. That is the argument we advance in this chapter, where we will aim to step away from assessing the democratic implications of the Internet on the basis of individual cases, countries, or outcomes to focus on how structural changes in the media are intertwined with changes in democratic politics.

We will set aside considerations of (important) individual phenomena like the Arab Spring, the indignados movement, and #MeToo, or (important) individual outcomes like the 2014 Indian general elections, the UK (Brexit) referendum on EU membership, or the 2016 US presidential elections, and instead identify a few key changes at the institutional level and the individual level that are part and parcel of the rise of digital media and discuss how this rise is in turn changing the institutions and infrastructures that enable free expression. Inspired by James Webster (2014) and his work on structuration, we examine structural change by considering the interplay between institutional change on the supply side and aggregate individual-level behaviour on the demand side.

We will do so through the lens of news, first the news media as an institution and second news as part of how individual citizens engage with public life. We focus on news as one of several key aspects of democratic politics, key to how we imagine it in its ideal forms and key to how we realize it imperfectly in practice. The structural changes we analyze are not dictated by technology but influenced by it and will play out in different ways in different contexts as technological momentum is shaped by cultural, economic, political, and social factors. Despite the enormity of the question "what does digital media mean for democracy?" and the impossibility of giving a single, clear, definite, universal answer to it, we believe it is useful to try to identify key, common aspects of global structural changes underway in democracies worldwide by synthesizing recent empirical research. We summarize these changes under the rubric of "democratic creative destruction" (and because of our focus on democracy, we are primarily concerned with developments in countries that are considered more or less free – currently accounting for somewhere in between a third and just over half of the world's population depending on one's definition of democracy and the index on which one relies).

We take the notion of creative destruction from the Austrian political economist Joseph Schumpeter, who used the term to capture ongoing structural changes in capitalism, to help us think about how structural changes in the media impact democracy. In his classic 1942 book *Capitalism, Socialism, and Democracy*, he argued that, in the long run, the history of social change is a history of ongoing evolution, but that the history of economic change specifically is a history of revolutions, of an ongoing process of creative destruction that "revolutionizes the economic structure from within, incessantly destroying the old one, incessantly creating a new one" (Schumpeter 1992, p. 83). Schumpeter suggested that, faced with this kind of dynamic change, any analysis that focuses on a given point in time (whether a high point or a low point) risks misunderstanding the structural changes underway, and that any analysis focused on any particular part (as important as it might be) risks missing the systemic implications. The moments and the parts are important, but we adopt Schumpeter's systemic view here. Our democracies are changing in response to many other, sometimes more important, factors than this kind of creative destruction, including those that political scientists and sociologists traditionally focus on, from changes in party systems (Mair 1997) and forms of governance (Rhodes 1997) to changes in trust in institutions (Norris 2011) and people's value systems (Ingelhart 1997). Yet because our democracies are intertwined with the news, and because the news is in turn intertwined with the market forces and technology that are central to creating, maintaining, and changing the institutions and infrastructures of free expression, Schumpeter's approach to thinking about structural transformations gives us a way of capturing a few key aspects of the big picture. We focus here on what it means for news, though by extension, as political scientists have long argued, information revolutions often involve fundamental change in how governments, political parties, interests groups, and social movements operate too, because most of the institutions that enable democracy are interdependent (see, e.g., Bimber 2003).

News is important here because of the different roles it plays in democracies. We should not romanticize how well actually existing journalism in actually existing democracies has in fact lived up to the various ideals we might have for journalism and for democracy. Yet with its many imperfections, at least in North America and Western Europe, empirical research suggests that independent, professionally produced news has helped inform the public, helped people make sense of the world through analysis, interpretation, and the portrayal of contending forces, and helped members of the public connect with one another to see themselves as part of a community and act in concert to influence public affairs (van Zoonen 1998; Curran et al. 2009; Couldry et al. 2010). Beyond these, perhaps the most visible democratic role of news, investigative journalism specifically can also produce a range of "positive externalities" that benefit the whole public – even those who do not actually engage with a particular story – by ensuring more efficient local government, reducing corruption, and increasing how responsive elected officials are to their constituents (Brunetti and Weder 2003; Besley and Prat 2006; Snyder and Strömberg 2008). Again, we do not want to romanticize journalism as we knew it. News is necessarily always imperfect, and for much of the twentieth century much of it was all too often by white men, about white men, for white men, uncomfortably close to political elites and oriented toward the affluent, often not trusted, and not always trustworthy. Yet while journalism arguably has been able to do less for democracy than many journalists and academics like to think (Gans 2003), and sometimes plays a more ambiguous role, news is integral to actually existing democracies, because it helps citizens navigate the (public) world beyond personal experience.

In the rest of the chapter, we identify key aspects of the move to digital, mobile, and platform-dominated media first for the institutions that underpin the professional production of news (Cook 1998), then at the individual level to see how it affects the "public connections" that news can enable (Couldry et al. 2010), before finally turning to a discussion of the democratic implications. We argue that the result of the democratic creative destruction we describe is an explosion in the amount of public communication overall (from organized, self-interested actors as well as billions of individual end users) combined with a drastic reduction in the number of professional journalists and the emergence of a media environment where everyone can speak (resulting in a far more intense competition for attention and used for many and often ambiguous purposes) and where news media still serve as gatekeepers to the news agenda but are increasingly supplemented by platform companies serving as secondary gatekeepers in terms of reaching a wide audience. This is a media environment that challenges many established institutions, including news media, gives technology companies more institutional and infrastructural roles (and power), and in many ways empowers individual media users, making democracy relatively more demotic and popular, even as many people are also exposed to more abuse and harassment and many frequently use digital media in ambiguous ways, including ways that challenge established norms and values associated with liberal democracy.

STRUCTURAL TRANSFORMATIONS IN THE NEWS MEDIA

The ongoing move to a more digital, more mobile, and more platform- dominated media environment has made news more abundant and more accessible but existentially threatens the business models that funded professional news production in the twentieth century, resulting in a marked decline in news industry revenues and in newsroom employment, thus challenging incumbent institutions, even as the large technology companies that dominate this environment are growing rapidly and are gradually being institutionalized as they are forced to accept (and sometimes actively embrace) a wider range of formal and informal obligations than just that to their own bottom line and mission statement.

The destructive side of creative destruction is clear to see in the decline of legacy news media, the creative side too, with the rise of platform companies like Google, Facebook, and Twitter, the multitude of ways in which many different actors make use of digital technologies broadly and platform products and services specifically, and in how news media, both legacy and digital-born, are evolving and adapting to a new media environment.

Instead of tracing the fortunes of individual news media organizations, whether legacy ones like the New York Times or digital-born ones like BuzzFeed, we can consider the news media of a given country as an institution, a set of organizations generally seen within a society as presiding over a particular social sphere, in this case the production of news (Cook 1998,p. 70). Such institutions are defined by a set of cross-organizational formal and informal norms, routines, and procedures, in the case of news media broadly shared news values, work flows, and a common orientation toward the events, ideas, preoccupations, strategies, and politics of powerful officials, as well as a sense of professional ethics among journalists and an orientation toward public service. Not all news media are exactly alike, but they share many features, and not all (national) news institutions are identical (Hallin and Mancini 2004). At least within high-income liberal democracies, however, they have much in common, including their integral role in politics – an institutional role, Timothy Cook (1998) has suggested, "without which .. government could not act and could not work" (pp. 2–3) and without which individual citizens would struggle to stay informed about and engage with complex political processes far removed from personal experience.

News is thus intertwined with politics but also with the marketplace. In high- income democracies, news is a public good overwhelmingly produced by professional journalists working for private sector news media operating for- profit. Historically, news production has been funded in a variety of ways, including subsidies from political actors and media proprietors interested in power to pursue their own ends and through various forms of non-profit models, backed by private philanthropists or politically mandated investment of public resources. Yet, in the second half of the twentieth century, news in North America and Western Europe was increasingly the province of journalists working for for-profit businesses based on selling content to audiences and selling audiences to advertisers (Hamilton 2004). Even in a country like the United Kingdom, home to the license-fee funded public service BBC, an estimated 79 percent of investment in news production comes from for-profit private sector media companies (primarily newspapers), and, in the United States, where public media enjoy less political support, print publishers still account for the majority of reporters employed and broadcasters for another quarter, with online media and "information services" at just 10 percent (Nielsen 2019).

In the business of news, we see clearly the destructive side of creative destruction, especially among newspapers. Newspapers are central to the news institution and the business of news, but print has been in structural decline in many countries for decades as more and more different forms of media compete for attention and advertising. In a country like the United States, per capita print circulation has been declining for more than half a century, the number of daily newspapers dropping (especially dramatically with the disappearance of evening newspapers as television grew), and newspapers' share of the overall advertising market shrinking in parallel (see Figure 7.1).

Surviving newspapers remained profitable, especially because many were near- monopolies for some forms of local advertising in the growing number of one- newspaper towns. Yet newspapers were clearly becoming a less important part of the media overall.

This long-term structural decline, accelerated in recent years by the rapid rise of digital media, has had dramatic implications for the business sustaining (and sometimes constraining) journalism. Newspapers provided the bulk of investment in news production in a media environment where individuals had low choice and news media high market power over advertisers (Hamilton 2004). Yet we are increasingly moving to an environment where individuals have high choice and news media have low market power over advertisers (Nielsen 2019). In this environment, people are voting with their attention, and they are not voting for news. Precise figures are hard to come by, but one can roughly estimate that about 20 percent of the time people spend with print media is spent with news, 12 percent of the time spent with television is spent with news, and at most 7 percent of the time spent with digital media is spent with news.1 (Consistent cross-platform measurements do not exist, and people often over report their news consumption in surveys, so the share may well be even lower. For digital media specifically, one behavioural tracking source estimates news accounts for just 3 percent of time spent; see Hindman 2018.)

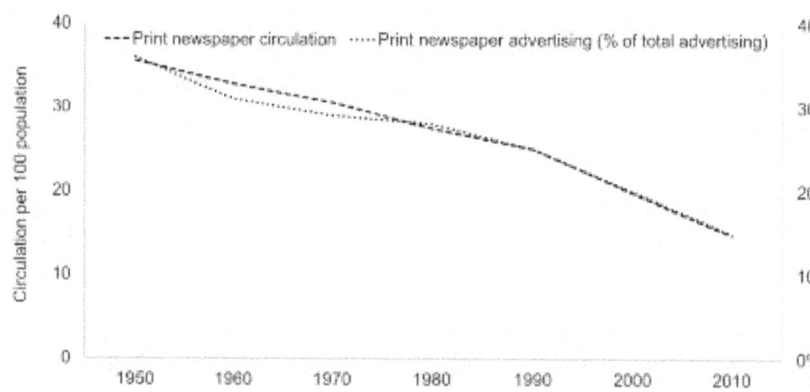

Fig: 7.1 US print newspaper circulation and advertising share Data. 2012 US Census and Historical Statistics of the United States: From Colonial times to 1970. Douglas Galbi (on advertising). Note, last data point on advertising is 2007. Additional information provided by Nielsen (2019).

As attention is going elsewhere, advertising is following, especially as people increasingly embrace platform products and services like search, social media, messaging applications, and the like that offer cheap, targeted advertising at scale. This means large technology companies like Google and Facebook have quickly come to dominate digital advertising, capturing a majority globally, leaving literally tens of thousands of other media organizations, including the entire news industry, competing for the rest (see Figure 7.2 – note that some of Google's and Facebook's revenues are shared with third parties, including publishers).

Thus, advertising revenues that in the twentieth century helped fund content creation for a mass public increasingly help fund the provision of platform products and services to individual users and are tied in with pervasive data collection, especially by the dominant technology companies (Turow and Couldry 2018).2

From the point of view of billions of end users worldwide, as well as for millions of advertisers and other third parties like app developers, gaming companies, and the like, the rise of platforms is an example of the creative side of creative destruction – in high-income democracies, digital media now account for half or more of all media use and will come to account for a similar share of advertising – even as this rise is an existential challenge to the traditional business of news. In this changing environment, advertising alone will be a much smaller and much less lucrative part of the business of news than it has been in print and television. Figures from the United States in 2011 give a sense of how different the rates for digital advertising are from offline advertising, in terms of CPMs ("cost per mille," the advertising cost per 1,000 views). That year, industry observers estimated a $60 average CPMs for print newspapers, $23 for primetime network television, between $3.50 and $2.50 for generic online advertising, $0.75 for mobile display advertising, and just$0.56 per 1,000 impressions on social networking sites (Nielsen 2019). The industry saying that analog dollars (100 cents) turn into digital dimes (10 cents) and mobile pennies (one cent) captures the stark differences in advertising rates between different media. As audiences and advertisers increasingly embrace digital media, the consequences are clear. In the United States alone, from 2008 to 2017, newspapers lost more than $20 billion in print advertising, close to half of total industry revenues, and cut newsroom employment by 45 percent. This decline of a net 32,000 professional journalists was far from offset by the growth in digital-born news media expanding their newsrooms from 7,000 to 13,000 in the same period (newsroom employment in radio and television was broadly stable) (Grieco 2020). These business changes have little to do with politics directly but could have potentially profound political implications, as news organizations cut their newsrooms, in many cases specifically getting rid of specialist beat reporters and closing local and international bureaus in favor of focusing on general, national news.

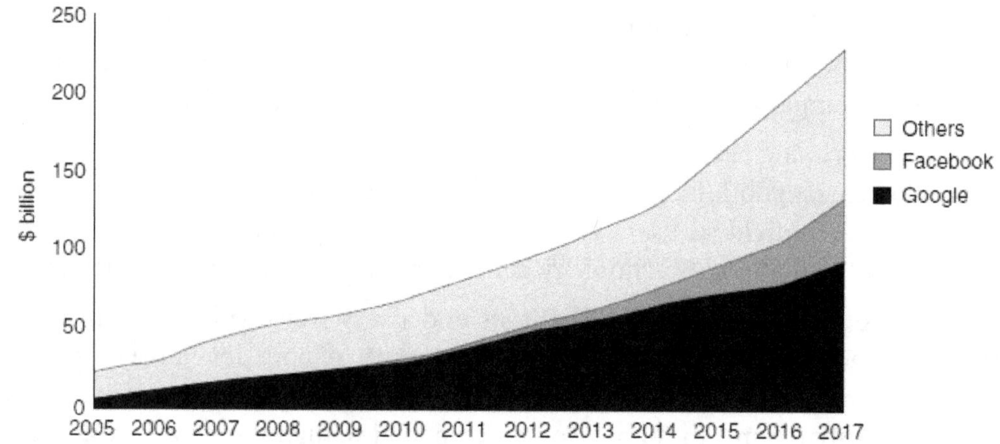

Fig 7.2 Developments in digital advertising

Note. *Both Google and Facebook share some of their advertising with partners through various revenue sharing arrangements. Data.* Nielsen (2019).

These institutional changes are not only about a structural shift of attention and advertising away from news media and to content and practices hosted, enabled, and moderated by large technology companies (with consequent cuts in newsroom employment). They also involve changes to the operations of news media themselves, as well as in other actors' and organizations' ability to communicate with a wide audience. The rise of platforms is thus the most obvious creative side of this process of creative destruction, but not the only one. New institutions are emerging, but old institutions – including the news media but also governments, political parties, interest groups, social movements, and many others – are adapting to change and renewing themselves (Chadwick 2017).

In the news media, the rise of digital media means that newsrooms frequently have to produce more news across more channels, at a faster pace than before, as a shrinking number of journalists publish to a website, multiple social media channels, and often a legacy media platform too (whether print or broadcast) (Bell et al 2017). Increasingly, inherited news values are supplemented with new editorial considerations focused on audience analytics, social media optimization, and search engine optimization as news media seek to build digital reach and compete for attention online. Especially new digital-born news media like BuzzFeed, HuffPost, and Vice have often aggressively embraced platforms and "worked towards the algorithms" to quickly build wide audiences via search engines and social media (Caplan and boyd 2018).

News media are thus actively embracing many of the products and services offered by some of their main competitors for attention and advertising, increasingly empowered by but also dependent on platform companies like Google and Facebook (Nielsen and Ganter 2017) that provide them with everything from audience research over analytics to ad tech solutions (Libert et al. 2018) – even as they also challenge the business of news and the relation news media have historically had with their audience. The often sudden and sometimes dramatic impact of changes implemented unilaterally by platform companies – a tweak to an algorithm, the discontinuation of a product or service – has revealed how news, like other forms of cultural production, is increasingly contingent on the infrastructure offered by platforms (Nieborg and Poell 2018) and involve them in, for example, data-collection practices that some critics see as fundamentally illiberal in their disregard for traditional conception of privacy (Glasius and Michaelsen 2018).

In parallel, other organizations too have embraced digital media to communicate with the public. The PR cliché that "every organization is a media organization" is increasingly becoming a reality (Davis 2013). Whereas the news institution in the twentieth century was the single most important gatekeeper due to mass media's control over the channels of communication, the rise of digital media (enabling virtually everybody with internet access to publish) combined with the rise of new secondary gatekeepers in the form of search engines, social media, and other platforms that drive discovery and structure attention online represents a new situation (Nielsen 2016a; Kreiss and McGregor 2019).

INDIVIDUALS RANGING FROM ACTIVISTS TO ADVOCATES

Organizations, and think tanks, over political candidates, campaigns, and parties, to a multitude of private companies aggressively try to engage people in public affairs online. Even as the number of professional journalists employed by news organizations is in clear structural decline, the number of PR professionals employed by government agencies, interest groups, and corporations is on the rise, and far outstrips reporters (Davis 2013). Even if many of these forms of strategic communication often struggle to capture attention and engage people in effective and meaningful ways, some individual campaigns – from Barack Obama to Donald Trump, from the Tea Party to #MeToo, and, more darkly, in the form of extremist groups both foreign and domestic, as well as disinformation and information operations by states trying to undermine the democratic process and trust in institutions in other countries – have clearly managed to circumvent traditional gatekeepers and work with platform products and services to reach a wide public and in turn influence mainstream political debate (Chadwick 2017).

Finally, of course, billions of individual users are embracing digital media, not only to get news but also to express themselves, connect, and build communities. In the next section, we examine their aggregate individual-level choices, but it is important to recognize that these choices also have an informal, institutional dimension that helps structure our media environment and thus impact our politics. The rapid, global embrace of digital media was initially cast in very positive terms by some who saw it as a dawn of a more "participatory culture" (Jenkins 2006) superseding older forms of more passive mass media consumption, with trolling and the like as unfortunate and ultimately marginal aberrations. More extensive empirical research has challenged this benign interpretation and argued that, in deeply diverse and disputatious, irreducible plural societies, open and permissive systems are open to abuse, and many of the ways in which we use them are deeply ambivalent. Much of what some users may think of as forms of harmless "cultural play" online often involves deploying highly corrosive forms of speech, such as racist memes, sexist tropes, and the like that antagonize, silence, and marginalize people, especially historically disadvantaged communities including women and ethnic, religious, and sexual minorities (Phillips and Milner 2017). If the move to digital media and the increasing centrality of a few large technology companies to much of what we do with media point toward what José van Dijck (2013) has called "plat formed sociality," it is important to recognize that these formal structures come accompanied with informal structures we might think of as a "culture of connectivity" and that this culture is deeply ambivalent in enabling communication, engagement, and community-building for a wide variety of different ends and with a wide variety of different valences, refracting the values and activities of the societies they are used in.

Major platform companies like Facebook and Google thus clearly already operate a number of products and services with infrastructural properties (they are shared, widely accessible systems that are used by a wide range of actors for many different purposes) (Plantin et al. 2016), so far in ways primarily governed by inherited legal and regulatory frameworks and individual companies' own sense of mission and terms of service (Gillespie 2018). Yet we are beginning to see the institutionalization of platform organizations through an increasingly heated public debate over what formal rules and informal norms should govern their operations as well as the creation of joint trade groups and various multi-stakeholder forums (DeNardis 2014). In line with Schumpeter, the economic change has in many ways already been revolutionary, even as many of the social changes are more evolutionary.

INDIVIDUAL-LEVEL CHANGES IN HOW WE ENGAGE WITH NEWS

At the individual level, the ongoing move to a more digital, more mobile, more platform-dominated media environment involves a rapid move from direct access to news sources to a heavy reliance on distributed discovery via platform products and services like search engines and social media that provide us with new, supplementary ways of accessing, consuming, and engaging with news that broadly point to more diverse and sometimes participatory news use while also bringing with it widespread online harassment, exposure to disinformation, and the potential for more political polarization and social inequality in news use.

The creative side of this development is clear to see, with digital media enabling new ways of accessing, consuming, and engaging with news, including opportunities for individuals to express themselves, connect with others, and remix cultural products for a potentially large audience, leaving individuals simultaneously empowered by and dependent on the platform companies that provide many of the products and services we all increasingly rely on (van Dijck 2013).

Even if many fears are expressed, the precise nature of the destructive side of creative destruction is perhaps less easy to systematically substantiate, at least at scale. The move to digital media is accompanied by the relative decline of the kind of mass media experience associated in particular with mid- twentieth-century broadcasting, a shared, simultaneous experience of millions watching the same program – a single imagined community around a single news agenda (you can still watch the TV news, but it will never again mean what it once did), just as the limited share of attention going to news online raises the prospect of a marginalization of public affairs in favour of private concerns and entertainment. Yet many of the most frequently articulated fears concerning the democratic implications of our changing media environment are not supported by empirical research. As we will show in this section, and as Pablo Barberá documents in his contribution to this volume (Chapter 3), fears over, for example, audience fragmentation and filter bubbles remain unsubstantiated and are frequently complicated or flat- out contradicted by empirical evidence. Instead, destructive impacts may come in the form of sustained online harassment especially of vulnerable communities (which in turn may silence them and reduce their opportunities to participate in public life) and exposure to various forms of online disinformation, as well as the potential for greater political polarization and social inequality in news use.

The shift toward online news consumption is clear and visible in every high-income country. As the number of people who use offline media for news falls, and online news consumption grows, the centrality of each medium also changes, albeit gradually. Printed news consumption has declined to such a point that in 2018, across thirty-seven markets globally we surveyed, only around 10 percent of internet users regarded it as their main source of news (Newman et al. 2018). Television is still the most widely used news source in many countries, but its importance is waning. In the same survey, around 40 percent say television is their main source of news, and the audiences for most television news bulletins are both shrinking and aging. As especially print and increasingly television decline, online news use is growing. In 2018, around 45 percent say that it is their main source of news. In contrast to the television news audience, the online news audience skews younger (see Figure 7.3). Two-thirds (67 percent) of respondents between eighteen and twenty-four now say online is their main source of news, compared to just a quarter (24 percent) who name television. Social media alone – just one of the ways of getting news online – is more important for news for the youngest age group than television. With generational replacement, the shift toward the kind of digital-, mobile-, and platforms-first environment that most people below the age of thirty-five already live in (especially in high-income, highly connected societies) will only continue.

Of course, many of the most popular online news sources in most countries are legacy news brands that have their roots in broadcasting or print publishing – so the destruction only extends so far. Even as older channels of communication become less important, organizations built around them may still renew themselves and find a digital future (Chadwick 2017). The creative side, for individual users, is apparent. The shift toward digital news use not only has led to a massive increase in the number of available news sources both old and new (and thus massive increase in different types of coverage, perspectives, and styles that people have access to) but, perhaps more importantly, has enabled a change from an almost complete reliance on direct access to an increased reliance on distributed discovery via search engines, social media, and news aggregators. In practice, people arrive at news in many different ways, but our survey research shows that just one-third of people said that their main way of arriving at news was by going directly to the websites and apps of news publishers like the BBC or the New York Times (Newman et al. 2018). There maining two-thirds say that their main way of arriving at news was via search (24 percent), social media (23 percent), or email, mobile alerts, or news aggregators (6 percent each) (see Figure 7.4).

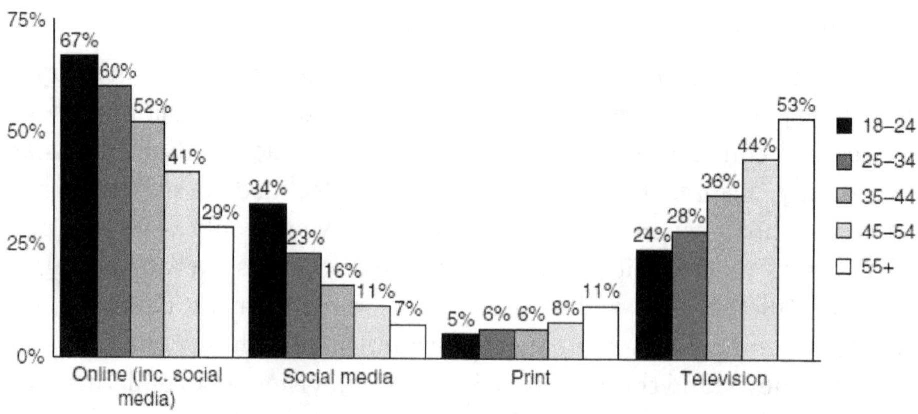

Fig. 7.3 Main source of news, by age group

Note. *Respondents across thirty-seven markets were asked: "You say you've used these sources of news in the last week, which would you say is your MAIN source of news?" Base: 72,192.*

Data. Newman et al. (2018). See www.digitalnewsreport.org for more information.

This is an epochal shift on how news is distributed and curated. Direct discovery has been a defining feature of the mass media environment in the twentieth century, but the twenty-first-century digital media environment is increasingly defined by algorithmically based forms of personalization, as people rely on products and services like search engines and social media that do not create content but help users discover content. Reliance on distributed discovery is even higher among the under thirty-fives, but there is considerable national variation. For example, in the Nordics and other countries characterized by democratic corporatist media systems (Hallin and Mancini2004), where loyalty to news brands is stronger and trust in the news media is higher, the importance of direct access has remained high. In much of Southern

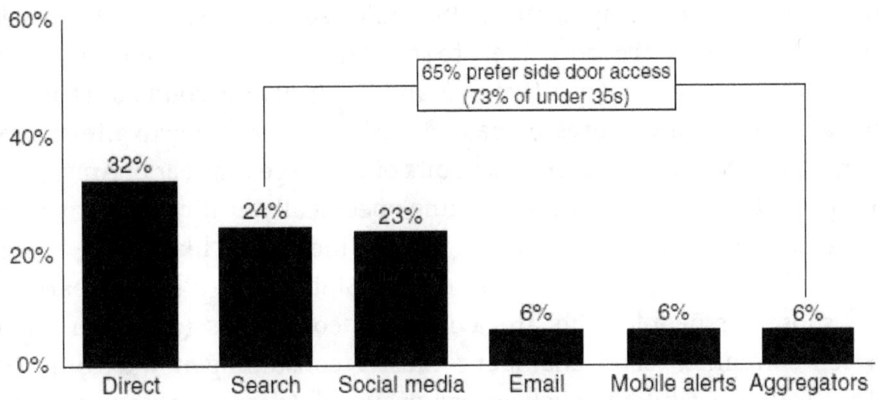

Fig. 7.4 Main way of accessing news online

Note. *Respondents across thirty-seven markets were asked: "Which of these was the MAIN way in which you came across news in the last week?" Base: 69,246.*

Data. *Newman et al. (2018). See www.digitalnewsreport.org for more information.*

Europe and other polarized pluralist countries, however, where the opposite is generally true, distributed discovery is clearly more widely used.

The difference between direct discovery and distributed discovery is key to many of the fears concerning the democratic implications of digital media, especially the fear that algorithmic personalization through search engines, social media, and the like will lead to audience fragmentation and the creation of filter bubbles. It is worth considering briefly how direct versus distributed forms of discovery can result in patterns of news use that are potentially democratically problematic.

Take direct discovery first, where people go directly to a preferred source of news. This form of discovery gives the individual user full, active control. Because it is not possible to consume all of the news that is available online (even from just a small pool of the most popular sources), those who primarily go to news sources directly have to decide where to get their news online. If they want to directly consume news from a particular source, they have to know it exists and then make a conscious decision to either type the web address into their browser or download the app onto their smart phone. Such choices are often characterized by what communications researchers and psychologists call "selective exposure," where people tend to favour sources that reflect their pre-existing beliefs and interests while avoiding sources that might contradict them. (We use terms like "choice" and "selective" in a broad sense here; much media use is habitual and not necessarily based on deliberate, discrete decisions.) These dynamics will vary from context to context and country to country, depending on people's dispositions. In terms of beliefs, for example, many US media users engage in partisan selective exposure, where people are more likely to select news sources that produce content aligned with their political views (Iyengar and Hahn 2009; Stroud 2011). In parallel, marked variation in how interested people are in news (relative to alternatives like entertainment) also shapes the media habits of the large number of Americans who are not very interested in politics. Looking specifically at direct discovery across offline media like print and broadcast and online media like going to websites and apps, this combination leaves the United States with a hyper- partisan and engaged subset of people who are avid news consumers (and some of whom live in self-contained "echo chambers" mostly consuming news from attitude-consistent sources) while a much larger group of Americans pay only sporadic attention to political news (Prior 2007). In contrast, empirical research from parts of Europe suggests that, in other contexts, levels of interests matter more than partisanship (Skovsgaard, Shehata, and Strömbäck 2016; Castro-Herrero, Nir, and Skovsgaard 2018).

The deeper issue here is that levels of interest in the news are likely to be reflected in other socioeconomic inequalities between different groups (Shehata and Amnå 2017; Kalogeropoulos and Nielsen 2018), with important knock-on consequences for their news consumption.

Distributed discovery through search engines, social media, and other platform products and services that rely at least in part on various forms of algorithmically curated personalized recommendation could potentially lead to similar outcomes, increased partisan polarization, and growing inequality between news lovers and a less interested majority as automated systems feed us more of what we click on and less of everything else. In these environments, our individual choices are increasingly structured for us through various forms of algorithmic filtering and recommendation. This development has often been associated with the idea of "filter bubbles" (Pariser 2011), whether in the form of audience fragmentation or narrowed news diets. So far, however, empirical research has not substantiated these concerns and has, in fact, often found that digital news and media use work very differently from how it is often assumed, or asserted, to work (again, see Barberá, Chapter 3, this volume).

First, despite the explosive growth in the number of sources available and the gradual erosion of many traditional mass audiences, empirical research suggests that the audiences of the most popular news outlets tend to overlap with one another (Webster and Ksiazek 2012; Fletcher and Nielsen 2017). Furthermore, when comparing offline environments (completely reliant on direct discovery and thus selective exposure) with online environments (where distributed discovery is far more important), online news audiences are in fact frequently less fragmented and more overlapping than their offline counterparts (Fletcher and Nielsen 2017), perhaps in part because search engines and social media often lead people to broadly used, widely shared major news brands.

Second, in contrast to the concern that platform products and services would be associated with a narrowing of news diets where people are only fed more of the same, in fact most empirical research finds use of social media and search engines associated with more diverse news use (Flaxman, Goel, and Rao 2016; Dubois and Blank 2018; Fletcher and Nielsen 2018a).

Our own research has suggested two central causal mechanisms that supplement the tendency for forms of selective exposure that dominate direct discovery (often in ways that may point to polarization and inequality, as well as fragmentation and echo chambers), namely incidental exposure and automated serendipity. Incidental exposure refers to situations where people use social media or video sharing services for reasons that have nothing to do with news (staying in touch with friends, sharing things, entertainment) and in the process are incidentally exposed to sources of news they would not have come across otherwise. We have documented how incidental exposure leads to significantly more diverse news diets across different platforms like Facebook, Twitter, and YouTube (Fletcher and Nielsen 2018a). Automated serendipity refers to how people who use search engines to access news in the process are led to more and different sources of news than those they access by going directly, and we have demonstrated empirically how people who use search engines for news both are likely to consume news from a left-leaning and right-leaning news source and have more politically balanced news repertoires than people who do not use search engines for news (Fletcher and Nielsen 2018b).

This does not mean that echo chambers and filter bubbles do not exist in some form, or that people who are heavily reliant on distributed discovery have perfectly diverse and healthy news diets.3 Yet we need to keep in mind that direct access and distributed discovery both create personalization, either because people personalize their own news consumption or because an algorithm does it for them (Zuiderveen Borgesius et al. 2016). It appears that the self-selected personalization that results from selective exposure is more powerful than the preselected exposure that results from algorithmic selection, meaning that people who rely on distributed discovery are left with larger and more diverse news diets.

Whether people trust these news sources is a separate matter. In parallel to the growth of distributed discovery, we have also seen steady year-on-year declines in trust in the news media. Despite being stable in most countries from 1980 to 2010 according to the World Values Survey (Hanitzsch, van Dalen, and Steindl 2018), more recent data from 2015 onward suggest that trust in the news media is falling in both traditionally low-trust countries like France (down 14 percentage points since 2015) and traditionally high-trust countries like Germany (down 13 percentage points since 2015) (Newman et al. 2019). In most countries, trust in news from search engines and social media is significantly lower than trust in the news media as a whole (Newman et al. 2019), but at the moment it is far from clear that the move to distributed discovery is to blame for the overall declines. Indeed, when it comes to evaluating different types of news selection, people have what we call "generalized skepticism," where those skeptical of primary gatekeepers (publishers) are often skeptical of secondary gatekeepers (platforms) too – and usually for similar reasons. People often do not understand how editorial processes, let alone algorithmic news selection, work, but that does not mean they uncritically accept what they come across (Fletcher and Nielsen 2019).

In parallel with the move from direct to distributed discovery, we have seen the move to a digital media environment that affords people with more opportunities for more participatory forms of news and media use, in the process also exposing many to widespread online harassment and potentially various forms of disinformation disseminated online and especially via platforms. Digital media offers everyone with internet access a range of both "web 1.0" and "web 2.0" ways of engaging in more participatory forms of news and media use, ranging from commenting on news sites and sharing via email to commenting and/or sharing via social media sites. While all internet users have access to this participatory potential, it is important to recognize that the majority does not in practice use it, though a large minority does, relying especially on social media (Newman et al. 2018). Looking more closely at who comments and shares news online, across web 1.0 and social media, in most countries, the most active tend to be those who have most enthusiastically embraced a wide range of different social media platforms and often use them for many other purposes than news, specifically political partisans and people with high levels of interest in news (Kalogeropoulos et al. 2017). Unlike other forms of political participation, which tend to skew toward older men (Verba et al. 1995), all these forms of participation are as widespread among the young and among women (Valeriani and Vaccari 2016; Kalogeropoulos et al. 2017).

Not all forms of participation, of course, are equally benign or pro-social. The Internet, and the use we make of it, is profoundly ambiguous. Various forms of online harassment and trolling once thought to be relatively marginal and sub-cultural phenomena are now mainstream and widely experienced, enabled by digital technologies but fed by culturally sanctioned impulses and often amplified by political actors as well as the corporate interest of some publishers and platform companies (Phillips 2015). The scale and scope of these issues will differ from country to country and are experienced very differently by different groups (especially along lines of gender, race, and religion), but survey research from the United States can serve to illustrate how widespread they are (Duggan 2017). In 2017, 41 percent of Americans said they had personally been subjected to online harassment, and 66 percent has witnessed such behaviours directed at others. (These numbers are higher than the percentage of people who use digital media to actively comment on or share news online.) Almost one in five (18 percent) reported having been subjected to particularly severe forms of online harassment, for example, physical threats, harassment over a sustained period, sexual harassment, or stalking. Different groups are subject to different kinds of harassment – while only 3 percent of white Americans report having been subject to racial harassment online, one-in-four black Americans have. Similarly, while only 5 percent of men say they have been harassed online because of their gender, 11 percent of women have. Strikingly, the ambivalence about what exactly constitutes harassment is not exclusively on the side of the perpetrators but also clear among the victims. Twenty-eight percent of those whose most recent encounter with online harassment involved severe types of abusive behavior – such as stalking, sexual harassment, sustained harassment, or physical threats – answered in the 2017 survey that they do not think of their own experience as constituting “online harassment.” Yet, however defined, such widespread, sustained, and unequally distributed intimidation will lead some to take a less active part in online public life than they would otherwise want to, a dynamic only further compounded in political contexts where people may feel reluctant to discuss news openly or share their political views for fear of social or other repercussions (Newman et al. 2018) or where some political leaders amplify and encourage various forms of harassment (see Siegel, Chapter 4, this volume.).

Other forms of problematic online participation may take the form of good-faith, bottom-up dissemination of false or potentially harmful information online by ordinary users or, more nefariously, foreign or domestic extremism and organized for-profit or political disinformation campaigns. The same digital media that have dramatically lowered the barriers to entry and allowed everyone to publish online, the same platform products and services that demonstrably lead people to more diverse news and enable more participatory forms of news and media use also serve to disseminate various forms of misinformation and disinformation (Wardleand Derakhshan 2017). The risks are great, and we are only beginning to see significant amounts of empirical research in this area (see Guess and Lyons, Chapter 2, this volume). On the one hand, there are clearly real issues around bottom-up disinformation shared among users, for-profit disinformation from various unscrupulous low-quality publishers, and, perhaps most worryingly, various organized disinformation campaigns by both domestic and foreign political actors; it is also worth noting that the best available evidence from the United States currently suggests that overall exposure to much of this content is low, fleeting, and largely confined to those who already hold partisan views (Guess, Nyhan, and Reifler 2018;Nelson and Taneja 2018). Digital media has undoubtedly provided a structure for large-scale misinformation and disinformation to exist, and very real and very worrying attempts to abuse these structures are clearly afoot, but this does not mean that there will inevitably be dramatic democratic consequences in terms of individuals' attitudes and behaviours.

WHAT ARE THE MAIN CONSEQUENCES OF THIS PHENOMENON KNOWN AS "DEMOCRATIC CREATIVE DESTRUCTION?"

It is clear that democracy has historically evolved in part through creative destruction in the media environment. Think, for example, of broadcasting – starting with radio, then terrestrial television, then post-broadcast television. Similarly, democracy has evolved through other dramatic societal changes, from institutional changes in party systems (Mair 1997) and forms of governance (Rhodes 1997) to changes in individual-level aggregate levels of trust in institutions (Norris 2011) and in people's value systems (Ingelhart 1997). So far, we have described more recent creative destruction in the media at both the institutional and the individual level, but what is the impact of this process of creative destruction on democracy?

This of course depends on what one means by democracy. Historically, communications researchers have offered a range of different theoretical conceptions based on normative political philosophy, including ideal models of procedural democracy, competitive democracy, participatory democracy, and deliberative democracy (see, e.g., Strömbäck 2005). Increasingly, those interested in discussing the democratic implications of digital media are drawing on similar theoretical models, asking what we would want algorithmic curation to look like from different idealistic starting points, whether participatory or deliberative (Helberger 2019). These are important discussions but also often rather abstract and a bit removed from the hustle and bustle of actually existing and highly imperfect democratic politics, so we will instead follow Joseph Schumpeter a step further and focus on the implications in terms of a fairly minimal conception of democracy as liberal, representative, and based on relatively diverse and inclusive elite competition that offers a basic structure for making and implementing political decisions but no guarantee that these decisions will be "good" ones that ultimately ensure peace, prosperity, and personal fulfillment (Nielsen 2016b). If we start with this more minimalist view of democracy, and consider the changes we have summarized, the systemic implications for democracy in our view are likely to (1) be often indirect and institutional through an (incessant) revolution of the institutions that enable popular government (news media but also, by extension, interdependent other institutions like political parties, etc.), (2) be limited in terms of short-term impact on people's attitudes and behaviours, and (c) leave most individuals and many institutions simultaneously increasingly empowered by and increasingly dependent on a small number of large, for-profit, US-based platform companies like Facebook and Google.

At the institutional level, many of the institutions that animated twentieth-century democracy, including political parties, member-based interest groups, as well as the news media itself, are seriously challenged by the rise of digital media and platform companies. Some adapt and others implode, even as new actors that have for some time enjoyed power with limited responsibility are increasingly (and imperfectly) being institutionalized and bound by both informal norms and formal rules.4 As individuals, we are empowered by digital media even as we are also becoming dependent on them, exposed to more diverse news, offered new potential for participation, but also exposed to online harassment and disinformation, as the same platforms that enable us to find or share baby photos, cat videos, and dad jokes are integral to everything from #MeToo to populist campaigns by domestic politicians and attempts by foreign states to interfere with our elections. Advertising spending that used to support the private (for-profit) provision of news as a public good now increasingly support the private (for-profit) provision of platform products and services we use to access information and connect with one another.

This diagnosis of democratic creative destruction moves us away from more utopian early visions about the impact of online digital media on democracy but also departs from the newer, more dystopian visions that see the impact of online digital technologies on democracy as profoundly negative. We might call this position "complex realism," in recognition that the impact on democracy is neither fantastically benign nor completely disastrous – but profound, complicated, varied, and contextual. Much depends on the transition of old institutions and the institutionalization of new actors; and the political and social consequences are fundamentally political and social questions at least as much as they are about business and technology. Thus, for us as people, the move a more digital, more mobile, and more platform-dominated media environment may point to a more popular democracy, democracy with more focus on the demotic demos- part of demos-kratos, even as some of the institutions that are central to the -kratos are challenged and new institutions developing. For publishers, and many other twentieth-century legacy institutions integral to our democracies, there is still an important but more precarious role. For platforms, commercial success and rapid growth in use come with great complexity, enormous responsibility, and increasingly intense political and public scrutiny. For public authorities, there are questions about how they can ensure the protection of fundamental rights (free expression, privacy, etc.), the existence of an enabling environment for citizens and for news, while protecting the integrity of public debate and political processes in a changing media environment increasingly influenced by a few very large US-based technology companies.

Based on current trends, we can imagine three consequences specifically for the news media's role in democracy that could result from the huge changes to how it is financed: (1) restoration, where the news media finds a way to fund itself that allows it to play the same democratic role, even as new challenges arise (such as the concern that the move to pay models may exacerbate information inequalities); (2) renewal, where the news media finds a way to fund itself to play a different democratic role, either because it no longer has the resources to play the previous role or because the wider context has changed to such a degree that a new role is required; or (3) retreat, where the news media is able to fund itself but cannot play any meaningful democratic role at the level of mass politics (e.g., beyond the role played by high culture). Some of these paths would clearly be better for democracy than others. Beyond this it is vital that we avoid a fourth scenario we might call (4) relegation, where the vestiges of media power are co-opted and relegated to serve various political or commercial ends that have little to do with news (Schiffrin 2017) – a form of instrumentalization common in history and seen all over the world today too where media are weak. This will probably be bad for democracy and bad for almost everyone else. We as individuals would have plenty of choice, and many platform products and services, but what we would have to choose from would be captured media focused on manipulating us for ulterior ends, not independent news media serving the public, however imperfectly.

How we use digital media is up to us individually and collectively (even if we do not use them under conditions of our own choosing). In deeply divided, unequal, and disputatious societies there are no guarantees we will use them in ways that various elites or parts of the establishment will consider democratic or that we will all find substantially benign or to our liking – but it will almost certainly be more demotic, popular, often diverse, and sometimes majoritarian (in addition to being incredibly profitable for the most successful platform companies). This interplay is a classic tension between, on the one hand, liberal values, norms, and established institutions that many see as key to democracy and, on the other hand, popular sentiments and forms of representation that sometimes challenge these values, norms, and institutions. The challenge to the norms, values, and institutions of the -kratos is real and serious, especially so in countries where many of these seem fragile, but the opportunities for many people, around the popular, demotic, demos- are real too, and unease with specific political outcomes, potentially disastrous as they may be in other ways, should not lead people to jump to conclusions about whether current changes in our media environment are fundamentally antidemocratic. We may be moving toward a version of democracy where traditional elites, the media, and others parts of the establishment are relatively disempowered and ordinary people are empowered (as are a few for-profit platforms that urgently need to be institutionalized). Those experiencing a sense of relative disempowerment may be surprised and frustrated when the democratic process does not produce the outcomes they want. Whatever each of us individually think about these outcomes substantially, even if they may be malign, that does not make them undemocratic. Liberal representative democracy, minimally conceived, makes no guarantees about outcomes. We may have to accept that politics and the media can be both more democratic (at least in the sense of being more demotic and more popular) and bad for many people, particularly parts of established elites as well as for various vulnerable groups exposed to newly empowered majority groups.

Schumpeter thought the process of (economic) creative destruction would lead to the ultimate collapse of capitalism. We are less pessimistic about democratic creative destruction and more hopeful we will be able to renew and develop institutions in the future that hold powerful platforms to account (as news media have been, imperfectly, in the past) and also enable an empowered public of individual citizens to take a meaningful part in self- government in the future. In democracies, elites and establishments come and go, and that is part of the point. The question is whether people play a substantive role in that process. We believe they have, can, and will.

REFERENCES

Bell, E. J., Taylor, O., Brown, P. D., Hauka, C., & Rashidian, N. (2017). The Platform Press: How Silicon Valley Reengineered Journalism. Tow Center for Digital Journalism, Columbia University report. https://academiccommons.columbia.edu/catalog/ac:15dv41ns27

Besley, T., & Prat, A. (2006). Handcuffs for the grabbing hand? Media capture and government accountability. The American Economic Review, 96(3), 720–736.

Bimber, B. A. (2003). Information and American Democracy: Technology in the Evolution of Political Power. Cambridge: Cambridge University Press.

Brunetti, A., & Weder, B. (2003). A free press is bad news for corruption. Journal of Public Economics, 87(7–8), 1801–1824. https://doi.org/16/S0047-2727(01)00186-4

Caplan, R., &boyd, d. (2018). Isomorphism through algorithms: Institutional dependencies in the case of Facebook. Big Data & Society, 5(1). https://doi.org/10.1177/2053951718757253

Castro-Herrero, L., Nir, L., & Skovsgaard, M. (2018). Bridging gaps in cross-cutting media exposure: The role of public service broadcasting. *Political Communication*, *35*(4), 542–565.

Chadwick, A. (2017). *The Hybrid Media System: Politics and Power* (2nd ed.). New York: Oxford University Press.

Cook, T. E. (1998). *Governing with the News: The News Media As a Political Institution.* Chicago: University of Chicago Press.

Couldry, N., Livingstone, S. M., & Markham, T. (2010). *Media Consumption and Public Engagement: Beyond the Presumption of Attention* (rev. ed.). Basingstoke: Palgrave Macmillan.

Curran, J., Iyengar, S., Lund, A. B., & Salovaara-Moring, I. (2009). Media system, public knowledge and democracy. European Journal of Communication, 24(1), 5–26. https://doi.org/10.1177/0267323108098943

Davis, A. (2013). Promotional Cultures: The Rise and Spread of Advertising, Public Relations, Marketing and Branding. Cambridge: Polity Press.

DeNardis, L. (2014). *The Global War for Internet Governance.* New Haven, CT: Yale University Press.

Dubois, E., & Blank, G. (2018). The echo chamber is overstated: The moderating effect of political interest and diverse media. *Information, Communication & Society*, *21* (5), 729–745.

Duggan, M. (2017). Online harassment 2017. Pew Research Center, July 10. www.pewinternet.org/2017/07/11/online-harassment-2017/

Flaxman, S., Goel, S., & Rao, J. M. (2016). Filter bubbles, echo chambers, and online news consumption. Public Opinion Quarterly, 80 (Special Issue), 298–320.

Fletcher, R., & Nielsen, R. K. (2017). Are news audiences increasingly fragmented? A cross-national comparative analysis of cross-platform news audience fragmentation and duplication. Journal of Communication, 67(4), 476–498.

Fletcher, R., & Nielsen, R. K. (2018a). Are people incidentally exposed to news on social media? A comparative analysis. New Media & Society, 20(7), 2450–2468.

Fletcher, R., & Nielsen, R. K. (2018b). Automated Serendipity: The Effect of Using Search Engines on the Diversity and Balance of News Repertoires. Digital Journalism, 8(6), 976–989.

Fletcher, R., & Nielsen, R. K. (2019). Generalised scepticism: How people navigate news on social media. Information, Communication & Society, 22(12), 1751–1769. https://doi.org/10.1080/1369118X.2018.1450887

Gans, H. J. (2003). Democracy and the News. Oxford: Oxford University Press. Gillespie, T. (2018). Custodians of the Internet: Platforms, Content Moderation, and the Hidden Decisions That Shape Social Media. New Haven, CT: Yale University Press.

Glasius, M., & Michaelsen, M. (2018). Authoritarian practices in the digital age| Illiberal and authoritarian practices in the digital sphere. International Journal of Communication, 12, 3795–3813. http://ijoc.org/index.php/ijoc/article/view/8899

Grieco, E. (2020). U.S. newspapers have shed half of their newsroom employees since2008. Pew Research Center, April 20. www.pewresearch.org/fact-tank/2018/07/ 30/newsroom-employment-dropped-nearly-a-quarter-in-less-than-10-years-with- greatest-decline-at-newspapers/

Guess, A., Nyhan, B., & Reifler, J. (2018). Selective exposure to misinformation: Evidence from the consumption of fake news during the 2016 US presidential campaign. www.dartmouth.edu/~nyhan/fake-news-2016.pdf

Hallin, D. C., & Mancini, P. (2004). Comparing Media Systems: Three Models of Media and Politics. Cambridge: Cambridge University Press.

Hamilton, J. (2004). All the News That's Fit to Sell: How the Market Transforms Information into News. Princeton: Princeton University Press.

Hanitzsch, T., van Dalen, A., & Steindl, N. (2018). Caught in the nexus: A comparative and longitudinal analysis of public trust in the press. The International Journal of Press/Politics, 23(1), 3–23. https://doi.org/10.1177/1940161217740695

Helberger, N. (2019). On the democratic role of news recommenders. Digital Journalism, 7(8), 993–1012. https://doi.org/10.1080/21670811.2019.1623700 Hindman, M. (2018). The Internet Trap: How the Digital Economy Builds Monopolies and Undermines Democracy. Princeton: Princeton University Press.

Inglehart, R. (1997). Modernization and Post-modernization: Cultural, Economic, and Political Change in 43 Societies. Princeton: Princeton University Press.

Iyengar, S., & Hahn, K. S. (2009). Red media, blue media: Evidence of ideological selectivity in media use. Journal of Communication, 59(1), 19–39.

Jenkins, H. (2006). Convergence Culture: Where Old and New Media Collide. New York: New York University Press.

Kalogeropoulos, A., Negredo, S., Picone, I., & Nielsen, R. K. (2017). Who shares and comments on news? A cross-national comparative analysis of online and social media participation. Social Media & Society, 3(4). https://doi.org/10.1177/2056305117735754

Kalogeropoulos, A., & Nielsen, R. K. (2018). Social Inequalities in News Consumption. Reuters Institute factsheet.

Kim, Y. M., Hsu, J., Neiman, D. et al. (2018). The stealth media? Groups and targets behind divisive issue campaigns on Facebook. Political Communication, 35(4), 515–541. https://doi.org/10.1080/10584609.2018.1476425

Kreiss, D., & McGregor, S. C. (2019). The "arbiters of what our voters see": Facebook and Google's struggle with policy, process, and enforcement around political advertising. Political Communication, 36(4), 499–522. https://doi.org/10.1080/10584609.2019.1619639

Libert, T., Graves, L., & Nielsen, R. K. (2018). Changes in Third-Party Content on European News Websites after GDPR. Reuters Institute factsheet.

Mair, P. (1997). Party System Change: Approaches and Interpretations. Oxford: Clarendon Press.

Nelson, J. L., & Taneja, H. (2018). The small, disloyal fake news audience: The role of audience availability in fake news consumption. New Media & Society, 20(10), 3720–3737.

Newman, N., Fletcher, R., Kalogeropoulos, A., Levy, D. A. L., & Nielsen, R. K. (2018). Reuters Institute Digital News Report 2018. Reuters Institute.

Newman, N., Fletcher, R., Kalogeropoulos, A., & Nielsen, R. K. (2019). Reuters Institute Digital News Report 2019. Reuters Institute.

Nieborg, D. B., & Poell, T. (2018). The platformization of cultural production: Theorizing the contingent cultural commodity. New Media & Society, 20(11), 4275–4292. https://doi.org/10.1177/1461444818769694

Nielsen, R. K. (2016a). Democracy. In B. Peters (Ed.), Digital Keywords: A Vocabulary of Information Society and Culture (pp. 81–92) (Princeton Studies in Culture/Power/History). Princeton: Princeton University Press.

(2016b). News media, search engines and social networking sites as varieties of onlinegatekeepers. In C. Peters & M. Broersma (Eds.), Rethinking Journalism Again: Societal Role and Public Relevance in a Digital Age (pp. 81–96). London: Routledge.

(2019). The changing economic contexts of journalism. In T. Hanitzsch & K. Wahl-Jorgensen (Eds.), Handbook of Journalism Studies.

Nielsen, R. K., & Ganter, S. A. (2017). Dealing with digital intermediaries: A case study of the relations between publishers and platforms. New Media & Society, 20(4), 1600–1617. https://doi.org/10.1177/1461444817701318

Noble, S. U. (2018). Algorithms of Oppression: How Search Engines Reinforce Racism. New York: University Press.

Norris, P. (2011). Democratic Deficit: Critical Citizens Revisited. Cambridge: Cambridge University Press.

Pariser, E. (2011). Filter Bubbles: What the Internet Is Hiding from You. London: Penguin.

Phillips, W. (2015). This Is Why We Can't Have Nice Things: Mapping the Relationship between Online Trolling and Mainstream Culture (Information Society Series). Cambridge, MA: MIT Press.

Phillips, W., & Milner, R. M. (2017). The Ambivalent Internet: Mischief, Oddity, and Antagonism Online. Cambridge: Polity Press.

Plantin, J.-C., Lagoze, C., Edwards, P. N., & Sandvig, C. (2016). Infrastructure studies meet platform studies in the age of Google and Facebook. New Media & Society, 20(1), 293–310. https://doi.org/10.1177/1461444816661553

Prior, M. (2007). Post-Broadcast Democracy: How Media Choice Increases Inequality in Political Involvement and Polarizes Elections. Cambridge: Cambridge University Press.

Rhodes, R. A. W. (1997). Understanding Governance: Policy Networks, Governance, Reflexivity and Accountability. Bristol: Open University Press.

Schiffrin, A. (Ed.) (2017). In the Service of Power: Media Capture and the Threat toDemocracy. Washington, DC: Center for International Media Assistance.

Schumpeter, J. A. (1992). Capitalism, Socialism, and Democracy (5th ed.). London: Routledge.

Shehata, A., & Amnå, E. (2017). The development of political interest among adolescents: A communication mediation approach using five waves of panel data. Communication Research, 46(8), 1055–1077.

Skovsgaard, M., Shehata, A., & Strömbäck, J. (2016). Opportunity structures for selective exposure: Investigating selective exposure and learning in Swedish election campaigns using panel survey data. International Journal of Press/Politics,21(4), 527–546.

Snyder, J. M., & Strömberg, D. (2008). Press coverage and political accountability. NBER Working Paper No. 13878. www.nber.org/papers/w13878

Strömbäck, J. (2005). In search of a standard: Four models of democracy and their normative implications for journalism. Journalism Studies, 6(3), 331-345. https:// doi.org/10.1080/14616700500131950

Stroud, N. J. (2011). Niche News: The Politics of News Choice. Oxford: Oxford University Press.

Turow, J., & Couldry, N. (2018). Media as data extraction: Towards a new map of a transformed communications field. Journal of Communication, 68(2), 415-423. https://doi.org/10.1093/joc/jqx011

Valeriani, A., & Vaccari, C. (2016). Accidental exposure to politics on social media as online participation equalizer in Germany, Italy, and the United Kingdom. New Media & Society, 18(9), 1857–1874. https://doi.org/10.1177/1461444815616223

Van Dijck, J. (2013). The Culture of Connectivity: A Critical History of Social Media. Oxford: Oxford University Press.

Van Zoonen, L. (1998). A day at the zoo: Political communication, pigs and popular culture. Media, Culture & Society, 20(2), 183–200. https://doi.org/10.1177/016344398020002002

Verba, S., Schlozman, K. L., & Brady, H. E. (1995). Voice and Equality: Civic Voluntarism in American Politics. Cambridge, MA: Harvard University Press.

Wardle, C., & Derakhshan, H. (2017). Information Disorder: Toward an Interdisciplinary Framework for Research and Policy Making. Council of Europe Report No. DGI(2017)09).

Webster, J. G. (2014). The Marketplace of Attention : How Audiences Take Shape in a Digital Age. Cambridge, MA: MIT Press.

Webster, J. G., & Ksiazek, T. B. (2012). The dynamics of audience fragmentation: Public attention in an age of digital media. Journal of Communication, 62(1), 39–56.

Zuiderveen Borgesius, F. J., Trilling, D., Möller, J., Bodó, B., de Vreese, C. H., & Helberger, N. (2016). Should we worry about filter bubbles? Internet Policy Review, 5(1), 1–16.

FOOTNOTE

1. These are rough estimates. See https://rasmuskleisnielsen.net/2017/11/30/how-much-time-do- people-spend-with-news-across-media/
2. Our focus here is on news but it is worth mentioning that such cheap, targeted, and tailored digital advertising is of course also increasingly important for political communication, whether candidate campaigns, interest groups, political parties, and the like (Kreiss and McGregor 2019) or more problematic actors like astroturf groups, and fundamentally unidentifiable groups, including foreign entities (see, e.g., Kim et al. 2018).
3. Beyond the specific issues of news diversity that we examine here, algorithmic and automated ranking systems can embed various forms of discrimination and reinforce oppressive social relations as, for example, Noble (2018) shows.
4. Importantly, the platforms that increasingly dominate media markets in most democracies are all US-based. They often seem and are seen as primarily responsive to American political and public pressures and disinclined to customize their content moderation practices, terms of service, policies, and so on to other countries.

08 MISINFORMATION AND ITS CORRECTION

INTRODUCTION: AN OVERVIEW

In an age where information flows freely and rapidly through various media channels, the issue of misinformation has become an increasingly pressing concern. Misinformation, often driven by a myriad of sources, from social media platforms to traditional news outlets, can lead to significant societal challenges. This includes the erosion of trust in institutions, the proliferation of false beliefs, and even the incitement of panic and fear. In response to this, efforts to correct and combat misinformation have gained prominence, as individuals, organizations, and governments seek to restore accuracy and veracity in public discourse. This intricate interplay between the dissemination of false information and its correction forms a critical dynamic in the information landscape of the 21st century. This essay delves into the complex realm of misinformation, exploring the methods and challenges involved in its correction, and the broader implications for our societies.

Fake news is big news. From the diffusion of rumours and conspiracies in the United States to the spread of disinformation by Russian troll farms, misinformation is a hot topic among academics and journalists alike. How can we understand and correct such misinformation? A logical starting point is to fight fiction with fact. Indeed, many proposed solutions to the problem of misinformation assume that the proper remedy is merely to provide more information. In this view, if citizens were only better informed, misinformation would lose its power. However, ample research suggests that the answer is not so simple. Misinformation may continue to endure post- correction for several reasons. First, corrections are rarely able to fully eliminate reliance on misinformation in later judgments. Even when people recall hearing a retraction, the original misinformation may still influence their attitudes and beliefs (what is known as the continued influence effect). Worse yet, people may come to believe in misinformation even more strongly post-correction. In particular, retractions that run counter to individuals' prior attitudes may bolster beliefs in the original misinformation (what are known as worldview backfire effects). These worldview backfire effects have their roots in directionally motivated reasoning; individual's process misinformation and corrections through the lens of their preexisting beliefs and partisan attachments, so they may actively dispute corrections that contradict their broader worldviews.

Although political misinformation is not a new phenomenon, the topic has received renewed attention in recent years, in conjunction with sweeping changes in the contemporary media environment. As the Internet and, particularly, social media become an increasingly common source for political information (Shearer and Matsa 2018), citizens receive more and more of their news in an uncontrolled and minimally regulated setting where misinformation may easily spread (Vosoughi, Roy, and Aral 2018). Validating these concerns, numerous studies of "fake news" spotlight social media platforms, including both Facebook and Twitter, as the primary incubators of misinformation during the 2016 US presidential election (e.g., Allcott and Gentzkow 2017; Guess, Nyhan, and Reifler 2020). However, even if the sources of misinformation have fundamentally changed, best practices for correcting misinformation have not. While many of the pieces cited in this chapter do not focus explicitly on the Internet or social media, these works can still inform scholarly understanding of how to correct misinformation on these platforms.

The cognitive processes we highlight are likely to translate to the digital realm and are thus crucial to understand when developing prescriptions for social media-based misinformation. Nevertheless, we also spotlight a number of recent studies that examine methods for correcting misinformation in the context of social media.

PREVIOUS REVIEW PIECES

Several excellent review articles have already greatly enriched our knowledge of misinformation and its correction. Each is a valuable resource for deeper reading on this subject. In the interest of not rehashing existing work, we have made a conscious choice to showcase topics not already covered in these reviews. However, for the benefit of the reader, we summarize the primary takeaways from each piece and preview how we build on the groundwork they laid. First, Lewandowsky et al. (2012) provide a comprehensive summary of the literature on misinformation and its correction. In particular, they delve into the psychological roots of the continued influence effect and backfire effects and recommend appropriate interventions for practitioners seeking to mitigate these effects. However, since the article's publication in 2012, the field has evolved in notable ways – especially regarding the existence and magnitude of different types of backfire effects. Swire and Ecker (2018) thus provide an updated summary of the literature and offer several new strategies for effectively correcting misinformation. We pick up where these two articles leave off; we discuss newer research on both the continued influence effect and backfire effects and suggest ways for future work to continue to flesh out these topics in even greater detail.

Second, Flynn, Nyhan, and Reifler (2017) offer a more recent review of the misinformation literature, with a specific focus on the relationship between directionally motivated reasoning and political misperceptions. In their view, individuals' preexisting beliefs strongly affect their responses to corrections, such that individuals with different partisan or ideological leanings may respond to the same political facts in profoundly different ways. Importantly, the authors document a number of individual and contextual moderators of directionally motivated reasoning that predispose certain subsets of the population to be more vulnerable to worldview backfire effects. However, motivated reasoning is not the sole reason why misinformation persists over time. As studies of the continued influence effect demonstrate, individuals may continue to hold misinformed beliefs post-correction, even in the absence of strong prior attitudes. As such, we take a closer look at the full range of psychological mechanisms that may impede attempts to correct misinformation.

Finally, Tucker et al. (2018) focus on the interplay of social media and political polarization in enabling the spread of misinformation, with particular emphasis on the specific actors who manufacture misinformation. However, though they present a wide-ranging and thorough analysis of the contemporary research on the production of digital misinformation, these authors devote substantially less attention to best practices for correction. As a complement to this work, we discuss recent research on strategies to correct misinformation appearing on social media platforms, including Facebook and Twitter.

ORGANIZATION OF THE CHAPTER

In this chapter, we synthesize recent work on misinformation and its correction. Knowledge of this subject is still rapidly developing, and many questions remain unanswered and unresolved.[1] Here, we pay particular attention to one of these important questions: Why does misinformation persist even after it has been corrected? To this end, we first provide a definition of misinformation and specify the core criteria that help to discriminate between the many related concepts in this area. Second, we discuss two key perspectives on the perseverance of misinformation post-correction: backfire effects and the continued influence effect. Third, we outline a number of individual and contextual moderators that might make certain individuals or groups especially susceptible to misinformation. Finally, we conclude with a series of recommendations for future research.

DEFINITION OF MISINFORMATION: MAPPING KEY CRITERIA

To understand how best to tackle the problem of misinformation, it is essential to first define what this term means. However, scholarly notions of what constitutes misinformation often differ significantly across works and across disciplines. These definitions are highly variable, ranging from simple statements about the misleading nature of misinformation to commentaries on the motivation for the spread of misinformation. Some scholars broadly characterize misinformation as false information; for example, Fetzer (2004) defines it as "false, mistaken, or misleading information" (p. 231), and Berinsky(2017) defines it as "information that is factually unsubstantiated" (p. 242). Other scholars take a more restricted view, contrasting the term with other concepts, such as disinformation. For instance, Wardle (2018) argues that misinformation is "information that is false, but not intended to cause harm" (p. 5), whereas disinformation is "false information that is deliberately created or disseminated with the express purpose to cause harm" (p. 4). Finally, a third approach emphasizes the temporal nature of misinformation processing, arguing that misinformation's primary feature is that it is first presented as true but later revealed to be false. Ecker et al. (2015) state that misinformation is "information that is initially presented as factual but subsequently corrected" (p. 102). Similarly, Lewandowsky et al. (2012) define misinformation as "any piece of information that is initially processed as valid but that is subsequently retracted or corrected" (pp. 124–125). In this sense, information only becomes misinformation when it is first believed and later corrected, separating misinformation from other false information that goes unrebutted.

Compounding the problem is the fact that the term "misinformation" is often confounded with other similar concepts. For instance, as noted in the previous paragraph, some authors attempt to draw a line between misinformation and disinformation, or "information that is false and deliberately created to harm a person, social group, organization, or country" (Wardle and Derakhshan 2017, p. 20). Other scholars speak of misperceptions, or "cases in which people's beliefs about factual matters are not supported by clear evidence and expert opinion" (Nyhan and Reifler 2010, p. 305). Still others make reference to conspiracy theories, which offer unconventional explanations of the causes of events in terms of the "significant causal agency of a relatively small group of persons – the conspirators – acting in secret" (Keeley 1999, p. 116; see also Oliver and Wood 2014). Similar to, though broader in scope than, conspiracy theories are political rumors, which are "unverified stories or information statements people share with one another" (Weeks and Garrett 2014, p. 402). Finally, since the 2016 US presidential election, there has been much talk of fake news, which shares many similarities with disinformation but differs in its presentation. In particular, recent work defines fake news as "fabricated information that mimics news media content in form but not in organizational process or intent" (Lazer et al. 2018, p. 1094).

The multitude of definitions of misinformation speaks to the need for clarity on what exactly we, as a scholarly community, mean when we talk about misinformation. In an attempt to provide such structure, we compiled a wide variety of definitions of misinformation and related terms. Looking for common threads, we identified four overarching criteria for differentiating types of misinformation.2 First, we found that different definitions of misinformation place more or less emphasis on the truth value of the information – that is, whether the information has been proven to be untrue or whether it is merely unsubstantiated. Second, we noted that definitions of misinformation vary in their area of focus, particularly whether they emphasize the effects of false information versus false beliefs. Third, we found that scholars distinguish forms of misinformation based on their format, including whether or not the presentation of the information is designed to resemble traditional news sources. Finally, we noted differences in the perceived intentions of the actors who spread misinformation, in terms of their level of awareness that the information was false.

FOUR KEY CRITERIA

First, *truth value*: All forms of misinformation, at least to some degree, rest on shaky factual foundations. That is, all misinformation is in some way inaccurate. In some cases, misinformation is characterized by a lack of conclusive evidence to support a particular position, whereas, in others, it involves statements that run counter to mainstream consensus or expert opinion. However, the extent to which information is untrue varies across forms of misinformation; some subtypes may be definitively false (e.g., disinformation or fake news), whereas others may be merely misleading or unverified (e.g., political rumours).

Second, the area of focus: It is important to separate the presence of false information (misinformation) from the endorsement of false beliefs (misperceptions). This distinction is valuable because, as Thorson (2015)highlights, misperceptions are not exclusively caused by misinformation. Even if individuals only encounter true information, they may still arrive at inaccurate beliefs for other reasons, such as cognitive biases or misinterpretation of available facts. In this sense, the appropriate tools for correction may depend heavily on whether false beliefs are the clear product of misinformation or if they instead originate via other channels.

Third, format: Different types of misinformation may be presented in different ways. In some cases, misinformation may be embedded within otherwise accurate reports, whereas, in other cases, it may exist as standalone content. This is especially relevant to the study of fake news, or fabricated articles that imitate the appearance of traditional news stories (Allcott and Gentzkow 2017; Lazer et al. 2018). Fake news is a form of disinformation, as it is spread despite being known to be false, but it may be distinguished from other types of disinformation by its unique format – namely, its emulation of legitimate media outlets (Pennycook and Rand 2018). In addition to fake news, recent work also looks beyond textual forms of misinformation to other types of media, including manipulated images and videos (Kasra, Shen, and O'Brien 2016; Schwarz, Newman, and Leach 2016; Shen et al. 2019).

Finally, intentionality: Does the person transmitting misinformation sincerely believe it to be true or are they aware that it is false? By most accounts, this is the primary means of distinguishing between misinformation and disinformation (for a review, see Wardle 2018). On the one hand, misinformation may circulate without any intent to deceive. For instance, in the wake of breaking news events, people increasingly turn to the Internet, and especially social media, for real-time updates. As new information is released in a piecemeal fashion, individuals may inadvertently propagate information that later turns out to be false (Nyhan and Reifler 2015a; Zubiaga et al. 2016). On the other hand, disinformation is false or inaccurate information that is deliberately distributed despite its inaccuracy (Stahl 2006; Born and Edgington 2017). People may choose to share fictitious stories, even when they recognize that these stories are untrue. Why might people knowingly promulgate false information? One answer relates to the disseminators' motivations; although misinformation is typically not designed to advance a particular agenda, disinformation is often spread in service of concrete goals. For instance, fake news is often designed to go viral on social media (Pennycook and Rand 2018; Tandoc, Lim, and Ling 2018), enabling rapid transmission of highly partisan content and offering a reliable stream of advertising revenue (Tucker et al. 2018). In practice, however, determining a person or group's intentions is extremely difficult. It is hard to uncover people's "ground truth" beliefs about the veracity of a piece of information, and it is even harder to ascertain their underlying motivations. That said, recognizing the range of motivations for spreading misinformation is valuable, even if these motivations are hard to disentangle in the wild.

For the purposes of this chapter, we consider "misinformation" an umbrella term under which many associated concepts are subsumed. Moving forward, we recommend misinformation as the default term to use, unless explicitly referring to one of these more specific constructs. Given the difficulty of proving the motivations underlying the spread of false information, we adopt an intent-agnostic approach; we make no assumptions about what compels individuals or groups to broadcast misinformation. Instead, we take the view that misinformation – in all of its forms – may have a considerable, harmful impact on people's beliefs and behaviour. As such, in the discussion that follows, we cite examples of corrective strategies targeted at all different types of misinformation.

RESPONSES TO CORRECTIONS: CONTINUED INFLUENCE AND BACKFIRE EFFECTS

Detailing types of information is not a mere technical exercise. A well- functioning democratic society does not necessarily need to be guided by fully informed citizens, but an environment rife with misinformation can easily derail democracy. An uninformed citizenry is arguably far less pernicious than a misinformed citizenry (Kuklinski et al. 2000); as Hochschild and Einstein (2015) write, "people's unwillingness or inability to use relevant facts in their political choices may be frustrating, but people's willingness to use mistaken factual claims in their voting and public engagement is actually dangerous to a democratic polity" (p. 14). When the public holds misinformed beliefs, this can not only affect their individual attitudes and behaviours but also shape large- scale policy outcomes (e.g., health care reform, see Nyhan 2010; Berinsky 2017). Correcting misinformation is therefore a worthy goal; but how can it best be accomplished?

Previous research suggests that not all corrections are effective in reducing individuals' reliance on misinformation. There are two pathways through which misinformation might continue to shape attitudes and behaviours post-correction: the continued influence effect and backfire effects. Engrained in the former is the notion that corrections are somewhat, but not entirely, effective at dispelling misinformation. More concerning, however, are the latter, in which corrections not only fail to reduce but actually strengthen beliefs in the original misinformation. Neither of these phenomena offers a particularly sanguine take on the ability to curtail the spread of misinformation. However, each offers its own unique predictions about the most promising avenues for corrections. We begin by reviewing the extant literature on backfire effects and then turn to the continued influence effect.

BACKFIRE EFFECTS

Providing factual corrections of misinformation may, under certain circumstances, only make things worse. Specifically, retractions that challenge people's worldviews may entrench beliefs in the original misinformation. This phenomenon is known as a backfire effect or, more precisely, a worldview backfire effect.3 Nyhan and Reifler (2010) sounded the first alarm bells about the possibility of these worldview backfire effects. Across a series of studies, they found that, when certain subjects were presented with factual corrections that contradicted their political beliefs, they responded by becoming more, rather than less, wedded to their previous misperceptions. Since their highly influential piece was published, concerns about worldview backfire effects have taken hold both in popular media and in academic circles. This widespread interest has spawned an entire line of work dedicated to elucidating the psychological mechanisms that drive these effects.

Worldview backfire effects can be understood as a product of directionally motivated reasoning (for a comprehensive review, see Flynn et al. 2017). According to theories of motivated reasoning, individuals are motivated to process information in ways that align with their ultimate goals (Kunda 1990). In particular, individuals must balance several competing impulses, including directional goals (to attain a desired outcome) and accuracy goals (to reach the correct conclusion). Worldview backfire effects transpire when directional motivations take precedence over accuracy goals – a frequent occurrence in the realm of politics (Lodge and Taber 2013).

Two complementary processes are at the heart of these effects. First, confirmation bias: Individuals tend to seek out and interpret new information in ways that validate their pre-existing views. Along these lines, individuals also tend to perceive congenial information as more credible or persuasive than opposing evidence (Guess and Coppock 2018; Khanna and Sood 2018). Second, disconfirmation bias: When exposed to ideologically dissonant information, individuals will call to mind opposing arguments (counter arguing).4 In combination, these two processes can cultivate worldview backfire effects; when individuals are confronted with a correction that contradicts their past beliefs, they will act to both discount the correction and bolster their prior views.

Several studies have investigated the potential for worldview backfire effects in the context of misinformation. Although Nyhan and Reifler issued the earliest warnings about this phenomenon, it has since been reproduced across other settings. First, worldview backfire effects have been tied to message presentation, with individuals most resistant to message framing that contradicts their broader worldviews (Zhou 2016). Second, world view backfire effects have been linked to source cues. For instance, several studies find that Republicans are averse to corrections from Democratic elites (Berinsky 2017) or nonpartisan fact-checking sources (Holman and Lay 2019). Finally, worldview backfire effects extend to the behavioural realm; across multiple studies, exposure to pro-vaccine corrections decreased future vaccination intentions among those already hesitant to get vaccinated (Skurnik, Yoon, and Schwarz 2007; Nyhan et al. 2014; Nyhan and Reifler 2015b; but see Haglin 2017).

Empirical studies have also taught us about the mechanisms that undergird worldview backfire effects. Consistent with a motivated reasoning perspective, worldview backfire effects appear rooted in counter arguing. In one experiment, Schaffner and Roche (2017) examine differences in survey response times following the release of the October 2012 jobs report, which announced a sharp decrease in the unemployment rate under the Obama administration. They find that those Republicans who took longer to provide estimates of the unemployment rate after the report's release were less accurate in their responses, suggesting that worldview backfire effects may arise out of deliberate, effortful processes. However, more work beyond this initial study is certainly needed to isolate the mechanisms that underlie worldview backfire effects.

AVOIDING WORLDVIEW BACKFIRE EFFECTS

In light of mounting concerns about the potential for worldview backfire effects, scholars have explored several tactics for correcting misinformation while circumventing these effects. Although many routes to correction are possible, all designed to counteract directionally motivated reasoning, we summarize here two main subcategories of these corrections focused on source credibility and worldview affirmation.

First, the source of misinformation – as well as its correction – may have a profound impact on responses to corrections. When evaluating the accuracy of a claim, individuals rely heavily on source cues (Schwarz et al. 2016), which signal a source's expertise or trustworthiness. In terms of expertise, if sources are depicted as authorities on a given subject, they are likely to be deemed more credible (Vraga and Bode 2017). In fact, expert consensus is considered a key "gateway belief" that can override directional impulses. For example, communicating the broad scientific agreement about climate change reduces partisan differences in climate change attitudes (van der Linden et al. 2015; van der Linden et al. 2017; Druckman and McGrath 2019; but see Kahan, Jenkins-Smith, and Braman 2011). However, the trustworthiness of a source seems to matter even more than expertise when countering misinformation (McGinnies and Ward 1980; Guillory and Geraci 2013). People are more likely to view sources as trustworthy if they share similar traits. As a result, corrections that are attributed to an in-group member (e.g., a leader of one's preferred party) may be more effective than those credited to an out-group member (e.g., an opposing partisan, see Swire, Berinsky et al. 2017). Furthermore, though corrections are most frequently issued by elites, individuals are also receptive to corrections from members of their social circles (Margolin, Hannak, and Weber 2018; Vraga and Bode 2018), who may not be experts but may still be deemed trustworthy. Finally, trustworthiness is a function of one's perceived stake in an issue. Recent research on "unlikely sources" (Berinsky 2017; Benegal and Scruggs 2018; Wintersieck, Fridkin, and Kenney 2018; Holman and Lay 2019) indicates that corrections are most persuasive when they come from sources who stand to benefit from the spread of misinformation (e.g., a Democratic politician or left-leaning publication correcting a fellow Democrat).

Second, where possible, corrections should be tailored to their target audience: the subset of people for whom these corrections would feel most threatening. Framing corrections to be consonant with, rather than antagonistic to, this group's values and worldviews may thus be a successful corrective strategy (Kahan et al. 2010; Feinberg and Willer 2015; for reviews, see Lewandowsky et al. 2012; Swire and Ecker 2018). In a similar vein, some scholars propose using self-affirmation exercises (Cohen, Aronson, and Steele 2000; Cohen et al. 2007) to subdue directional motivations (Trevors et al. 2016; Carnahan et al. 2018); if people feel validated in their global self-worth, corrections that impugn their political views may provoke a less defensive response (but see Nyhan and Reifler 2019).

BACKLASH AGAINST WORLDVIEW BACKFIRE EFFECTS

The previous discussion presumes that worldview backfire effects are not only dangerous but prevalent. Recently, however, there has been backlash against the very notion of worldview backfire effects, with some suggesting they are extremely rare in practice. Wood and Porter (2019) attempt to detect worldview backfire effects across a wide array of divisive issues and find little evidence to support their existence, even when using language identical to Nyhan and Reifler (2010). When examining several highly polarized issues, including gun control and capital punishment, Guess and Coppock (2018) likewise fail to uncover any worldview backfire effects in response to counter-attitudinal information. Instead, individuals seem to accommodate novel information into their later assessments of issues, even if that information runs counter to their beliefs (see also Porter, Wood, and Kirby 2018). However, even if corrections largely improve belief accuracy, these messages seem to have little impact on individuals' subsequent attitudes, evaluations of politicians, or policy preferences (Swire, Berinsky et al. 2017; Aird et al. 2018; Nyhan et al. 2019; Porter, Wood, and Bahador 2019; Barrera et al. 2020).

What accounts for the discrepancies in results across studies? The answer may be both theoretical and methodological. First, there is a large body of work on the theoretic side. Some scholars have suggested that worldview backfire effects are more likely when corrections necessitate attitude change versus only pertain to a single, specific event (Ecker et al. 2014; Ecker and Ang 2019). Why are people better able to absorb ideologically dissonant corrections for one-off events? To answer this question, Ecker and Ang (2019) draw on stereotype subtyping theory (Richards and Hewstone 2001). According to this theory, individuals possess stereotypes about the customary behaviour of different groups (e.g., members of a political party). Subtyping is a common response when group members act in ways that flout a well-established stereotype; rather than forming a new stereotype, individuas instead label contrary cases as exceptions to the broader rule. If misinformation pertains to a single, isolated event, individuals may thus be able to internalize disconfirming corrections without altering their deep-seated worldviews. It is much harder, however, to dismiss general patterns of behaviour as anomalous. As such, people are more likely to resist corrections that, on acceptance, would require a large-scale shift in their core beliefs.

Redlawsk, Civettini, and Emmerson (2010) provide a somewhat different perspective on the boundaries of worldview backfire effects. They posit an "affective tipping point" at which individuals cease to engage in motivated reasoning and instead revise their beliefs to be more accurate – in other words, the point at which individuals pivot from directional to accuracy goals. As people encounter more and more disconfirming information, they may reach a critical threshold at which they are no longer motivated to defend their previous views. In this view, worldview backfire effects will occur until enough contradictory evidence accumulates. After this point, individuals will begin to rationally update their beliefs in response to corrections rather than double down on their previously misinformed views. This theoretical account generates somewhat divergent predictions from Ecker and Ang. For both sets of authors, general cases of misinformation should provoke heightened discomfort. However, if enough contrary evidence comes to light, Redlawsk and colleagues anticipate a diminished likelihood of worldview backfire effects, whereas Ecker and Ang seem to predict the exact opposite. Further work may be needed to adjudicate between these two explanations. In particular, efforts to pinpoint the precise location of this tipping point may prove fruitful.

Methodological differences may play a role as well. Worldview backfire effects may not be immediately apparent post-correction. Instead, they may only emerge after some time has elapsed (Peter and Koch 2016; Pluviano, Watt, and Della Sala 2017). However, most research on worldview backfire effects just measures the effect of corrections after a short distraction task. In contrast, studies that do incorporate lengthy time delays (e.g., Berinsky 2017; Swire, Berinsky et al. 2017) find that the benefits of corrections quickly dissipate. Worldview backfire effects may therefore only be visible after a delay. Studies of these effects should therefore aim to measure responses at multiple points in time. In addition, worldview backfire effects are more probable for high-salience issues where individuals have strong prior attitudes (Flynn et al. 2017). Nevertheless, the deep-rooted nature of these issues may limit the range of effect sizes that a single experimental manipulation can elicit. As a result, worldview backfire effects may be especially hard to detect for highly polarized issues – the veryissues where we would expect the most pervasive effects.

On a related note, it is essential to come to some consensus regarding what, exactly, we consider a "backfire effect." In particular, worldview backfire effects may be an artifact of the baseline against which they are measured. Scholars generally define worldview backfire effects as cases where the presentation of both misinformation and its correction is worse than presenting misinformation uncorrected. Yet when considering the deleterious effects of misinformation in society, a more expansive definition may be appropriate. Worldview backfire effects are commonly measured experimentally by comparing respondents who were exposed to misinformation to respondents who were exposed to both misinformation and corrections. However, when examining information that has already spread through society – beliefs about President Obama's citizenship, for example – a better baseline might be people's beliefs if they had not been re-exposed to misinformation as part of an experiment. If providing a correction to misinformation is worse than providing no information at all, strategies for mitigating misinformation may require substantial adjustment.

CONTINUED INFLUENCE EFFECT

The ubiquity of worldview backfire effects remains an open question. However, even if these effects are overblown, valid concerns about the unintended consequences of corrections remain. In particular, the format in which corrections are delivered may bolster beliefs in misinformation, even in the absence of worldview backfire effects. A near-universal finding in the misinformation literature is that, even after its correction, misinformation continues to influence people's attitudes and beliefs (for a review, see Walterand Tukachinsky 2019). This is known as the continued influence effect (Wilkes and Leatherbarrow 1988; Johnson and Seifert 1994). Importantly, people may correctly recall a retraction yet still use outdated misinformation when reasoning about an event. From this perspective, corrections can partially reduce misperceptions but cannot fully eliminate reliance on misinformation in later judgments.

Why does misinformation linger post-correction? Scholars suggest two potential reasons for the continued influence effect. First, according to the mental model theory, individuals construct models of external events in their heads, which they continuously update as new information becomes available (Johnson and Seifert 1994; Swire and Ecker 2018). However, retractions often threaten the internal coherence of these models (Gordon et al. 2017; Swire and Ecker 2018). As a result, even if individuals explicitly recall corrections, they may nevertheless continue to invoke misinformation until a plausible alternative takes its place. Numerous studies find that corrections are more effective when they contain alternative causal accounts rather than just negate the original misinformation (Johnson and Seifert 1994; Ecker, Lewandowsky, and Tang 2010; Nyhan and Reifler 2015a; but see Ecker et al. 2015).

Secondly, the continued influence effect can be understood through dual-process theory. Dual-process theory distinguishes between two types of memory retrieval: automatic and strategic. Automatic processing is fast and unconscious, whereas strategic processing is deliberate and effortful. In addition, automatic processing is relatively a contextual, distilling information down only to its most essential properties, whereas strategic processing is required to retrieve specific details about a piece of information(Ecker et al. 2011). As a result, individuals may be able to remember a piece of misinformation but not recall relevant features, such as its source or perceived accuracy (Swire and Ecker 2018). In this view, the continued influence effect constitutes a form of retrieval failure; misinformation is automatically retrieved, but its retraction is not. This emphasis on automatic versus strategic processing is also consistent with an online processing model of misinformation (Lodge and Taber 2013; Thorson 2016). According to this model, initial misinformation is encoded with a stronger affective charge than its correction, meaning that misinformation will continue to dominate subsequent evaluations until individuals engage in the strategic processing necessary to explicitly recall a correction.

Most direct studies of the continued influence effect use variants of the same research design, based on the "warehouse fire" script (Wilkes and Leatherbarrow 1988; Johnson and Seifert 1994). In this scenario, the cause of a fire is initially attributed to volatile chemicals stored in a closet, but the closet is later revealed to have been empty. Subsequent studies have adapted this narrative to other contexts, such as police reports or political misconduct, but all follow a similar format in which information about a breaking news event is relayed over a series of short messages. Experimenters randomly assign some subjects to read a critical piece of misinformation (e.g., the presence of flammable materials) as well as its retraction (e.g., the empty closet). However, this communication technique is arguably ill-suited to the study of political misinformation. First, many of these studies present misinformation and corrections as coming from the same source. However, in the realm of politics, the sources most likely to issue corrections may be the ones least likely to spread the misinformation in the first place. Second, the sequencing of messages may not accurately mimic how individuals encounter information in the real world, where the temporal distance may be either much shorter (instantaneous, if people see a correction before or concurrently with the original misinformation) or much longer (if corrections are issued at a later date). Finally, these studies usually rely on fictional scenarios that do not implicate social identities or prior attitudes (but see Ecker et al. 2014), both ofwhich may increase the likelihood of the continued influence effect.

Accordingly, recent work has sought to investigate the presence of the continued influence effect in the political domain. Most notably, Thorson (2016) introduces the concept of "belief echoes," a version of the continued influence effect focused on attitudes rather than causal inferences. According to her theory, misinformation may continue to influence political attitudes through two separate processes. First, automatic belief echoes develop as a by-product of online processing. Even when individuals accept corrections as true, misinformation may still be automatically activated, thereby continuing to affect attitudes outside of conscious awareness. Deliberative belief echoes, on the other hand, occur when individuals assume that the existence of one piece of negative information – even if it is known to be false – increases the likelihood that other relevant negative information is true (a "where there's smoke, there's fire" philosophy). Together, these automatic and deliberative belief echoes may contribute to the perpetuation of misinformation post-correction.

FAMILIARITY BACKFIRE EFFECTS

The continued influence effect suggests that corrections are somewhat, though not entirely, effective in reducing belief in misinformation. In fact, contrary to worldview backfire effects, the continued influence effect does not require the existence of strong prior attitudes. However, backfire effects might occur even in the absence of worldview threat. In particular, corrections that repeat misinformation may amplify its influence, constituting an alternate form of backlash known as familiarity backfire effects. Of note, within the political science literature, the term "backfire effect" almost exclusively refers to worldview backfire effects. However, familiarity backfire effects are a much more common area of focus within the psychology literature. To avoid confusion, we treat these concepts as separate phenomena.

Familiarity backfire effects involve cases in which retractions increase, rather than reduce, reliance on misinformation by making misinformation feel more familiar. These effects are primarily studied in the context of repetition. In particular, familiarity backfire effects are considered the product of the illusory truth effect, wherein "repeated statements are easier to process, and subsequently perceived to be more truthful, than new statements" (Fazio et al.2015, p. 993). The illusory truth effect operates through a series of complementary psychological mechanisms. First, repeating information strengthens its encoding in memory, enabling easier retrieval later on (for reviews, see Lewandowsky et al. 2012; Peter and Koch 2016). Second, the difficulty with which information is processed influences its perceived authenticity. This is tied to the meta cognitive experience of "processing fluency" (Schwarz, et al. 2007); information that is easier to process feels more familiar, and familiarity is a key criterion by which individuals judge accuracy (Alter and Oppenheimer 2009). Accordingly, if individuals have repeated contact with a piece of misinformation, they may perceive it as more credible than if they encounter it only once, regardless of its content.

The illusory truth effect is of particular concern in regard to misinformation correction, given the standard format of corrections. In particular, as part of the debunking process, most corrections directly reference the original misinformation. For instance, the commonly employed "myths vs. facts" strategy involves repeating misinformation (the "myth") while simultaneously discrediting it (the "fact"). As such, repeated exposure to misinformation – even during its correction – may activate the familiarity heuristic and therefore enhance the perceived accuracy of misinformation. Indeed, familiarity backfire effects have been detected across numerous studies of this specific correction style (Schwarz et al. 2007; Peter and Koch 2016; but see Cameron et al. 2013).

Familiarity backfire effects may be especially prominent after a time delay. Though individuals are typically able to differentiate fact from fiction immediately after viewing a correction, they may soon forget the details of the correction and retain only the gist of the original misinformation. For example, Skurnik et al. (2007) find that subjects were able to distinguish between mythsand facts about the flu vaccine right after reading an informational flyer but, after only a short break, were significantly more likely to mistake myths for facts than the reverse. In addition, in a study of healthcare reform, Berinsky (2017)notes that the effectiveness of corrections faded rapidly over time, with subjects exposed to corrections no more likely than those in a control group to reject a rumour about "death panels" after just a week. Even if corrections are initially able to reduce misperceptions, their benefits may be short-lived.

Familiarity backfire effects are also likely to be relatively universal, as the illusory truth effect is largely robust across individuals and situations. Even when they have prior knowledge about a subject, individuals tend to rate repeated statements as truer than new statements (Fazio et al. 2015). In addition, the illusory truth effect is only modestly associated with dispositional skepticism (DiFonzo et al. 2016) and is uncorrelated with several psychological traits, such as analytical thinking and need for closure, that are otherwise connected to the processing of misinformation (De keersmaecker et al. 2020). Finally, the illusory truth effect appears independent of motivated reasoning; across both politically consistent and discordant statements, repeated exposure corresponds to higher accuracy ratings (Pennycook, Cannon, and Rand 2018).

Not all scholars, though, have found evidence of familiarity backfire effects. Although most scholars acknowledge that familiarity affects the processing of corrections, some dispute the negative relationship between repetition of misinformation and belief accuracy (e.g., Swire, Ecker, and Lewandowsky 2017; Pennycook et al. 2018). In fact, Ecker, Hogan, and Lewandowsky (2017) find that retractions that include reminders of the original misinformation are more effective than retractions without this repetition.5 They attribute these results to the benefits of coactivating misinformation and corrections (see also Swire and Ecker 2018). When misinformation and its correction are summoned simultaneously, individuals are better able to detect discrepancies between the original misinformation and the factual evidence. This "conflict detection" expedites the knowledge revision process, leading to more efficient belief updating. In light of these contradictory findings, it remains unclear how concerned we should be about familiarity backfire effects when correcting misinformation. However, we discuss a number of strategies in the following section to minimize the risk of these effects, regardless of their prevalence.

AVOIDING FAMILIARITY BACKFIRE EFFECTS

What strategies exist to correct misinformation while evading familiarity backfire effects? The most obvious solution is to focus on the correction without alluding to the original misinformation. However, several of the pieces cited in this chapter suggest that avoiding repetition is not a magic bullet; at times, providing details about a piece of misinformation can aid in the correction process. Moreover, even if avoiding repetition is the goal, this may not always be possible. In many cases, misinformation is published by one source and corrected by another. Rather than just affirm the facts, corrections may need to invoke the original misinformation in order to provide proper contextualization. Instead of avoiding repetition of *misinformation*, it may thus be more valuable to focus on reiterating *corrections*, as a means of increasing the familiarity of accurate information (Ecker et al. 2011).

Furthermore, processing fluency is not solely a function of repetition (Schwarz et al. 2007). On the whole, information that is easier to process will be perceived as more familiar (and therefore more valid). Consequently, corrections may be more successful when they are less cognitively taxing. For example, visual corrections may be easier to digest than long-form fact- checking articles (Alter and Oppenheimer 2009; Schwarz et al. 2016). Previous studies using photographs (Garrett, Nisbet, and Lynch 2013), infographics (Nyhan and Reifler 2019), and videos (Young et al. 2018) largely corroborate this hypothesis (but see Nyhan et al. 2014). Similarly, corrections that employ simple words or grammatical structures may be more decipherable than linguistically complex corrections (Alter and Oppenheimer 2009). The readability of corrections is thus another important consideration for future research to explore. Finally, it may be optimal for corrections to combine multiple approaches. For instance, corrections that pair pithy images (e.g., PolitiFact's Truth-O-Meter) with accompanying descriptive text may be especially effective (Amazeen et al. 2016).

INDIVIDUALS AFFECTED BY MISINFORMATION: FACTORS INFLUENCING THE SPREAD OF MISINFORMATION AND STRATEGIES FOR ITS CORRECTION

Overall, misinformation appears both pervasive and difficult to correct once it spreads. However, not all misinformation is created equal, nor are all individuals equally susceptible to its influence. Thus, it is important to examine which groups are most likely to be affected by misinformation in society. In the sections that follow, we outline several factors – both individual and contextual – that may affect the persistence of misinformation among certain groups, by making individuals either more likely to believe misinformation or more resistant to its correction.

INDIVIDUAL FACTORS

We first discuss several individual-level moderators of receptiveness to misinformation and responsiveness to corrections. These factors may be bifurcated into two strands: those that are explicitly political in nature and those that reflect more fundamental personal or psychological orientations.

Political Factors

Two main political factors contribute to the nature and severity of misinformation effects: political sophistication and ideology. One of the most frequently studied moderators of correction effectiveness is political sophistication, which includes aspects of political knowledge, engagement, and education (for a review, see Flynn et al. 2017). At first glance, more politically sophisticated individuals should be less susceptible to misinformation than less-informed citizens, as they can draw on their superior knowledge to discern fact from fiction. Along these lines, Berinsky (2012) finds that more politically engaged individuals are, on the whole, more likely than others to reject political rumours. However, he also finds that politically sophisticated Republicans are more likely to accept rumours about Democrats, suggesting that political knowledge does not entirely inoculate individuals against misinformation.

In fact, belief in misinformation may actually be more prevalent within this more educated and engaged group. Recent research finds that individuals who are more politically active and engaged are more likely to share misinformation via social media, thereby contributing to the spread of misinformation to other members of the public (Valenzuela et al. 2019). Moreover, politically sophisticated individuals may be more resistant to corrections. In general, politically sophisticated individuals tend to evince the strongest directional motivations (Lodge and Taber 2013), corresponding to greater endorsement of misinformation that reinforces their prior beliefs (Nyhan, Reifler, and Ubel 2013; Miller, Saunders, and Farhart 2016; Jardina and Traugott 2019). Nyhan and Reifler (2010) propose two mechanisms by which this might be the case: a biased information search and biased information processing. First, politically sophisticated individuals may be more likely to selectively consume ideologically consistent media (confirmation bias), thereby filtering out the sources most likely to publish attitude-incongruent corrections. Second, when encountering attitude-incongruent corrections, politically sophisticated individuals may be best equipped to counter-argue against these corrections (disconfirmation bias).

The most politically sophisticated individuals seem the least amenable to corrections when misinformation supports their pre-existing beliefs. As a result, corrections may fail to reduce and may even enhance belief in misinformation among this small but consequential group. From this perspective, political sophistication is a crucial determinant of responses to misinformation and its correction. Highly sophisticated partisans have both the motivation and the expertise to discount corrections that run counter to their predispositions. Furthermore, less engaged citizens are unlikely to be exposed to corrections in the first place. When considering solutions to the spread of misinformation, the standard prescription is merely to provide more information. However, this heightened susceptibility to misinformation among the most informed citizens exposes the limits to this approach; when individuals are knowledgeable about and involved in politics, this engagement may ironically engender the strongest opposition to corrections. Thus, a more informed populace may not be a panacea if corrections continue to heighten directional motivations.

Political Ideology and Partisanship

An active debate in the misinformation literature concerns potential asymmetries in responses to misinformation based on political ideology and partisan identification (for a review, see Swire, Berinsky et al. 2017).

Specifically, some scholars claim that conservatives and Republicans are especially vulnerable to misinformation. In a widely cited article, Jost et al. (2003) catalog a laundry list of predictors of conservatism (e.g., close- mindedness, intolerance of ambiguity), many of which could engender openness Jost et al. (2018) highlight several other factors associated with conservatism, including an emphasis on in-group consensus and homogeneous social networks, that may give rise to "echo chambers" in which misinformation can easily spread (see also Nam, Jost, and Van Bavel 2013; Ecker and Ang 2019). Taken together, these pieces paint a picture of conservatives as resistant to change, averse to uncertainty, and drawn to one-sided information environments – all of which mightpredispose those on the right to favour misinformation, relative to their moderate or liberal counterparts.

These theoretical expectations have some empirical backing. Recent research finds that, during the 2016 election, Republicans were more likely than Democrats to read and share fake news (Grinberg et al. 2019; Guess, Nagler, and Tucker 2019; Guess et al. 2020). Furthermore, ideology and partisanshipare associated with differences in responses to corrections. For example, Nyhan and Reifler (2010) report evidence of ideological asymmetry in responses to corrections. Although they find that, regardless of partisan leaning, corrections were generally less effective when they were attitude-incongruent, worldview backfire effects were visible for Republicans but not Democrats (see also Ecker and

Ang 2019).6 These individual-level differences may be exacerbated by system-wide differences in conservative versus liberal media. Although misinformation originates in both liberal and conservative circles, the insular nature of the conservative media ecosystem may be more conducive to the spread of misinformation (Faris et al. 2017; see also Barberá, Chapter 3, this volume), and conservative media sources are more likely than liberal sites to dismiss or otherwise derogate nonpartisan fact-checkers (Iannucci and Adair 2017). Finally, these system-wide differences also extend to individual behaviour. In an analysis of tweets about the 2012 presidential election, Shin and Thorson (2017) find that Republicans retweeted or replied much less frequently to fact-checking sites than Democrats – and their replies tended to be more acrimonious. Similarly, across both Facebook and Twitter, Amazeen, Vargo, and Hopp (2018) find that liberal-leaning individuals tend to be more likely than others to share fact-checking information.

However, this emphasis on the psychological profiles of political conservatives is not without controversy. Kahan and colleagues contend that motivated reasoning is not a uniquely right-wing phenomenon. Instead, all individuals are motivated to express and maintain beliefs similar to those of other members of their identity groups (the "cultural cognition thesis," e.g., Kahan et al. 2011; Kahan 2013). In line with this perspective, several recent works suggest that liberals are not, in fact, immune to the effects of misinformation (Aird et al. 2018; Guess et al. 2019). Across numerous fields, ranging from science to politics, both conservatives and liberals evince similar levels of motivated reasoning (Nisbet, Cooper, and Garrett 2015; Meirick and Bessarabova 2016; Frimer, Skitka, and Motyl 2017; Swire, Ecker et al. 2017; Ditto et al. 2019). While conservatives may disproportionately display the motivational tendencies associated with belief in misinformation, these proclivities do not necessarily translate to behavioural differences.

While political knowledge has been firmly established as a key moderator of misinformation effects, via its relationship to directionally motivated reasoning, the jury is still out regarding the role of political ideology and partisanship. Although conservatives and Republicans may, under certain conditions, be more sensitive to misinformation than others, this divide may be overstated. Are observed cases of ideological asymmetry a function of deeply rooted psychological traits, or do they instead reflect systematic differences in conservative versus liberal media environments (or in the misinformation itself)? Future work should continue to grapple with this tricky distinction.

Individual and Psychological Factors

Misinformation, however, is not contained to the political sphere. More basic personal and psychological factors may predispose certain individuals to champion misinformation and disavow corrections across domains. We Reifler's

(2010) experiments rely on actual examples of misinformation (stem cell research and weapons of mass destruction in Iraq). While this approach has the benefit of greater external validity, these cases may diverge in notable ways beyond their ideological slant (e.g., issue salience or importance). Studies that focus on fabricated misinformation, rather than real-world rumours, may thus be better suited to identifying potential partisan or ideological asymmetries.

In particular, Nyhan and highlight four of these potential moderators, namely age, analytical thinking, need for closure, and psychological reactance.7 Scholars highlight age as a key demographic variable influencing both exposure and responses to misinformation. Several recent studies find that older adults are more likely than others to share fake news stories on social media (Grinberg et al. 2019; Guess et al. 2019). However, other work finds that old age is also associated with greater sharing of fact-checks on social media (Amazeen et al. 2018), suggesting that older cohorts may engage differently with political content on social media, relative to their younger counterparts.

Scholars have also identified analytical thinking, or a person's capacity to override gut feelings and intuitions, as another determinant of their responses to misinformation. In this sense, individuals who are more prone to careful, deliberate processing of information (or "cognitive reflection") seem to be less susceptible to misinformation. Analytical thinking is associated with reduced belief in conspiracy theories (Swami et al. 2014) and increased accuracy in judging fake news headlines (Pennycook and Rand 2018; Bronstein et al. 2019; Pennycook and Rand 2020). Furthermore, highly analytical individuals are more willing than others to adjust their attitudes post-correction, even after controlling for a host of other variables (De keersmaecker and Roets 2017; see also Tappin, Pennycook, and Rand 2018). While most studies conceptualize analytical thinking as a dispositional trait, recent work suggests that interventions designed to encourage greater deliberation may also prove an effective tool for correcting misinformation (Bago, Rand, and Pennycook 2020).

Need for closure may also shape an individual's susceptibility to misinformation. Need for closure refers to "the expedient desire for any firm belief on a given topic, as opposed to confusion and uncertainty" (Jost et al. 2003, p. 348, italics in original). This motivation fosters two main behavioural inclinations: the propensity to seize on readily available information and the tendency to cling to previous information (Jost et al. 2003; Meirick and Bessarabova 2016; De keersmaecker et al. 2020). Consequently, individuals with a high need for closure may be more trusting of initial misinformation, which provides closure through explaining the causes of events, and more resistant to corrections, which may sow feelings of confusion and uncertainty (Rapp and Salovich 2018). Need for closure, however, is primarily used as a control variable in studies of misinformation and is rarely the main construct of interest. Indeed, the few studies connecting a need for closure to misinformation focus solely on the endorsement, rather than correction, of misinformation (e. g., Leman and Cinnirella 2013; Moulding et al. 2016; Marchlewska, Cichocka, and Kossowska 2018). Nevertheless, need for closure may also moderate the effectiveness of corrections. For instance, individuals with a high need for closure may be especially vulnerable to the continued influence effect; if these individuals are less acceptant of gaps in their mental models of an event, they may be more likely to retain misinformation in the absence of plausible alternative explanations. Moving forward, future research should continue to probe the extent to which a high need for closure predisposes certain individuals to disregard corrections.

Finally, high levels of psychological reactance may trigger backfire effects by stimulating counter arguing. Psychological reactance occurs when individuals perceive a threat to their intellectual or behavioural freedoms, such as when they feel strong pressure to adopt a certain attitude or belief (Sensenig and Brehm 1968). In short, many people do not like being told what or how to think. As a result, they may actively defy corrections that seem overly authoritative (Garrett et al. 2013; Weeks and Garrett 2014). Misperceptions may thus be even more difficult to remedy for individuals who eschew conformity. Indeed, across countries, anti-vaccination attitudes are significantly and positively correlated with psychological reactance (Hornsey, Harris, and Fielding 2018). Moreover, several studies document a link between psychological reactance and resistance to climate change messaging (Nisbet et al. 2015; Ma, Dixon, and Hmielowski 2019). A deeper focus on psychological reactance may therefore help reconcile previously perplexing findings in the misinformation literature. Some accounts of the continued influence effect posit that individuals continue to endorse misinformation because they do not believe corrections to be true (Guillory and Geraci 2013). This tendency may be heightened among those with a contrarian streak. In addition, several scholars caution against providing too many corrections ("overkill" backfire effects, see Cook and Lewandowsky 2011; Lewandowsky et al. 2012; Ecker et al. 2019). The purported perils of overcorrection may have their roots in psychological reactance (Shu and Carlson 2014); inundating people with a surfeit of corrections may provoke feelings of reactance, particularly among those already liable to reject consensus views.

CONTEXTUAL FACTORS

Along with individual-level moderators of misinformation effects, contextual factors may play an important role in guiding responses to misinformation and its correction. These variables include the *content* of misinformation as well as the *environments* in which misinformation is consumed and corrected.

CONTENT-BASED FACTORS

The actual substance of misinformation – including its subject matter and tone – is an important determinant of its correctability. First, corrections maybe differentially effective across issue areas. For example, in a meta-analysis of studies of misinformation correction, Walter and Murphy (2018) find that corrections are more effective for health-focused misinformation than for political and scientific misinformation. Second, misinformation may vary in its affective content. Negatively valenced misinformation tends to be more durable than positive or neutral misinformation (Forgas, Laham, and Vargas2005; Guillory and Geraci 2016; but see Mirandola and Toffalini 2016). Moreover, the emotions that misinformation arouses may also influence its persistence (Vosoughi et al. 2018). In particular, Weeks (2015) finds that feelings of anger tend to encourage directionally motivated processing of corrections, whereas feelings of anxiety tend to reduce partisan differences in responses to corrections. However, misinformation does not seem to inspire these emotions in equal measure. Text analysis of comments on Facebook posts containing misinformation finds that responses to misinformation are more frequently characterized by anger as opposed to anxiety (Barfar 2019).

ENVIRONMENTAL FACTORS

How people encounter misinformation may also influence both their contact with and their responses to corrections. Although misinformation is an age- old problem, the topic has garnered attention in recent years due to concerns about how the *Internet* – and especially *social media* – might extend its reach.

Many producers of misinformation use social media sites as their main means of disseminating misinformation (Tucker et al. 2018). Reflecting this fact, several recent studies emphasize the role of social networking sites, including Facebook and Twitter, in amplifying exposure to fake news content (Allcott and Gentzkow 2017; Allcott, Gentzkow, and Yu 2019; Guess, Nyhan, and Reifler 2020). However, some work suggests that exposure to fake news on social media is limited to only a small subset of the population (Grinberg et al. 2019; Guess et al. 2019), and others find that social media use is only weakly associated with the endorsement of false information (Garrett 2019).

Even if misinformation may propagate easily via social media, these platforms may be essential to combating its spread. After all, social media can spread corrections in addition to misinformation (Vraga 2019). Much work focuses on efforts by social media sites to prevent the spread of misinformation or other harmful rhetoric in the first place (for reviews, see Guess and Lyons, Chapter 2, and Siegel, Chapter 4, this volume). However, social media platforms can also play an active role in correcting misinformation after the fact. To this end, scholars have studied the effectiveness of two types of social media-based corrections: algorithmic and social corrections. Some social media sites have built-in functionalities that can be deployed to combat misinformation. For example, Bode and Vraga (2015, 2018) focus on Facebook's "related stories" feature, which recommends relevant articles underneath shared links, and find that fact-checking articles publicized through this system may be effective in increasing belief accuracy – especially on issues where individuals do not possess strong prior attitudes. Another proposed form of algorithmic correction relies on "crowd sourced" data on the trustworthiness of different news outlets to decrease the likelihood that individuals will encounter posts from unreliable sources (Pennycook and Rand 2019). In Addition to These Algorithmic

Corrections, other social media users (e.g., Facebook friends or Twitter followers) can intervene to provide corrections (Vraga and Bode 2018). These social corrections may be especially effective, as individuals are more likely to accept corrections from people they already know (Friggeri et al. 2014; Margolin et al. 2018).

However, some scholars caution about the potential for social media to undermine the correction of misinformation. The "social" nature of social media may increase levels of exposure to misinformation, as individuals are more likely to read news that has been shared or endorsed by members of their social networks (Messing and Westwood 2014; Anspach 2017). The nature of the social media environment may also inhibit corrections of misinformation; Jun, Meng, and Johar (2017) warn that people are less likely to fact-check statements in social settings – a form of "virtual bystander effect." Furthermore, even if corrections circulate on social media, individuals may be more attentive to user comments on these posts than to the actual fact-checking messages themselves. If these comments distort or otherwise misrepresent corrections, individuals may not become better informed, despite their exposure to fact-checking information (Anspach and Carlson 2018).

Finally, and most importantly, corrective efforts on social media may have unintended consequences. Given the difficulties of correcting misinformation post exposure, many scholars recommend preemptive interventions designed to induce skepticism prior to misinformation exposure (Ecker et al. 2010; Peter and Koch 2016; Cook, Lewandowsky, and Ecker 2017). Specifically, some scholars recommend training individuals to detect and resist misinformation by highlighting the techniques commonly deployed by creators of misinformation (Roozenbeek and van der Linden 2019a, 2019b). Social networking sites have adopted similar models. For example, after the 2016 US presidential election, Facebook rolled out a new system to flag potentially inaccurate stories as disputed or false. Warning labels of this sort may be effective in reducing the sharing of flagged stories (Mena 2019).

However, false stories that go undetected by this system may be viewed as more accurate than they would have were the system never put in place (Pennycook et al. 2020). Similarly, general warnings about the potentially misleading nature of social media posts may decrease beliefs in the accuracy of true headlines (Clayton et al. 2019), suggesting that corrections issued on social media might inadvertently erode trust in credible media content.

EXPOSURE TO FACT CHECKS

Only a small subset of the population will likely encounter both misinformation and corrections. On the misinformation side, while some types of misinformation are widespread (e.g., the birther movement), many remain fringe beliefs. Despite rampant fears about "fake news," fake newssites during the 2016 and 2018 elections received the bulk of their traffic from a very small set of highly partisan consumers (Grinberg et al. 2019; Guess et al. 2019, 2020). On the corrections side, a limited number of people view a limited number of corrections. Relatively few people ever visit professional fact-checking sites, such as PolitiFact or Factcheck.org, without external prompting; the public appreciates fact-checking in theory but shows little interest in practice (Nyhan and Reifler 2015c). These low levels of engagement are exacerbated by patterns of selective exposure to and sharing of fact-checking messages on social media platforms (Shin and Thorson 2017; Zollo et al. 2017; Hameleers and van der Meer 2020), as partisans tend to seek out and share fact checks that reinforce their prior attitudes. If highly engaged members of the public cherry-pick favourable fact- checking messages to share with others, those exposed to these messages may observe only a narrow, unrepresentative slice of the available set of corrections.

Finally, even if individuals do take the initiative to visit fact-checking sites, these sites frequently choose to cover markedly different topics. In fact, even when their coverage does overlap, fact-checking organizations often reach diametrically opposed conclusions about the factual basis for a given piece of information (Marietta, Barker, and Bowser 2015). These potential discrepancies are consequential, as several studies of fact-checking messages find that the content of these messages (e.g., affirming or refuting information) matters more than their source (e.g., Fox News, MSNBC, or PolitiFact) in increasing belief accuracy (Wintersieck 2017; Wintersieck et al. 2018).

SUMMARY

Within both popular media and academia, concerns abound regarding the prevalence and persistence of misinformation. In an age where misinformation can diffuse rapidly via the Internet and social media, it is more imperative than ever to think creatively about how best to debunk misinformation. Although misinformation may take many forms – ranging from political rumours to disinformation – each of these forms presents a potential threat to democracy by distorting attitudes, behaviour, and public policy. Definitional concerns should therefore take a backseat to mitigating the harmful effects of misinformation. Given the potential dangers of misinformation, devising effective strategies for correction is crucial, yet previous prescriptions have often come up short. In this review, we have discussed two phenomena that may contribute to the durability of misinformation post-correction: the continued influence effect and backfire effects. Though scholars have found evidence that each of these processes undermines the effectiveness of corrections, recent works have cast doubt on their pervasiveness. In light of these findings, several areas merit further research. First, although worldview backfire effects may be less widespread than originally thought, the existence of these effects remains an open question. Efforts to isolate the conditions, both theoretical and methodological, under which worldview backfire effects are most likely to occur may help to resolve this ongoing debate. Similarly, though scholars frequently discourage the repetition of misinformation within corrections, more recent studies have cast doubt on the prevalence of familiarity backfire effects. Given that traditional methods of correction often cite the original misinformation, understanding whether and how this repetition might undercut their effectiveness is important. In particular, clarifying the conditions under which repetition is a benefit versus a hindrance may yield practical recommendations for improving the success of fact-checking sites. Finally, misinformation does not affect all individuals equally, nor is all misinformation equally persuasive. Continuing to identify these places of heterogeneity may enable more active targeting of corrections to those subgroups where misinformation is most likely to take root.

REFERENCES

Aird, M. J., Ecker, U. K. H., Swire, B., Berinsky, A. J., & Lewandowsky, S. (2018). Does truth matter to voters? The effects of correcting political misinformation in an Australian sample. Royal Society Open Science, 5(12), 180593. https://doi.org/ 10.1098/rsos.180593

Allcott, H., & Gentzkow, M. (2017). Social media and fake news in the 2016 election. Journal of Economic Perspectives, 31(2), 211–236. https://doi.org/10.1257/ jep.31.2.211

Allcott, H., Gentzkow, M., & Yu, C. (2019). Trends in the diffusion of misinformation on social media. Research & Politics, 6(2), 2053168019848554.https://doi.org/ 10.1177/2053168019848554

Alter, A. L., & Oppenheimer, D. M. (2009). Uniting the tribes of fluency to form a meta cognitive nation. Personality and Social Psychology Review, 13(3), 219–235. https://doi.org/10.1177/1088868309341564

Amazeen, M. A., Thorson, E., Muddiman, A., & Graves, L. (2016). Correcting political and consumer misperceptions: The effectiveness and effects of rating scale versus contextual correction formats. Journalism & Mass Communication Quarterly, 95 (1), 28–48. https://doi.org/10.1177/1077699016678186

Amazeen, M. A., Vargo, C. J., & Hopp, T. (2018). Reinforcing attitudes in a gate watching news era: Individual-level antecedents to sharing fact-checks on social media. Communication Monographs, 86(1), 112–132. https://doi.org/ 10.1080/03637751.2018.1521984

Anspach, N. M. (2017). The new personal influence: How our Facebook friends influence the news we read. Political Communication, 34(4), 590–606. https://doi.org/10.1080/10584609.2017.1316329

Anspach, N. M., & Carlson, T. N. (2018). What to believe? Social media commentary and belief in misinformation. Political Behaviour, 1–22. https://doi.org/10.1007/ s11109-018-9515-z

Bago, B., Rand, D., & Pennycook, G. (2020). Fake news, fast and slow: Deliberation reduces belief in false (but not true) news headlines. Journal of Experimental Psychology: General. https://doi.org/10.1037/xge0000729

Barfar, A. (2019). Cognitive and affective responses to political disinformation inFacebook. Computers in Human Behavior, 101, 173–179. https://doi.org/10.1016/j.chb.2019.07.026

Barrera, O. D., Guriev, S. M., Henry, E., & Zhuravskaya, E. (2020). Facts, alternative facts, and fact checking in times of post-truth politics. Journal of Public Economics, 182, 104123. https://doi.org/10.1016/j.jpubeco.2019.104123

Benegal, S. D., & Scruggs, L. A. (2018). Correcting misinformation about climate change: The impact of partisanship in an experimental setting. Climatic Change, 148(1–2), 61–80. https://doi.org/10.1007/s10584-018-2192-4

Berinsky, A. J. (2012). Rumours, truths, and reality: A study of political misinformation. Working Paper, Massachusetts Institute of Technology. (2017). Rumours and health care reform: Experiments in political misinformation. British Journal of Political Science, 47(2), 241–262. https://doi.org/10.1017/ S0007123415000186

Bode, L., & Vraga, E. K. (2015). In related news, that was wrong: The correction of misinformation through related stories functionality in social media: In related news. Journal of Communication, 65(4), 619–638. https://doi.org/10.1111/ jcom.12166

(2018). See something, say something: Correction of global health misinformation on social media. Health Communication, 33(9), 1131–1140. https://doi.org/10.1080/ 10410236.2017.1331312

Born, K., & Edgington, N. (2017). Analysis of Philanthropic Opportunities to Mitigate the Disinformation/Propaganda Problem. Hewlett Foundation report. https://hewlett.org/ wp-content/uploads/2017/11/Hewlett-Disinformation-Propaganda-Report.pdf

Bronstein, M. V., Pennycook, G., Bear, A., Rand, D. G., & Cannon, T. D. (2019). Beliefin fake news is associated with delusionality, dogmatism, religious fundamentalism, and reduced analytic thinking. Journal of Applied Research in Memory and Cognition, 8(1), 108–117. https://doi.org/10.1016/j.jarmac.2018.09.005

Cameron, K. A., Roloff, M. E., Friesema, E. M. et al. (2013). Patient knowledge and recall of health information following exposure to "facts and myths" message format variations. Patient Education and Counseling, 92(3), 381–387. https://doi.org/10.1016/j.pec.2013.06.017

Carnahan, D., Hao, Q., Jiang, X., & Lee, H. (2018). Feeling fine about being wrong: The influence of self-affirmation on the effectiveness of corrective information. Human Communication Research, 44(3), 274–298. https://doi.org/10.1093/hcr/hqy001

Chan, M. S., Jones, C. R., Hall Jamieson, K., & Albarracín, D. (2017). Debunking: A meta-analysis of the psychological efficacy of messages countering misinformation. Psychological Science, 28(11), 1531–1546. https://doi.org/ 10.1177/0956797617714579

Clayton, K., Blair, S., Busam, J. A. et al. (2019). Real solutions for fake news? Measuring the effectiveness of general warnings and fact-check tags in reducing belief in false stories on social media. Political Behaviour, 1–23. https://doi.org/10.1007/s11109- 019-09533-0

Cohen, G. L., Aronson, J., & Steele, C. M. (2000). When beliefs yield to evidence: Reducing biased evaluation by affirming the self. Personality and Social Psychology Bulletin, 26(9), 1151–1164. https://doi.org/10.1177/01461672002611011

Cohen, G. L., Sherman, D. K., Bastardi, A., Hsu, L., McGoey, M., & Ross, L. (2007).Bridging the partisan divide: Self-affirmation reduces ideological closed-mindedness and inflexibility in negotiation. Journal of Personality and Social Psychology, 93(3), 415–430. https://doi.org/10.1037/0022-3514.93.3.415

Cook, J., & Lewandowsky, S. (2011). The Debunking Handbook. St. Lucia: University of Queensland. http://sks.to/debunk

Cook, J., Lewandowsky, S., & Ecker, U. K. H. (2017). Neutralizing misinformation through inoculation: Exposing misleading argumentation techniques reduces their influence. PLoS ONE, 12(5), e0175799. https://doi.org/10.1371/journal.pone.0175799

De keersmaecker, J., & Roets, A. (2017). "Fake news": Incorrect, but hard to correct. The role of cognitive ability on the impact of false information on social impressions. Intelligence, 65, 107–110. https://doi.org/10.1016/j.intell.2017.10.005

De keersmaecker, J., Dunning, D., Pennycook, G. et al. (2020). Investigating the robustness of the illusory truth effect across individual differences in cognitive ability, need for cognitive closure, and cognitive style. Personality and Social Psychology Bulletin, 46(2), 204–215. https://doi.org/10.1177/0146167219853844

DiFonzo, N., Beckstead, J. W., Stupak, N., & Walders, K. (2016). Validity judgments of rumours heard multiple times: The shape of the truth effect. Social Influence, 11(1), 22–39. https://doi.org/10.1080/15534510.2015.1137224

Ditto, P. H., Liu, B. S., Clark, C. J. et al. (2019). At least bias is bipartisan: A meta-analytic comparison of partisan bias in liberals and conservatives. Perspectives on Psychological Science, 14(2), 273–291.

Druckman, J. N., & McGrath, M. C. (2019). The evidence for motivated reasoning in climate change preference formation. Nature Climate Change, 9(2), 111–119. https://doi.org/10.1038/s41558-018-0360-1

Ecker, U. K. H., & Ang, L. C. (2019). Political attitudes and the processing of misinformation corrections. Political Psychology, 40(2), 241–260. https://doi.org/ 10.1111/pops.12494

Ecker, U. K. H., Hogan, J. L., & Lewandowsky, S. (2017). Reminders and repetition of misinformation: Helping or hindering its retraction? Journal of Applied Research in Memory and Cognition, 6(2), 185–192. https://doi.org/10.1016/j.jarmac.2017.01.014

Ecker, U. K. H., Lewandowsky, S., Cheung, C. S. C., & Maybery, M. T. (2015). He did it! She did it! No, she did not! Multiple causal explanations and the continued influence of misinformation. Journal of Memory and Language, 85, 101–115. https://doi.org/10.1016/j.jml.2015.09.002

Ecker, U. K. H., Lewandowsky, S., Fenton, O., & Martin, K. (2014). Do people keep believing because they want to? Pre-existing attitudes and the continued influence of misinformation. Memory & Cognition, 42(2), 292–304. https://doi.org/10.3758/ s13421-013-0358-x

Ecker, U. K. H., Lewandowsky, S., Jayawardana, K., & Mladenovic, A. (2019). Refutations of equivocal claims: No evidence for an ironic effect of counter argument number. Journal of Applied Research in Memory and Cognition, 8(1), 98–107. https://doi.org/10.1016/j.jarmac.2018.07.005

Ecker, U. K. H., Lewandowsky, S., Swire, B., & Chang, D. (2011). Correcting false information in memory: Manipulating the strength of misinformation encoding and its retraction. Psychonomic Bulletin & Review, 18(3), 570–578. https://doi.org/ 10.3758/s13423-011-0065-1

Ecker, U. K. H., Lewandowsky, S., & Tang, D. T. W. (2010). Explicit warnings reduce but do not eliminate the continued influence of misinformation. Memory & Cognition, 38(8), 1087–1100. https://doi.org/10.3758/MC.38.8.1087

Faris, R., Roberts, H., Etling, B., Bourassa, N., Zuckerman, E., & Benkler, Y. (2017). Partisanship, propaganda, and disinformation: Online media and the 2016 U.S. presidential election. Berkman Klein Center for Internet & Society at Harvard University research publication. https://dash.harvard.edu/handle/1/33759251 Fazio, L. K., Brashier, N. M., Payne, B. K., & Marsh, E. J. (2015). Knowledge does not protect against illusory truth. Journal of (5), 993–1002. https://doi.org/10.1037/xge0000098

Feinberg, M., & Willer, R. (2015). From gulf to bridge: When do moral arguments facilitate political influence? Personality and Social Psychology Bulletin, 41(12), 1665–1681. https://doi.org/10.1177/0146167215607842

Fetzer, J. H. (2004). Disinformation: The use of false information. Minds & Machines,14(2), 231–240.

Flynn, D. J., Nyhan, B., & Reifler, J. (2017). The nature and origins of misperceptions: Understanding false and unsupported beliefs about politics. Political Psychology, 38(S1), 127–150. https://doi.org/10.1111/pops.12394

Forgas, J. P., Laham, S. M., & Vargas, P. T. (2005). Mood effects on eyewitness memory:Affective influences on susceptibility to misinformation. Journal of Experimental Social Psychology, 41(6), 574–588. https://doi.org/10.1016/j.jesp.2004.11.005

Friggeri, A., Adamic, L. A., Eckles, D., & Cheng, J. (2014). Rumor cascades. In Proceedings of the Eighth International AAAI Conference on Weblogs and Social Media (pp. 101–110). Palo Alto, CA: AAAI Press.

Frimer, J. A., Skitka, L. J., & Motyl, M. (2017). Liberals and conservatives are similarly motivated to avoid exposure to one another's opinions. Journal of Experimental Social Psychology, 72, 1–12. https://doi.org/10.1016/j.jesp.2017.04.003

Garrett, R. K. (2019). Social media's contribution to political misperceptions in U.S. presidential elections. PLoS ONE, 14(3), e0213500. https://doi.org/10.1371/journal.pone.0213500

Garrett, R. K., Nisbet, E. C., & Lynch, E. K. (2013). Undermining the corrective effects of media-based political fact checking? The role of contextual cues and naïve theory. Journal of Communication, 63(4), 617–637. https://doi.org/10.1111/jcom.12038

Gordon, A., Brooks, J. C. W., Quadflieg, S., Ecker, U. K. H., & Lewandowsky, S. (2017). Exploring the neural substrates of misinformation processing. Neuropsychologia, 106, 216–224. https://doi.org/10.1016/j.neuropsychologia.2017.10.003

Grinberg, N., Joseph, K., Friedland, L., Swire-Thompson, B., & Lazer, D. (2019). Fake news on Twitter during the 2016 U.S. presidential election. Science, 363(6425), 374–378.

Guess, A., & Coppock, A. (2018). Does counter-attitudinal information cause backlash? Results from three large survey experiments. British Journal of Political Science, 1- 19. https://doi.org/10.1017/S0007123418000327

Guess, A., Nagler, J., & Tucker, J. (2019). Less than you think: Prevalence and predictors of fake news dissemination on Facebook. Science Advances, 5(1), eaau4586.

Guess, A., Nyhan, B., & Reifler, J. (2020). Exposure to untrustworthy websites in the 2016 US election. Nature Human Behaviour, 1–9. https://doi.org/10.1038/s41562- 020-0833-x

Guillory, J. J., & Geraci, L. (2013). Correcting erroneous inferences in memory: The role of source credibility. Journal of Applied Research in Memory and Cognition, 2(4), 201–209. https://doi.org/10.1016/j.jarmac.2013.10.001

Guillory, J. J., & Geraci, L. (2016). The persistence of erroneous information in memory: The effect of valence on the acceptance of corrected information. Applied Cognitive Psychology, 30(2), 282–288. https://doi.org/10.1002/acp.3183

Haglin, K. (2017). The limitations of the backfire effect. Research & Politics, 4(3), 1–5. https://doi.org/10.1177/2053168017716547

Hameleers, M., & van der Meer, T. G. L. A. (2020). Misinformation and polarization in a high-choice media environment: How effective are political fact-checkers? Communication Research, 47(2), 227–250.

Hart, P. S., & Nisbet, E. C. (2012). Boomerang effects in science communication: Howmotivated reasoning and identity cues amplify opinion polarization about climate mitigation policies. Communication Research, 39(6), 701–723. https://doi.org/ 10.1177/0093650211416646

Hochschild, J. L., & Einstein, K. L. (2015). Do Facts Matter? Information and Misinformation in American Politics (1st ed.). Norman: University of Oklahoma Press.

Holman, M. R., & Lay, J. C. (2019). They see dead people (voting): Correcting misperceptions about voter fraud in the 2016 U.S. presidential election. Journal of Political Marketing, 18(1–2), 31–68. https://doi.org/10.1080/ 15377857.2018.1478656

Hornsey, M. J., Harris, E. A., & Fielding, K. S. (2018). The psychological roots of anti- vaccination attitudes: A 24-nation investigation. Health Psychology, 37(4), 307– 315. https://doi.org/10.1037/hea0000586

Iannucci, R., & Adair, B. (2017). Heroes or Hacks: The Partisan Divide Over Fact- Checking. DukeReporters' Labreport. https://drive.google.com/file/d/ 0BxoyrEbZxrAMNm9HV2tvcXFma1U/view?usp=embed_facebook

Jardina, A., & Traugott, M. (2019). The genesis of the birther rumour: Partisanship, racial attitudes, and political knowledge. The Journal of Race, Ethnicity, and Politics, 4 (1), 60–80. https://doi.org/10.1017/rep.2018.25

Johnson, H. M., & Seifert, C. M. (1994). Sources of the continued influence effect: Whenmisinformation in memory affects later inferences. Journal of Experimental Psychology: Learning, Memory, and Cognition, 20(6), 1420–1436. https://doi.org/10.1037/0278-7393.20.6.1420

Jost, J. T., Glaser, J., Kruglanski, A. W., & Sulloway, F. J. (2003). Political conservatism as motivated social cognition. Psychological Bulletin, 129(3), 339–375. https://doi.org/10.1037/0033-2909.129.3.339

Jost, J. T., van der Linden, S., Panagopoulos, C., & Hardin, C. D. (2018). Ideological asymmetries in conformity, desire for shared reality, and the spread of misinformation. Current Opinion in Psychology, 23, 77–83. https://doi.org/ 10.1016/j.copsyc.2018.01.003

Jun, Y., Meng, R., & Johar, G. V. (2017). Perceived social presence reduces fact-checking. Proceedings of the National Academy of Sciences, 114(23), 5976–5981. https://doi.org/10.1073/pnas.1700175114

Kahan, D. M. (2013). Ideology, motivated reasoning, and cognitive reflection. Judgment and Decision Making, 8(4), 407–424.

Kahan, D. M., Braman, D., Monahan, J., Callahan, L., & Peters, E. (2010). Cultural cognition and public policy: The case of outpatient commitment laws. Law and Human Behavior, 34(2), 118–140. https://doi.org/10.1007/s10979-008-9174-4

Kahan, D. M., Jenkins-Smith, H., & Braman, D. (2011). Cultural cognition of scientific consensus. Journal of Risk Research, 14(2), 147–174. https://doi.org/10.1080/ 13669877.2010.511246

Kasra, M., Shen, C., & O'Brien, J. (2016). Seeing is believing: Do people fail to identify fake images on the Web? Paper presented at AoIR 2016: The 17th Annual Conference of the Association of Internet Researchers, October 5–8, Berlin, Germany.

Keeley, B. L. (1999). Of conspiracy theories. The Journal of Philosophy, 96(3), 109–126. https://doi.org/10.2307/2564659

Khanna, K., & Sood, G. (2018). Motivated responding in studies of factual learning. Political Behavior, 40(1), 79–101. https://doi.org/10.1007/s11109-017-9395-7

Kuklinski, J. H., Quirk, P. J., Jerit, J., Schweider, D., & Rich, R. F. (2000). Misinformation and the currency of democratic citizenship. The Journal of Politics, 62(3), 790–816.

Kunda, Z. (1990). The case for motivated reasoning. Psychological Bulletin, 108(3), 480–498.

Lazer, D. M. J., Baum, M. A., Benkler, Y. et al. (2018). The science of fake news. Science, 359(6380), 1094–1096. https://doi.org/10.1126/science.aao2998

Leman, P. J., & Cinnirella, M. (2013). Beliefs in conspiracy theories and the need for cognitive closure. Frontiers in Psychology, 4(378), 1–10. https://doi.org/10.3389/ fpsyg.2013.00378

Lewandowsky, S., Ecker, U. K. H., Seifert, C. M., Schwarz, N., & Cook, J. (2012). Misinformation and its correction: Continued influence and successful debiasing. Psychological Science in the Public Interest, 13(3), 106–131. https://doi.org/ 10.1177/1529100612451018

Lodge, M., & Taber, C. S. (2013). The Rationalizing Voter. Cambridge: Cambridge University Press.

Ma, Y., Dixon, G., & Hmielowski, J. D. (2019). Psychological reactance from reading basic facts on climate change: The role of prior views and political identification. Environmental Communication, 13(1), 71–86. https://doi.org/ 10.1080/17524032.2018.1548369

Marchlewska, M., Cichocka, A., & Kossowska, M. (2018). Addicted to answers: Need for cognitive closure and the endorsement of conspiracy beliefs. European Journal of Social Psychology, 48(2), 109–117. https://doi.org/10.1002/ejsp.2308

Margolin, D. B., Hannak, A., & Weber, I. (2018). Political fact-checking on Twitter: When do corrections have an effect? Political Communication, 35(2), 196–219. https://doi.org/10.1080/10584609.2017.1334018

Marietta, M., Barker, D. C., & Bowser, T. (2015). Fact-checking polarized politics: Does the fact-check industry provide consistent guidance on disputed realities? The Forum, 13(4), 577–596. https://doi.org/10.1515/for-2015-0040

McGinnies, E., & Ward, C. D. (1980). Better liked than right: Trustworthiness and expertise as factors in credibility. Personality and Social Psychology Bulletin, 6(3),467–472.

Meirick, P. C., & Bessarabova, E. (2016). Epistemic factors in selective exposure and political misperceptions on the right and left: Epistemic factors in news use and misperceptions. Analyses of Social Issues and Public Policy, 16(1), 36–68. https:// doi.org/10.1111/asap.12101

Mena, P. (2019). Cleaning up social media: The effect of warning labels on likelihood of sharing false news on Facebook. Policy & Internet. https://doi.org/10.1002/ poi3.214

Messing, S., & Westwood, S. J. (2014). Selective exposure in the age of social media: Endorsements trump partisan source affiliation when selecting news online. Communication Research, 41(8), 1042–1063. https://doi.org/10.1177/0093650212466406

Miller, J. M., Saunders, K. L., & Farhart, C. E. (2016). Conspiracy endorsement as motivated reasoning: The moderating roles of political knowledge and trust. American Journal of Political Science, 60(4), 824–844. https://doi.org/10.1111/ ajps.12234

Mirandola, C., & Toffalini, E. (2016). Arousal – but not valence – reduces false memories at retrieval. PLoS ONE, 11(3) https://doi.org/10.1371/journal.pone.0148716

Moulding, R., Nix-Carnell, S., Schnabel, A. et al. (2016). Better the devil you know than a world you don't? Intolerance of uncertainty and worldview explanations for belief in conspiracy theories. Personality and Individual Differences, 98, 345–354. https:// doi.org/10.1016/j.paid.2016.04.060

Nam, H. H., Jost, J. T., & Van Bavel, J. J. (2013). "Not for all the tea in China!" Political ideology and the avoidance of dissonance-arousing situations. PLoS ONE, 8(4), e59837. https://doi.org/10.1371/journal.pone.0059837

Nisbet, E. C., Cooper, K. E., & Garrett, R. K. (2015). The partisan brain: How dissonant science messages lead conservatives and liberals to (dis)trust science. The ANNALS of the American Academy of Political and Social Science, 658(1), 36–66. https://doi.org/10.1177/0002716214555474

Nyhan, B. (2010). Why the "death panel" myth wouldn't die: Misinformation in the health care reform debate. The Forum, 8(1). https://doi.org/10.2202/1540- 8884.1354

Nyhan, B., Porter, E., Reifler, J., & Wood, T. J. (2019). Taking fact-checks literally but not seriously? The effects of journalistic fact-checking on factual beliefs and candidate favorability. Political Behaviour. https://doi.org/10.1007/s11109-019- 09528-x

Nyhan, B., & Reifler, J. (2010). When corrections fail: The persistence of political misperceptions. Political Behaviour, 32(2), 303–330. https://doi.org/10.1007/ s11109-010-9112-2

(2015a). Displacing misinformation about events: An experimental test of causal corrections. Journal of Experimental Political Science, 2(1), 81–93. https://doi. org/10.1017/XPS.2014.22

(2015b). Does correcting myths about the flu vaccine work? An experimental evaluation of the effects of corrective information. Vaccine, 33(3), 459–464. https://doi.org/10.1016/j.vaccine.2014.11.017

(2015c). Estimating fact-checking's effects: Evidence from a long-term experiment during campaign 2014. Working Paper, American Press Institute.

(2019). The roles of information deficits and identity threat in the prevalence of misperceptions. Journal of Elections, Public Opinion, and Parties, 29(2), 222– 244. https://doi.org/10.1080/17457289.2018.1465061

Nyhan, B., Reifler, J., Richey, S., & Freed, G. L. (2014). Effective messages in vaccine promotion: A randomized trial. Pediatrics, 133(4), e835–e842. https://doi.org/ 10.1542/peds.2013-2365

Nyhan, B., Reifler, J., & Ubel, P. A. (2013). The hazards of correcting myths about health care reform. Medical Care, 51(2), 127–132. https://doi.org/10.1097/ MLR.0b013e318279486b

Oliver, J. E., & Wood, T. J. (2014). Conspiracy theories and the paranoid style(s) of mass opinion. American Journal of Political Science, 58(4), 952–966. https://doi.org/ 10.1111/ajps.12084

Pennycook, G., Bear, A., Collins, E. T., & Rand, D. G. (2020). The implied truth effect: Attaching warnings to a subset of fake news stories increases perceived accuracy of stories without warnings. Management Science. https://doi.org/10.1287/ mnsc.2019.3478

Pennycook, G., Cannon, T. D., & Rand, D. G. (2018). Prior exposure increases perceived accuracy of fake news. Journal of Experimental Psychology: General, 147(12), 1865–1880. https://doi.org/10.1037/xge0000465

Pennycook, G., & Rand, D. G. (2018). Lazy, not biased: Susceptibility to partisan fake news is better explained by lack of reasoning than by motivated reasoning. Cognition, 188, 39–50. https://doi.org/10.1016/j.cognition.2018.06.011

(2019). Fighting misinformation on social media using crowd sourced judgments of news source quality. Proceedings of the National Academy of Sciences, 116(7), 2521–2526. https://doi.org/10.1073/pnas.1806781116

(2020). Who falls for fake news? The roles of bullshit receptivity, over claiming, familiarity, and analytic thinking. Journal of Personality, 88(2), 185–200. https:// doi.org/10.1111/jopy.12476

Peter, C., & Koch, T. (2016). When debunking scientific myths fails (and when it does not): The backfire effect in the context of journalistic coverage and immediate judgments as prevention strategy. Science Communication, 38(1), 3–25. https:// doi.org/10.1177/1075547015613523

Pluviano, S., Watt, C., & Della Sala, S. (2017). Misinformation lingers in memory: Failure of three pro-vaccination strategies. PLoS ONE, 12(7), 1–15. https:// doi.org/10.1371/journal.pone.0181640

Porter,E.,Wood,T.J.,&Bahador,B.(2019).Canpresidentialmisinformationonclimate changebecorrected?EvidencefromInternetandphoneexperiments. Research & Politics, 6(3). https://doi.org/10.1177/2053168019864784

Porter, E., Wood, T. J., & Kirby, D. (2018). Sex trafficking, Russian infiltration, birth certificates, and pedophilia: A survey experiment correcting fake news. Journal of Experimental Political Science, 5(2), 159–164. https://doi. org/10.1017/XPS.2017.32

Rapp, D. N., & Salovich, N. A. (2018). Can't we just disregard fake news? The consequences of exposure to inaccurate information. Policy Insights from the Behavioural and Brain Sciences, 5(2), 232–239.

Redlawsk, D. P., Civettini, A. J. W., & Emmerson, K. M. (2010). The affective tipping point: Do motivated reasoners ever "get it"? Political Psychology, 31(4), 563–593. https://doi.org/10.1111/j.1467-9221.2010.00772.x

Richards, Z., & Hewstone, M. (2001). Subtyping and subgrouping: Processes for the prevention and promotion of stereotype change. Personality and Social PsychologyReview, 5(1), 52–73. https://doi.org/10.1207/ S15327957PSPR0501_4

Roozenbeek, J., & van der Linden, S. (2019a). Fake news game confers psychological resistance against online misinformation. Palgrave Communications, 5(1), 1–10. https://doi.org/10.1057/s41599-019-0279-9

(2019b). The fake news game: Actively inoculating against the risk of misinformation. Journal of Risk Research, 22(5), 570–580. https://doi.org/10.1080/13669877.2 018.1443491

Schaffner, B. F., & Roche, C. (2017). Misinformation and motivated reasoning. Public Opinion Quarterly, 81(1), 86–110. https://doi.org/10.1093/poq/nfw043

Schwarz, N., Newman, E., & Leach, W. (2016). Making the truth stick & the myths fade: Lessons from cognitive psychology. Behavioural Science & Policy, 2(1), 85–95. https://doi.org/10.1353/bsp.2016.0009

Schwarz, N., Sanna, L. J., Skurnik, I., & Yoon, C. (2007). Meta cognitive experiences and the intricacies of setting people straight: Implications for debiasing and public information campaigns. Advances in Experimental Social Psychology, 39, 127– 161. https://doi.org/10.1016/S0065-2601(06)39003-X

Sensenig, J., & Brehm, J. W. (1968). Attitude change from an implied threat to attitudinal freedom. Journal of Personality and Social Psychology, 8(4, Pt.1), 324–330. https://doi.org/10.1037/h0021241

Shearer, E., & Matsa, K. E. (2018). News Use Across Social Media Platforms 2018. Pew Research Center report. https://www.journalism.org/2018/09/10/news-use-across- social-media-platforms-2018/

Shen, C., Kasra, M., Pan, W., Bassett, G. A., Malloch, Y., & O'Brien, J. F. (2019). Fake images: The effects of source, intermediary, and digital media literacy on contextual assessment of image credibility online. New Media & Society, 21(2), 438–463.

Shin, J., & Thorson, K. (2017). Partisan selective sharing: The biased diffusion of fact-checking messages on social media: Sharing fact-checking messages on social media. Journal of Communication, 67(2), 233–255. https://doi.org/10.1111/jcom.12284

Shu, S. B., & Carlson, K. A. (2014). When three charms but four alarms: Identifying the optimal number of claims in persuasion settings. Journal of Marketing, 78(1), 127– 139. https://doi.org/10.1509/jm.11.0504

Skurnik, I., Yoon, C., & Schwarz, N. (2007). "Myths & Facts" about the flu: Health education campaigns can reduce vaccination intentions. http://webuser.bus.umich.edu/yoonc/research/Papers/ Skurnik%5 FYoon%5 FSchwarz% 5 F 2005 % 5 FMyths% 5 FFacts% 5 FFlu%5 FHealth% 5F Education%5F Campaigns%5F JAMA.pdf Stahl, B. C. (2006). On the difference or equality of information, misinformation, and disinformation: A critical research perspective. Informing Science: The International Journal of an Emerging Trans-discipline, 9, 83–96. https://doi.org/ 10.28945/473

Swami, V., Voracek, M., Stieger, S., Tran, U. S., & Furnham, A. (2014). Analytic thinking reduces belief in conspiracy theories. Cognition, 133(3), 572–585. https://doi.org/10.1016/j.cognition.2014.08.006

Swire, B., Berinsky, A. J., Lewandowsky, S., & Ecker, U. K. H. (2017). Processing political misinformation: Comprehending the Trump phenomenon. Royal Society Open Science, 4(3), 160802. https://doi.org/10.1098/rsos.160802

Swire, B., & Ecker, U. (2018). Misinformation and its correction: Cognitive mechanisms and recommendations for mass communication. In B. Southwell, E. A. Thorson, &L. Sheble (Eds.), Misinformation and Mass Audiences (pp. 195–211). Austin, TX: University of Texas Press. *https://utpress.utexas.edu/books/southwell-thorson-sheble-misinformation-and-mass-audiences*

Swire, B., Ecker, U. K. H., & Lewandowsky, S. (2017). The role of familiarity in correcting inaccurate information. Journal of Experimental Psychology: Learning, Memory, and Cognition, 43(12), 1948–1961. https://doi.org/10.1037/xlm0000422

Tandoc, E. C., Lim, Z. W., & Ling, R. (2018). Defining "fake news": A typology of scholarly definitions. Digital Journalism, 6(2), 137–153. https://doi.org/10.1080/ 21670811.2017.1360143

Tappin, B. M., Pennycook, G., & Rand, D. (2018). Rethinking the link between cognitive sophistication and identity-protective bias in political belief formation. PsyArXiv.org. https://doi.org/10.31234/osf.io/yuzfj

Thorson, E. (2015). Identifying and correcting policy misperceptions. Unpublished paper. http://www.americanpressinstitute.org/wp-content/uploads/2015/04/ Project-2-Thorson-2015-Identifying-Political-Misperceptions-UPDATED-4-24.pdf

(2016) Belief echoes: The persistent effects of corrected misinformation. Political Communication, 33(3), 460–480. https://doi.org/10.1080/10584609.2015.1102187

Trevors, G. J., Muis, K. R., Pekrun, R., Sinatra, G. M., & Winne, P. H. (2016). Identity and epistemic emotions during knowledge revision: A potential account for the backfire effect. Discourse Processes, 53(5–6), 339–370. https://doi.org/10.1080/ 0163853X.2015.1136507

Tucker, J., Guess, A., Barbera, P. et al. (2018). Social media, political polarization, and political disinformation: A review of the scientific literature. SSRN. https://doi.org/ 10.2139/ssrn.3144139

Valenzuela, S., Halpern, D., Katz, J. E., & Miranda, J. P. (2019). The paradox of participation versus misinformation: Social media, political engagement, and the spread of misinformation. Digital Journalism, 7(6), 802–823. https://doi.org/ 10.1080/21670811.2019.1623701 van der Linden, S. L., Leiserowitz, A. A., Feinberg, G. D., & Maibach, E. W. (2015). The scientific consensus on climate change as a gateway belief: Experimental evidence. PLoS ONE, 10(2), 1–8. https://doi.org/10.1371/ journal. pone.0118489

van der Linden, S. L., Leiserowitz, A., Rosenthal, S., & Maibach, E. (2017). Inoculating the public against misinformation about climate change. Global Challenges, 1(2), 1–7. https://doi.org/10.1002/gch2.201600008

Vosoughi, S., Roy, D., & Aral, S. (2018). The spread of true and false news online.Science, 359(6380), 1146–1151. https://doi.org/10.1126/science. aap9559Misinformation and Its Correction 197

Vraga, E. K. (2019). What can I do? How to use social media to improve democratic society. Political Communication, 36(2), 315–323. https://doi.org/10.1080/10584609.2019.1610620

Vraga, E. K., & Bode, L. (2017). Using expert sources to correct health misinformation in social media. Science Communication, 39(5), 621–645. https://doi.org/10.1177/ 1075547017731776

(2018). I do not believe you: How providing a source corrects health misperceptions across social media platforms. Information, Communication & Society, 21(10), 1337–1353. https://doi.org/10.1080/1369118X.2017.1313883

Walter, N., & Murphy, S. T. (2018). How to unring the bell: A meta-analytic approach to correction of misinformation. Communication Monographs, 85(3), 423–441. https://doi.org/10.1080/03637751.2018.1467564

Walter, N., & Tukachinsky, R. (2019). A meta-analytic examination of the continued influence of misinformation in the face of correction: How powerful is it, why does it happen, and how to stop it? Communication Research, 47(2), 155–177. https:// doi.org/10.1177/0093650219854600

Wardle, C. (2018). Information Disorder: The Essential Glossary. Harvard Kennedy School Shorenstein Center on Media, Politics, and Public Policy. https:// firstdraftnews.org/wp-content/uploads/2018/07/ infoDisorder_glossary.pdf

Wardle, C., & Derakhshan, H. (2017). Information Disorder: Toward an Interdisciplinary Framework for Research and Policymaking. Council of Europe Report No. DGI(2017)09. https://rm.coe.int/information-disorder-toward-an- interdisciplinary-framework-for-researc/168076277c

Weeks, B. E. (2015). Emotions, partisanship, and misperceptions: How anger and anxiety moderate the effect of partisan bias on susceptibility to political misinformation. Journal of Communication, 65(4), 699–719. https://doi.org/10.1111/jcom.12164

Weeks, B. E., & Garrett, R. K. (2014). Electoral consequences of political rumours: Motivated reasoning, candidate rumors, and vote choice during the 2008 U.S. presidential election. International Journal of Public Opinion Research, 26(4), 401–422. https://doi.org/10.1093/ijpor/edu005

Wilkes, A. L., & Leatherbarrow, M. (1988). Editing episodic memory following the identification of error. The Quarterly Journal of Experimental Psychology Section A, 40(2), 361–387. https://doi.org/10.1080/02724988843000168

Wintersieck, A., Fridkin, K., & Kenney, P. (2018). The message matters: The influence off act-checking on evaluations of political messages. Journal of Political Marketing,1–28. https://doi.org/10.1080/15377857.2018.1457591

Wintersieck, A. L. (2017). Debating the truth: The impact of fact-checking during electoral debates. American Politics Research, 45(2), 304–331. https://doi.org/ 10.1177/1532673X16686555

Wood, T., & Porter, E. (2019). The elusive backfire effect: Mass attitudes' steadfast factual adherence. Political Behaviour, 41(1), 135–163. https://doi.org/10.1007/ s11109-018-9443-y

Young, D. G., Jamieson, K. H., Poulsen, S., & Goldring, A. (2018). Fact-checking effectiveness as a function of format and tone: Evaluating FactCheck.org and FlackCheck.org. Journalism & Mass Communication Quarterly, 95(1), 49–75. https://doi.org/10.1177/1077699017710453

Zhou, J. (2016). Boomerangs versus javelins: How polarization constrains communication on climate change. Environmental Politics, 25(5), 788–811. https://doi.org/10.1080/09644016.2016.1166602

Zollo, F., Bessi, A., Del Vicario, M. et al. (2017). Debunking in a world of tribes. PLoS ONE, 12(7), e0181821. https://doi.org/10.1371/journal.pone.0181821

Zubiaga, A., Liakata, M., Procter, R., Wong Sak Hoi, G., & Tolmie, P. (2016).Analysing how people orient to and spread rumours in social media by looking at conversational threads. PLoS ONE, 11(3), 1–29. https://doi.org/10.1371/ journal. pone.0150989.

FOOTNOTE

1. Indeed, though we attempt to provide a comprehensive review of the literature on misinformation correction, the field is moving so fast that this review may soon be out of date.
2. We are certainly not the first to propose such a typology (see Born and Edgington 2017; Tucker et al. 2018; Wardle 2018). However, we take a more comprehensive view than many of these previous works in that we seek to integrate a larger number of related concepts into a common theoretical framework.

3. Other terms for worldview backfire effects include "boomerang effects" (Hart and Nisbet 2012; Garrett, Nisbet, and Lynch 2013; Zhou 2016) or "backlash" (Guess and Coppock 2018).
4. Counter arguing typically involves generating arguments to dispute a correction. Inverting this process, Chan et al. (2017) also find that corrections are generally less effective when people are asked to record arguments in favour of the original misinformation.
5. As they note, however, their experimental design includes only a short distraction task (30 minutes) separating the presentation of misinformation and its correction from measurement of their dependent variables. Although this time interval is consistent with previous studies (e.g., Skurnik, Yoon, and Schwarz 2007), it is possible that their results would be different after a longer delay.
6. This observed asymmetry, however, cannot be definitively ascribed to individual-level differences across ideological groups. For instance, there may be qualitative differences between conservative- and liberal-leaning misinformation that make the former stickier. In particular, Nyhan and Reifler's (2010) experiments rely on actual examples of misinformation (stem cell research and weapons of mass destruction in Iraq). While this approach has the benefit of greater external validity, these cases may diverge in notable ways beyond their ideological slant (e.g., issue salience or importance). Studies that focus on fabricated misinformation, rather than real-world rumours, may thus be better suited to identifying potential partisan or ideological asymmetries.
7. Of course, these factors may be correlated with political sophistication and ideology and may therefore be at the root of some of the empirical regularities cited in the "Political Factors" section.

09 CONTRASTING MEDIA REGULATION APPROACHES:

UNITED STATES AND EUROPE

INTRODUCTION: AN OVERVIEW

Media regulation is a critical aspect of the modern information landscape, ensuring the responsible dissemination of content while safeguarding freedom of expression. In this context, a comparative analysis of media regulation in the United States and Europe offers valuable insights into the contrasting approaches and their implications. The United States, known for its strong emphasis on the First Amendment, has historically favoured minimal government intervention in media, emphasizing self-regulation and market forces. In contrast, Europe has implemented a more interventionist regulatory framework, driven by concerns about protecting public interest and cultural diversity. This examination of the media regulation systems in both regions will shed light on the complexities of striking a balance between free expression and responsible media practices, making it essential in an era characterized by the rapid exchange of information and ideas.

In current debates over the Internet's impact on global democracy, the prospect of state regulation of social media has been proffered as a solution to problems like fake news, hate speech, conspiracy-mongering, and similar ills. For example, US Senator Mark Warner has proposed a bill that would enhance privacy protections required of internet platforms, create rules for labeling bot accounts, and change the legal terms of the platforms' legal relationship with their users. In Europe, regulation has already been enacted in the form of the European Union's General Data Protection Regulation (GDPR) and new laws like the Network Enforcement Law (NetzDG). This chapter will survey this rapidly developing field, putting current efforts of liberal democracies to regulate internet content in the broader perspective of legacy media regulation. As we will see, there are very different national approaches to this issue among contemporary liberal democracies, and in many respects the new internet regulations, actual and proposed, are extensions of existing practices. We conclude that, in the US case, content regulation will be very difficult to achieve politically and that antitrust should be considered as an alternative.

Media regulation is a sensitive and controversial topic in all liberal democracies. The US Constitution's First Amendment protects freedom of speech, while media freedom is guaranteed in various legal instruments governing the European Union and the Council of Europe, as well as in the European Convention on Human Rights. Freedom of speech is normatively regarded as critical to the proper functioning of a liberal democracy, and the

Francis Fukuyama is a senior fellow at the Freeman Spogli Institute for International Studies (FSI) and Mosbacher Director of the Center on Democracy, Development and the Rule of Law, Stanford University. Andrew Grotto is the William J. Perry International Security Fellow at FSI's Cyber Policy Center and Director of the Program on Geopolitics, Technology and Governance, and a visiting fellow at the Hoover Institution. The authors thank Barby Cantu, Ben Gaiarin, Veronica Kim, Bryan Metzger, and Michal Skreta for outstanding research support.

Internet was seen in its early days as a great boon to democratic discourse. Nonetheless, all modern democracies regulate media in various ways; even in the United States, where the First Amendment is regarded with great reverence, the state has over the centuries seen fit to draw boundaries around what can be said or shown on various media platforms.

In addition to normative hostility to restrictions on speech, many observers have maintained that it is not technologically possible to regulate media in the age of the Internet. The explosion of bandwidth for communications of all sorts that has occurred since the 1980s has made state control vastly more difficult than in the days when citizens relied on a handful of local and national newspapers and two or three broadcasting channels operating over finite, government-allocated radio spectrum. Regulating content on the Internet was said to be like "nailing jello to a wall" (Allen-Ebrahimian 2016) because rapid technological change would quickly outpace any government mechanisms for censorship. The sentiment that normative and technical constraints undermine state control of online content is evident in John Perry Barlow's "Declaration of the Independence of Cyberspace," in which governments were told "You have no sovereignty where we gather" (Segal 2018).

China may ultimately prove that Barlow was wrong and that a high-capacity authoritarian government is perfectly capable of controlling speech on the Internet. Indeed, China envisions applying AI/big data techniques to the monitoring of citizen behaviour under a "social credit" system. Short of this level of control, however, governments in modern liberal democracies that want to protect freedom of speech nonetheless use various mechanisms to regulate legacy media, mechanisms that have been carried forward into the digital era.

There are, however, not only large systematic differences in approach between Europe and the United States with regard to the role of the state but important differences as well among European countries. We focus here on France and Germany. These differences did not begin with internet regulation but are evident in the long prior experience of dealing with legacy media.

Modern liberal democracies do not typically regulate speech via censorship directed by the state, as in authoritarian regimes, that is, by having a government official approve or alter the content carried by a media channel. Rather, the mechanisms tend to be indirect and include controlling access to media channels through licensing; managing sources of revenue to support private media; setting broad guidance as to what type of content is deemed acceptable or not; promoting certain content through public broadcasting and other mechanisms; and establishing more or less permissive regimes for private citizens, including politicians and other public figures, to press defamation and invasion of privacy claims. In addition, states have sought to encourage self- regulation by content providers. These are the same techniques that have been carried forward into the Internet Age. An alternative approach to media regulation is antitrust. The logic here is that, in the marketplace of ideas, fair competition among ideas depends in part on meaningful competition among the platforms that carry ideas. Media pluralism, therefore, is a source of resiliency against propaganda, demagoguery, and extremism coming to dominate democratic discourse. Thus, in most liberal democracies, print media have not been subject to extensive content regulation because these markets are usually decentralized and competitive. In contrast, broadcast media, and in particular TV, have been much more highly regulated everywhere because of the formerly oligopolistic or monopolistic position of broadcasters. Today, one could argue that internet platforms like Google and Facebook occupy a position similar to that of legacy television networks: Because of their scale and reach, decisions that they take with regard to content moderation are far more consequential than for print media. An alternative to state regulation of content would therefore be antitrust actions designed to increase the number of platforms and reduce the reach of the current internet giants.

MEDIA REGULATION IN FRANCE AND GERMANY

France and Germany are the two largest media markets in continental Europe. Though media governance in France and Germany has much in common when contrasted against other European countries and the United States, noteworthy distinctions emerge when the two countries are contrasted with each other. These distinctions are interesting in their own right and as illustrations of how the two largest media markets on the European continent approach media governance. These distinctions are also important contextual factors to consider as France,

Germany, and other actors within the European Union grapple with whether and how to pursue national and/or European approaches to addressing disinformation.

Of particular relevance to the present discussion is how France and Germany differ in their respective conceptions of media pluralism and especially in the role envisioned for the state in safeguarding or promoting media pluralism. As we shall see, the two countries' initial forays into regulating problematic content on online platforms already show signs of these differences, which emerge as important historical themes in how the two countries have regulated legacy media. Hallin and Mancini (2004) present a framework for comparing media systems among the Western liberal democracies of Europe and North America based on four dimensions: the developmental arc of a mass circulation press; the nature and extent of linkages between the media and the broader political system, or political parallelism; norms and practices associated with journalistic professionalism; and the role of the state in shaping the media system. Using this framework, the authors describe three archetypical models for the relationship between a political system and its media (Hallin and Mancini 2004, pp. 73–75). These models – Polarized Pluralist, Democratic Corporatist, and Liberal – provide a useful analytic framework for assessing recent developments in the media landscape in Europe and the United States.

The media systems in these countries existed well before the Internet became a global force, and key concepts, traditions, and assumptions from these legacy governance frameworks help frame debates about whether and how to regulate internet platforms and the content they carry.

Countries described by the Polarized Pluralist model (France, Greece, Italy, Portugal, and Spain) feature an elite-oriented print media with relatively small circulation and a comparatively more popular broadcast media. Freedom of the press and the rise of commercial media industries developed relatively late in these countries. Linkages between the media and politics tend to be durable and mutually reinforcing and characterized by advocacy journalism, political parallelism, and the instrumental use of the media by political and commercial actors through regulation and/or ownership to advance their broader political and economic interests. The state tends to play a large role in regulating, owning, and/or financing media, and public broadcasting tends to be politicized.

In contrast to the Polarized Pluralist countries, the Democratic Corporatist countries (Austria, Belgium, Denmark, Finland, Germany, the Netherlands, Norway, Sweden, and Switzerland) experienced early development of press freedom and a robust commercial media industry, especially in print media where readership and circulation levels are still among the highest in Europe. Newspapers affiliated with political parties and interest groups have been common throughout their recent history, however, and political parallelism is relatively high, though declining. Advocacy journalism remains an important feature of the media landscape but coexists alongside neutral, information- oriented reporting. The media is regarded as an important social institution worthy of state support and protection, and the profession is marked by high degrees of professionalism and formal organization. Democratic Corporatist countries tend to have long traditions of liberal democracy (with Germany standing out as a notable exception, as we will see) and well-organized social groups coexisting within a corporatist framework that emphasizes consensus and rational-legal authority.

The third model is the Liberal model, which Hallin and Mancini most closely associate with Canada, Ireland, the United Kingdom, and the United States. Like the Democratic Corporatist countries, the Liberal countries also feature strong traditions of press freedom, a commercial mass-circulation press, and early development of liberal institutions. Unlike the Democratic Corporatists, however, the role of the state is generally more limited, and the media is shaped largely by market forces as opposed to partisan, ideological, or other instrumental purposes.

In both France and Germany, achieving and sustaining media pluralism is a fundamental goal of policy because it is viewed as essential to a vibrant, competitive marketplace for ideas and thus vital to democratic discourse. In France, this ideal can be traced back to the 1881 Law on the Freedom of the

Press, which established a liberal regime for the press that reflected the view of French elites in the Third Republic that the primary threat to pluralism was excessive state control of the press and that safeguards against excessive state interference were needed. The consensus among the ruling former French Resistance elites after World War II, however, was that the pendulum had swung too far in the direction of liberalization during the interwar period, with the result that press barons had accumulated too much control over the media. As Raymond Kuhn (2011) explains, "[w]hereas in 1881 the concern of the legislators had been to promote the liberty of the press by protecting it from political control of the state, in 1944 the emphasis was placed on removing economic threats to press freedom from capitalist owners" (p. 12). Thus, in 1944 France put in place a number of measures to shield the press from market pressures, including a framework for provision of financial aid from the state to print media – a practice that continues today.

For France, however, media pluralism means more than just a competitive media market; for broadcast media especially, it means a pluralism of distinctly French media that upholds and delivers French linguistic and other politico- cultural values to French citizens, in an increasingly competitive global media marketplace dominated by American popular culture (Kuhn 2011; Eko 2013).

Though France has on occasion engaged in outright censorship – perhaps most notably in the 1950s and early 1960s during the Algerian war of independence – it has more typically directed policy and state resources to promoting preferred content, through subsidies and content requirements, over outright censorship of disfavoured content. The French approach of promoting preferred content canbe seen in the political competition for influence over public broadcasting, where such competition resulted in a changing series of regulators, the Haute Autorité de la communication audiovisuelles (HACA), the Commission nationale de la communication et des libertés (CNCL), and finally the Conseilsupérieur de l'audiovisuel (CSA) in 1989.

For Germany, media pluralism is viewed as a bulwark against the return of totalitarianism. The structure of German public broadcasting, with its devolution of broadcasting governance to the Länder, reflects this orientation. Instead of establishing one or a small number of national-level public broadcasting outlets, as the British and French did, German public broadcasting is organized and managed at the German state, or Länder, level. This decentralized structure was imposed on Germany by the Allied Powers following World War II as a way of guarding against the monopolization of media power by any single political actor (Hallin and Mancini 2004). Indeed, concern about the monopolization of the German media by illiberal forces – and the concomitant emphasis in Germany on media pluralism – is a recurring theme in Germany's governance frameworks for media, which generally seek to "limit state power in order to avoid the recurrence of totalitarianism" (Hallinand Mancini 2004, p. 161).

The public broadcasting ideal in Europe has been codified by the Council of Europe, and all of the Council's members are required to establish public broadcasters conforming to it (Mutu and Corral 2013). For example, German public broadcasters in the Länder are governed by independent boards comprised of representatives from political parties on an apportioned basis and members of civil society, such as trade unions and professional associations – a typically corporatist approach to governance. A recommendation adopted by the Council of Ministers in December 2000 (Council of Europe 2000) calls on member states to guarantee the independence of broadcasting regulators, referring in turn to Article 10 of the European Convention on Human Rights and decisions of the European Court of Human Rights that define freedom of information as a fundamental right. Control over content and determination of what constitutes the public interest is not to be set directly by governments but rather delegated to a professional body whose standards, in theory, reflect a belief in impartiality, non-partisanship, and a broad sense of public interest.

Another way in which this orientation manifests is print media, by way of contrast with France. On the one hand, both France and Germany have traditionally had vibrant local and regional newspaper markets. As recently as 2013, for example, half of all newspapers sold in Germany were regional papers (Stelzig 2015, p. 71). The French display an even more marked preference for regional papers over the national press (Kuhn 2011, p. 38). Overall readership of newspapers, however, is declining in both countries (Kuhn 2011, p. 38; Kolo and Weichart 2013; Lardeau and Le Floch 2013). Matthieu Lardeau and Patrick Le Floch highlight the comparatively high cover prices of French newspapers, due to declining advertising revenues and long-standing production and distribution in efficiencies in the French print industry, as a major factor turning readers away. Kuhn agrees, and identifies changing consumer preferences and competition from free newspapers as additional relevant factors (Kuhn 2011, pp. 40–42). In the case of Germany, Castulus Kolo and Stephan Weichart point to changing consumer preferences and competition from internet platforms for advertising dollars as critical factors impacting the German newspaper industry. French newspapers benefit from an elaborate system of direct and indirect subsidies that keep many otherwise nonviable newspapers alive. Germany, however, has no tradition of direct subsidies, limiting its state support instead to indirect measures, such as preferential tax treatment. As Kolo and Weichart (2013) explain, "[t]raditionally, Germany's postwar governments have decided not to directly support their press as fears of intervention into editorial affairs of newspapers remained widespread" (p. 215). How to support the newspaper industry while steering clear of French- style direct support remains, as of this writing, a matter of considerable debate in Germany (Kolo and Weichart 2013).

The examples of public broadcasting and print media highlight how France and Germany differ with respect to the appropriate role of the state in promoting media pluralism. France has tended to pursue a more direct, interventionist role for the state in promoting a particular brand of media pluralism that emphasizes French nationalist and cultural values, from subsidizing French newspapers to mandating that broadcasters carry French cultural content. Germany, however, has purposefully avoided comparable forms of direct intervention, out of concern that the state might abuse these powers to undermine pluralism in pursuit of illiberal ends.

When we turn to digital media, we find that recent developments in both countries aimed at addressing misinformation and other problematic content reflect the experience with legacy media. On November 20, 2018, French lawmakers, with French President Macron's backing, passed a "law on the fight against the manipulation of information". The law establishes an expedited judicial procedure for adjudicating complaints by individuals and organizations, including the French government, about alleged "fake news" and its proliferation in the period leading up to elections. It also imposes heightened transparency obligations on platforms during these periods and requires them to police their platforms for fake content between elections. The French broadcasting regulator, the Higher Audiovisual Council (CSA), is empowered under the law to strip broadcasters of their licenses if the CSA determines that the broadcaster is spreading offending content on behalf of a foreign government.

Germany has also enacted a new law to address problematic content, the "Act to improve the enforcement of the law in social networks," also known as NetzDG. Rather than endow the federal German state with new authorities for initiating and adjudicating complaints about content, however, NetzDG puts that responsibility in the first instance on the platforms. One of the "Frequently Asked Questions" that the German Federal Ministry of Justice and Consumer Protection (BMJV) poses to itself about NetzDG is, "Why should social networks decide what is legal and what is not? Is that not the job of law enforcement agencies?" The BMJV goes on to answer:

This obligation is already set out in section 10 of the Telemedia Act. According to this Act, service providers are obliged to delete unlawful content as soon as they become aware of it. It is therefore up to service providers themselves to decide whether content is unlawful when such content is reported. Those who operate services and/or infrastructure and make these available to third parties have a duty to limit their own role – whenever still possible – in any abuse of the infrastructure and/or services they provide. Operators themselves are responsible for doing this after receiving specific indications that such abuse is taking place. There is no general judicial-scrutiny provision in German civil law which would imply that any issues surrounding disputed content could, orindeed must, first be resolved by the courts.1This approach, according to the BMJV, helps "guarantee a free, open and democratic culture of communication."To be sure, both governments have maintained close political ties with media that add important nuance to the relationships between the state and media in each country. According to Hallin and Mancini (2004, p. 168), for example, Germany's corporatist governance of public broadcasting is criticized by some as falling short of the corporatist ideal of pluralistic multi-stakeholder governance, since the stakeholders that comprise the governance boards often have partisan or ideological leanings that are consistent with the political representatives on the board, such that a board may in fact be comprised mainly of like-minded partisans. Media policy making in France, on the other hand, is political in a different way – it is usually conducted by the president in a deliberative context dominated by elites, including the media organizations themselves (Kuhn 2011). Indeed, French presidents have routinely sought to, and in most cases succeeded in, at least partially refashion elements of French media governance to advance one or more political objectives (e.g., Kuhn 2011, p. 21). In this respect, Macron's Paris Call in November 2018 and his initiatives on press subsidies are in step with a line of media-related measures initiated by his predecessors. In addition, the media in both countries have in the past adhered to norms that have had the practical effect of shielding politicians and incumbent parties from political threats. In France, for example, journalistic norms about not reporting on politicians' private lives have protected political figures, perhaps most notably former French president François Mitterrand, from scrutiny of their character (Kuhn 2011). In Germany, mainstream media have for decades refused to give much media exposure to the far right, which Antonis Ellinas (2010) argues is an important reason for why the German far right has lagged behind its ideological brethren in Austria, where the far right has experienced greater electoral success.

Media and technology have always had a deeply intimate, symbiotic relationship. Advances in communications technology inevitably impact the development, distribution, and consumption of media. At the same time, consumer demand for content and new media experiences can in turn drive the market for new communications technology. A salient feature of the French approach to media governance, in contrast to Germany and that country's traditional export orientation, is France's strong dirigiste streak. This streak is evident in France's various efforts to support French media outlets in the face of international competition. According to Lardeau (2013), "while French regulators in the 1980s claimed to be preoccupied with efforts to limit concentration and thwart the voracious appetite of domestic press barons, today's emphasis has shifted to enabling French media empires to grow sufficiently large and prosperous to compete with international rivals" (p. 196). The dirigiste streak is also evident in its deployment of media policy in the service of wider French industrial policy initiatives. For example, Kuhn (2011, p. 16) suggests that one of the motivations behind France's decision to extend the daily broadcast schedule for television in the 1960s was to help French television manufacturers sell more televisions.

A particularly compelling example of French industrial policy relating to the media is Minitel, the "[p]rofoundly French" internet platform (Mailland and Media Regulation in the United States and Europe 207Driscoll 2017). Minitel was a modem-based videotex platform and network service developed and implemented in the 1980s by the French postal and telecommunications regulator PTT; Minitel remained in service until 2012, when it was retired. The catalyst behind the French government's considerable investment in Minitel- which included giving a Minitel video device costing several hundred dollars to every household in France for free – was a report commissioned in 1976 by French President Valéry Giscard d'Estaing on telecommunications and computers from two leading French experts, Simon Nora and Alain Minc. Giscard was deeply concerned about the state of France's telecommunications infrastructure, which lagged far behind other industrial countries, and about the country's ability to compete with the United States in both the technological and the cultural spheres, as advances in telecommunications and computers created new opportunities–and risks–for content creation and distribution. Giscard initiated a major overhaul of France's telecommunications infrastructure in 1975 and directed Nora and Minc to look ahead at how France should approach digitization. Nora and Minc's 1978 book-length report, The Computerization Society, was a bestseller in France and was a call to arms for the French government to intervene decisively with industrial policy aimed at building a competitive "telematics" industry in France – Nora and Minc's phrase for the increasing convergence of the telecommunications and computer industries (Nora and Minc 1981, p. 4). The authors predicted a "computer revolution" that "will alter the entire nervous system of social organization" and "affect the economic balance, modify power relationships, and increase the stakes of sovereignty" (Nora and Minc 1981, pp. 3–4). Especially in light of the "IBM challenge" from the United States, which threatened to "encroach upon a traditional sphere of government power, communications" (Nora and Minc 1981, p. 6), France needed "a deliberate policy of social change":

It must support the [French] companies that provide computer-related services, a sector that is dynamic but fragmented; it must allow powerful public intervention in the field of research, provided incentives linked to the activities of the manufacturers for the component parts of the computer industry, and finally, once its strategy has been determined, it must allot a proper role to the national manufacturer of large computers. (Nora and Minc 1981, p. 8)President Giscard, a conservative, approved a videotex pilot program in 1978 (Mailland and Driscoll 2017, p. 55), and his successor, François Mitterrand, a socialist, brought Minitel to market five years later.

REGULATION OF MEDIA IN THE UNITED STATES

There is an extensive literature on American exceptionalism that documents the ways in which the United States has always been an outlier among other developed liberal democracies with regard to state regulation. Seymour Martin Lipset, among others, has noted that the American state modernized later than did the state in other advanced societies, was less extensive, and achieved a lower degree of professionalization (Lipset 1995). American political culture remains highly suspicious of concentrated political power and has created an expansive set of political institutions to protect citizens from government power. The private sector has a much more positive valence as the locus of entrepreneurship and individual freedom. In Europe, by contrast, the private sector is regarded with greater suspicion, while government is generally regarded more as a protector of public interest that is needed to safeguard citizens from excessive private power. How European governments exercise this protector role, however, is itself an important source of variation in how democracies regulate media.

These broad generalizations show up in a variety of domains related to technology regulation. European regulators, for example, in recent decades have primarily focused on protecting consumers from abuse of their privacy rights by private corporations, as exemplified by the EU GDPR, which establishes a comprehensive framework for consumer privacy. In the United States, there is no such comprehensive framework; instead, privacy protections are embedded in a variety of sector-specific laws and regulations, such as the Health Insurance Portability and Accountability Act (HIPAA) and the Fair Credit Reporting Act (FCRA), which govern health- and credit-related data, respectively. In addition, Europeans have always been more willing to regulate speech than Americans; many European countries enacted laws banning certain forms of hate speech (e.g., publication of Nazi propaganda and symbols) well before the rise of the Internet, in contrast to the United States where such speech is legally protected. Private speech is also more constrained in certain European countries as a result of tougher libel laws that facilitate civil litigation against private individuals.

The United States has typically relied much more heavily on industry self-regulation than have European democracies, and this tradition has carried on into the digital age. Neither the Federal Communications Commission (FCC) nor any other federal regulators have sought to lay down formal rules as to the kinds of content that internet platforms can carry. Government agencies have expressed concern over certain forms of content like child pornography or terrorist training materials that might be deemed illegal per se – and not simply because they were posted on the Internet. Digital platforms have responded to such pressures by taking down such content to avoid criminal and reputational liability but not necessarily because the government was endowed with special powers through a law like the German NetzDG.

Indeed, the internet platforms were spared from the threat of private liability for content they hosted by Section 230 of the Communications Decency Act of 1996. This section is frequently misinterpreted as requiring that internet companies act like neutral platforms (i.e., by not curating content) if they are not to lose this protection from private lawsuits. In fact, the intention of the legislation was the opposite: Were such liability to exist, the platforms would respond by not seeking to moderate content at all for fear of being held liable for their editorial decisions. This protection was seen as an effort to promote the rapid growth of internet platforms and placed the burden of content curation squarely on the platforms themselves. The latter sometimes try to argue that they are simply neutral conveyors of other people's content, but it is clear that they have been able to promote or demote various forms of content at their own discretion.

The nature of this self-regulation has shifted dramatically as a result of Russian involvement in the 2016 American election, the Cambridge Analytica scandal, and the realization that extremist views and polarization were being fostered by platform algorithms that promoted conspiracy theories and

outlandish personal attacks over high-quality information. Politicians on both the left and the right began suggesting that platforms might need more overt forms of regulation to protect American democracy.[2] Facebook founder and CEO Mark Zuckerberg went so far as to suggest that his industry needed some form of government regulation. Facebook and Google began to tune their algorithms and started to make more overtly political kinds of decisions as to what constituted acceptable content. Google's YouTube, for example, banned conspiracy theorist Alex Jones from using its services. Facebook, for its part, tweaked its algorithms and beefed up its human content moderation staff substantially beginning in 2017. It is also in the process, as of this writing, of establishing an independent appeals process for adjudicating complaints alleging improper content mediation decisions by Facebook.

There is plenty of precedent for private, for-profit companies making these sorts of prudential decisions. The US First Amendment does not protect the right of individuals to use privately owned platforms; indeed, the First Amendment protects the right of those platforms to carry whatever content they see fit. Only the government can be accused of censorship under its terms. Private corporations like those that own the *New York Times* or the *Wall Street Journal* make decisions about appropriate content all the time; that is what media companies do.

The problem with self-regulation by companies like Facebook and Google is not a legal one; the issue they raise is one of basic legitimacy, brought on by their scale. Traditional newspapers like the *New York Times* make decisions to carry only certain content and not others in a print media market that is still relatively decentralized and competitive. Consumers have the option of switching from the *Times* to a different print media outlet if they dislike its coverage.

The same is not true in the world of online platforms. Owing to economies of scale and scope, the large internet platforms (predominantly Facebook and Google) have grown to such a size that they effectively constitute the public square, not just in the United States but in dozens of other countries around the world. A takedown by YouTube is far more consequential than a decision by alegacy media company not to carry a particular writer or point of view, since there are few other channels for reaching so wide an audience. Facebook exercises government-like powers, even though it is not a government; it is a private, for-profit company largely controlled by a single individual, whose primary objective is not necessarily to serve the public interest of his political community. Facebook can try to acquire the trappings of a government, like its own internal Supreme Court or its own currency, but these efforts in the end do not make its behaviour more democratically legitimate.

This is not a new or unprecedented situation. Democracies have faced the issue of monopolistic or oligopolistic media companies in the past, during the heyday of broadcast television. The universal response by liberal democracies was to regulate broadcast media, and many continue to do so to varying degrees. This power to regulate media exists despite the commitment of all modern liberal democracies to protect fundamental freedom of speech and is as true in the United States as it is in Europe or Asia. In order to understand the possibilities for state regulation of internet platforms in the United States, it is therefore useful to look at the history of regulation of legacy media.

REGULATION, COMPETITION, AND PRIVATIZATION OF LEGACY BROADCAST MEDIA

Lack of competition is what initially induced democratic countries to regulate broadcast media, since the introduction of radio and then television offered new channels of mass communication with limited bandwidth. This was true in the United States as in other democracies. Congress began regulating radio broadcasting with the Radio Act of 1927, which created a temporary Federal Radio Commission whose primary job was to allocate scarce broadcast spectrum (Head and Sterling 1982, pp. 140–141; Spar 2001). Federal authority over broadcasting was expanded by the passage of the Communications Act of 1934, which established the FCC as the principal national regulator, first of radio and then of television broadcasting.

From the beginning, there were constitutional challenges to the FCC's ability to regulate broadcasting, not just from the perspective of the First Amendment but also regarding the national government's authority over interstate commerce and its ability to deprive private actors of property by denying them a license under the Fifth Amendment's takings clause. The latter two issues were ultimately decided in the government's favour by the courts, but the first issue – the state's right to regulate content – has remained controversial up to the present. The 1934act also stated that broadcast media were not "common carriers" like railroads or trucking companies that could be forced to accept content from all comers – an issue that is potentially important in the context of present-day debates over net neutrality (Head and Sterling 1982, pp. 405–409).

The grounds for content regulation in American law were initially laid by the "public interest" standard written into the Radio Act of 1927 and carried forward by the Communications Act of 1934. This standard said that private broadcasters were expected to serve not just their own commercial interests but a broader public interest as well. The act did not define what that interest was but left it up to the FCC to establish guidelines. In practice, the FCC did not write highly detailed rules defining public interest; rather, there was a general expectation that broadcasters would include content relevant to their local communities and would provide balanced coverage of political issues. This standard was enforced by the threat that the FCC might not renew a broadcaster's license if it did not deem it compliant with its general guidance (Head and Sterling 1982, pp. 410–412).

The argument for public broadcasting was made initially on the basis of spectrum scarcity, which evaporated with the development of cable television and the Internet. The oligopolistic or quasi-monopolistic positions of broadcasters began to give way in virtually every country to a much broader and more diverse media landscape. State regulatory authorities, beginning in the United States and Britain, began opening up their broadcast sectors to private actors. Competition began in Britain with the introduction of ITV in the 1950s and expanded in the 1980s with the growth of powerful private

channels like Rupert Murdoch's Sky TV. These private broadcasters began to compete vigorously with each other and with the incumbent public broadcasters. The latter lost significant market share and saw a large erosion of their revenue base as user fees declined and advertisers shifted to alternative platforms.

This shift was not just technological. The 1980s saw the rise of politicians like Ronald Reagan and Margaret Thatcher, who attacked the regulatory state as the source rather than the solution to public problems and who believed that free markets would ultimately produce a fairer distribution of resources than heavily regulated markets. They received intellectual support from an economics profession dominated by a rising form of market orthodoxy that argued that prices constituted accurate reflections of relative scarcities – the so-called Chicago School (Appelbaum 2019).

This pro-market revolution in economic thought had major implications for media regulation. In the early days of the FCC, there was a presumption that the government was a guardian of public interest and that commercial interests on their own would not necessarily produce positive outcomes in terms of either efficiency or democratic control – hence the "public interest" mandate in the 1934 Communications Act. Even Herbert Hoover, long regarded as the epitome of a free-market enthusiast, argued that the broadcast sector was crying out for regulation (Head and Sterling 1982, pp. 139–140). By the 1980s, however, this view had changed to one that held that largely unregulated media markets would best serve public interest and that state regulation did not serve a neutral "public interest" but was politically driven.

The pro-market revolution of the 1980s had consequences for the other form of possible state intervention: antitrust. Led by Robert Bork, Aaron Director, George Stigler, and others, a number of conservative legal scholars and economists began arguing for a much narrower understanding of the grounds on which the government could launch antitrust actions. Bork argued that the original Sherman Act envisioned only one standard for public concern, which was consumer welfare as measured by prices and/or quality. Government antitrust suits against technology companies like IBM and Microsoft, which dragged on for years and ended up costing large amounts of money, were criticized for being wasteful and misdirected.

The growing hostility toward media regulation was best illustrated by the rise and fall of the FCC's "Fairness Doctrine." The latter had its origins in the "public interest" provision of the Communications Act and was strengthened in 1959 when Congress amended the act's Section 315 which had exempted broadcasters from having to provide equal time coverage for certain kinds of news programs. The new law stated "Nothing ... shall be construed as relieving broadcasters ... from the obligation imposed upon them under this Act to operate in the public interest and to afford reasonable opportunity for the discussion of conflicting views on issues of public importance" (Head and Sterling 1982, pp. 476–477). The FCC interpreted this as a statutory endorsement of equal time coverage and an elaboration of the public interest provision of the original act. The FCC could, in other words, behave a bit like a European public broadcaster in forcing private media to provide what the agency regarded as balanced coverage of political events.

The FCC interpreted the Fairness Doctrine as permitting it to force broadcast stations to allow responses to personal attacks. The Supreme Court took up the question of whether this exercise of state power was compatible with the First Amendment in the 1969 Red Lion Broadcasting v. FCC case. In a preview of contemporary controversies over conspiracy theories and fake news, the FCC wanted to compel a Christian radio station to allow replies to a conservative commentator who alleged plots by the FBI and CIA in attacking a critic. The Court upheld the constitutionality of the FCC's action on the grounds of spectrum scarcity, the uniqueness of broadcasting, public interest, and the state's fiduciary responsibility (Headand Sterling 1982, pp. 477–478).

The Fairness Doctrine continued to be controversial, especially among conservatives. They believed that it was being used by the government to shut down conservative voices and that the FCC could never be truly impartial in its enforcement of the rule. By the 1980s, there was also a growing belief among economists that markets, left to their own devices, would be self-correcting. This view was used to critique antitrust actions, under the assumption that large scale implied efficiency rather than an undue use of market power (Wu 2018).

Yet it was also applied to the market for ideas; in line with classic First Amendment thinking, it was argued that good ideas would eventually drive out bad ideas and that the government did not have a legitimate role in policing thought. Consider this passage from a 1985 law review article:

> [W]ere there no fairness regulations, the most a broadcaster could hope to gain from misinforming or misleading its listeners is the allegiance of those already ideologically committed to the broadcaster's point of view. That allegiance, probably depending on the issue addressed, may or may not counterbalance the loss of viewers who are not ideologues. But, in the absence of the doctrine, broadcasters would have almost no incentive to provide erroneous or one-sided information to those who do not want it or to refuse all coverage of issues that interest have to convince some many viewers or listeners. They do, after all, have to convince someone to turn on the set and tune in their frequency. (Krattenmaker and Powe 1985, p. 160)

It was also argued that the Fairness Doctrine would stifle rather than encourage free speech, by deterring broadcasters from airing controversial content in the first place for fear of provoking an FCC action. The Fairness Doctrine was eventually rescinded by the FCC itself under Republican chairman Denis Patrick in 1987, in a 4–0 vote. The Democrats in Congress have subsequently tried unsuccessfully to reinstate the doctrine on several occasions but faced strong opposition from Republican administrations, including a veto by President Reagan and a threatened veto by President George H. W. Bush.

In contrast to its European counterparts, then, the United States by the early twenty-first century had taken a much more relaxed position than its European counterparts toward the regulation of legacy media. This was driven both by the explosion of bandwidth provided by cable and internet technology and by an ideological shift toward greater distrust of government regulation. The Europeans, facing similar pressures, have themselves backed away from pervasive state control over legacy media and permitted greater market competition, though their public broadcasters remain powerful players in many European countries. It is not the case, however, that the United States never took a more European-style approach to media regulation. The Supreme Court has upheld the constitutionality of the Fairness Doctrine in the Red Lion case; its abolition was the result of an administrative decision on the part of the FCC.

CONCISE SUMMARY

Regulation of legacy media may seem to be irrelevant to contemporary discussions of whether the Internet should be regulated in the interests of protecting democracy, in light of the huge differences between the technologies involved. Yet many of the older controversies remain the same and may provide legal precedents for future action.

As we have seen, the governments of modern liberal democracies have reconciled their efforts to regulate legacy media with their commitment to freedom of the press on the grounds of spectrum scarcity. As technology evolved during the 1980s and 1990s, this concern seemed increasingly outdated. The efforts by liberals to reinstate the Fairness Doctrine were driven in large measure by their unhappiness with the growth of Fox News, AM talk radio, and a host of new conservative media outlets that challenged the mainstream media's dominance of the political and social narrative. Conservatives answered these criticisms by arguing that the new channels simply provided political balance in a media market that was diverse and highly competitive. If Fox News was attracting more viewers than CNN, that was the result of individual consumer choice and not a mandate by the government. In this they were correct; the legacy media market is not dominated by a single political point of view, however much one may object to biases by one outlet or another. If one does not like Fox News, one is always free to switch the dial to MSNBC.

The Internet at the outset promised to be as diverse and competitive as legacy media when it first came into existence as a public platform in the 1990s. Since then, however, it has moved in the direction of the broadcast media of the 1950s. Two very large platforms, Facebook and Google, and a third somewhat smaller one, Twitter, now serve as the primary channels of communication for hundreds of millions of people, not just in the United States but worldwide. It can be argued that the platforms have put themselves in a position comparable to the three main broadcast networks in the United States back in the heyday ofover-the-air television. The platforms may not be monopoly providers of information, but neither were the broadcast networks; what they have in common is extraordinary influence over what millions of people see and hear through their decisions to prioritize certain content over others.

None of the internet platforms are necessarily promoting a single point of view. Yet, through their terms of service, they have maintained the right to police content, a right that is further protected by Section 230 of the Communications Decency Act, which shields them from liability for what they decide to carry. In addition, as private actors they enjoy free speech rights protected by the First Amendment. This has led to the paradoxical outcome wherein the platform's ability to restrict speech on behalf of a foreign authoritarian government is actually protected constitutionally from US government regulation (Keller 2018).

In the early days of the Internet, content moderation centered around relatively uncontroversial issues like terrorist incitement, child pornography, cyber bullying, and the like. Yet, with the weaponization of social media by Russia and a host of other political actors, they have come under increasing pressure to restrict fake news, conspiracy theories, hate speech, and other toxic content flying around the Internet. They are, in other words, being asked to perform the same kinds of editorial functions that legacy media organizations like newspapers and TV channels have traditionally undertaken.

The question today, however, is whether the platforms' near-monopoly or oligopoly position puts them in a similar position to the broadcast networks back in the early days of television. Because the market for social media is less competitive, a decision to remove certain content is much more consequential than the decision of, say, *USA Today* not to carry it.

As the platforms have grown more active in policing more political forms of speech in recent years, complaints have grown that they are showing political bias (Wakabayashi and Kang 2018). This in turn has led to a number of law suits against them, in some cases demanding that they be required to carry opposing political viewpoints. These "must carry" demands replicate the logic of the old Fairness Doctrine, that is, that the government could override the free speech rights of a private actor and compel it to carry certain material for the sake of political balance. To date, the courts have not supported such suits, but in light of precedents like *Red Lion* and subsequent Supreme Court cases, it is not clear in what ways contemporary internet platforms are different from legacy broadcast media.

There are two basic approaches to solving the problem of platform dominance. The first is to accept that dominance as an inevitable fact and to try to regulate platforms in the manner of legacy broadcasting. This has been one leg of the European approach to date. It is very unclear, however, what sorts of regulation would uphold public interest. Forcing the internet platforms to carry certain kinds of content in the name of political balance might have similar effects to the Fairness Doctrine, discouraging them from carrying controversial content in the first place. It is also not at all clear what a proportionate and legitimate approach to internet regulation along these lines might look like, in light of political polarization within societies and, given the global scope of service provision by internet platforms, different conceptions across countries of the appropriate role for the state in intervening in media markets. A number of European countries continue to enjoy a degree of political consensus that allows them to support public broadcasters that promote balanced coverage believed to be in the public interest. This would not seem to be possible in a highly polarized country like the United States currently.

The boundaries of acceptable discourse have been challenged by the highest political authorities; expecting a federal agency like the FCC to police political debate is highly unrealistic.

The second, and not necessarily mutually exclusive, approach is to pursue policies aimed at increasing the degree of competition among internet platforms. As we have seen, liberal democracies have pursued a variety of mechanisms to support competition and pluralism, albeit with mixed degrees of success and based on different conceptions of pluralism and the role of the state. There is growing interest and focus on the competitive practices of large internet companies, but it is not immediately obvious how and whether alternative internet media platforms would affect the quality of civic discourse online and the incidence of disinformation (Cremer, de Montjoye, and Schweitzer 2019).

There is a growing consensus that antitrust law needs to be broken out of the framework established by the Chicago School back in the 1980s and modernized to meet the needs of the digital age. There are several prongs to this reassessment (Wu 2018; Khan 2018). The first is to broaden the courts' understanding of potential harms arising from excessive concentration of power in the hands of a small number of private corporations. Robert Bork was insistent that the legislative history behind the Sherman Act encompassed only economic harms to consumer welfare and not potential political harms (Bork 1966). It is not clear that he was correct in this assertion, since Senator Sherman himself articulated deep concerns about the political effects of concentrated private power on American democracy.

The chief political harm that contemporary platform power poses today is the one that we have just explored: The editorial decisions taken by Facebook and Google, while perhaps justified in themselves, have enormous power to affect overall political discourse in the countries in which they operate due to their sheer scale. They are not public institutions and have no legitimacy as, in effect, custodians of public interest. This problem would not be nearly as severe if there were greater competition among platforms, in the manner of legacy print media.

In terms of economic harms, it is clear that the existing consumer welfare standard measured by prices needs to be rethought. Many internet services are offered at zero price. The real costs to consumers arise elsewhere: foregone privacy when the platform sells their information to third parties or uses it to advance their own self-interest; foregone innovation when a large platform buys a start-up that is a potential competitor, and lost opportunities when platforms use their enormous data on consumer preferences to pursue exclusionary policies in adjacent markets (Khan 2017).

If one accepts the premise that large platforms create new categories of harms through reduced competition, the question then turns to potential remedies.

Here, the very nature of digital markets poses severe constraints. Modern internet platforms enjoy enormous economies of scale and scope; the larger they are, the more potentially useful they are to advertisers and consumers. Competition exists not for market share but for the market itself, since scale and scope economies reward a single dominant player (Cremer et al., 2019). If a government were to try to break up Facebook, for example, in the way that it broke up AT&T, it is likely that one of the "baby Facebooks" would eventually come to assume the same dominant position that the original Facebook enjoyed.

It is beyond the scope of this chapter to review all of the possible antitrust remedies that have been suggested. One idea is to increase data portability, so as to make it easier for users to switch to alternative platforms. The idea of data portability has already been built into European regulations like GDPR; but privacy rules like GDPR themselves limit portability, since one's network connections are part of one's individual profile but also "belong" to those connections. For a group to move to another platform from Facebook would require consent by all the network members, something that is unlikely for a number of behavioural reasons.

A second idea is to restrict exclusionary behaviour through the purchasing of potentially competitive start-ups. Facebook has already been subject to substantial criticism for its purchases of Instagram and WhatsApp and is busy seeking to integrate them with its existing services to make it harder for regulators to force a later disgorgement. This kind of scrutiny would require a redefinition of anticompetitive behaviour away from the focus on total market share used in classic antitrust cases. In a Schumpeterian world of creative destruction, the most dangerous competitors are often not large rivals but small, nimble ones with good ideas.

Another suggestion for facilitating antitrust actions is to shift the standards of proof for potential harms from ones based on a strict rule of reason to structural remedies. One of the consequences of the Chicago School revolution in antitrust thinking was the establishment of a rule of reason standard that required antitrust enforcers to provide extensive empirical market analyses and projections of consequences for future markets of a given enforcement action. This increased the time and cost necessary to bring an antitrust action against a company and explains why the IBM and Microsoft cases dragged on for as many years as they did. A structural standard, by contrast, would define a certain market structure as per se anticompetitive, avoiding the need for such lengthy litigation. While both US and European competition law have been influenced by Chicago School thinking, there are more grounds for structural remedies in the latter case. The problem with this approach is knowing what structural standard to apply in a highly fluid technological world, one that is not arbitrary and likely to impede rather than promote competition.

The political climate surrounding internet regulation has shifted dramatically since 2016. The large platforms, and especially Facebook, have come under sustained criticism for their past behaviour in facilitating Russian interference in the US election and for increasing domestic polarization by facilitating extremist speech, conspiracy theories, and the like. The Europeans have shifted in this direction earlier and more decisively than American regulators, imposing national-level laws like NetzDG or Europe-wide ones like GDPR and initiating antitrust actions against the large platforms. In the face of these shifting views, American regulators have been taking a fresh look at platform behaviour. It is, nonetheless, not clear whether this will result in a consensus regarding either regulatory or antitrust remedies to the problems at hand. Regulation and antitrust are to some extent substitutes for one another; the problem of content moderation on the Internet could be dealt with under both approaches or the two in combination. Both approaches face substantial obstacles to implementation in practice, particularly in the United States where partisanship and polarization have reached new heights in recent years. Whether platform behaviour will actually change in the face of these shifts in public opinion and state policies remains to be seen.

REFERENCES

Allen-Ebrahimian, B. (2016). The man who nailed jello to the wall. Foreign Policy, June 29.

Appelbaum, B. (2019). The Economists' Hour: False Prophets, Free Markets, and the Fracture of Society. Boston: Little, Brown.

Bork, R. H. (1966). Legislative intent and the policy of the Sherman Act. Journal of Law and Economics, 9, 7–48.

(1993). The Antitrust Paradox: A Policy at War with Itself. New York: Free Press. Council of Europe (2000). Recommendation No. R (2000) 23 of the Committee of Ministers to Member States on the Independence and Functions of Regulatory Authorities for the Broadcasting Sector. (Adopted by the Committee of Ministers on December 20, 2000, at the 735th meeting of the Ministers' Deputies).

Cremer, J., de Montjoye, Y.-A., & Schweitzer, H. (2019). Competition Policy for the Digital Era. European Commission's Directorate-General for Competition, Committee for the Study of Digital Platforms, Market Structure and Antitrust Subcommittee (Booth School Stigler Center, Chicago) report.

Eko, L. S. (2013). American Exceptionalism, the French Exception, and Digital Media Law. New York: Lexington Books.

Ellinas, A. A. (2010). The Media and the Far Right in Western Europe: Playing the Nationalist Card. Cambridge: Cambridge University Press.

Hallin, D. C., & Mancini, P. (2004). Comparing Media Systems: Three Models of Media and Politics. Cambridge: Cambridge University Press.

Head, S. W., & Sterling, C. H. (1982). Broadcasting in America: A Survey of Television, Radio, and New Technologies (4th ed.). Boston: Houghton Mifflin.

Khan, L. M. (2017). Amazon's Antitrust Paradox, Yale Law Journal, 126, 710–805. (2018). The New Brandeis Movement: America's antimonopoly debate. Journal of European Competition Law and Practice, 9, 131–132.

Keller, D. (2018). State and private censorship in the new public square. Unpublished paper, Stanford Center for Internet and Society.

Kolo, C., & Weichart, S. (2013). Germany: Evaluating alternatives to finance quality journalism. In P. Murschetz (Ed.), State Aid for Newspapers, Media Business and Innovation (pp. 000–000). Berlin: Springer-Verlag.

Krattenmaker, T. G., & Powe, L. A. Jr. (1985). The Fairness Doctrine today: A constitutional curiosity and an impossible dream. Duke Law Journal, 17, 151–176. Kuhn, R. (2011). The Media in Contemporary France. Maidenhead: Open University Press.

Lardeau, M. & Le Floch, P. (2013). France: Press subsidies – inefficient but enduring. In P. Murschetz (Ed.), State Aid for Newspapers, Media Business and Innovation (pp. 000–000). Berlin: Springer-Verlag.

Lipset, S. M. (1995). American Exceptionalism: A Double-Edged Sword. New York: W. W. Norton.

Mailland, J., & Driscoll, K. (2017). Minitel. Cambridge, MA: MIT Press. p.49. McNamee, R. (2019). Zucked: Waking Up to the Facebook Catastrophe. New York: Penguin Press.

Mutu, A., & Corral, J. B. (2013). Broadcasting regulation in Europe: A theoretical design for comparative research, Tripodos, 32, 13–28.

Nora, S., & Minc, A. (1981).The Computerization of Society. Cambridge, MA: MIT Press.

Segal, A. (2018). When China rules the Web, Foreign Affairs, 97(September-October). Spar, D. L. (2001). Ruling the Waves: Cycles of Discovery, Chaos, and Wealth from the Compass to the Internet. New York: Harcourt.

Stelzig, K. (2015). Germany. In B. Schwarzer & S. Spitzer (Eds.), The European Newspaper Market: Social Media Use and New Business Models (p. 71). Baden: Nomos.

Wakabayashi, D., & Kang, C. (2018). Google's Pichai faces privacy and bias questions in Congress. New York Times, December 11.

Wu, T. (2018). The Curse of Bigness: Antitrust in the New Gilded Age. Columbia Global Reports, 2018.

FOOTNOTE

1. German Federal Ministry of Justice and Consumer Protection, "Questions and answers: Act to Improve Enforcement of the Law in Social Networks." www.bmjv.de/SharedDocs/FAQ/EN/ NetzDG/NetzDG.html
2. For an account of Facebook's role in these scandals, see McNamee (2019).

10 FACTS AND WHERE TO FIND THEM

EMPIRICAL INVESTIGATION OF INTERNET PLATFORMS AND CONTENT OVERSIGHT

INTRODUCTION: AN OVERVIEW

In an era where digital information and online interactions have become integral parts of our daily lives, understanding the mechanisms governing internet platforms and their content moderation is of paramount importance. This empirical investigation delves into the realm of internet platforms, seeking to unearth the facts and realities that shape the ways in which content is managed, disseminated, and controlled on these platforms. The digital age has ushered in an unprecedented wealth of information, and with it, the challenge of ensuring the accuracy, fairness, and responsibility of this information. As we navigate the digital landscape, discerning the truth from the noise becomes increasingly essential. This study embarks on a journey to unravel the intricacies of content moderation on internet platforms, shedding light on the methods, policies, and their real-world impact. By examining the available data and conducting rigorous research, we aim to provide valuable insights into the multifaceted landscape of internet content governance.

We live in an era of increasing worry that internet platforms like Facebook or Twitter, which mediate our online speech, are also fomenting hatred, spreading misinformation, and distorting political outcomes. The 2016 US presidential election, in particular, unleashed a torrent of concern about platform-borne harms. Policymakers around the world have called for laws requiring platforms to do more to combat illegal and even merely "harmful" content.

From the perspective of platforms themselves, these proposals have a lot in common. Regardless of their substantive mandates – to address content that is misleading, hateful, or violent, for example – they all require similar operational processes to comply. Platforms already have these processes in place to enforce current laws and their discretionary Community Guidelines. Any new efforts to regulate content online will likely build on existing systems, personnel, and tools – and inherit both their strengths and their weaknesses. That makes it important to understand those systems.

Reliable information about platforms' content-removal systems was, for many years, hard to come by; but data and disclosures are steadily emerging as researchers focus on the topic and platforms ramp up their transparency efforts. This chapter reviews the current and likely future sources of information.

Some content takedowns are required by law, while others are performed voluntarily. Legal takedowns are shaped by intermediary liability laws, which tell platforms what responsibility they have for unlawful content posted by users. Platforms operating under legal frameworks like the US Digital Millennium Copyright Act (DMCA) or the EU's eCommerce Directive typically meet their legal obligations using "notice-and-takedown" systems. Larger platforms invest heavily in these operations and sometimes supplement them with proactive efforts to identify and eliminate illegal material. However, the evidence we review suggests that platforms perform poorly at enforcing the law consistently at scale.

Platforms' voluntary content removals are based on private rule sets: Community Guidelines. These private standards often prohibit a broad margin of lawful speech beyond that which actually violates the law. Community Guidelines may draw on platform operators' own moral beliefs or social norms. They may also simply aim to shape the user experience for business purposes. A real estate listing site, for example, might exclude photos that do not show buildings and property. Most websites prohibit spam, pornography, and harassment for comparable reasons. Platforms can also use Community Guidelines to simplify their legal enforcement efforts and avoid conflict with governments, by simply prohibiting more speech than the law does. Governments, for their part, may avoid challenges under constitutions or human rights law if removal of legal content is attributed to private, rather than state, action (Angelopoulos et al. 2016). Therefore, as policymakers and the public have increasingly demanded that platforms remove content that is harmful or offensive, but not necessarily illegal, these discretionary rules have become ever more important.

New platform efforts to weed out prohibited content will, inevitably, have a lot in common with these existing systems. That is partly good news, because policymakers are not drafting on a blank slate. Lawyers, researchers, and platform employees have two decades of experience in the ways that content- removal systems work in practice. It is also, however, partly bad news. Evidence suggests that platforms do not do a great job as enforcers of speech rules. Even when they apply their own, self-defined Community Guidelines, the results often appear erratic. It is hard for independent researchers to quantify platforms' accuracy in applying Community Guidelines standards, though, since the rules themselves are poorly understood and there is little reliable information about the specific text, images, videos, or other content removed. Platforms' performance under laws like US copyright law or German hate speech law can be easier to research, in part simply because the rules come from public law rather than platforms' discretionary Community Guidelines. There is also somewhat more information available about how platforms apply legal rules and what specific content they take down. 1 This has allowed independent experts to assess the platforms' removal practices – and document significant problems. Platforms that receive notices alleging illegality, and hence exposing them to legal risk, commonly err on the side of caution, removing even lawful information. Some simply take down any content identified in a complaint. This "over-removal" is a constant by-product of notice-and-takedown systems. Platforms have removed information ranging from journalism and videos documenting police brutality in Ecuador (Vivanco 2014) to media coverage of fraud investigations in the United States (Cushing 2017) to criticism of religious organizations (Galperin 2008) to scientific reporting (Oransky 2013; Timmer 2013).

Platforms historically have had little incentive to share detailed information about content removal with the public. Compiling records of evolving content takedown processes, which may use different tools and standards or be managed by different internal teams over time, is burdensome; and any disclosure, particularly one that admits error, can be used against platforms in court or in the press. Yet the longer-term benefits of greater transparency, for both society and platforms themselves, are becoming ever more evident. Without it, public debates about platform responsibility can become exercises in speculation. Laws passed without a practical foundation in platforms' real-world operations and capabilities can be burdensome for the companies and their users, yet fail to achieve lawmakers' legitimate goals.

Whether in recognition of this problem, or because of increasing pressure from civil society, academia, and other quarters, some platforms have provided substantially more public transparency in recent years. This chapter will review major sources of information released by platforms, as well as independent research concerning content takedown operations. We will begin in the section "Takedown and Intermediary Liability Laws" by very briefly reviewing intermediary liability law, which plays a central role in structuring platforms' content-removal operations. One particularly robust academic study will serve to illustrate common platform takedown practices and research themes.

The section titled "Sources of Information," which makes up the bulk of the chapter, provides a broader review of the current empirical literature and likely sources of future information. First, we discuss disclosures from platforms and other participants in content moderation, such as users and governments. Second, we discuss independent research from third parties such as academics and journalists, including data analysis, interviews, and surveys. Finally, before concluding the chapter, we will list specific questions and areas for future empirical research.

Debates about proposed new laws ranging from the EU's Terrorist Content Regulation to Singapore's "fake news" law should be informed by empirically grounded assessments of platforms' capacity to comply and the potential unintended consequences of their compliance efforts. Without better information about platforms' true strengths and weaknesses as speech regulators, we should not expect to see well-designed laws.

TAKEDOWN AND INTERMEDIARY LIABILITY LAWS

This section discusses intermediary liability laws, which form the legal backdrop for content-moderation discussions. As we explain, these laws determine when and how platforms are legally required to remove content. Following a brief legal analysis, we show how such laws operate in practice with the help of one particularly thorough study: "Notice and takedown in everyday practice" (Urban, Karaganis, and Schofield 2016).

Intermediary Liability Laws

Intermediary liability laws tell internet intermediaries such as ISPs, search engines, or social media companies what legal responsibility they have for their users' speech. As a matter of black-letter law, they are typically separate from underlying substantive legal doctrines that define things like defamation or hate speech. Yet by prescribing when and how platforms must take action, intermediary liability laws strongly influence what speech actually gets taken down.

At a high level, intermediary liability laws must balance three, often competing goals. The legal details in national law typically reflect lawmakers' judgment about how best to balance them. One goal is to prevent harm. Generally, the better job a law does of incentivizing platforms to take down illegal or otherwise harmful content, the more it will serve this goal. Another, often competing goal is to protect lawful online speech and information. A law that requires aggressive policing by platforms may run afoul of this goal, leading platforms to take down lawful and valuable speech in order to avoid legal risk. A third goal is to promote innovation. Early intermediary liability laws were conceived in part as means to protect nascent industries. Today, intermediary liability laws may profoundly affect competition between incumbent platforms and start-ups.

The balance of priorities between these three goals is a matter of national values and policy choices; but the question of what specific legal rules will, in practice, serve each goal is in part an empirical one, tied to the real-world practices of platforms responding to the law's requirements and incentives.2

Internationally, most intermediary laws share two basic elements. First, platforms are immune from legal claims arising from users' unlawful speech as long as they do not get too involved in developing that speech. National laws diverge as to how "neutral" platforms must be to qualify for immunity and the degree of content moderation they can engage in without being exposed to liability. One relative outlier in this respect is the US Communications DecencyAct (CDA), which grants platforms unusually broad immunities, even when they become aware of unlawful content, for the express purpose of encouraging them to moderate and weed out "objectionable" content.3

Second, most intermediary liability laws give platforms obligations once they "know" about illegal content. In much of the world, platforms that learn about material like defamation or terrorist propaganda on their services must take down that content or face legal consequences. Laws vary substantially, however, in what counts as "knowledge." Under some national rules, platforms can only be legally required to take down users' speech if a court has adjudicated it unlawful.4 Elsewhere, the law leaves platforms to decide for themselves what speech violates the law.

Within this framework, one important source of variation comes from the procedures that the law provides for platforms taking content down. The US Digital Millennium Copyright Act (DMCA) is one of the most procedurally detailed intermediary liability laws.5 It spells out formal prerequisites for "notices" from right sholders, steps for "counter-notice" by accused users, and other details including penalties for bad-faith notices against lawful speech. The Manila Principles, a set of model intermediary liability rules endorsed by civil society groups around the world and supported in the human rights literature, lists additional procedural protections – including public transparency requirements to illuminate errors, bias, or abuse in notice-and-takedown systems.6

A rapidly developing intermediary liability policy debate concerns platforms' potential obligations to proactively monitor or police users' speech. Until recently, most countries' laws built on the assumption that platforms could not, realistically, monitor user speech on an ongoing basis and accurately identify illegality. Important laws like the US DMCA and EU eCommerce Directive expressly disclaimed monitoring obligations,7making platforms responsible only for unlawful content they became aware of, usually through notice from third parties. Platforms' voluntarily-developed filtering tools have since changed policymakers' expectations, though the exact operation of those tools is poorly understood. One major new law, the EU's Copyright Directive, effectively equires filtering.8 Other proposals in areas like terrorist content are pending.9 Critics ranging from technologists to three UN rapporteurs have raised serious concerns about filters (Cannataci et al. 2018; O'Brian and Malcolm 2018). As a 2019 letter from civil society organizations including European Digital Rights (EDRi), Article 19, and the American Civil Liberties Union (ACLU) put it, filters remain "untested and poorly understood technologies to restrict online expression," with great potential to silence protected expression ranging from parody to human rights reporting, with resulting harm to "democratic values and individualhuman rights."10

Another emerging issue comes from both platforms' and governments' reliance on Community Guidelines instead of law as a basis for removing online content. Platforms' discretionary rules often prohibit legal expression, and until recently it was generally assumed that platforms had extremely wide latitude to do so.11 National constitutions and human rights laws protect internet users from state interference with their legal exercise of speech rights, but platforms are generally free to ban any speech they want; and, because Community Guidelines are privately defined and enforced, platforms' decisions are generally not subject to review by courts.

In recent years, though, governments, particularly in Europe, have increasingly turned to platforms' Community Guidelines as enforcement mechanisms. For example, both the European Commission's Hate Speech Code of Conduct and Disinformation Code of Practice call on platforms to voluntarily prohibit specified content, often in reliance on Community Guidelines.12 Law enforcement bodies including Europol, for their part, often use Community Guidelines or Terms of Service rather than law as a basis for asking platforms to take down content (Europol 2016; Chang 2018). Civil liberties organizations have decried these arrangements, saying they replace democratic lawmaking and courts with privatized and unaccountable systems (European Digital Rights 2016; see also Chang 2018).

A Case Study: Notice and Takedown in Everyday Practice

By far the most thorough analysis of intermediary liability compliance operations is "Notice and takedown in everyday practice" (Urban et al. 2016). To produce it, researchers reviewed takedown notices affecting some 4,000 individual webpage URLs in Google's web search and image search products and interviewed platform operators, right sholders, and other participants in the notice-and-takedown ecosystem. Although focused on copyright (the area for which the richest public dataset is available), its thorough analysis documents trends and issues with close analogs for content removal under other laws. Many of its lessons, particularly those relating to automation and large-scale operations, are relevant to removal under Community Guidelines as well.

One of the study's most important findings is the divergence between the operations and capabilities of mega-platforms like Google and other, more modest internet intermediaries (Urban et al. 2016, pp. 28–29, 73–74). Smaller or more traditional companies generally employed teams of three or fewer people for this function and carried out substantive individual review of each notice (Urban et al. 2016, pp. 29, 36). Many described "opting to take down content even when they are uncertain about the strength of the underlying claim" in order to avoid exposure to liability (Urban et al. 2016, p. 41). They also reported notifiers' "deliberate gaming" of the takedown process, "including to harass competitors, to resolve personal disputes, to silence a critic, or to threaten the [platform]" (Urban et al. 2016, p. 40).

The picture for larger players was very different. The difference began with scale: In contrast to the dozens or hundreds of notices received by smaller operations, Google received more than 108 million removal notices for web search during the study's six-month period (Urban et al. 2016, pp. 29, 77). Both large-scale notifiers and platforms relied heavily on automation. Rights holders and their outsourced vendors automated the notification process, for example by using search queries to identify lists of URLs (Urban et al. 2016, p. 92). The resulting "robonotices" sometimes included errors, like a request from the musician Usher to take down a film version of Edgar Allan Poe's Fall of the House of Usher (Urban et al. 2016, pp. 90–91).

Platforms reported automatically accepting many such automated requests, in particular from "trusted" sources. As a result, some provided no human review at all for the majority of automated notices they received (Urban et al. 2016, p. 29). Some also proactively policed content, using "measures such as exante filtering systems, hash-matching based 'staydown' systems, [and] direct back-end takedown privileges for trusted rights holders" (Urban et al. 2016, p. 29).

In their quantitative analysis, Urban and colleagues documented considerable error in DMCA operations. Among notices submitted to Google web search, for example, they found questionable legal claims in 28 percent (Urban et al. 2016, p. 88). Some 4.2 percent – which extrapolates to 4.5 million requests across the six-month dataset – seemed to be simple errors, requesting removal of material that did not relate to the notifier's legal claim (Urban et al. 2016, p. 88). Among notices submitted to Google's image search product, the figure was 38 percent (Urban et al. 2016, pp. 98–99). Fully 70 percent of image search notices were called into serious doubt if calculations included one individual's barrage of improper takedown demands (Urban et al. 2016, pp. 98–99).13

Platforms interviewed for the Urban study also reported a low rate of DMCA counter-notices from users challenging erroneous takedowns. Many platforms received no counter-notices at all (Urban et al. 2016, p. 44). This finding is consistent with figures released by the Motion Picture Association of America in 2013, showing a 0.000032 percent rate of counter-notices to DMCA removal requests filed by member companies; only 8 counter-notices were identified for 25,235,151 notified

URLs (Boyden 2013). Platform transparency reports, similarly, typically report counter-notice rates of well below 1 percent for copyright claims (Bridy and Keller 2016). Given the widespread documentation of over-removal, these figures suggest that wrongful removals are going unchallenged.

SOURCES OF INFORMATION

This section reviews numerous sources of empirical information, both from platforms and other participants involved in content takedown and from independent researchers. Some, including major platform transparency reports, are published on regular schedules and should be fruitful sources of future information.

Disclosures by Platforms and Other Participants in Content Takedown

Platforms reveal information about content moderation in manifold ways. These include (1) periodic transparency reports; (2) primary source information shared with academic research archives such as Harvard's Lumen Database; (3) notices to affected individuals about takedown decisions; and (4) incidental public statements and other disclosures about specific content issues. Increasingly, (5) governments also require platforms to perform public filings about content moderation, and some also publish data about their own involvement in takedown procedures. (6) Third-party audits also reveal information about takedown practices, as do (7) leaked information from platforms.

Transparency Reports

Many platforms publish periodic transparency reports, which typically disclose aggregate data about requests for content removal. An index of transparency reports maintained by the civil society organization Access Now lists reports from more than seventy companies,[14] ncluding Google,[15] Facebook,[16] Twitter,[17] Amazon,[18] Tumblr,[19] Medium,[20] Reddit,[21] Github,[22] and Word Press.[23] These can provide important quantitative overviews of the big picture – or at least part of it. They typically aggregate data about removal requests, along with the platform's rate of compliance. They may also disclose the frequency with which users accused of wrongdoing choose to appeal or challenge platforms' decisions. Transparency reports have historically focused on legal removal requests. In 2018, however, Facebook,[24] Twitter,[25] and YouTube[26] all published their first Community Guidelines enforcement reports.

Transparency reports have major limitations. The aggregated data in transparency reports only shows the platforms' own assessments, and not the merits of the underlying cases. That means researchers cannot evaluate the accuracy of takedown decisions or spot any trends of inconsistent enforcement. Also, most transparency reports only cover particular categories of takedowns – often only those initiated by governments or copyright-holders. This leaves open questions about platforms' responses to legal allegations brought by individuals under, say, French defamation law or Brazilian privacy law.

Transparency reports also vary widely in the ways they classify data, making apples-to-apples comparisons between companies difficult. In particular, reports that track how many notices a company received cannot fruitfully be compared to reports tracking how many items of content they were asked to remove, since one notice may list any number of items.

Transparency reports also vary greatly in detail. Take, for instance, the aforementioned Community Guideline reports. YouTube's report documents the number of channels and videos removed for eleven different types of standards violations (e.g., spam, nudity, promotion of violence and extremism) (Google 2018a). It also specifies how these videos were detected, whether through automated flagging, individual trusted flaggers, users, NGOs, or government agencies. Facebook's report is even more detailed; it also registers how often users appealed against removal decisions and how often content was later restored (either proactively by Facebook or following a user appeal) (Facebook 2018b). In addition to this numerical reporting, Facebook provides details about operations. Its expected staff of more than 20,000 people are working on content moderation, including native speakers of more than 50 languages and teams working around the clock. Separately, Facebook has published a detailed public version of its Community Standards (Facebook 2018b) and a guide to understanding the figures from the report (Facebook 2018). Twitter's report, on the other hand, is significantly less detailed. It only documents the number of unique accounts reported and actioned for six different categories of violations, without specifying appeal or reinstatement rates or reporting mechanisms other than those from known government entities (Twitter 2018).

One important external assessment of company transparency reports' strengths and weaknesses can be found in the Electronic Frontier Foundation's periodic Who Has Your Back report (Gebhart 2018). Another can be found in the Ranking Digital Rights Corporate Accountability Index, which rates technology companies on numerous measures relating to transparency and protection of users' free expression and privacy rights.27 The Open Technology Institute's Transparency Reporting Toolkit also provides a valuable comparison of existing reports and recommendations for improved practices (Open Technology Institute 2018). It draws on the widely endorsed Santa Clara Principles, which call for "numbers, notice, and appeal" as essential elements in platforms' content-removal operations.[28]

Primary Source Information Shared by Platforms

For researchers to draw their own conclusions about platforms' content- removal practices, they need to know what content was actually removed. To date, the best source for such information has been the Lumen database ("Lumen"), an archive hosted at Harvard's Berkman Klein Center.

Lumen archives legal takedown notices from any platform–or sender–that chooses to share them. Senders' personal information, and occasionally–as in the case of child abuse content–content location URLs are redacted, but researchers can otherwise review the entire communication. At last check, the database held some 9.3 million notices, targeting approximately 3.35 billion URLs.29 The majority comes from Google; other contributors include Twitter, Word Press, the Internet Archive, Kickstarter, Reddit, and Vimeo. Because the notices identify material that is often still available at the listed URL, researchers can look at the specific content alleged to be illegal and assess whether a platform made the right decision. The Lumen database has enabled extensive academic research.30

Demands for other forms of "primary source" transparency are increasing. An important recent proposal from the French government, for example, calls for transparency sufficient for auditors to review specific takedown decisions.31 Similarly, proposed amendments to the German Network Enforcement Law (Netzwerkdurschsetzungsgesetz, or NetzDG) – discussedin further detail in the section titled "Public Filings and Other Government Disclosures" – also call for the auditing of content moderation practices and the creation of a public "clearing house" to adjudicate user complaints about wrongful removals (German Parliament 2018). Such independent oversight mechanisms, if they proved operationally and economically feasible, might also allow more detailed third-party research into the substance of content- moderation decisions.

Notice to Affected Individuals

Platforms also provide potentially useful information to individuals affected by takedown requests. In particular, they may (1) respond to a person who requested removal, letting them know if the request was honoured; (2) notify the user whose content was taken down; or (3) "tombstone" missing material, putting up a notice for users who are trying to visit a missing page or find information. YouTube's "this video is not available" notices are perhaps the most visually familiar example for many internet users.

Information gleaned from notices in individual cases often drives news cycles about particularly controversial decisions. It cannot show researchers the big picture, but it can play an important role in surfacing errors, by putting information in the hands of the people most likely to care and take action.

Issue-Specific Platform Disclosures

For high-profile content-moderation issues, platforms are increasingly issuing in-depth public statements to explain their policies. Some offer detailed information on platforms' assessment of individual cases, which is typically lacking from aggregate transparency reports.

An important example is the terrorist attack on Christchurch of March 15, 2019. Video footage of the attack was live streamed on Facebook and spread virally to several other websites. Facebook ultimately issued two public announcements describing their efforts to remove this graphic footage. They provide detailed timelines of events, starting with the first livestream, as well as data on how often it was subsequently viewed, shared, re-uploaded, and ultimately removed.[32] In its response to the Christchurch incident, Facebook also took the unprecedented step of inviting a legal academic, Kate Klonick, tosit with response teams. Klonick later published her observations (Klonick2019).

Facebook also issued several statements regarding its efforts to remove "coordinated inauthentic behaviour," to protect elections in, for example, Ukraine,[33] Israel,[34] India, and Pakistan[35] and targeting fake accounts originating from Russia[36] and Iran.[37] These posts explain how the platform identifies inauthentic behaviour, what patterns it has found, and what removal decisions it made including examples as well as aggregate data.

Cloudflare, a web infrastructure company, published a particularly influential blog post about content moderation in the aftermath of the Charlottesville riots of August 11, 2018. It explained why the company had decided to terminate its services to The Daily Stormer, a white supremacist website. The author, CEO Matthew Prince, was remarkably self-critical and highlighted the "the risks of a company like Cloudflare getting into content policing" (Cloudflare 2017).

Perhaps the most in-depth example of issue-specific reporting is Google's report on Three Years of the Right to Be Forgotten (Google 2018b). This document is unique in the degree of detail it provides about the company's internal process in assessing individual removal requests. It provides anonymized examples of individual cases, such as one request to remove search results for "an interview[the notifier] conducted after surviving a terrorist attack" and another for "a news article about [the notifier's] acquittal for domestic violence on the grounds that no medical report was presented to the judge confirming the victim's injuries" (Google 2018b, p. 10; Google took down both). The report lists several specific factors and classifications Google uses to resolve requests. One factor, for example, is the identity of the "requesting entity." Google classifies the requesting entity for each item of disputed online content using the six categories in Table 10.1 (Google2018b,

p. 5). Based on these granular criteria, Google generates aggregate numbers and statistical analysis.

Table 10.1 Breakdown of all requested URLs after January 2016 by the categories of requesting entities

Requesting entity	Requested URLs	Breakdown	Delisting rate
Private individual	858,852	84.5%	44.7%
Minor	55,140	5.4%	78.0%
Nongovernmental public figure	41,213	4.1%	35.5%
Government official or politician	33,937	3.3%	11.7%
Corporate entity	22,739	2.2%	0.0%
Deceased person	4,402	0.4%	27.2%

Note. Private individuals make up the bulk of requests.

The report is also valuable because it illustrates concretely how a platform might break down complex claims into standardized elements or checkboxes for rapid, large-scale processing. Independent researchers could review these elements to assess, for example, how adequate they seem as an alternative to judicial review of parties' competing privacy and free expression rights. They could also use the reported factors and elements as a concrete, debatable starting point in discussing what information platform employees should reasonably track and report about each takedown decision.

Official Government Records and Public Disclosures

Valuable information about platform operations sometimes surfaces to the public through court or other public filings.38 Documents made public in the Viacom v. YouTube case, for example, made headlines for their revelations about both parties to the suit (Anderson 2010; YouTube 2010). Information disclosed in response to consultations by governments or transnational bodies has appeared in publications including a 2012 European Commission staff report (European Commission 2012) and reports from the office of the UN Free Expression Rapporteur (Kaye 2017).

More recently, large platforms including Facebook, YouTube, and Twitter have published important reports as part of their compliance with Germany's NetzDG law.39 That law is best known for its unusually strict content-removal rules, but it also imposes unprecedented public reporting requirements. Platforms' biannual reports include information such as staffing numbers, wellness resources available to staff, operational processes, the number of consultations with external legal counsel, and turnaround time for responding to notices, broken down by the specific legal violation alleged. While researchers have no independent means of assessing accuracy of the platforms' legal determinations, the reports are rich in other statistics and operational detail.

For example, in the second half of 2018, YouTube received NetzDG notices identifying more than 250,000 items. The most reported category was Hate Speech or Political Extremism (83,000 plus complaints), followed by Defamation or Insults (51,000 plus) and Sexual Content (36,000 plus). In response, YouTube removed 54,644 items, with takedown rates varying per content category (Google 2018c). The report also shows whether notices were submitted by users vs. German government agencies.

As Figure 10.1 from the report shows, YouTube also relied heavily on Community Guidelines. Nonetheless, it looked to German law to resolve the legal status of more than 10,000 items.

Facebook's NetzDG reports paint a very different picture. In the same period, they reportedly received only 500 NetzDG complaints, involving 1,048 items of content – only a fraction of what YouTube and other major platforms received (Facebook 2018b). This is likely because their NetzDG complaint form was less visible on their website compared to YouTube or Twitter. Yet Facebook's Community Guideline removals in the same period numbered in the millions and were not included in the NetzDG report. On July 2, 2019, Germany's Federal Office of Justice fined Facebook €2 million for incomplete reporting, claiming that, because it was unclear which complaints based on Community Guidelines had in fact identified unlawful material, "the number of received complaints about unlawful content is incomplete," and the reports therefore created a "distorted picture" (Bundesamt für Justiz 2019). This raises the question whether NetzDG also requires platforms to assess and report on the lawfulness of content decisions that are not referred to them under the NetzDG framework.

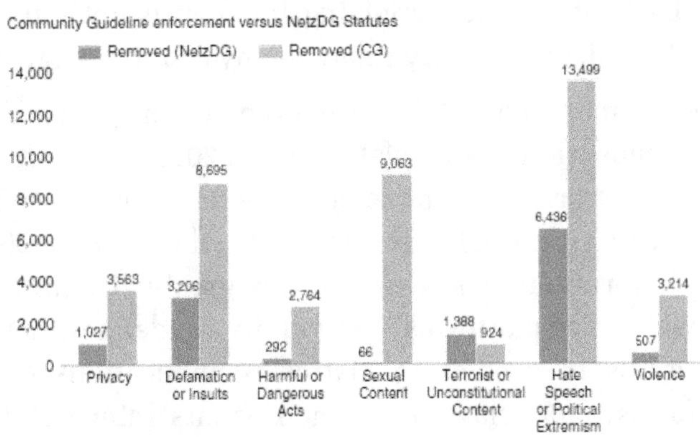

Fig 10.1 Community guideline enforcement versus NetzDG statutes Source. Google (2018c)

The European Commission also persuaded Twitter, Google, and Facebook to publish monthly compliance reports in the run-up to the EU elections of May 2019, as part of the Code of Practice on Disinformation (European Commission 2018b). These reports describe a range of activity related to disinformation, including media literacy and fact-checking efforts but also certain forms of content moderation. Importantly, these are some of the few reports to discuss the enforcement of advertising standards, including procedural information on the approval, review, and transparency mechanisms for political advertising as well as quantitative data on advertising activity and removal decisions. In May 2019, for instance, Google detected 16,690 EU-based Google accounts in violation of its misrepresentation policies, and Twitter removed 1,418 ads in violation of their Unacceptable Business Practices Policy (which prohibits, e.g., misleading content) (Google 2019; Twitter 2019). Finally, the US House Intelligence Committee has also published important datasets, obtained from Facebook, about Russian political advertising during the 2016 US presidential elections (US House of Representatives 2019).

Platforms also disclose takedown information to the European Commission for inclusion in the Commission's reporting on the Hate Speech Code of Conduct (European Commission 2016, 2017). Under the Code of Conduct, expert organizations notify participating platforms about content the organizations have identified as illegal hate speech. Platforms complied with 28 percent of such notices in the Commission's first review and 59 percent in its second – a development billed by the Commission as "important progress." Yet the figures represent only notifiers' and platforms' rate of agreement about what content should come down; and, while the Code of Conduct refers to "illegal" hate speech, platforms (and perhaps also notifiers) presumably actually assess notices under their Community Guidelines. Without independent access to notices and affected content, we cannot know what standards either side is applying, how consistently and accurately those standards are enforced, or how they relate to any country's laws.40

Some related but more modest disclosures come from governments themselves, sometimes in conjunction with platforms. A 2016 report from Europol, for example, discusses terrorist content referred by its Internet Referral Unit (IRU) to platforms for takedown (Europol 2016). As of then, the IRU had referred 9,787 items to 70 different platforms. Its success rate was greater than 90 percent. Because IRUs seek removal under platforms' Community Guidelines, however, this figure reflects only success in predicting platforms' applications of those rules – or convincing platforms to adopt law enforcement agents' interpretation. Independent researchers have no means of ascertaining what portion of referred or removed content violates any laws.

Some European states also operate their own IRUs at the national level. Their operations have been criticized for a lack of transparency, but occasional disclosures have occurred. The UK's Counter-Terrorist Information Referral Unit (CTIRU) published data on its website on December 2016 claiming that it was instigating the removal of more than 2,000 pieces of content per week and was on course to have removed more than 250,000 pieces of content in total by the end of the year (UK Metropolitan Police 2016). The CTIRU has also published information in Parliamentary Hearings41 and in response to Freedom of Information requests submitted by University College Dublin law professor T. J. McIntyre (2018).

More government reporting about their involvement in content moderation may one day be required by law. The EU Parliament's draft of the Terrorist Content Regulation, for example, includes detailed requirements for transparency about law enforcement referrals to platforms.42

Audits

Published reports from independent auditors represent a small but likely growing category of disclosure. The Global Network Initiative has published reports of privacy and content-removal practices going back to 2013 for companies including Facebook, Google, LinkedIn, Microsoft, and Yahoo, for example. The reports, which draw on internal but non-privileged information shared by the companies, include general assessments and case studies.43 Other presumably also honor notifications – and Commission counts them as "successful" – for content that does not violate the law but does violate the platforms' Community Guidelines. The increase from 28 percent compliance to 59 percent could mean that notifiers got better at predicting platforms' internal rules.

One-off independent audits have become a common response to tech industry scandals and may produce relevant information going forward.44

A Human Rights Audit of the Internet Watch Foundation ("IWF Audit") report provides insights into an important non-platform participant in content takedowns (MacDonald 2014).45 The UK's Internet Watch Foundation (IWF) is a private, non-profit organization that works with police, companies, and the public to identify child sexual abuse material online. It then conveys lists of URLs to intermediaries to be blocked. The IWF Audit, prepared at IWF's request by an outside human rights expert, details the group's internal operations and suggests improved processes for, among other things, appeals and difficult legal judgment calls. This report is unique among empirical research – and important to developments well beyond child protection – in its focus on the interplay of state and private action. For example, it discusses the role that IWF as a private organization plays in speeding takedown requests initiated by police – requests that would otherwise require additional judicial process (MacDonald 2014, p. 5).

Leaked Information

In addition to their publicly available Community Guidelines, platforms also issue more detailed rules and instructions for their content-moderation staff. These documents are confidential, but they have been leaked to the press on several occasions. They shed some light on the way that platforms' general principles are enforced in practice; in order to instruct their moderators at scale, platforms are often forced to reduce complex speech issues to simplified rules of thumb.

For instance, Facebook instruction manuals leaked to *The Guardian* told content moderators that the phrase "Someone should shoot Trump" was a credible threat of violence, whereas "Let's beat up fat kids" was not (Hopkins 2017). In documents leaked to the *Süddeutsche Zeitung*, Facebook instructed moderators to treat people as public figures, with fewer privacy protections, as long as they "were mentioned in news reports five times or more in the past two years" (Krause and Grasegger 2016). Gawker's 2012 leaks alleged that Facebook contractors were instructed to "escalate" to Facebook employees any "maps of Kurdistan," "burning Turkish flag(s)," and "All attacks on Ataturk (visual and text)" – suggesting that Facebook made concessions to public pressure from Turkey (Chen 2012). More recently, the *New York Times* has also published similar documents (Fisher 2018).

Independent Research

A growing and important body of information about platforms' takedown practices comes from outside researchers. Some (1) analyze data released by platforms, while others (2) perform surveys and interviews with platform staff and other participants in the takedown ecosystem.[46] (3) Others haverun their own tests and experiments with platform services and associated software.

Analysis of Data Disclosed by Platforms

As mentioned in the section on "Primary Source Information Shared by Platforms," researchers using the Lumen database can do an important thing most others cannot: review the content that platforms actually removed. A handful of Lumen-based reports, like *Notice and Takedown*, take this approach (Urban et al. 2016). Most concern copyright, since the bulk of the data Lumen holds relates to the US DMCA.[47]

One recent exception came from law professor Eugene Volokh, who discovered that numerous claimants had falsified court orders and used them to convince Google to take content out of its search results (Volokh and Levy 2016). Volokh's detective work, which involved hiring an actual detective, turned on clues like the dates and official stamp numbers that appeared on the putative court documents – details that were only available because Lumen gives researchers access to exact copies.

Reporting and Interviews with Participants in Takedown Processes

Other researchers have carried out the painstaking work of tracking global developments and seeking out and interviewing individual participants. Rebecca McKinnon laid important groundwork for this in her 2012 book *Consent of the Networked* (MacKinnon 2012). The *Notice and Takedown* report, discussed in the section titled "A Case Study: Notice and Takedown in Everyday Practice," builds on interviews and extensively documents the self- reported behaviours of copyright owners, platforms, and other players in the notice-and-takedown ecosystem (Urban et al. 2016, pp. 10–13, 116–117).

Noteworthy contributions relating to Community Guidelines enforcement include Kate Klonick's article "The new governors: The people, rules, and processes governing online speech," for which the author reviewed public reporting to date on the topic and interviewed early platform content moderators to understand the growth of their rules. Facebook, for example, started with vague rules, remembered by one employee as "Feel bad? Take itdown" (Klonick 2018). Tarleton Gillespie explored content moderation at length in a 2018 book (Gillespie 2018). Other researchers have reported on platforms' publicly documented removal rules (Venturini et al. 2016; York et al. 2018).

Reporters like Julia Angwin have experimented with platform content toleration, documenting things like anti-Semitic ad targeting terms on Facebook (Angwin, Varner, and Tobin 2017). Academics and civil society advocates affiliated with Onlinecensorship.org have used crowd sourcing to gather and quantify users' reportsofexperienceswithplatformtakedowns(Anderson,Carlsonetal. 2016; Anderson, Stender et al. 2016), including apparent disparate impact on vulnerable and minority groups (York and Gullo 2018). Documentarians have produced at least two films about the on- the-ground experience of individual frontline content moderators working in places like India or the Philippines for vendors under contract with US-based platforms.48 Daniel Kreiss and Shannon McGregor have performed in-depth interviews with Facebook and Google's advertising staff, in order to study how company standards around political advertising are developed and enforced (Kreiss and McGregor 2019); and academics including Sarah Roberts have analyzed more closely the role – and vulnerability – of this global workforce (Roberts 2019).

Academics also engage with platform employees at conferences and other discussion events, such as the Content Moderation at Scale (or "COMO") series initiated by Professor Eric Goldman of Santa Clara University.49

Independent Trials and Experiments

Because platforms' content-removal decisions are taken behind closed doors, some researchers have been creative in nosing out useful information. European researchers in the early 2000s, for example, experimented with posting famous out-of-copyright literature – John Stuart Mill's On Liberty in one case (Ahlert, Marsden, and Yung 2004) and an essay by the nineteenth-century Dutch satirist Multatuli in another (Leyden 2004) – and then submitting copyright infringement notices to see if intermediaries would take them down. Most intermediaries complied. More recently, the researcher Rishabh Dara sent a wide array of content-removal requests to intermediaries in India and tracked their responses in detail (Dara 2011). There, too, platforms generally erred on the side of caution. Dara's research is relatively unique in its focus on non- copyright claims. For example, by invoking a law against advocacy of gambling, he caused a news site to take down user comments concerning a proposed change in Indian gambling law (2011, p. 15).50 University of Haifa researchers Mayaan Perel and Niva Elkin-Koren did similar research in Israel to assess the use of algorithms in copyright takedown processes – a method they call "black box tinkering" (Perel and Elkin-Koren 2017).

Independent research may be particularly relevant for the study of algorithmic content filtering systems, which have become increasingly central to legal debates and large platforms' moderation practices. Reliance on these technologies concerns civil rights activists, since they perform poorly in decisions that require nuanced assessments of context.51 Distinguishing terrorist propaganda from journalist commentary on terrorism, for instance, or distinguishing content piracy from parody or other fair uses, is difficult to automate.

In a 2018 report, the Center for Democracy and Technology reviewed commercially available text-based filters and found an accuracy rate in the 70–80 percent range (Center for Democracy and Technology 2017). Filters performed particularly poorly in assessing jokes or sarcasm or in languages not spoken by their developers (Center for Democracy and Technology 2017, pp. 14, 19). A 2017 report by Princeton Computer Science professor Nick Feamster and Evan Engstrom of the start-up–advocacy group Engine provides greater technical detail, analyzing one of the few open-source (and hence publicly reviewable) filtering tools, Echoprint (Engstrom and Feamster 2017). The authors found a 1–2 percent error rate in simple duplicate matching, including both false positive and false negatives. Under a broader view of content moderation, platforms also shape discourse through the design of their ranking and recommender algorithms, such as Facebook's News Feed and YouTube's Recommended videos (Keller 2019b). A growing body of literature in computer science and communications science seeks to ascertain the operation and effects of these complex systems.52 The design of these algorithms is currently unregulated, but several governments have recently proposed to do so.53 Most of these initiatives also explicitly demand greater transparency in algorithmic recommendations.54

CONSEQUENCES OF PLATFORM CONTENT REMOVAL

Most empirical research on platform content takedowns focuses on removal decisions themselves. Research on more complex questions about how removals affect individual users or society at large is generally harder to come by.

One possible exception is the growing body of research on online influence and the distortion of democratic political processes. Areas of empirical inquiry include "fake news," Russian electoral interference, bot-based message amplification, and political bias in platforms' content-moderation policies. Current and likely future work in this area is comparatively robust and is discussed throughout this volume. A promising source for future research is Facebook's Social Science One project with the Social Science Research Council, which will provide some access to anonymized user data for independent research on "the effects of social media on democracy and elections."55

Another relevant issue is the charge, increasingly raised in the United States, Germany, and elsewhere, that major California-based platforms are biased against political conservatives. Individual takedown decisions often drive news coverage or social media concern about this possibility. To meaningfully assess the claim, however, researchers would need for more information about overall takedown patterns. Even with that data, researchers may continue to disagree on what qualifies as legitimate political speech and which speakers fall into the category of "conservatives." For example, commentators have disagreed on the appropriate classification of the American Nazi Party (Hanania 2019; Graves 2019).

Beyond election-related topics, empirical research on the broader impact of platform takedown decisions is rare. One particularly pressing question concerns the connection between online speech and offline violence. Observers around the world have pointed to social media as a causal factor in violence in areas from Myanmar to Libya (Walsh and Zway 2018; McLaughlin 2018). A 2018 study from Germany, claiming to quantify Facebook's impact on physical assaults against immigrants, drew both headlines and condemnation of its methodology (Taub and Fisher 2018; Masnick 2018).

Research on terrorism, radicalization, and recruitment is comparatively advanced, but experts are divided on the true role of online materials. A 2017 review of literature to date, for example, cited divergent opinions but some movement toward "consensus that the internet alone is not generally a cause of radicalisation, but can act as a facilitator and catalyser of an individual's trajectory towards violent political acts" (Meleagrou-Hitchens and Kaderbhai 2017, pp. 19, 39; Keller 2018).

Other researchers have cited data suggesting that open platforms, which permit public visibility and counter-speech, may be less conducive to real- world violence than more isolated internet echo chambers (Benesch 2014; Munger 2017).56 A related empirical question concerns online speech and public participation by members of vulnerable or minority groups. Many thinkers express concern, for example, that toleration for lawful but offensive or threatening speech on platforms like Twitter effectively diminishes the public presence of ethnic minorities, women, and other frequently attacked groups (West 2017). Civil rights organizations have also charged platforms with disproportionately silencing members of minority groups.57 Questions about disparate impact or bias in takedown operations are all but impossible to truly answer, however, in the absence of representative datasets revealing individual content-removal decisions.

Other consequences of platform takedown operations may affect any user. Individuals who are locked out of their accounts with major platforms like Facebook or Google, for example, may find themselves unable to access other online services that depend on the same login information. Those who depend on hosting services to maintain their writing or art may find their own sole copies deleted (Macdonald 2016); and several studies suggest that internet users who believe their speech is being monitored curtail their writing and research (Marthews and Tucker 2017, Pen America 2013, Penney 2016).

Empirical Questions about Platform Content Takedowns

The empirical research summarized in this chapter answers some important questions about platform content takedowns and illuminates others. Key considerations that should inform policy decisions are listed here. Current and future research addressing these questions will improve both our understanding and public decision-making on questions involving platforms and online speech.

- **Accuracy rates in identifying prohibited material**
    - In notices from third parties generally
    - In notices from expert or "trusted" third parties
    - In flags generated by automated tools
    - In platform decision-making
- **Areas of higher or lower accuracy**
    - For different claims (such as defamation or copyright)
    - For different kinds of content (such as images vs. text; English language vs. Hindi; news articles vs. poems)
    - For different kinds of notifiers (such as "trusted experts")

- Success rates of mechanisms designed to prevent over-removal
  - Legal obligations or penalties for notifiers
  - Legal obligations or penalties for platforms
  - Counter-notice by users accused of posting unlawful content
  - Audits by platforms
  - Audits by third parties
  - Public transparency
- Costs
  - Economic or other costs to platforms
  - Economic or other costs to third parties when platforms under-remove (prohibited content persists on platforms)
  - Economic or other costs to third parties when platforms over-remove (when platforms take down lawful or permitted content)
- Filters
  - Accuracy in identifying duplicates
  - Accuracy in classifying never-before-seen content
  - Ability to discern or assess when the same item of content appears in a new context (such as news reporting)
  - Relative accuracy for different kinds of prohibited content (such as nudity vs. support of terrorism)
  - Relative accuracy for different kinds of files or media (such as text vs. MP3)
  - Effectiveness of human review by platform employees to correct filtering errors
  - Cost, including implementation and maintenance costs for platforms that license third-party filtering technology
  - Impact on subsequent technical development (such as locking in particular technical designs)
- Community Guidelines
  - Rules enforced
  - Processes, including appeal
  - Accuracy and cost of enforcement
  - Governments' role in setting Community Guidelines

- Governments' role in specific content-removal decisions
- Consequences of removal, over-removal, and under-removal
  - Public information and discourse, including trust in media
  - Electoral outcomes
  - Violence
  - Commercial interests of notifiers
  - Commercial interests of businesses impacted by removals
  - Disparate impact based on race, gender, etc.

SUMMARY

Public understanding of platforms' content-removal operations, even among specialized researchers, has long been limited. This information vacuum leaves policymakers poorly equipped to respond to concerns about platforms, online speech, and democracy. A growing body of independent research and company disclosures, however, is beginning to remedy the situation. Through improved public transparency by platforms, and thoughtful inquiry and evaluation by independent experts, we may move toward new insights and sounder public policy decisions.

REFERENCES

Access Now. (2016). Transparency Reporting Index. Access Now report. www.accessnow.org/transparency-reporting-index/

Ahlert, C., Marsden, C., & Yung, C. (2004). How "liberty" disappeared from cyberspace: The mystery shopper tests internet content self-regulation. Programme in Comparative Media Law & Policy at the Oxford Centre for Socio-Legal Studies research paper.

Amazon. (2015). Amazon Information Request Report. Amazon report. http://d0.awsstatic.com/certifications/Transparency_Report.pdf

Anderson, J., Carlson, K., Stender, M., West, S. M.,& York, J. C. (2016). Censorship in Context: Insights from Crowdsourced Data on Social Media Censorship. Onlinecensorship.org report. https://onlinecensorship.org/news-and-analysis/ onlinecensorship-org-launches-second-report-censorship-in-context-pdf

Anderson, J., Stender, M., West, S. M., & York, J. C. (2016). Unfriending Censorship: Insights from Four Months of Crowdsourced Data on Social Media Censorship. Onlinecensorship.org report. https://onlinecensorship.org/ news-and-analysis/onlinecensorship-org-launches-first-report-download

Anderson, N. (2010). Smoking guns, dark secrets aplenty in YouTube-Viacom filings. Ars Technica, March 18. https://arstechnica.com/tech-policy/2010/03/smoking- guns-dark-secrets-spilled-in-youtube-viacom-filings/

Angelopolous, C., Brody, A., Hins, A. W. et al. (2016). Study of Fundamental Rights Limitations for Online Enforcement Through Self-Regulation. Report. https://perma.cc/8QAW-79QT

Angwin, J., Varner, M., & Tobin, A., (2017). Facebook enabled advertisers to reach "Jew haters." ProPublica, September 14. www.propublica.org/article/facebook- enabled-advertisers-to-reach-jew-haters

Automattic. (n.d.). Transparency Report. Automattic report. https://transparency.automattic.com

Bar-Ziv, S., & Elkin-Koren, N. (2017). Behind the scenes of online copyright enforcement: Empirical evidence on notice & takedown. Connecticut Law Review, 50(2), 1–46.

Benesch, S. (2014). Countering dangerous speech to prevent mass violence duringKenya's 2013 elections. Dangerous Speech Project website, February 9. https:// dangerousspeech.org/countering-dangerous-speech-kenya-2013

Benesch, S., & Matias, J. N. (2018). Launching today: New collaborative study to diminish abuse on Twitter. Medium, April 6. https://medium.com/@susanbenesch/launching-today-new-collaborative-study-to-diminish-abuse-on- twitter-2b91837668cc

Boyden, B. (2013). The Failure of the DMCA Notice and Takedown System. George Mason University Center for the Protection of Intellectual Property. https://sls.gmu.edu/cpip/wp-content/uploads/sites/31/2013/08/Bruce-Boyden-The-Failure-of-the- DMCA-Notice-and-Takedown-System1.pdf

Bridy, A., & Keller, D. (2016). U.S. Copyright Office Section 512 Study: Comments in Response to Notice of Inquiry, March 31. (2017). U.S. Copyright Office Section 512 study: Comments in response to second notice of inquiry. SSRN. https://papers.ssrn.com/sol3/papers.cfm?abstract_id=2920871

Bundesamt fuer Justiz. (2019). Bundesamt für Justiz erlässt Bußgeldbescheid gegen Facebook. Bundesjustizamt.de. www.bundesjustizamt.de/DE/Presse/Archiv/2019/ 20190702.html

Cannataci, J., Kaye, D., & Ní Aoláin, F. (2018). Mandates of the Special Rapporteur on the promotion and protection of the right to freedom of opinion and expression; the right to privacy; and promotion and protection of human rights and fundamental freedoms while countering terrorism.

United Nations Special Rapporteur communication OL OTH 71/2018, December 7. https://spcommreports.ohchr.org/TMResultsBase/DownLoadPublicCommunicationFile?gId=24234

Center for Democracy and Technology. (2017). Mixed Messages? The Limits of Automated Social Media Content Analysis. Center for Democracy and Technology report. https://cdt.org/insight/mixed-messages-the-limits-of-automated-social-media- content-analysis/

Chang, B. (2018). From Internet Referral Units to international agreements: Censorship of the Internet by the UK and EU. Columbia Human Rights Law Review, 49(2), 114–212.

Chen, A. (2012). Inside Facebook's outsourced anti-porn and gore brigade, where "camel toes" are more offensive than "crushed heads." Gawker.com, February16. http://gawker.com/5885714/inside-facebooks-outsourced-anti-porn-and-gore- brigade-where-camel-toes-are-more-offensive-than-crushed-heads

Cloudflare. (2017). Why we terminated Daily Stormer. Cloudflare.com (blog), August16. https://blog.cloudflare.com/why-we-terminated-daily-stormer/

Copyright Alliance. (2016). Comments of the Copyright Alliance Before the U.S. Copyright Office, Docket No. 2015-7. https://copyrightalliance.org/wp-content/ uploads/2016/11/Copyright-Alliance-Section-512-Comments1.pdf

Cornia, A., Sehl, A., Levy, D., & Nielsen, R. K. (2018). Private Sector News, Social Media Distribution, and Algorithm Change. Reuters Institute Digital News Projectreport. https://reutersinstitute.politics.ox.ac.uk/our-research/private-sector-news- social-media-distribution-and-algorithm-change

Cushing, T. (2017). Someone under Federal Indictment Impersonates a Journalist to File Bogus DMCA Notice. Techdirt, May 23. www.techdirt.com/articles/ 20170518/09500537404/someone-under-federal-indictment-impersonates-journalist-to-file-bogus-dmca-notice.shtml

Dara, R. (2011). Intermediary Liability in India: Chilling Effects on Free Expression on the Internet. https://cis-india.org/internet-governance/intermediary-liability- in-india.pdf

Duguay, S., Burgess, J., & Suzor, N. (2018). Queer women's experiences of patchwork platform governance on Tinder, Instagram, and Vine. Convergence, 26(2), 237– 252. https://doi.org/10.1177/1354856518781530

Engstrom, E., & Feamster, N. (2017). The Limits of Filtering: A Look at the Functionality & Shortcomings of Content Detection Tools. Engine report. www.engine.is/the-limits-of-filtering

European Commission. (2016). Code of Conduct on Countering Illegal Hate Speech Online: First Results on Implementation. European Commission report. http://ec.europa.eu/information_society/newsroom/image/document/2016-50/factsheet- code-conduct-8_40573.pdf

(2017). Code of Conduct on Countering Online Hate Speech: Results of Evaluation Show Important Progress. European Commission report. http://ec.europa.eu/ newsroom/just/item-detail.cfm?item_id=71674

(2018a). Public consultation on measures to further improve the effectiveness of the fight against illegal content online. Europa.eu. https://ec.europa.eu/digital-single- market/en/news/public-consultation-measures-further-improve-effectiveness-fight- against-illegal-content-online

(2018b). EU Code of Practice on Disinformation. Europa.eu. https://ec.europa.eu/digital-single-market/en/news/code-practice-disinformation

European Digital Rights. (2016). Europol: Non-transparent cooperation with IT companies. EDRi.org. https://edri.org/europol-non-transparent-cooperation-with- it-companies/

Europol. (2016). EU Internet Referral Unit: Year One Report. Europol report. www.europol.europa.eu/sites/default/files/documents/eu_iru_1_year_report_highlights.pdf Facebook. (2018a). Facebook Government Requests. Facebook report. https:// govtrequests.facebook.com

(2018b). NetzDG Transparency Report (January–June 2018). Facebook report. https://fbnewsroomus.files.wordpress.com/2018/07/facebook_netzdg_july_2018_ english-1.pdf

(2019a). A further update on the New Zealand terrorist attack. FacebookNewsroom, March 20. https://newsroom.fb.com/news/2019/03/technical- update-on-new-zealand/

(2019b). Update on New Zealand. Facebook Newsroom, March 18. https://newsroom.fb.com/news/2019/03/update-on-new-zealand/

(2019c). More coordinated inauthentic behaviour from Russia. Facebook Newsroom,May 6. https://newsroom.fb.com/news/2019/05/more-cib-from-russia/(

2019d). Removing coordinated inauthentic behaviour from Israel. Facebook Newsroom, May 16. https://newsroom.fb.com/news/2019/05/removing-coordinated-inauthentic- behavior-from-israel/

(2019e). Removing coordinated inauthentic behaviour and spam from India and Pakistan. Facebook Newsroom, April 1. https://newsroom.fb.com/news/2019/04/ cib-and-spam-from-india-pakistan/

(2019f). More coordinated inauthentic behaviour from Russia. Facebook Newsroom,May 6. https://newsroom.fb.com/news/2019/05/more-cib-from-russia/

(2019g). Removing more coordinated inauthentic behaviour from Iran. Facebook Newsroom, May 28. https://newsroom.fb.com/news/2019/05/removing-more-cib- from-iran/

Fisher, M. (2018). Inside Facebook's secret rulebook for global political speech. New York Times, December 27. www.nytimes.com/2018/12/27/world/ facebook-moderators.html

Ford, G. S. (2017). Notice and takedown in everyday practice: A review. SSRN. https://papers.ssrn.com/sol3/papers.cfm?abstract_id=2963230

French Secretary of State for Digital Affairs. (2019). Interim Mission Report: Creating aFrench Framework to Make Social Media Platforms More Accountable. Mission report. www.numerique.gouv.fr/uploads/Regulation-of-social-networks_Mission- report_ENG.pdf

Galperin, E. (2008). Massive takedown of anti-Scientology videos on YouTube. Electronic Frontier Foundation, September 5. www.eff.org/deeplinks/2008/09/ massive-takedown-anti-scientology-videos-youtube

Gebhart, G. (2018). Who has your back? Censorship edition 2018. Electronic Frontier Foundation, September 10. www.eff.org/who-has-your-back-2018

German Parliament. (2018). Proposal of Representative Kunast and Others to Further Develop the Network Enforcement Law. Document 19/5950. http://dip21. bundestag.de/dip21/btd/19/059/1905950.pdf

Gillespie, T. (2018). Custodians of the Internet: Platforms, Content Moderation, and the Hidden Decisions That Shape Social Media. New Haven, CT: Yale University Press.

GitHub. (2015). GitHub's 2014 Transparency Report. Github report. https://github.com/blog/1987-github-s-2014-transparency-report

Goldman, E. (2018). COMO: Content moderation at scale conference recap. Eric Goldman (blog). https://blog.ericgoldman.org/archives/2018/07/como-content- moderation-at-scale-conference-recap.htm

Google. (n.d.). Google Transparency Report. Google report. https://transparencyreport.google.com

(2018a). YouTube Community Guidelines Enforcement Report. Google report. https://transparencyreport.google.com/youtube-policy/removals?hl=en

(2018b). Three Years of the Right to be Forgotten. Google report. https://g.co/research/rtbf_report

(2018c). Removals under the Network Enforcement Law. Google report. https:// transparencyreport.google.com/netzdg/youtube(2019). EU Code of Practice: May Report. Google report. https://ec.europa.eu/newsroom/dae/document.cfm?doc_id=60042

Graves, Z. (2019). Does Twitter have an anti-conservative bias, or just a Nazi bias? Techdirt, July 18. www.techdirt.com/articles/20190221/16154641652/does-twitter- have-anti-conservative-bias-just-anti-nazi-bias.shtml

The Guardian. (2017). YouTube changes restrictions on gay-themed content following outcry. The Guardian, March 21. www.theguardian.com/music/2017/mar/21/ youtube-changes-restrictions-gay-lgbtq-themed-content-tegan-sarah

Hanania, R. (2019). It isn't your imagination: Twitter treats conservatives more harshly than liberals. Quillette, July 18. https://quillette.com/2019/02/12/it-isnt-your- imagination-twitter-treats-conservatives-more-harshly-than-liberals/

Hargreaves, E., Agosti, C., Menasche, D., Neglia, G., Reiffers-Mason, A., & Altman, E. (2018). Biases in the Facebook News Feed: A case study on the Italian elections. arXiv.org. https://arxiv.org/abs/1807.08346

Heins, M., & Beckles, T. (2005). Will Fair Use Survive? Free Expression in the Age of Copyright Control. Brennan Center for Justice report. www.brennancenter.org/ publication/will-fair-use-survive-free-expression-age-copyright-control

Helberger, N., Leerssen, P., & van Drunen, M. (2019). Germany proposes Europe's first diversity rules for social media platforms. LSE Media Policy Project (blog), May 29. https://blogs.lse.ac.uk/mediapolicyproject/2019/05/29/germany-proposes-europes-first-diversity-rules-for-social-media-platforms/

Hopkins, N. (2017). Revealed: Facebook's internal rulebook on sex, terrorism and violence. The Guardian, May 21. www.theguardian.com/news/2017/may/21/ revealed-facebook-internal-rulebook-sex-terrorism-violence

Human Rights Watch. (2006). "Race to the Bottom": Corporate Complicity in Chinese Internet Censorship. Human Rights Watch report. www.hrw.org/reports/2006/ china0806/china0806web.pdf

Kaye, D. (2017). Report of the Special Rapporteur on the Promotion and Protection of the Right to Freedom of Opinion and Expression, A/HRC/35/22, United Nations, August 18. https://documents-dds-ny.un.org/doc/UNDOC/GEN/G17/077/46/PDF/ G1707746.pdf? OpenElement

Keller, D. (2018). Internet platforms: Observations on speech, danger and money. Hoover Institution Aegis Paper Series No. 1807. www.hoover.org/research/internet-platforms-observations-speech-danger-and-money

(2019a). Build your own Intermediary Liability law: A kit for policy wonks of all ages. Balkinization (blog), June 11. https://balkin.blogspot.com/2019/06/build-your- own-intermediary-liability.html?m=1

(2019b). Who do you sue? State and platform hybrid power over speech. Hoover Institution Aegis Paper Series No. 1902. www.hoover.org/sites/default/files/research/docs/who-do-you-sue-state-and-platform-hybrid-power-over-online-speech_0.pdf

Klonick, K. (2018). The new governors: The people, rules, and processes governing online speech. Harvard Law Review, 131 (6), 1599–1669.

(2019). Inside the team at Facebook that dealt with the Christchurch shooting. The New Yorker, July 18. www.newyorker.com/news/news-desk/inside-the-team-at-facebook-that-dealt-with-the-christchurch-shooting

Krause, T., & Grasegger, H. (2016). Facebook's secret rules of deletion. Süddeutsche Zeitung Internet Archive. https://web.archive.org/web/20170103040043/http://international.sueddeutsche.de/post/154543271930/facebooks-secret-rules-of-deletion

Kreiss, D., & McGregor, S. (2019). The "arbiters of what our voters see": Facebook and Google's struggle with policy, process, and enforcement around political advertising. Political Communication, 36(2). www.tandfonline.com/eprint/9IUFbkGmZ4YHtNXM7sQ2/full?target=10.1080/10584609.2019.1619639

Kuczerawy, A. (2017). The power of positive thinking: Intermediary liability and the effective enjoyment of the right to freedom of expression. Journal of Intellectual Property, Information Technology and E-Commerce Law, 8(3), 226–237.

Levin, S. (2017). Civil rights groups urge Facebook to fix "racially biased" moderationsystem. The Guardian, January 18. www.theguardian.com/technology/2017/jan/18/facebook-moderation-racial-bias-black-lives-matter

Leyden, J. (2004). How to kill a website with one email: Exploiting the European E- commerce Directive. The Register, September 10. www.theregister.co.uk/2004/10/ 14/isp_takedown_study

Macdonald, F. (2016). Google's deleted an artist's blog, along with 14 years of his work. Science Alert, July 18. www.sciencealert.com/google-has-deleted-an-artist-s-blog- with-14-years-of-his-work

MacDonald, K. (2014). A Human Rights Audit of the Internet Watch Foundation. Lord MacDonald Report. www.iwf.org.uk/sites/default/files/inline-files/Human_Rights_Audit_web.pdf

MacKinnon, R. (2012). Consent of the Networked: The Worldwide Struggle For Internet Freedom. New York: Hachette Book Group.

Marthews, A., & Tucker, C. E. (2017). Government surveillance and internet search behavior. SSRN. https://papers.ssrn.com/sol3/papers.cfm?abstract_id=2412564

Masnick, M. (2018). Dubious studies and easy headlines: No, a new report does not clearly show Facebook leads to hate crimes. Techdirt, August 3. www.techdirt.com/articles/20180823/00122840491/dubious-studies-easy-headlines-no-new-report-does-not-clearly-show-facebook-leads-to-hate-crimes.shtml?threaded=true

McIntyre, T. J. (2018). Internet censorship in the United Kingdom: National schemesand European norms. In L. Edwards (Ed.), Law, Policy and the Internet (pp. 291– 330). Oxford: Hart Publishing.

McLaughlin, T. (2018). How Facebook's rise fueled chaos and confusion in Myanmar. Wired, September 10. www.wired.com/story/how-facebooks-rise-fueled-chaos- and-confusion-in-myanmar

Medium. (2015). Medium's 2015 Transparency Report. Medium report. https://blog.medium.com/medium-s-2015-transparency-report-5c6205c48afe

Meleagrou-Hitchens, A., & Kaderbhai, N. (2017). Research Perspectives on Online Radicalisation: A Literature Review, 2006–2016. VOX-Pol report. www.voxpol.eu/new-vox-pol-report-research-perspectives-online-radicalisation

Munger, K. (2017). Tweetment effects on the tweeted: Experimentally reducing racist harassment. Political Behavior, 39(3), 629–649. https://link.springer.com/article/ 10.1007/s11109-016-9373-5

O'Brian, D., & Malcolm, J. (2018). 70+ internet luminaries ring the alarm on EU copyright filtering proposal. Electronic Frontier Foundation, June 12. www.eff.org/deeplinks/2018/06/internet-luminaries-ring-alarm-eu-copyright-filtering-proposal

Ong, T. (2018). Facebook is recruiting external advisers to tackle claims of bias on its platform. The Verge, May 2. www.theverge.com/2018/5/2/17310894/facebook- recruiting-external-advisers-bias-minority-conservative

Open Technology Institute. (2018). The Transparency Reporting Toolkit: Content Takedown Reporting. Open Technology Institute report. www.newamerica.org/ oti/reports/transparency-reporting-toolkit-content-takedown-reporting/

Oransky, I. (2013). WordPress removes Anil Potti posts from Retraction Watch in error after false DMCA copyright claim. Retraction Watch, February 5. https://retractionwatch.com/2013/02/05/wordpress-removes-anil-potti-posts-from- retraction-watch-in-error-after-false-dmca-copyright-claim

Pen America (2013). Chilling Effects: NSA Surveillance Drives U.S. Writers to Self-Censor. Pen America report. https://pen.org/chilling-effects

Penney, J. (2016). Chilling effects: Online surveillance and Wikipedia use. Berkeley Technology Law Journal, 31(1), 172. https://papers.ssrn.com/sol3/papers.cfm? abstract_id=2769645

Perel, M., & Elkin-Koren, N. (2017). Black box tinkering: Beyond disclosure in algorithmic enforcement. Florida Law Review, 69(181). https://papers.ssrn.com/ sol3/papers.cfm?abstract_id=2741513

Regulation 2019/1150, 2019 O.J. (L 186) 57 (EU)

Reda, J. (2017).When filters fail: These cases show we can't trust algorithms to clean up the internet. Julia Reda website. https://juliareda.eu/2017/09/when-filters-fail/

Reddit, Inc. (2015). Reddit, Inc. Transparency Report, 2015. www.reddit.com/wiki/transparency/2015

Roberts, S. T. (2016). Commercial content moderation: Digital laborers' dirty work. Media Studies Publications, Paper No. 12. https://ir.lib.uwo.ca/cgi/viewcontent.cgi?article=1012&context=commpub

(2019). Behind the Screen: Content Moderation in the Shadows of Social Media. New Haven, CT: Yale University Press.

Seng, D., (2015). "Who watches the watchmen?" An empirical analysis of errors in DMCA takedown notices. SSRN. https://papers.ssrn.com/sol3/papers.cfm? abstract_id=2563202

Taub, A., & Fisher, M. (2018). Facebook fueled anti-refugee attacks in Germany, new research suggests. New York Times, August 21. www.nytimes.com/2018/08/21/ world/europe/facebook-refugee-attacks-germany.html

Timmer, J. (2013). Site plagiarizes blog posts, then files DMCA takedown on originals. Ars Technica, February 5. https://arstechnica.com/science/2013/02/site-plagiarizes- blog-posts-then-files-dmca-takedown-on-originals

Torrent Freak. (2018). Google Drive uses hash matching to detect pirated content. TorrentFreak.com. https://torrentfreak.com/google-drive-uses-hash-matching-detect- pirated-content

Tumblr. (n.d.). Transparency Report. Tumblr report. www.tumblr.com/transparency Twitter. (2017). Twitter Transparency Report Copyright Notices January – June 2017.

Twitter Report. https://transparency.twitter.com/en/copyright-notices.html#copyright- notices-jan-jun-2017

(2018a). Twitter Rules Enforcement Report. Twitter report. https://transparency.twitter.com/en/twitter-rules-enforcement.html

(2018b). Twitter Netzwerkdurchsetzungsgesetzbericht: Januar – Juni 2018. Twitter report. https://cdn.cms-twdigitalassets.com/content/dam/transparency-twitter/data/ download-netzdg-report/netzdg-jan-jun-2018.pdf

(2019). EU Code of Practice: May Report. Twitter report. https://ec.europa.eu/newsroom/dae/document.cfm?doc_id=60043

UK Metropolitan Police. (2016). 250,000th piece of online extremist/terrorist material to be removed. Archive.org. https://web.archive.org/web/20180306202125/http://news.met.police.uk/news/250000th-piece-of-online-extremist-slash-terrorist-material-to- be-removed-208698

Urban, J. M., Karaganis, J., & Schofield, B. (2016). Notice and takedown in everyday practice. UC Berkeley Public Law Research, Paper No. 2755628. http://ssrn.com/ abstract=2755628

(2017). Response to "Notice and takedown in everyday practice: A review." The Takedown Project. http://takedownproject.org/770-2

Urban, J. M., & Quilter, L. (2006). Efficient process or "chilling effects": Takedown notices under Section 512 of the Digital Millennium Copyright Act. Santa Clara High Tech Law Journal, 22(4): 621–693.

US Copyright Office. (2015). Section 512 Study. US Copyright Office report. www.copyright.gov/policy/section512/

US House of Representatives. (2019). Social Media Advertisements. Intelligence. House.Gov. https://intelligence.house.gov/social-media-content/social-media-advertisements.htm

US Patent and Trademark Office. (2015). Multistakeholder Forum on the DMCA Notice and Takedown System. USPTO.Gov. www.uspto.gov/learning-and-resources/ip- policy/copyright/multistakeholder-forum-dmca-notice-and-takedown-system

Venturini, J., Louzada, L., Maciel, M., Zingales, N., Stylianou, K., & Belli, L. (2016). Terms of Service and Human Rights: An Analysis of Online Platform Contracts. Report. http://bibliotecadigital.fgv.br/dspace/handle/10438/18231

Vivanco, J. M. (2014). Censorship in Ecuador has made it to the Internet. Human Rights Watch news release, December 15. www.hrw.org/news/2014/12/15/censorship- ecuador-has-made-it-internet

Volokh, E., & Levy, P. A. (2016). Dozens of suspicious court cases, with missing defendants, aim at getting web pages taken down or deindexed. Washington Post, October 10. www.washingtonpost.com/news/volokh-conspiracy/wp/2016/10/10/dozens-of-suspicious-court-cases-with-missing-defendants-aim-at-getting-web-pages-taken-down-or-deindexed/?utm_term=.b61e8a5967b2

Walsh, D., & Zway, S. A. (2018). A Facebook war: Libyans battle on the streets and on screens. New York Times, September 4. www.nytimes.com/2018/09/04/world/ middleeast/libya-facebook.html

West, L. (2017). I've left Twitter. It is unusable for anyone but trolls, robots and dictators. The Guardian, January 3. www.theguardian.com/commentisfree/2017/ jan/03/ive-left-twitter-unusable-anyone-but-trolls-robots-dictators-lindy-west

York, J. C., Faris, R., Deibert, R., & Heacock, R. (2018). Policing content in the quasipublic sphere. OpenNet Initiative bulletin, September. https://opennet.net/policing- content-quasi-public-sphere

York, J. C., & Gullo, K. (2018). Offline/Online project highlights how the oppressionmarginalized communities face in the real world follows them online. Electronic Frontier Foundation, March 6. www.eff.org/deeplinks/2018/03/offlineonline- project-highlights-how-oppression-marginalized-communities-face-real

YouTube. (2010). Broadcast yourself. YouTube (official blog), March 18. https://youtube.googleblog.com/2010/03/broadcast-yourself.html

FOOTNOTE

Daphne Keller directs the Program on Platform Regulation at the Stanford Cyber Policy Center and was formerly Associate General Counsel to Google. Paddy Leerssen is a PhD candidate at the Institute for Information Law (IViR), University of Amsterdam, and a nonresident fellow at the Stanford Center for Internet and Society.

1. This chapter does not attempt to list the research on content takedown in more strongly speech- repressive countries such as China. See, e.g., Human Rights Watch (2006).
2. Many laws provide somewhat different rules for different claims (like copyright vs. terrorism) or different kinds of intermediaries (like hosts vs. ISPs). For a review of doctrinal variables, see Keller (2019a).

3. 47 U.S.C. § 230.
4. Marco Civil da Internet, Federal Law no. 12.965 (2014) (Brazil); Copyright Act, Law No. 20.435 (Chile); Corte Suprema de Justicia de la Nacion, 8/10/2014, Rodriguez, Maria Belen c. Google Inc. / da.os y perjuicios (Argentina). U.S.C. § 512.
5. Manila Principles on Intermediary Liability, www.manilaprinciples.org; David Kaye, the UNSpecial Rapporteur on Freedom of Expression, has reported that the Manila Principles "establish baseline protection for intermediaries in accordance with freedom of expression standards" (Kaye 2017).
6. 17 USC 512(m); Council Directive 2000/31, 2000 O.J. (L 178) 1 (EC) ("eCommerce Directive"), Article 15.
7. Directive 2019/790, 2019 O.J. (L130) 92 (EC)("Copyright Directive"), Article 17.
8. European Parliament. Legislative resolution of April 17, 2019 on the proposal for a regulation of the European Parliament and of the Council on preventing the dissemination of terrorist content online (provisional edition), P8_TA-PROV(2019)0421. www.europarl.europa.eu/doceo/docu- ment/TA-8-2019-0421_EN.pdf
9. Center for Democracy and Technology. Civil Society Letter to the European Parliament on the proposed Regulation on Preventing the Dissemination of Terrorist Content Online, February 2019. https://cdt.org/files/2019/02/Civil-Society-Letter-to-European-Parliament-on-Terrorism- Database.pdf
10. US courts have consistently upheld platforms' right to take down users' lawful speech.
11. Internationally, a different picture may be emerging. In 2018, first instance courts in both Germany and Brazil upheld user claims in this situation. See Keller (2019b), pp. 12–13. Experts have raised concerns that states may violate human rights obligations when they rely on private Community Guidelines to prohibit online expression and information. See Angelopolous et al. (2016), pp. 50–51; Kuczerawy (2017).
12. European Commission (2016) (agreement with Microsoft, YouTube, Twitter, and Facebook); European Commission (2018b) (agreement with Facebook, Twitter, and Google). While the Hate Speech Code (European Commission 2016) calls for removal of content posted by users, the Disinformation Code (European Commission 2018b) concerns advertising content and counsels against prohibiting "false" content from ordinary users.
13. Any study's assessment of error rates, while particularly essential for policymaking, is also subject to challenge – since it requires researchers, like the platforms themselves, to make judgment calls in legal gray zones. Some critics disputed Urban, Karaganis, and Schofield's (2016) study methodology on these and other grounds. See, e.g., Ford (2017). Urban, Karaganis, and Schofield (2017) and other experts – including one of this chapter's authors and law professor Annemarie Bridy – defended the study's standards for classifying notices. See Urban et al. (2017); Bridy and Keller (2017).

14. Access Now (2016).
15. Google (n.d.).
16. Facebook (2018a).
17. Twitter (2017).
18. Amazon (2015).
19. Tumblr (n.d.).
20. Medium (2015).
21. Reddit, Inc. (2015).
22. GitHub (2015).
23. Automattic (n.d.).
24. Facebook (2018a).
25. Twitter (2018).
26. Google (2018a).
27. The Ranking Digital Rights 2018 Corporate Accountability Index. https://rankingdigitalrights .org/index2018/
28. The Santa Clara Principles. https://santaclaraprinciples.org/
29. Email correspondence with Adam Holland, Lumen Project Manager.
30. This includes Urban, Karaganis, and Schofield (2017) and numerous other scholarly works including those cited in Section III.B.1, below. See also Brief of Amici Curiae Chilling Effects Clearinghouse Leaders in Support of Appellee at *8–16, Perfect 10, Inc. v. Google, Inc., 653 F.3d 976 (9th Cir. 2011), 2010 WL 5813411, www.eff.org/document/amicus-brief-chilling-effects (citing other works). Equivalent transparency for removal of hosted content, while highly valuable, would be more difficult. It would require either the host or Lumen to actively preserve allegedly illegal content, in the face of a removal request. In many cases, as with privately shared Facebook posts, disclosing the content could also conflict with privacy obligations to users.
31. See French Secretary of State for Digital Affairs (2019), p. 20, which calls for an "independent and extra-judicial mechanism for reviewing the platform's decision."
32. "The first user report on the original video came in 29 minutes after the video started, and 12 minutes after the live broadcast ended. In the first 24 hours, we removed more than 1.2 million videos of the attack at upload. Approximately 300,000 additional copies were removed after they were posted" (Facebook 2019a).
33. Facebook (2019c). 34 Facebook (2019d). 35 Facebook (2019e). 36 Facebook (2019f).
34. Facebook (2019g).
35. See, e.g., European Commission (2018a); US Copyright Office (2015); US Patent and Trademark Office (2015); Torrent Freak (2018) (citing testimony of Google legal director disclosing use of hash matching on Google Drive).

36. Netzwerkdurchsetzungsgesetz vom 1. September 2017 (BGBl. I S. 3352). ("Network Enforcement Law" or "NetzDG"). www.gesetze-im-internet.de/netzdg/BJNR335210017.html; Google (2018c); Twitter (2018b); Facebook (2018b).
37. The Code covers "illegal hate speech," and the Commission says its reports quantify platforms' compliance with "notifications concerning illegal hate speech." In practice, platforms.
38. Hansard. 2017. HL Deb 787 Col. 1261. http://bit.ly/2kctmPL
39. European Parliament. Legislative resolution of 17 April 2019 on the proposal for a regulation of the European Parliament and of the Council on preventing the dissemination of terrorist content online (provisional edition), P8_TA-PROV(2019)0421. www.europarl.europa.eu/doceo/docu- ment/TA-8-2019-0421_EN.pdf
40. Global Network Initiative, Company Assessments. https://globalnetworkinitiative.org/com- pany-assessments/
41. For instance, Facebook recently responded to accusations of bias with new auditing measures, in which "one adviser will conduct an audit of Facebook's impact on minority communities and communities of color, while another will advise the company on the potential bias against conservative perspectives" (Ong 2018).
42. An additional valuable resource documenting content removal mechanisms by IWF and other UK entities is McIntyre (2018).
43. Platforms have recently taken a few steps toward greater disclosures to independent researchers. Facebook, for example, committed to the Social Science One data-sharing project discussed in the main text; and Twitter agreed to experiment with new means of surfacing rules to users in a joint project with researchers (Benesch and Matias 2018). These are important developments, but it is not clear if either will lead to new public information specifically on the topic of contentremoval.
44. Heins and Beckles (2005) found 47 percent of notices stated weak claims or involved speech with important legal defenses; Urban and Quilter (2006), pp. 621, 641, noted 55 percent of notices involved disputes between commercial competitors and 31 percent presented significant legal questions; Bar-Ziv and Elkin-Koren (2017) found a few notifiers accounted for a high 66 percent rate of abusive requests on Israel's .il domain, but the remainder of requests had a rate perhaps as low as 5 percent invalid or questionable requests; Seng (2015), p. 1, found that 8.3 percent of notices had "formal" errors and 1.3 percent had "substantive" errors. A member survey by the Copyright Alliance, a copyright-holder advocacy organization, provided a rare quantification of notifiers' experiences. Of 219 respondents to a survey, 62 percent reported filing DMCA notices that received no response at all from platforms. Examples in the report suggested many may have been smaller companies (see Copyright Alliance 2016).

45. The Cleaners (2018), directed by Hans Block and Moritz Riesewieck (Berlin: Gebrueder Beetz Filmproduktion); Field of Vision – The Moderators (2017), directed by Ciaran Cassidy and Adrian Chen (New York: First Look Media), YouTube video, April 14. www.youtube.com/ watch?v=k9m0axUDpro
46. 49 Santa Clara University School of Law, 2018. Content Moderation & Removal at Scale con-ference, Santa Clara, CA, February 2. https://law.scu.edu/event/content-moderation-removal- at-scale. In one widely reported session, Emma Llansó of the Center for Democracy and Technology and Mike Masnick of the blog Techdirt invited the audience to "make the call" on a series of vexing take-down decisions – and found, even within the relative cultural homo- geneity of a Washington, DC audience, no consensus (Goldman 2018).
47. This research might be difficult to replicate, given ethics concerns about targeting the lawful speech of real-world internet users for unjustified removal.
48. 51 Article 1. 2018. Joint Letter on European Commission regulation on online terrorist content.
49. www.article19.org/resources/joint-letter-on-european-commission-regulation-on-online-ter- rorist-content/; Reda (2017).
50. E.g. see Hargreaves et al. (2018) on documenting patterns in Facebook content recommenda- tions for Italian news media, based on observational data from dummy accounts; see Cornia et al. (2018) on surveying the effects of changes to the Facebook news feed on various news organizations.
51. Helberger, Leerssen, and van Drunen (2019). See also French Secretary of State for Digital Affairs (2019), p. 3, which proposes an "[o]bligation of transparency of the function of ordering content" and a "duty of care towards [platforms'] users"; The European Commission (2018b), in its Code of Practice on Disinformation, requires platforms to "[d]ilute the visibility of disinformation by improving the findability of trustworthy content."
52. European Commission (2018b). See also: Regulation 2019/1150 (EU).
53. Social Science One. https://socialscience.one
54. Research by Susan Benesch, for instance, indicated that speech believed to be correlated to violence during Kenyan election was overrepresented in closed Facebook discussion, compared to public exchanges on Twitter (Benesch 2014).
55. 57 In 2017, for example, seventy civil rights and social justice organizations wrote to Facebook to complain of bias in its content-removal decisions (Levin 2017). In 2018, YouTube faced public outcry from LGBTQ users who said their videos were unfairly penalized (The Guardian 2017); see also Duguay, Burgess, and Suzor (2018). One author of this chapter has argued elsewherethat platforms' overzealous efforts to counter Islamist extremism can be expected to dispropor- tionately harm users speaking Arabic or talking about Islam (Keller 2018, pp. 20–26).

11 MANAGING MISINFORMATION

EVALUATING THE CASE FOR AMENDMENT OF SECTION 230 OF THE COMMUNICATIONS DECENCY ACT

INTRODUCTION: AN OVERVIEW

In an age where the rapid dissemination of information and the influence of online platforms are more pronounced than ever before, the management of misinformation has become a pressing concern. This study delves into the intricacies of managing misinformation, with a specific focus on evaluating the case for potential amendments to Section 230 of the Communications Decency Act. Section 230, a pivotal legal framework in the United States, has long shielded online platforms from liability for the content posted by users, while granting them the authority to moderate such content. This investigation explores the evolving challenges surrounding disinformation and assesses the merits and drawbacks of potential changes to Section 230 in an effort to strike a balance between safeguarding free expression and curbing the spread of harmful misinformation. The aim is to provide a comprehensive understanding of the complex dynamics at play in the regulation of online content and the potential implications of legislative amendments in addressing the misinformation conundrum.

Revelations surrounding Russian interference in the 2016 US presidential election and the role that "fake news" may have played in shaping voter preferences have sparked a broad conversation among researchers, policymakers, technologists, and others on how to combat the spread and influence of disinformation online. Emerging from this conversation has been a number of legislative or regulatory proposals that would make it more difficult for disinformation to flow through the Web.

Given the fragmented nature of information creation across the Web, many of these proposals rely on the central role that online platforms such as Google, Facebook, and Twitter play in shaping the distribution of information throughout the Web. By creating incentives – or penalties – encouraging platforms to take a more proactive role in removing or combating disinformation, these interventions seek to leverage the unique position of these companies as potentially the most effective "least cost avoiders" in addressing the challenge posed by disinformation.

To that end, these interventions will confront the long-standing legal protections provided by Section 230 of the Communications Decency Act of1996 (CDA 230), a key legal provision that broadly shields platforms from legal liability for the actions of third-party users of their services. For the past two decades, this provision has been seen as a major driver in the growth of online services and a cornerstone supporting free expression on the Web. Simultaneously, CDA 230 has also been argued to inhibit platform responsiveness to the harms posed by harassment, defamation, child pornography, and a host of other activities online. The present-day debates on how to address "fake news" will join the legacy of efforts to reform or eliminate the shield provided by CDA 230.

This chapter seeks to address three questions given this historical background. First, would modifications to CDA 230 pave the way to an effective response to the challenges posed by disinformation online? Second, if so, should such modifications be made? Finally, how should such modifications be crafted?

"Part 1: The Disinformation Challenge" frames the challenge posed by disinformation online, specifically the threat posed by the confluence of politically motivated actors, financially motivated media outlets, and online "troll" culture. "Part 2: How Does CDA 230 Shape Efforts to Combat Online Political Disinformation?" examines the legislative history and case law surrounding CDA 230 and evaluates its impact on contending with the challenge of online disinformation. "Part 3: Should CDA 230 Be Modified to Address Political Disinformation?" takes up the challenge of whether or not CDA 230 should be modified in light of this analysis, concluding that partial amendment focused on the techniques leveraged by disinformation campaigns is warranted.

PART 1: THE DISINFORMATION CHALLENGE

"Fake news" has become a commonplace term for characterizing the prevalence of false or inaccurate stories circulating online, considered a symptom of the poor state of information quality throughout media and society generally. These stories were widely distributed during the 2016 US presidential election, with one survey suggesting that close to one in five US adults saw headlines claiming (falsely) that the Pope had endorsed then-candidate Donald Trump and that protestors had been paid #3,500 to disrupt a Trump rally (Silverman and Singer-Vine 2016). These stories were also considered credible, with 64 percent and 79 percent of respondents reporting that they believed the stories to be "very or somewhat accurate," respectively (Silverman and Singer-Vine 2016).

However, as has been observed by others, the use of "fake news" as a conceptual frame is problematic on a number of levels (Oremus 2016; Sullivan 2017; Nielsen and Graves 2017). In and of itself, the spreading of false information under the pretense of truth is, of course, not a novel phenomenon, either online or in channels of communications more generally (Barnoux 1966; Mulford 2008). Moreover, there are numerous problems with defining the contours of the "fake news" phenomena. Should it apply only to the outright fabrication of events and assertions about reality? Or does it also include the partial presentation of information or an unfair characterization of events?

A sharper framing of the nature of the purported threat is necessary to evaluate the case for modifying or eliminating CDA 230. This chapter focuses on three major developments that have been drivers motivating the post-2016 discussion around online disinformation and its regulatory response. This includes (1) the active spreading of disinformation by governments and state-owned media, (2) financially motivated actors pushing disinformation for the purposes of obtaining advertising revenue, and (3) the activities of online "troll" communities as a vector for spreading disinformation. This chapter narrows in specifically on campaigns of political disinformation, false information targeted to shape perceptions around some aspect of political discourse, rather than efforts which spread inaccurate stories on other topics such as corporate acquisitions or celebrity deaths (Lee 2017).

As they have been less of a primary focus in the regulatory debates around what to do with "fake news," this chapter also excludes some other types of falsity. It does not cover the inadvertent spread of false or misleading information through the Web that does not result from a coordinated effort. Similarly, this chapter focuses on activities primarily targeted at disseminating disinformation – distinguishing it from cases in which a campaign simply attempts to amplify a point of view or spread awareness of a fact.

There is no doubt these categories are by necessity blurry at the edges; a disinformation campaign may leverage an existing misconception spreading organically, or an effort to bring attention to a certain point of view may strategically frame the truth or even shade into falsehood. Issues frequently bleed across the fuzzy boundary between "political" and "non political" discourse, such as debunked theories around the dangers of vaccines promoted by "antivax" activists. However, through this rough framework, this section seeks to offer background context around some of the activities that have provided the impetus for recent calls for legislative and regulatory action on online disinformation.

Disinformation from State Actors

Perhaps the primary trigger for calls for a regulatory response to the challenges posed by disinformation threats online has been confirmation by the intelligence community that Russian state actors engaged in an active effort to shape discourse around the 2016 US presidential election (NCCIC 2016; National Intelligence

Council 2017). The 2016 Russian campaign was a multifaceted effort aimed at undermining trust in targeted political figures. This included conspiracy theories suchas "Pizzagate," whichspreadthenotionthatDemocraticnomineeHillaryClinton and Clinton campaign chairman John Podesta were members of an underground sex trafficking ring (Robb 2017). Beyond efforts to spread disinformation, the effort also included attempts to exacerbate political polarization, in one case stoking racial controversy around law enforcement between activist Black Lives Matter and Blue Lives Matter groups (Alcindor 2017; Seetharaman 2017).

The campaign also operated through a range of different channels. State-owned media outlets such as Sputnik and Russia Today were leveraged to create and disseminate disinformation widely. These more obvious channels operated alongside more subtle "grassroots" infiltration of online communities and the purchase of targeted advertising across various social media platforms. Beyond the spread of disinformation, the campaign also engaged in hacking targeted at compromising private information held by political parties and candidates on both sides of the electoral race.

Although the 2016 Russian campaign has been a widely discussed example of state-driven online disinformation, the use of these techniques is not new. Researchers have tracked similar online disinformation campaigns launched by Russia to influence political discourse throughout Central and Eastern Europe, as well as the Middle East, in recent years (Chen 2015; Lange-Ionatamishvili, Svetoka, and Geers 2015; NPR 2017; Wintour 2017).

Nor are these campaigns specific to Russia. Researchers have found that social media has been leveraged for political disinformation purposes in a range of different contexts in recent years. Incidents include efforts seen in Mexico, Brazil, Canada, and China, to name a few (Finley 2015; Robertson et al. 2016; Woolley and Howard 2017). These campaigns have been launched by state actors as in the Russian case, but have also been launched by a range of independent groups (Robertson et al. 2016).

Financial Incentives for Disinformation

Recognition that politically motivated actors engaged in efforts to influence the 2016 election has emerged alongside a growing number of commentators highlighting the financial incentives driving the creation and dissemination of disinformation. Online advertising, in particular, has been seen as a motivatorto create false but highly sharable content that drives monetizable page views to content online.

In the context of the 2016 US presidential election, businesses both within the country and abroad engaged in the creation of sites spreading disinformation through the Web. Media outlets included such sites as "The Denver Guardian," which spread a range of conspiracy theories, such as one story connecting Clinton to the murder of an FBI agent investigating her use of a private email server, shared millions of times across Facebook (Coler 2016). While the site was designed with the appearance of a local paper in Colorado, it was in actuality operated by a Los Angeles–based entrepreneur who also ran a collection of other sites profiting from the sharing of disinformation (Coler 2016).

Outside the United States, journalists have uncovered groups of entrepreneurs in Macedonia and elsewhere profiting by selling advertisements running alongside disinformation catering to right-wing readers online (Tynan 2016; Subramanian 2017). Stories included "news" of Pope Francis endorsing then-candidate Trump and fabricated reports of the candidate slapping a protestor at a campaign rally (Subramanian 2017). These sites sometimes acted as an amplifier rather than an originator of disinformation, copying content from other sites online and promoting them through swarms of fake accounts on social media platforms like Twitter and Facebook (Subramanian 2017).

Discussion around financial incentives for disinformation has not been limited to discussing the outlets producing and promoting this content online. Since many of the most prominent online platforms such as Google and Facebook are themselves reliant on advertising, critics and researchers have also underscored that the companies hosting this activity may have perverse incentives to harbour it, given that disinformation content is often widely shared and viewed (Allcott and Gentzkow 2017; Thompson 2017). For their part, these platforms have disputed this notion in numerous public statements and have taken action to restrict distributing advertising against disinformation (Wingfield, Isaac and Benner 2016; Ling 2017).

"Trolling Culture" As a Disinformation Source

Beyond the activities of politically and financially motivated actors, the participation of grassroots online "troll" culture has also been a force in facilitating political disinformation. Crowd activity – often performed anonymously – to shock and harass private citizens, public figures, and institutions for pure entertainment purposes has been a long-standing feature of social behaviour on the Internet (Coleman 2015). These activities in the past have leveraged a wide array of tactics, from the manipulation of online polls to the strategic targeting of journalists and "swatting"– false emergency reports to law enforcement aimed at bringing police officers North 2017). In recent years, many of these communities have been radicalized by far-right groups to "spread white supremacist thought, Islamophobia, and misogyny through irony and knowledge of internet culture," as researchers Alice Marwick and Rebecca Lewis have documented (Marwick and Lewis 2017; Schreckinger 2017).

In the context of the 2016 US presidential election, many of these communities were involved in coordinated campaigns to spread political disinformation. This included promoting conspiracy theories that philanthropist George Soros was engaged in a nationwide campaign to fund protests against Trump and claims that Democratic National Committee (DNC) staffer Seth Rich was assassinated as part of a cover-up connected to the 2016 leak of emails from the DNC (Dreyfuss 2017).

Effectively, these campaigns drew on the efforts of volunteers, a loosely coordinated, informal coalition of overlapping "alt-right" groups. This brought together a wide range of actors, including gamer communities, users of the popular online discussion board Reddit, members of the white supremacist community Stormfront, and "alt-light" news outlets echoing some of the messages of the far-right but excluding some of the more controversial views, to name a few (Marwick and Lewis 2017, p. 26). These techniques drew explicitly on these earlier "trolling" efforts. As Mike Cernovich, one prominent alt-right figure involved in both earlier campaigns against feminists in the video-game industry and in the 2016election, put it, "troll tactics" were a means with which to "build [his] brand" (Marantz 2016).

The involvement of these communities in targeted campaigns of political disinformation highlights the important point that these three sources – state-run, financially driven, and trolling – do not operate independently. Instead, numerous ties link these engines of online disinformation into an ecosystem of overlapping, occasionally cooperating groups. Notably, state-run efforts coordinated by Russia leveraged paid agents who in turn worked to infiltrate and mobilize online communities to spread political disinformation (Kosoff 2017). Similarly, state-run efforts also subsidize and support a variety of financially motivated media channels to spread "fake news" and disinformation through the Web (Belford, Cvetkovska, Sekulovska, and Dojcˇinovic´ 2017). These groups also operate on their own, acting independently for their own reasons to engage in the distribution of disinformation.

The (Ambiguous) Impact of Online Disinformation

While all the activities discussed in this section are well documented, it is important to recognize that, at the time of writing, clear empirical evidence of their actual influence over political outcomes is still unclear. While some researchers have concluded that disinformation efforts did have an impact on the 2016 US presidential election, the issue remains a matter of scholarly debate (Howard and Kollanyi 2017; Kollanyi, Bradshaw, and Neudert 2017). Given the limited visibility into the operations of various disinformation activities and the data around overall political participation on social media and other platforms, it is likely that this issue will remain ambiguous for some time.

If they are indeed effective, the potential risk to democratic institutions and processes seem clear. The capability of foreign powers to effectively manipulate political discourse within a country raises difficult questions about the representativeness of elected officials and the decisions made by them. To the extent that much disinformation seen during the 2016 US presidential campaign focused on exacerbating political conflict and cementing polarization, such activities might also erode the ability for democracies to effectively act as engines for compromise between segments of society (Epstein and Graham 2007). Yet evidence on this front is ambiguous. It is unclear that the Internet is in fact increasing polarization (Boxell, Gentzkow, and Shapiro 2017). Moreover, it is unclear whether a more partisan media writ large is in turn making the public more polarized (Prior 2013).

However, regardless of whether or not they are indeed effective, these politically targeted activities - and public knowledge about them - still may raise threats to the health of democratic processes. Disinformation campaigns might accelerate erosion in public trust of institutions seen as critical to the maintenance of democracy. First, skepticism around the veracity of online information generally might also limit the influence of journalistic channels producing and distributing accurate information (Barthel and Mitchell 2017).

This may hinder the ability for democracies to engage in authentic, effective deliberation and arrive at decisions considered "legitimate."1Second, regardless of actual effectiveness, a broadly held perception that these disinformation campaigns do indeed have an impact may itself create distrust in the legitimacy of elected officials, particularly those supported by foreign governments and interests. This has been the case in the aftermath of the 2016 campaign, with numerous congressional inquiries and an ongoing special investigation attesting to the continued concerns by policymakers and the public as a whole.

Though ambiguity still exists, these risks and others have encouraged a live debate as to the set of responses - regulatory or otherwise - needed to combat these activities and limit their potential influence on the media and information ecosystem. These proposals confront the framework ofCDA 230.

PART 2: HOW DOES CDA 230 SHAPE EFFORTS TO COMBAT ONLINE POLITICAL DISINFORMATION?

Because of its potential threat to democratic processes and institutions, policymakers and scholars have begun to propose a range of legal and regulatory responses to online political disinformation. As is the case in other contexts, attention has turned toward the central role that online platforms play in hosting and facilitating the objectionable activity.[2] One recent examination of online media and sharing behaviour during the 2016 election season concluded simply that "[d]isinformation and propaganda are rooted in partisanship and are more prevalent on social media" (Faris et al. 2017). Specifically, the study found that the set of websites which receive a disproportionate amount of attention on Facebook were also cited by independent sources and media reporting as creators and distributors of "inaccurate if not blatantly false reporting" (Faris et al. 2017, p. 15).

Across a range of issues, these platforms serve as "least cost avoiders" – actors best positioned to manage the risk from certain activities. In the online disinformation context, platforms possess highly granular data about the activity across their services and have the ability to influence the distribution of content. This might be done algorithmically by modifying systems of recommendation that promote certain content over others or financially through the barring of ads supporting certain types of content online. In the case of large platforms such as Google and Facebook, the companies are also perceived to possess the resources and technical competence to effectively create effective systems of detection and mitigation.3

Without the cooperation of these platforms, proposals to address political disinformation confront a recurring, more general challenge with the enforcement of policy online, namely the challenge of identifying and pursuing particular actors that break rules (Lessig 1999). Laws broken by perpetrators of online political disinformation, and new laws that might be passed against these types of activities, will likely be limited by the costly requirements of identifying and enforcing rules against a disparate and continually evolving ecosystem of disinformation perpetrators.

To the extent that legislative and regulatory action will seek to shape the incentives that online platforms have to combat online political disinformation, these efforts will take place in the shadow of CDA 230, which provides strong protections shielding platforms from liability for actions taken by their users.

This provision does in part inhibit the effectiveness of existing and novel legal levers that would target online political disinformation.

Two routes remain by which legal action might combat these campaigns while leaving CDA 230 untouched. One, which would build on the legal precedent set by the Ninth Circuit in the Roommates.com case, would leave courts to engage in line drawing around the degree to which platforms might elicit illegal disinformation activity. Second, legislation and regulation targeting the platforms themselves and focusing on changing the information environment surrounding online political disinformation, rather than creating liability for the acts themselves, would also avoid having to amend CDA 230.

A CONCISE OVERVIEW OF THE HISTORY OF SECTION 230 OF THE COMMUNICATIONS DECENCY ACT

Passed in 1996, CDA 230 provides that "no provider or user of an interactive computer service shall be treated as the publisher or speaker of any information provided by another information content provider," subject to a set of exceptions for criminal, intellectual property, state, and communication privacy laws.[4]

This legislation was passed in response to the decision in Stratton Oakmontv. Prodigy Services, a 1995 decision that suggested that online service providers could be held liable for the defamatory content posted by users on their platforms to the extent that they exercised editorial control over that content.5 This decision represented an application of established common law principles around the liability of distributors and publishers. Under that framework, "distributors" exercising limited editorial control over content they distributed – such as bookstores and libraries – only faced liability for defamation if they had knowledge of the content and failed to remove it. In contrast, "publishers" exercising more active editorial control and judgment – such as newspapers and magazines – were deemed to be liable for defamatory content as if they had originally published it regardless of knowledge.6 Stratton Oakmont raised concerns that platforms would be unsustainable if exposed to liability for the acts of any individual user and would be deterred from taking proactive action to filter for offensive content (Reidenberg et al. 2012, pp. 5–6). To that end, the original impetus for CDA 230, as evidenced by its caption, was to protect platforms from liability for "Good Samaritan" acts to remove offensive content (Reidenberg et al. 2012, p. 7). However, Congress also had a range of other objectives in the passage of CDA 230, including an intent to "promote the continued development of the Internet and other interactive computer services and other interactive media" and "preserve the vibrant and competitive free market that presently exists for the Internet and other interactive computer services, unfettered by Federal or State regulation."7 Over the subsequent two decades, courts reviewing CDA 230 interpreted the doctrine to shield online platforms from liability for a broad range of acts taken by their users.8 In 1997, the Fourth Circuit in Zeran v. American Online concluded that CDA 230 worked to shield platforms from both traditional categories of publisher and distributor liability, rejecting an argument by the plaintiff that the provision only worked to block publisher liability.9 In 2003, the Ninth Circuit in Batzel v. Smith concluded that the phrase "interactive computer services" in CDA 230 was not limited to services providing access to the Internet as in Zeran and earlier cases but also included "any information service or other systems" such as a listserv.10 Later cases also confirmed that users who were independent of an online service provider could invoke the protection of CDA 230.11 In 2008, the Fifth Circuit in Doe v.

MySpace found that CDA 230 immunity applied broadly to tort claims, not just those premised on defamation as in the Stratton Oakmont decision.12 This broad view of CDA 230 was followed a year later by the Ninth Circuit in Barnes v. Yahoo!13. In that case, the Ninth Circuit clarified that the scope of CDA 230 could apply beyond causes of action sounding in tort to include any cause of action that "inherently requires the court to treat the defendant as the 'publisher or speaker' of content provided by another."14Together, these decisions have established CDA 230 as a broad shield for online intermediaries and influence the scope of available legal options in combating disinformation.

CDA 230 Shields Platforms from Acts of Online Disinformation Committed by Users CDA 230 and its impacts have been controversial, and the provision has remained the target of recurring efforts to modify it in various ways (Reidenberg et al. 2012, pp. 46-49).15 In the context of online political disinformation, CDA 230 conflicts with efforts to use existing causes of action and create new causes of action that would hold platforms liable for the illegal actions of its users.

There are a number of potentially applicable causes of action. Online political disinformation is often false information about an individual, and to that end might give rise to the tort of defamation or libel. Cases might include activities to spread conspiracy theories such as the sex trafficking "Pizzagate" rumour discussed in the section "Disinformation from State Actors" (Robb 2017).

Consistent with the cases discussed in the section "A Brief History of CDA 230," CDA 230 would prevent an online platform that hosted such defamatory content posted by a user from itself being held liable for defamation.16

Online political disinformation might also violate a number of other laws that are less prototypical cases for CDA 230. For instance, under federal law foreign nationals are prohibited from "making any contribution or donation of money or other thing of value, or making any expenditure, independent expenditure, or disbursement in connection with any federal, state or local election in the United States."17 This would include efforts by foreign actors to interfere in US elections through the purchase of advertising spreading falsehoods about a particular candidate. Courts reviewing the illegality of advertising in other circumstances beyond the election context have generally refused to impose liability on the platforms that host this material, absent some specific cases applying the holding in Roommates.com discussed in the section "Option One: Court-Driven Regulation via CDA 230."18 Accordingly, actions by agencies like the Federal Election Commission to enforce these laws against the platforms themselves would confront the limitations of CDA 230.19

New causes of action would likely face similar barriers, too. In the wake of the 2016 presidential election, California state legislators have proposed a bill that would make it illegal "for a person to knowingly and willingly make, publish or circulate on an Internet Web site ... a false or deceptive statement designed to influence the vote on ... (a) Any issue submitted to voters at an election, (b) Any candidate for election to public office."20 Beyond the range of potential First Amendment challenges to laws attempting to make creating or spreading political disinformation illegal, CDA 230 would still work to inhibit the enforceability of those rules on platforms.21

The impact of these limitations parallels long-standing critiques of CDA 230. Critics have argued since its passage that the shield provided by CDA 230 makes online platforms less responsive and proactive than they otherwise would be in dealing with defamatory content (Reidenberg et al. 2012, p. 26; Brown-Barbour 2015). Where information about the perpetrator of the defamation is scant, victims of defamation may be left without adequate routes for recovery.22 Similar discussions have played out in the context of enforcing laws against harassment in cyberspace.23 This challenge may be compounded where the perpetrators of this activity are operating outside of the United States, as it was during the 2016 US presidential election.

It should be observed that CDA 230 only operates to preclude the bringing of a suit against the platform seeking to find it liable as if it was the publisher of the defamatory content. Even if it did not, the fact that many acts of political disinformation will target public figures of various kinds may mean that claims like defamation and libel may as yet be relatively weak legal tools to bring to bear. For instance, even without CDA 230, a successful suit by a public figure would need to meet the standard set under New York Times Co. v. Sullivan, which requires proof of "actual malice." This is a challenging burden that requires plaintiffs to show that the act was committed with "sufficient evidence to permit the conclusion that the defendant in fact entertained serious doubts as to the truth of his publication."24

Even in light of the limitations imposed by CDA 230, it is important to underscore that the law does not in effect bar all legal or regulatory interventions that would incentivize platforms to combat online political disinformation. Two routes provide a potential basis for changing the state of play around this issue.

Option One: Court-Driven Regulation via CDA 230

Since *Zeran*, courts have consistently found that CDA 230 provides broad protections against online platforms being held liable for the activities of their users. However, a set of cases suggest that, under certain circumstances, courts may be willing to narrow the scope of the shield provided by CDA 230.

Fair Housing Council of San Fernando Valley v. Roommates.com concerned a claim against a website that provided a service connecting prospective renters with open apartments and rooms.25 The plaintiffs in the case alleged that the platform violated the federal Fair Housing Act (FHA) by eliciting information about the renters preferences around gender, sexual orientation, and family status. By publishing these preferences and allowing users to choose renters based on this criteria, the suit alleged a violation of FHA provisions that prohibited discrimination by landlords and tenants on this basis. Roommates. com invoked CDA 230, arguing that this would treat the platform as the one engaging in the discriminatory activity.

The Ninth Circuit – adopting a rationale parallel to that of the Seventh Circuit – held that Roommates.com did not receive immunity from CDA 230 since it played the role of a "information content provider" (Quist 2012). By designing a website registration process that included questions around categories like gender and sexual orientation, and providing a service that filtered based on these preferences, the court held that Roommates. comcontributed "materially to the alleged illegality of the conduct."26

The end result of the holding in Roommates.com is that the specific design decisions made around a website can contribute to the determination of whether or not it can claim immunity under CDA 230. Notably, the Ninth Circuit rejected a claim by the plaintiffs that the platform should be liable for discriminatory posts made by users in an open-ended, optional "Additional Comments" text field on user profiles.27 Since Roommates.com did not solicit a specific type of content in this text field, and published them as written, it was not a co-developer of the content and therefore received CDA 230 immunity for those activities.28

The holding in Roommates.com has been inconsistently applied across jurisdictions in the years following the decision, leading some scholars to suggest that the case is not settled law and in fact has a "checkered legacy" (Goldman 2017, p. 2). The Tenth Circuit in FTC v. Accusearch adopted the reasoning in Roommates. com in 2009, finding that a site that sold illegally acquired phone records was not entitled to CDA 230 immunity because it "specifically [encouraged] development of what [was] offensive about the content."29 In contrast, the application of Roommates.com by the First Circuit in Doe v. Backpage in 2016 allowed a site publishing ads for prostitution to obtain CDA 230 immunity, noting that an online platform's decisions in "structur[ing] its website and posting requirements are publisher functions entitled to section 230(c)(1) protection."30 Such a line of reasoning would seem to significantly limit the holding in Roommates. com.31 These differing applications of the rule raise doubts as to whether existing legal precedent will be a stable basis on which to combat online political disinformation (Feuerman 2016).

Yet, if it is applied, the Roommates.com holding suggests that – even absent a legislative modification – the immunities provided by CDA 230 might be effectively thinned by courts assessing whether or not activities associated with campaigns of political disinformation should create liability for online platforms. At issue will be the question of whether or not the specific design of the platform makes it "responsible, in whole or in part, for the creation or development of" the offending content.32 While this is an inquiry that will turn on the particular claim, the service under question, and the type of disinformation activity, the case provides some rough guidelines around what might not receive the benefit of CDA 230 immunity.

At the most basic level, under the Roommates.com holding it is unlikely that simply providing a space through which to engage in illegal acts around political disinformation will expose the platforms themselves to liability. Creating an open-ended box for posting content did not constitute co-development, enabling Roomates.com to obtain the benefit of CDA 230 at least for those elements of its platform. On this count, it is likely that simply making available the means of posting – even if leveraged by trolls, bots, and foreign agents to spread disinformation – will be a point on which platforms will be able to claim immunity.

However, the outcome is more ambiguous when considering other features common to web services. To the extent that disinformation campaigns operate through advertising channels provided by the platforms, a claim might be made that companies like Facebook and Google materially contribute to the illegality. Cases applying the Roommates.com holding have at times rejected the application of CDA 230 immunity in the advertising context. Merely profiting from advertisements that promote illegal services or are themselves illegal is insufficient33 However, a pricing arrangement that encourages the activity at issue may qualify as a material contribution. Courts have articulated a few possible scenarios here, including offering discounts to the problematic advertising and variable pricing structures that increase the profit of the platform in proportion to the value and volume of the illegal activity.34 Variable pricing is the reality online; most large platforms rely on auction-based systems for delivering advertising, with many buyers competing to deliver their content to a given user.35 To the extent that it can be shown that platforms systematically offer advertising that violates the law at a lower rate, there is potentially a claim of contribution that would block the application of CDA 230 immunity.

Also, content is typically curate, shaped, and personalized to users through an algorithmically generated "feed."36 This might be grounds to make an argument of co-development, particularly when one takes into account the fact that – in response to interest in a single piece of defamatory content – the platform may recommend further defamatory content. In this sense, it matches the search functionality in Roommates.com, in which the provision of a mechanism that highlighted content based on discriminatory criteria was seen to facilitate the illegal activity in a way that shed immunity under CDA230.37 Similar claims might also be made based on issues that have emerged in the advertising targeting context as well, in which the algorithmic generation of targeting criteria facilitates potentially illegal activity (Angwin, Varner, and Tobin 2017).

In spite of this, Roommates.com also provides ample opportunity to reframe the curation and co-creation of content in a feed in a more charitable light. Under the holding, a "website operator who edits user-created content ... retains his immunity for any illegality in the user-created content, provided that the edits are unrelated to the illegality"– examples include editing for length, correcting for spelling, or removing obscenity.38 Arguably platforms like Facebook do the same here, simply collaging and presenting the content as posted, as opposed to actually changing its meaning or otherwise "[contributing] to the alleged illegality."39

It is also not so clear that simply recommending additional defamatory content based on the interest of a user in defamatory content rises to the level of "co-development." In Roommates.com, the court focused on the fact that the platform used impermissibly discriminatory criteria in filtering and delivering apartment listings to users. However, in an effort to distinguish this case from other platforms that might arguably perform the same function, the court observed that the use of a "neutral [tool] to carry out what may be unlawful or illicit searches" on an "ordinary search engine" does not expose that service itself to liability.40 This is arguably the case here; a platform like Facebook does not explicitly solicit and then filter based on defamatory content. This sets the case apart from the design in Roommates.com, in which the platform presented a set of pre-defined categories that themselves were characteristics it was illegal to discriminate against. Instead, on a platform like Facebook, the user effectively "searches" on a neutral tool through their browsing behaviour, and the feed returns more content responsive to that behaviour, regardless of the specific topic.

As this brief analysis highlights, the end result of the Roommates.com holding is ambiguous and depends a great deal on the platform in question, a critique that was voiced by the dissent in that case.41 However, it seems clear that under certain circumstances platforms might not enjoy the benefits of CDA 230 immunity, and there appears to be at least a colourable claim that this would allow liability to be applied to the platforms for at least some of the tactics used by those driving political disinformation campaigns.

Option Two: Legislative Measures Apart from Modifying CDA 230

CDA 230 is simultaneously a broad and narrow provision. It is broad in the sense that platforms are shielded from liability against a wide range of illegal acts that their users might perpetrate. At the same time, it is narrow in the sense that it does not preclude a wide range of actions that might address campaigns of political disinformation outside the lever of applying user level liability to the platform. Three recent proposals made by researchers and policymakers focusing on this issue provide examples of the types of activities not inhibited by the framework laid down by CDA 230 and the case law interpreting the provision.

First, CDA 230 does not preclude the imposition of transparency requirements that would mandate that platforms disclose information relevant to evaluating the credibility of information. These might be interventions at the level of the user – helping to inform consumers about the provenance and verification of content. This might manifest as rules locking in a set of standards around "dispute flags" that would appear alongside posts online to signal that a story has been contested by an approved fact-checking organization, like those being experimented with at the time of writing (Kafka 2017). It might also include more extensive disclosures to particular regulators or expert research groups who might then work to enforce rules and inform the public at large (Diresta and Harris 2017). This would formalize the more ad hoc data provided by Facebook and other companies about advertising activity during the 2017 congressional hearings on this issue (Seetharaman and Wells 2017; Hwang and Woolley 2017).

Second, beyond greater transparency about the data platforms have "on hand," CDA 230 does not preclude measures mandating that platforms require greater disclosure from their users, as well. Proposals on this front have focused on the processes around online advertising, seen to be one channel for political disinformation in the 2016 US presidential election. Researchers have proposed "know your customer" requirements for online advertisers paralleling similar rules imposed in the financial sector, as well as more stringent rules around the labelling of anonymous and automated accounts (Diresta and Harris 2017, p. 82). The Honest Ads Act – bipartisan legislation originally proposed in October 2017 but seeing little subsequent action – would require that large online platforms maintain a public file of all electioneering communications beyond a certain monetary threshold.42 This file would include a copy of the advertisement, targeting data, as well as information about the purchaser of the advertisement.43 Similar approaches outside the advertising context might attempt to prevent bots and astroturfing by mandating more stringent requirements on the creation of new user accounts and profiles on a service.

Third, CDA 230 does not preclude more dramatic interventions that would change the actual flow of information through platforms. As a means of limiting the influence of online platforms in shaping public discourse, policymakers have called for a form of "net neutrality" to apply to the content layer of the Web, such that platforms like "Facebook, Google, and Amazon – like ISPs – should be'neutral' in their treatment of the flow of lawful information and commerce on their platforms" (Franken 2017). Other approaches might require that algorithms take into account certain machine-readable indicators of "credibility" in promoting and ranking information.44

All three of these approaches operate within the structure of CDA 230, enabling policymakers to address the tactics used by political disinformation campaigns without necessarily applying liability for individual acts to the platforms. This does not mean that they will not be otherwise rendered invalid. Courts have affirmed in a number of cases that algorithmic outputs are an exercise of the First Amendment rights of the platforms themselves.45

Regulation that would shape these outputs will thereby confront these constitutional protections. Interestingly, as Tim Wu (2013) has argued, First Amendment protections will not cover the algorithmic outputs of "functional" platforms whose "involvement with information is too distant or mechanical to be speech." These are circumstances in which CDA 230 immunity will be most likely to apply under Roommates.com because these platforms do not "materially contribute" to the offending content. To that end, the doctrines are somewhat complementary since regulations to directly shape algorithmic output will be most likely to survive First Amendment challenge in circumstances where the Roommates.com doctrine is likely to block attempts to impose liability on the platform.

Assuming an intervention met these constitutional requirements, these three approaches might enable action to be taken around these threats without a modification of the underlying law alongside the exception articulated in the Roommates.com case.

Summary: Some Routes Closed, Others Remain Open

Consistent with long-standing critiques of the provision on issues such as defamation and harassment, CDA 230 may provide perverse incentives for platforms to be less proactive on combating disinformation than would be preferable. It may also make online platforms less active on gathering and sharing information about perpetrators in a way that may hinder efforts to pursue these actors directly (Reidenberg et al. 2012).

At the same time, CDA 230 does not function as an absolute bar to action in the space. Under the holding in Roommates.com, judicial action might serve to impose liability on platforms to the extent that their specific design rises to the level of "co-development," which would make them complicit in the commission of illegal acts. Furthermore, since CDA 230 narrowly applies to claims that would treat the platform as a "publisher or speaker" of content, it does not conflict with legislative interventions that would place obligations on the platforms directly. Many of the proposals that would require greater transparency, user disclosure, and modifications to underlying content algorithms continue to be open options under the structure of CDA 230.

The question of whether or not to modify CDA 230 to contend with disinformation threats therefore depends on a careful weighing. At issue is whether or not these remaining options are sufficient to meet the threat posed by political disinformation – and, relatedly, the potential practicality, benefit, and cost of modifying CDA 230 to impose individual liability more directly on the platforms themselves.

PART 3: SHOULD CDA 230 BE MODIFI TO ADDRESS POLITICAL DISINFORMATION?

As public discussion around the challenge posed by online disinformation continues, there have been an increasing number of voices advocating for modification or removal of CDA 230. One recent op-ed in the Financial Times characterized the provision as a "loophole," arguing simply that platform operators "no longer deserve the sort of blanket exemptions from liabilities that companies in every other industry incur as a cost of doing business" (Foroohar 2017). The Economist characterized the provision as an "implicit subsidy" for online platforms, arguing that "giving platforms a free pass is increasingly difficult for regulators and courts: they simply have become too important for the economy and society more generally" (The Economist 2017).

The relationship between CDA 230 and efforts to combat disinformation is complex. This section seeks to assess the argument for modification or elimination of CDA 230 by answering the following questions. First, given the status quo, are the range of possible interventions sufficient to address the threat posed by campaigns of political disinformation? Second, what would be the potential positive and negative impacts produced by such a modification? Third, practically speaking, if one were to modify CDA 230, what modification would be appropriate to address the challenge posed by political disinformation?

Are Interventions Within the CDA 230 Framework Sufficient?

As discussed in "Part II: How Does CDA 230 Shape Efforts to Combat Online Political Disinformation?," CDA 230 does not function as a categorical block to potential legal interventions to address the challenges of political disinformation. Its impact is considerably more specific: It limits interventions that would serve to treat the platform as the publisher or speaker of an act, applying the liability of a given user to the platform as a whole. It does not hinder a range of potential legislative actions to mandate greater transparency from the platforms, enforce more robust disclosure on the part of users, or even modify the mechanics of how information is distributed by services like Facebook or Google. Nor does CDA 230 serve to block potential actions by courts using the precedent set in *Roommates.com* to selectively eliminate immunity. An immediate question is whether or not CDA 230 is merely adistraction. Are the potential tools that are available without modifying CDA 230 sufficient by themselves to contend with modern campaigns of political disinformation?

One significant challenge to regulatory or court-driven action in this space is the speed at which online disinformation campaigns are evolving. Russian political disinformation tactics have continuously incorporated new techniques, and their intervention in 2016 represents the culmination of years of previous experimentation in the space (Chivvis 2017). To that end, even if a given fix is successful in limiting the influence of these tactics in the short term, it may become rapidly obsolete as perpetrators change their approach. A robust solution will be able to adapt quickly as the landscape of strategies evolves; and, in that respect, it is unclear if the options discussed in “Option One: Court- Driven Regulation via CDA 230” or “Option Two: Legislative Actions Beyond Amending CDA 230” will provide a sufficiently nimble response.

For example, laws that would mandate that platforms require greater disclosure of information from users and advertisers might be quickly rendered a dead letter as perpetrators of these campaigns find new ways to mask their identity. Particularly in the case of sophisticated disinformation campaigns of the most concern, such as those seen in the 2016 presidential election, perpetrators of these efforts may have the means by which to mask their involvement through corporate shells and other aliases (Lapowsky 2017). We might expect in this case that defining a fixed set of reporting requirements would be easily evaded.

The current focus on advertising may also be too narrow. Although tools to block perpetrators of political disinformation from advertising platforms may limit easy access to powerful tools for targeting a given message, it is important to note that these campaigns can proceed even without access to paid promotion. Well-resourced campaigns may have access to the distribution capabilities of state-run media infrastructure, informal promotion relationships existing outside a platform’s advertising tools, and “grassroots” supporters willing to spread a given message.[46] Even narrower regimes focusing on limitations around *political* advertising in particular would miss efforts that seek to target and produce conflict outside the context of an election or campaign. The Facebook events staged by Russia to stoke conflict between Black Lives Matter and Blue Lives Matter groups, for instance, may not be activities hindered by "know your customer"-style laws.[47]

Intervention by the courts to selectively apply CDA 230 immunity without amendment of the underlying language seems similarly fraught. Roommates.com and its progeny depend on a highly fact-specific inquiry that turns on the precise design of an online platform. This is likely to leave untouched a number of channels through which campaigns of political disinformation might flowand remain effective. Recall in that decision that the provision of an open-ended text box for posting content was sufficiently "hands-off" such that the Roommates.com service was still able to obtain CDA 230 immunity for discriminatory content posted on that portion of the site. Extending such a rule to the political context would mean that platforms might, for instance, be granted immunity for activities occurring on its freeform posting features but not for algorithmic feeds where the platform plays a more active "co-development" role. The outcome might be that platforms take more proactive action to combat disinformation on some portions of their services more than others, leaving the overall problem unchecked.

Platforms may be left with considerable legal ambiguity as to the bounds of what may or may not incur intermediary liability, producing inconsistent implementation of policy across platforms. Beyond the fact-specific nature of decisions based on Roommates.com, courts have also applied the rule inconsistently across jurisdictions and in some cases articulated reasoning that would seem to reject the reasoning in that case.

A second difficulty is that much remains unknown about the societal impacts of political disinformation campaigns, which makes crafting an effective response in the near-term a challenge. For instance, proposals have proliferated that would require better signaling to consumers about the quality and provenance of content they encounter on online platforms (SantaClara University 2017). Yet it remains unclear whether or not labels indicating when a piece of content has been challenged by a fact-checking organization are indeed effective. One recent study suggests that simple repetition of "fake news" headlines are sufficient to increase user perceptions of accuracy, even when labeled as false or disputed (Pennycook, Cannon and Rand 2017). There is also evidence to suggest an "implied truth" effect, in which labeling "fake news" as such modestly reduces its perceived accuracy while perversely raising the perceived accuracy of disinformation that goes untagged (Pennycook and Rand 2017). In the political context, recent experimental results suggest that, even when a political leader's own statements are exposed as disinformation, the impact on actual voting intention may be limited (Swire et al. 2017). Further study will be needed to craft a meaningful response to these threats.

Finally, it is unclear if legislative and judicial bodies will have the technical competence to effectively administrate these interventions. Adopting a Roommates.com–based approach requires courts to play the primary role in interrogating specific design decisions and evaluating the extent to which they contribute to illegal conduct. Given that even specialists in the industry admit that the risks and complexity of managing these systems drive them to be conservative in their attempts to solve disinformation challenges, generalist courts48

Crafting a legislative intervention encounters similar hurdles. Many of the proposals discussed in "Option Two: Legislative Actions Beyond Amending CDA 230" suffer from a lack of sufficient coverage, making some techniques of disinformation more difficult while continuing to leave others open for exploitation. One option for overcoming this limitation is to expand the scope of legislation to more comprehensively deal with disinformation by, for instance, prescribing certain algorithms that would take defined elements of information quality into account or mandating the regular audit of algorithmic behaviour. Yet increasing the scope simultaneously expands the level of complexity, requiring legislators to engage more fully with the technical design of platforms at a detailed level. As in the judicial case, it is unclear if the legislative process will be able to do so effectively and in a timely manner.49

Benefits and Potential Costs of Modification

Modification of CDA 230 overcomes many of the deficiencies that are likely to hinder a regulatory or court-driven approach to the challenges posed by political disinformation. Importantly, exposing an "interactive computer service" to liability for illegal acts taken by users modifies the overall structure of incentives by shifting the burden to the platform. In essence, rather than specifying a detailed set of actions that should be taken to address disinformation, the government would set a priority about the activity to be minimized and delegate the decisions about how to achieve that end to the platform.

Such an arrangement avoids the challenges faced by the regulatory or court-driven approaches. Platforms are able to rapidly develop and implement measures to mitigate the impact of political disinformation. Importantly, they will be able to change tactics nimbly as the landscape of these campaigns continues to evolve, ensuring a more robust bulwark against these threats moving forward. Moreover, platforms are also best situated to assess the efficacy of certain proposed solutions and shed light on the current ambiguities about the impact and behavioural mechanisms underlying disinformation. The association of financial risk with failure to address the challenge would promote investment in this research work and empirically supported interventions based on it. Finally, modification of CDA 230 would shift responsibility to the actors with the technical expertise and deep understanding of the products necessary to develop a nuanced response to political disinformation.

That being said, the broad scope of CDA 230 means that modifications will create a range of downstream effects. While amendment or wholesale removal might limit the influence of political disinformation, it may produce a range of harms that will on net make such a change unwise.

First, applying user-level liability to platforms may render these services either insolvent or overly reactive in ways that harm freedom of expression. These are in some sense the "classic" arguments against creating exceptions within the CDA 230 framework (Reidenberg et al. 2012, pp. 35–37). On one hand, liability for the acts of any one of a large pool of users may threaten the financial viability of certain platforms Reidenberg et al. 2012, p. 36). This is particularly the case given the broad scope of "interactive computer service" under legal precedent, covering everything from a small blog or listserv to the biggest platforms operated by companies like Google and Facebook.50 Larger platforms will have the financial resources and legal expertise to absorb this risk, while smaller businesses and services run by volunteers may not be able to manage litigation based on the acts of their users. One effect may be to further accelerate and reinforce consolidation to the set of largest companies as less well-resourced platforms exit the market or merge with better-positioned competitors.

On the other hand, platforms may become overly reactive to even the minute threat of legal liability, favouring removal of potentially offending content by default rather than making a considered evaluation of the risk (Reidenberg et al. 2012, p. 36). Insofar as modification to CDA 230 attempts to confront the challenge of disinformation, the incentive to minimize legal risk might prompt platforms to pre-emptively remove content that is true and valuable but likely to be a source of controversy. These takedowns may also disproportionately reflect the interests of those most willing and able to pursue legal claims against the platforms. Ironically, the creation of platform liability for disinformation may create another route by which to suppress true information. Second, modification of CDA 230 may render platforms substantially less transparent and participatory than they would otherwise be. One concern motivating passage of CDA 230 in the 1990s was the notion that there was no practical means by which companies could effectively monitor the massive flows of user-generated content published through their services every day.51 However, as others have pointed out, this limitation has become less daunting with time, as advances in machine learning and processing power have made it more possible to monitor and moderate content at massive scale. Indeed, many such systems are today used to administrate monitoring of child pornography and intellectual property violations, laws that were exempted from the purview of CDA 230.

To the extent that modification of CDA 230 exposes platforms to liability around the disinformation activities perpetrated by their users, it is likely that the same automated, algorithmic approach will be deployed to maximize and accelerate identification and removal of offending content.52 Adoption of these automated methods to deal with questions of truth, falsity, and information quality may hinder other, alternative models that leverage user and community participation to filter for these criteria (Grimmelmann 2015; Rogers 2017). Wikipedia, the collaboratively edited encyclopaedia, has been relatively successful in resisting the influence of "fake news" through human moderation (Rogers 2017, pp. 359–362). Research indicates that users are driven by a sense of ownership and community identity to take an active role in disputing facts and eliminating falsehoods (Rogers 2017, p. 363). The presence of automated algorithms that moderate content can erode these motivations and inhibit the contributions of volunteers.53 In that respect, automated systems are in tension with community-driven approaches to the problem of disinformation.

There are qualities of community-driven filtration of disinformation that make it preferable to automated, algorithmic approaches. Algorithms are opaque, possessing hidden biases that can be difficult to ascertain as a user. Similarly, algorithms are designed and maintained by the platform, effectively delegating decisions over truth and falsity to the company operating the service. In contrast, a filtration approach that leverages community debate and moderation can take place in a more transparent manner and leaves decisions about disinformation to the users. Amending CDA 230 may incentivize platforms54

Third, as Nicholas Bramble (2012)has written, the immunity provided under CDA 230 represents a regulatory strategy to avoid data enclosure and regulatory capture in information infrastructure. Specifically, CDA 230 – and the immunity provided to platforms under Section 512 of the Digital Millennium Copyright Act – positions online intermediaries as a balancing force against the influence of network providers such as Comcast and AT&T on one hand and the influence of content providers like Disney, Viacom, and the New York Times on the other (Bramble 2012, p. 364). By limiting platform exposure to user-level liability, "network providers and content owners are no longer the sole entities to determine under what conditions user access, participation and innovation shall take place within these [online] spaces" (Bramble 2012). These exceptions also arrange financial incentives in a manner that, at least theoretically, positions online intermediaries as advocates for the communicative interests of its users against these other actors.55 The modification of CDA 230 would rewrite the balance of power between different interests with the ability to shape the broader information infrastructure in an undesirable way. This may outweigh the potential benefit gained by addressing the more narrow threats posed by political disinformation.

Meeting the specific challenge of political disinformation with a wholesale repeal of CDA 230 is unwarranted given the broader negative impacts that may result. To that end, the central question is one of tailoring: Precisely what kind of acts should be targeted by the crafting of an exception to CDA 230? Will the attribution of existing causes of action to the platforms be sufficient, or will new causes of action be needed?

What Modifications Are Practicable?

Particularly in the context of regulating information falsehood and quality, crafting an appropriate exception to CDA 230 is challenging. For one, as legal scholar Cass Sunstein (1992) has pointed out, "we do not know what a well- functioning marketplace of ideas would look like." Since it is difficult to specify an ideal end state with precision, it becomes similarly difficult to identify the set of incentives that society should impose on the platforms in addressing online disinformation.

For another, there is the difficult and practical choice of ascertaining precisely what causes of action, when taken by an individual user, should expose the platform to liability. There are not many relevant laws that make the spreading of falsehoods illegal. Defamation is one obvious tort that could be given an exception under CDA 230 given that political disinformation often concerns a specific individual's reputation or character. Yet, as discussed in "Part I: The Disinformation Challenge," disinformation campaigns may seek to spread falsehood about a far broader set of topics than those concerning an individual's reputation, and the standard for proving defamation against public figures is particularly high (Brown 2015).

Other activities that have been associated with political disinformation campaigns in the past would potentially run afoul of a host of laws, including statutes against cyber bullying and the tort of intentional infliction of emotional distress.[56] Insofar as a disinformation campaign made an effort to acquire and leak information, it might also commit invasion of privacy and violations of a state right to publicity.[57] These are all claims that could create liability for the platform if excepted from CDA 230 and in doing so encourage those platforms to combat perpetrators of these campaigns. While creating exceptions around these collateral acts might indirectly hinder the efficacy of a disinformation effort, they might still fail in addressing the core challenge: media manipulation and the spread of propaganda.

This scarcity of causes of action against individuals who perpetuate disinformation should come as no surprise. The First Amendment heavily limits regulations on the truth, falsity, or quality of information as *content-based* restrictions. The Constitution "demands that content-based restrictions on speech be presumed invalid."[58] In 2012, the Supreme Court examined the specific question on laws against false statements in *United States v. Alvarez.*[59] At issue in that case was the Stolen Valor Act of 2005, which made false statements about decorations awarded by the armed forces punishable by a fine or imprisonment up to six months.[60]

In evaluating the constitutionality of that law, a plurality of the Court noted that "falsity alone may not suffice to bring the speech outside the First Amendment" and rejected the argument that a government "interest in truthful discourse alone [was] sufficient to sustain a ban on speech."61 The Court argued for battling disinformation with counter-speech, stating "the remedy for speech that is false is speech that is true. This is the ordinary course in a free society ... [Society is] not well served when the government seeks to orchestrate public discussion through content-based mandates."62 Facing "the most exacting scrutiny," laws that would punish the distribution of information on basis of its falsity must pass a very high constitutional bar to be permissible.63

One approach may be to avoid the question of attempting to regulate against falsehood, or even political falsehood, per se. As in Alvarez, "some false statements are inevitable if there is to be an open and vigorous expression of views in public and private conversation, expression the First Amendment seeks to guarantee."64 The threat posed by coordinated campaigns of disinformation like those seen in the 2016 US presidential election and elsewhere is not simply that inaccurate information is being spread in the political realm. The distribution of political falsehoods is a long-standing feature of the history of US democratic institutions.65

What is unique is that disinformation is being spread through means that by themselves erode trust in the outcomes of democratic processes and hinder effective discourse around policy. Part of this is the perceived – and potentially actual – advantage that tools such as bots, advertisement micro-targeting, the financial resources of a foreign government, and other tactics confer to actors spreading a message and influencing the public. This advantage is independent of whether or not the information being spread is true or false, though in the immediate context it gives rise to the dramatic sense that the current state of affairs is one in which society is "counter[ing] a firehose of falsehood with a squirt gun of truth" (Paul and Courtney 2016). Rectifying that balance of power focuses on better equalizing the instrumentalities of discourse. Such a goal may be more tractable politically, legally, and intellectually than defining what the threshold of "truthiness" should be and delegating that to private actors and the government to interpret and enforce.

In short, while it may be difficult to specify concretely what an "ideal" marketplace of ideas looks like, it is more straightforward to articulate and halt what might be considered methods of unfair competition in the marketplace of ideas. Amendments to CDA 230 should be directed toward this aim rather than the broader objective of encouraging platforms to eliminate political falsehoods from the web writ large. To adopt the latter as a goal raises the risk of exceptions to CDA 230 that are entirely too broad and in the very least might require the creation of new causes of action that are of dubious legality under the First Amendment.

This approach would create exceptions to CDA 230 for a number of existing laws and potential new regulations. Portions of the Federal Election Campaign Act (FECA) would be excepted from CDA 230 to block foreign interference into political discourse.66 FECA prohibits foreign interests from engaging in election-related spending through advertising and other electioneering communications as they did during the 2016 US presidential election. By excepting these rules from the immunity provided by CDA 230, platforms would be liable for these acts and face incentives to minimize or eliminate this activity from their systems.

A range of rules have been proposed that would limit "micro targeting," the use of highly granular data to target messages to users in the elections context and beyond.67 Some ideas include regulation that would require that data brokers specializing in the collection and distribution of user data provide citizens with the ability to access the dossier compiled about them and opt out of certain uses.68 Another proposal would require provision of "comprehensive notices ... [of] data processing practices" from those engaging in the collection of voter data.69 If implemented, these rules might be subsequently reinforced by crafting an exception to CDA 230 that would align the incentives of the platforms with the enforcement of the law. This would increase the level of transparency available to the public around what kinds of targeting are in use and would block actors unwilling to provide that transparency from the platforms.

Limited exceptions for fraud to be built into CDA 230 might also be justified by the prevalence of unlabeled bots or paid agents purporting to be genuine users for the purposes of persuasion and mobilization. Such an exception would also work to align platforms with the objective of reducing or eliminating the creation of phony websites imitating or purporting to be local news outlets, as was seen in the 2016 election cycle (Coler 2016).

What techniques are "unfair competition in the marketplace of ideas" is rightly a matter of public debate, and such an open-ended inquiry may raise may concerns about the wide range of liability platforms might face. In the very least, the elimination of immunity from platforms that actively support the use of these techniques in influencing public discourse seems warranted and less controversial. Scholars Danielle Keats Citron and Benjamin Wittes have proposed such an approach, proposing an amendment that would explicitly prevent the limitation of liability for "Bad Samaritan" websites and other content hosts that "purposefully encourage" a defined set of illegal acts" (Citron and Wittes 2017). While their focus is on issues of sex trafficking and non-consensual pornography, a similar approach might be taken to contend with the challenges of political disinformation.

Combating disinformation would likely require a piecemeal fine-tuning of CDA 230. The incentive to engage in campaigns of political disinformation is not eliminated by simply making these efforts more challenging, and they will continue evolving as they have been in the past. Although exceptions to CDA 230 will likely make responses more agile than more rigid regulatory or judicial prescriptions, these campaigns are likely to find new channels through which to operate. We might alsoexpect that the impact of these campaigns may change over time. For example, a public increasingly on guard to the possibility of online disinformation campaigns might result in an overall reduction in the persuasive impact of those campaigns in the future. At the same time, ever-improving techniques for fabricating believable fakes in video and other media may increase the persuasive capability of these tactics overtime.70 Enabling an open-ended evolution of these exceptions permitsCDA 230 to adapt as our understanding of these techniques and the risk they pose changes over time.

CONCLUSION: THE TWILIGHT OF THE CROWD?

The rise of political disinformation, and the pervasiveness of disinformation more generally, represents an unexpected market failure in the figurative online marketplace of ideas. Much of the rhetoric in the early era of social media highlighted the extent to which the organic discourse of many participants – the much vaunted "wisdom of the crowds" – would help to weed out false information and produce a multifaceted representation of "the truth" (Surowiecki 2005; Taraborelli 2012). This was also implicit in the ideology of those designing the platforms now seen to be some of the greatest sources of disinformation. As Ev Williams, cofounder of Twitter, has stated "I thought once everyone could speak freely and exchange information and ideas, the world is automatically going to be a better place ... I was wrong about that"(Streitfeld 2017).

Early successes like Wikipedia did not generalize into a broader principle that crowds could effectively and reliably filter for truth and against falsity.[71] Regardless of its causal impact on voting behaviour and political perceptions, the 2016 US presidential election cycle demonstrated in the very least that concerted efforts to spread disinformation can be wildly successful in being shared online rather than quickly weeded out. Organic filtration by the wisdom of the crowds was less robust against deliberate manipulation than originally expected (Hwang 2017).

Efforts to amend or eliminate CDA 230 should be seen in the broader context of a retreat from open, participatory approaches to the problem of disinformation. In light of the perceived absence or weakness of a robust crowd, interventions have turned toward managing disinformation through legislative or judicial action or the judgments of private platform intermediaries. Making this shift can and should raise long-standing concerns about the influence and interests of platforms in regulating expression (Pasquale 2017). It also raises even longer-standing concerns about the role of government in regulating freedom of expression (Pasquale 2017, pp. 14–15).

However, the threat from political disinformation, particularly state-supported campaigns, continues to expand worldwide. Russian efforts leveraging these techniques continue to advance, and recent developments suggest that other nations like China are experimenting with the same playbook to advance their interests (Mozur 2017). In parallel, manipulation by far-right domestic actors continues to advance in the United States (Fang and Woodhouse 2017).

In light of this, well-calibrated modification of CDA 230 may go a long way in helping to give the public and civil society a fighting chance by encouraging platforms to stabilize and balance the marketplaces of ideas they own and operate. Of particular importance is the reduction or elimination of techniques of distribution that – regardless of the truth or falsity of the messages channeled through them – erode trust in public discourse and democratic processes.

Ultimately, the end goal should not be to fully delegate responsibility around the truth value of information to the government or to the platforms. Instead, the primary objective should be the encouragement of publics that are themselves robust against the ever-evolving nature of disinformation. If the wisdom of the crowds has been less robust than was expected a decade ago, it is in part because the online spaces in which they operate have failed to create the proper circumstances under which they could succeed. Fine-tuning the bounds of CDA 230 represents one step in realizing and revitalizing this original vision.

REFERENCES

Alcindor, Y. (2017). Black lawmakers pressure Facebook over racially divisive Russian ads. New York Times, September 28. www.nytimes.com/2017/09/28/us/politics/ facebook-russia-race-congressional-black-caucus.html

Allcott, H., & Gentzkow, M. (2017). Social media and fake news in the 2016 election. Journal of Economic Perspectives, 31(2), 211–236.

Angwin, J., Varner, M., & Tobin, A., (2017). Facebook enabled advertisers to reach "Jew haters." ProPublica, September 14. www.propublica.org/article/facebook- enabled-advertisers-to-reach-jew-haters

Arendt, H. (1971). Lying in politics: Reflections on the Pentagon Papers. The New York Review of Books, November 18. www.nybooks.com/articles/1971/11/18/lying-in- politics-reflections-on-the-pentagon-pape/

Barnouw, E. (1966). A Tower in Babel. New York: Oxford University Press.

Barthel, M., & Mitchell, A. (2017). Democrats, Republicans Now Split on Support for Watchdog Role. Pew Research Center report. www.journalism.org/2017/05/10/ democrats-republicans-now-split-on-support-for-watchdog-role

Belford, A., Cvetkovska, S., Sekulovska, B., & Dojcˇinovic´, S. (2017). Leaked documents show Russian, Serbian attempts to meddle in Macedonia. OCCRP, June 4. www.occrp.org/en/spooksandspin/leaked-documents-show-russian-serbian-attempts- to-meddle-in-macedonia/

Boxell, L., Gentzkow, M., & Shapiro, J. M. (2017). Greater Internet use is not associated with faster growth in political polarization among US demographic groups. Proceedings of the National Academy of Science, 114(40), 10612–10617.

Bramble, N. W. (2012). Safe harbors and the national information infrastructure. Hastings Law Journal, 64(2), 325–384.

Brown Barbour, V. S. (2015). Losing their license to libel: Revisiting § 230 immunity. Berkeley Technical Law Journal, 30(2), 1505–1560.

Chen, A. (2015). The Agency. New York Times, June 2. www.nytimes.com/2015/06/07/ magazine/the-agency.html

Chivvis, C. S. (2017). Understanding Russian "Hybrid Warfare": And What Can Be Done about It. RAND Corporation report. www.rand.org/pubs/testimonies/CT468.htmlAmendment of Section 230 281

Citron, D., & Wittes, B. (2017). The Internet will not break: Denying bad Samaritans Section 230 immunity 17. SSRN. https://papers.ssrn.com/abstract=3007720

Coleman, G. (2015). Hacker, Hoaxer, Whistleblower, Spy: The Many Faces of Anonymous. London: Verso.

Coler, J. (2016). We tracked down a fake-news creator in the suburbs. Here's what we learned. NPR.org, November 23. www.npr.org/sections/alltechconsidered/2016/11/ 23/503146770/npr-finds-the-head-of-a-covert-fake-news-operation-in-the-suburbs

Constine, J. (2017). Facebook security chief rants about misguided "algorithm" backlash. TechCrunch, October 7. http://social.techcrunch.com/2017/10/07/alex- stamos/

Diresta, R., & Harris, T. (2017). Why Facebook and Twitter can't be trusted to police themselves. POLITICO Magazine, November 1. http://politi.co/2zppJMA

Dreyfuss, B. (2017). Seth Rich, conspiracy theorists, and Russiagate "Truthers." The Nation, August 25. www.thenation.com/article/seth-rich-conspiracy-theorists-and-russiagate-truthers/

Dryzek, J. S. (2002). Deliberative Democracy and Beyond: Liberals, Critics, Contestations (1st ed.). New York: Oxford University Press.

The Economist. (2017). Internet firms' legal immunity is under threat. The Economist,February 11. www.economist.com/news/business/21716661-platforms-have- benefited-greatly-special-legal-and-regulatory-treatment-internet-firms

Epstein, D., & Graham, J. D. (2007). Polarized politics and policy consequences.Rand Corporation occasional paper. www.rand.org/content/dam/rand/pubs/occasional_papers/2007/RAND_OP197.pdf

Executive Office of the President. (2014). Big Data: Seizing Opportunities, Preserving Values. White House Washington report. https://obamawhitehouse.archives.gov/ sites/default/files/docs/big_data_privacy_report_may_1_2014.pdf

Fang, L., & Woodhouse, L. A. (2017). How white nationalism became normal online. The Intercept, August 25. https://theintercept.com/2017/08/25/video-how-white- nationalism-became-normal-online/

Faris, R., Roberts, H., Etling, B. et al. (2017). Partisanship, Propaganda, and Disinformation: Online Media and the 2016 US Presidential Election. Cambridge: Berkman Klein Center.

Feingold, R., Herman, L., Aravind, A. et al. (2017). Fake News & Misinformation: The Role of the Nation's Digital Newsstands Facebook, Google, Twitter, and Reddit. Stanford Law School Law and Policy Lab report. https://www-cdn.law.stanford.edu/wp-content/uploads/2017/10/Fake-News-Misinformation-FINAL-PDF.pdf

Feuerman, M. (2016). Court-side seats? The Communications Decency Act and the potential threat to Stub Hub and peer-to-peer marketplaces. Boston College Law Review, 57(1), 227–260.

Finley, K. (2015). Pro-government Twitter bots try to hush Mexican activists. Wired, August 23. www.wired.com/2015/08/pro-government-twitter-bots-try- hush-mexican-activists/

Foroohar, R. (2017). Facebook's self-policing needs an update. Financial Times, September 10. www.ft.com/content/f5d04d7e-9481-11e7-a9e6-11d2f0ebb7f0

Franken, A. (2017). We must not let Big Tech threaten our security, freedoms and democracy. The Guardian, November 8. www.theguardian.com/commentisfree/ 2017/nov/08/big-tech-security-freedoms-democracy-al-franken

Geiger, R. S. (2017). Beyond opening up the black box: Investigating the role of algorithmic systems in Wikipedian organizational culture. Big Data & Society. https://doi.org/10.1177/2053951717730735

Goldman, E. (2017). The ten most important Section 230 rulings. SSRN. https://papers. ssrn.com/abstract=3025943

Grimmelmann, J. (2015). The virtues of moderation. Yale Journal of Law and Technology, 17(1), 42–109.

Halfaker, A., Geiger, R.S., Morgan, J.T. (2013). The rise and decline of an open collaboration system: How Wikipedia's reaction to popularity is causing its decline. American Behavioural Scientist, 57(5), 664–688.

Howard, P., & Kollanyi, B. (2017). Social media companies must respond to the sinister reality behind fake news. The Observer, September 30. www.theguardian.com/ media/2017/sep/30/social-media-companies-fake-news-us-election

Hwang, T. (2017). The madness of the crowd. Logic Magazine, March 15. https://logicmag.io/01-the-madness-of-the-crowd/

Hwang, T., & Woolley, S. (2017). The most important lesson from the dust-up over Trump's fake Twitter followers. Slate, June 2. www.slate.com/articles/technology/ future_tense/2017/06/the_lesson_of_the_dust_up_over_trump_s_fake_twitter_followers.html

Jeong, S. (2015). The Internet of Garbage. New York: Vox Media.

Kafka, P. (2017). Facebook has started to flag fake news stories. Recode, March 4. www.recode.net/2017/3/4/14816254/facebook-fake-news-disputed-trump-snopes-politifact-seattle-tribune

Klein, D. O., & Wueller, J. R. (2017). Fake news: A legal perspective. SSRN. https://papers.ssrn.com/sol3/papers.cfm?abstract_id=2958790

Kollanyi, B., Bradshaw, S., & Neudert, L.-M. (2017). Social media, news and political information during the US election: Was polarizing content concentrated in swing states? Project on Computational Propaganda Data Memo No. 2017.8. http:// comprop.oii.ox.ac.uk/wp-content/uploads/sites/89/2017/09/Polarizing-Content- and-Swing-States.pdf

Kosoff, M. (2017). The Russian troll farm that weaponized Facebook had American boots on the ground. The Hive, October 18. www.vanityfair.com/news/2017/10/the-russian-troll-farm-that-weaponized-facebook-had-american- boots-on-the-ground

Lange-Ionatamishvili, E., Svetoka, S., & Geers, K. (2015). Strategic communication and social media in the Russia Ukraine conflict. In K. Geers (Ed.), Cyber War in Perspective: Russian Aggression Against Ukraine (pp. 103–111). Tallinn: NATOCCDCOE Publications.

Lapowsky, I. (2017). Russia wouldn't need Trump's digital team to spread fake news. Wired, July 13. www.wired.com/story/russia-trump-targeting-fake-news/

Lee, T. B. (2017). Dow Jones posts fake story claiming Google was buying Apple. Ars Technica, October 10. https://arstechnica.com/tech-policy/2017/10/dow-jones- posts-fake-story-claiming-google-was-buying-apple/

Lessig, L. (1999). Code and Other Laws of Cyberspace. New York: Basic Books.

Ling, J. (2017). Google chief says Google News will "engineer" Russian propaganda out of the feed. Motherboard, November 20. https://motherboard.vice.com/en_us/article/ pa39vv/eric-schmidt-says-google-news-will-delist-rt-sputnik-russia-fake-newsAmendment of Section 230 283

Marantz, A. (2016). Trolls for Trump. The New Yorker, October 31. www.newyorker.com/magazine/2016/10/31/trolls-for-trump

Marwick, A., & Lewis, R. (2017). Media Manipulation and Disinformation Online. Data & Society Research Institute report.

Meacham, J. (2013). Thomas Jefferson: The Art of Power. New York: Random House. Metz, C. (2015). Google is 2 billion lines of code – and it's all in one place. Wired, September 16. www.wired.com/2015/09/google-2-billion-lines-codeand-one-place/

Mina, A. X. (2017). Knight Prototype Fund supports the Credibility Working Group. MisinfoCon, June 22. https://misinfocon.com/knight-prototype-fund-supports-the- credibility-working-group-c3dcc6667569

Mozur, P. (2017). China spreads propaganda to U.S. on Facebook, a platform it bans at home. New York Times, November 8. www.nytimes.com/2017/11/08/technology/ china-facebook.html

Mulford, C. (2008). Benjamin Franklin's savage eloquence: Hoaxes from the press at Passy, 1782. Proceedings of the American Philosophical Society, 152(4), 490–530.

Museum of Hoaxes. Drunk Driving on the Internet. http://hoaxes.org/af_database/permalink/drunk_driving_on_the_internet

National Intelligence Council. (2017). Assessing Russian Activities and Intentions in Recent US Elections. Office of the Director of National Intelligence report, ICA2017-01D.

NCCIC (National Cyber-security and Communications Integration Center). (2016). GRIZZLY STEPPE – Russian Malicious Cyber Activity. Department of Homeland Security report, Jar-16-20296a.

Nielsen, R. K., & Graves, L. (2017). What do ordinary people think fake news is? Poor journalism and political propaganda. Columbia Journalism Review, October 24. www.cjr.org/analysis/fake-news-study.php

North, A. (2017). When a SWAT team comes to your house. New York Times, July 6. www.nytimes.com/2017/07/06/opinion/swatting-fbi.html

NPR. (2017). Russian bots tweeting calls to fire McMaster, former FBI agent says. NPR. org, August 20. www.npr.org/2017/08/20/544817844/russian-bots-tweeting-calls-to-fire-mcmaster-former-fbi-agent-says

Oremus, W. (2016). Stop calling everything "fake news." Slate, December 6. www.slate.com/articles/technology/technology/2016/12/stop_calling_everything_fake_news.html Pasquale, F. (2017). The automated public sphere. SSRN. https://papers.ssrn.com/abstract=3067552

Pasquale, F., & Bracha, O. (2007). Federal Search Commission? Access, fairness and accountability in the law of search. SSRN. https://papers.ssrn.com/abstract=1002453

Paul, C., & Courtney, W. (2016). Russian propaganda is pervasive, and America is behind the power curve in countering it. Rand Corporation (blog), September12. www.rand.org/blog/2016/09/russian-propaganda-is-pervasive-and-america- is-behind.html

Pennycook, G., Cannon, T. D., & Rand, D. G. (2017). Prior exposure increases perceived accuracy of fake news. SSRN. https://papers.ssrn.com/abstract=2958246

Pennycook, G., & Rand, D. (2017). Assessing the effect of "disputed" warnings and source salience on perceptions of fake news accuracy. SSRN. https://papers.ssrn.com/abstract=3035384

Prior, M. (2013). Media and political polarization. Annual Review of Political Science,16, 101–127.

Quist, M. D. (2012). "Plumbing the depths" of the CDA: Weighing the competing Fourth and Seventh Circuit standards of ISP immunity under Section 230 of the Communications Decency Act. George Mason Law Review, 20(1), 275–309.

Reidenberg, J. R., Debelak, J., Kovnot, J., & Miao, T. (2012). Section 230 of theCommunications Decency Act: A survey of the legal literature and reform proposals. SSRN. https://papers.ssrn.com/abstract=2046230

Robb, A. (2017). Pizzagate: Anatomy of a fake news scandal. Rolling Stone, November 16. www.rollingstone.com/politics/news/pizzagate-anatomy-of-a- fake-news-scandal-w511904

Robertson, J., Riley, M., & Willis, A. (2017). How to hack an election. Bloomberg Businessweek, March 31. www.bloomberg.com/features/2016-how-to-hack-an- election/

Rogers, J. (2017). Wikipedia and intermediary immunity: Supporting sturdy crowd systems for producing reliable information. Yale Law Journal Forum, 127, 358–372.

Rolling Stone. (2011). Musician Started Bon Jovi Death Hoax. Rolling Stone, December 28. www.rollingstone.com/music/news/musician-started-bon-jovi- death-hoax-20111228

Rubinstein, I. (2014). Voter privacy in the age of big data. SSRN. https://papers.ssrn.com/abstract=2447956

Santa Clara University. (2017). Leading news outlets establish transparency standards to help readers identify trustworthy news sources. The Trust Project, November16. www.scu.edu/ethics/focus-areas/journalism-ethics/programs/the-trust-project/trust-project-launches-indicators/

Schreckinger, B. (2017). World war meme. POLITICO Magazine, March/April. www.politico.com/magazine/story/2017/03/memes-4chan-trump-supporters-trolls-internet-214856

Seetharaman, D. (2017). Russian-backed Facebook accounts staged events around divisive issues. Wall Street Journal, October 30. www.wsj.com/articles/russian-backed- facebook-accounts-organized-events-on-all-sides-of-polarizing-issues-1509355801

Seetharaman, D., & Wells, G. (2017). Tech giants disclose Russian activity on eve of congressional appearance. Wall Street Journal, October 30. www.wsj.com/articles/ facebook-estimates-126-million-people-saw-russian-backed-content-1509401546

Silverman, C., & Singer-Vine, J. (2016). Most Americans who see fake news believe it, new survey says. BuzzFeed, December 6. www.buzzfeed.com/craigsilverman/fake- news-survey

Streitfeld, D. (2017). "The Internet is broken": @ev is trying to salvage it. New York Times, May 20. www.nytimes.com/2017/05/20/technology/evan-williams-medium-twitter-internet.html

Subramanian, S. (2017). Inside the Macedonian fake-news complex. Wired, February15. www.wired.com/2017/02/veles-macedonia-fake-news/

Sullivan, M. (2017). It's time to retire the tainted term "fake news." Washington Post, January 8. www.washingtonpost.com/lifestyle/style/its-time-to-retire-the-tainted-term- fake-news/2017/01/06/a5a7516c-d375-11e6-945a-76f69a399dd5_story.html

Sunstein, C. R. (1992). Free speech now. University of Chicago Law Review, 59,255–316.

Surowiecki, J. (2005). The Wisdom of Crowds. New York: Anchor Books.

Swire, B., Berinsky, A., Lewandowsky, S. et al. (2017). Processing political misinformation: Comprehending the Trump phenomenon. Royal Society Open Science. http://doi.org/10.1098/rsos.160802

Tapscott, D., & Williams, A. D. (2010). Wikinomics: How Mass Collaboration Changes Everything. New York: Penguin Group.

Taraborelli, D. (2012). Seven years after Nature, pilot study compares Wikipedia favourably to other encyclopaedias in three languages. Wikimedia Foundation (blog), August 2. https://blog.wikimedia.org/2012/08/02/seven-years-after-nature-pilot- study-compares-wikipedia-favorably-to-other-encyclopedias-in-three-languages/

Thompson, N. (2017). Our minds have been hijacked by our phones. Tristan Harris wants to rescue them. Wired, July 26. www.wired.com/story/our-minds-have-been- hijacked-by-our-phones-tristan-harris-wants-to-rescue-them/

Tremble, C. (2017). Wild Westworld: Section 230 of the CDA and Social Networks' Use of Machine-Learning Algorithms, Fordham Law Review 86 825.

Tynan, D. (2016). How Facebook powers money machines for obscure political "news" sites. The Guardian, August 24. www.theguardian.com/technology/2016/aug/24/ facebook-clickbait-political-news-sites-us-election-trump

Volokh, E., & Falk, D. M. (2012). First Amendment protection for search engine search results. White Paper commissioned by Google. www.volokh.com/wp-content/ uploads/2012/05/SearchEngineFirstAmendment.pdf

Wingfield, N., Isaac, M., & Benner, K. (2016). Google and Facebook take aim at fake news sites. New York Times, November 14. www.nytimes.com/2016/11/15/technology/ google-will-ban-websites-that-host-fake-news-from-using-its-ad-service.html

Wintour, P. (2017). Russian hackers to blame for sparking Qatar crisis, FBI inquiry finds. The Guardian, June 7. www.theguardian.com/world/2017/jun/07/russian- hackers-qatar-crisis-fbi-inquiry-saudi-arabia-uae

Woolley, S. C., & Howard, P. N. (2017). Computational propaganda worldwide: Executive summary. Project on Computational Propaganda Working Paper No.2017.11. http://comprop.oii.ox.ac.uk/publishing/working-papers/computational- propaganda-worldwide-executive-summary/

Wu, T. (2013). Machine speech. University of Pennsylvania Law Review, 161,1495–1533.

FOOTNOTE

1. For a review of theories of democracy based on the role of deliberation, see generally Dryzek (2002); see also Arendt (1971).
2. For a preliminary review of the role that different platforms have played in distributing disin- formation, see Feingold et al. (2017).
3. This perception is frequently bolstered by projects launched by the companies themselves. This includes systems like YouTube's Content ID (www.youtube.com/watch?time_continue= 2&v=9g2U12SsRns) that automate detection of IP infringement. It also includes technologies like Perspective (www.perspectiveapi.com/), a product that automates the detection of "toxic" comments online.
4. 47 U.S.C. § 230.
5. See Stratton Oakmont, Inc. v. Prodigy Services Co., 1995 WL 323710 (N.Y. Sup. Ct. 1995).
6. Id.
7. 47 U.S.C. § 230(a).
8. For a general review of leading cases in this space, see Goldman (2017).
9. Zeran v. American Online, Inc., 129 F.3d 32 (4th Cir. 1997).
10. Batzel v. Smith, 333 F.3d 1018 (9th Cir. 2003).
11. Barrett v. Rosenthal, 9 Cal.Rptr.3d 142 (Cal. Ct. App. 2004).
12. Doe v. MySpace, Inc. 528 F.3d 413 (5th Cir. 2008).
13. Barnes v. Yahoo!, 570 F.3d 1096 (9th Cir. 2009).
14. Id. at 1102.
15. See also Allow States and Victims to Fight Online Sex Trafficking Act of 2017, Pub. L. No. 115- 164, 132 Stat. 1253 (2018).
16. See, e.g., Zeran v. American Online, Inc., 129 F.3d 32 (4th Cir. 1997).
17. 52 U.S.C. § 30121. See also, 11 CFR 110.20.
18. See Jane Doe No. 1 v. Backpage.com, LLC, 817 F.3d 12 (1st Cir. 2016) (ads for prostitution); Chicago Lawyers' Committee for Civil Rights under the Law v. Craigslist, 519 F.3d 666 (housingads violating the Fair Housing Act).
19. See Federal Trade Commission v. Accusearch, Inc., 570 F.3d 1187 (10th Cir. 2009) (suits by an agency to enforce federal law still subject to CDA 230 analysis).
20. A.B. 1104, 2017–18 Cal. State Leg. (Cal. 2017).

21. See California A.B. 1104 Opposition Letter, Electronic Frontier Foundation (2017), www.eff.org/document/california-ab-1104-opposition-letter. This notes a number of First Amendment challenges to this type of legislation.
22. For a review of the large literature on this topic, see Reidenberg et al. (2012), pp. 29–31.
23. See Reidenberg et al. (2012), pp. 26-27; Jeong (2015).
24. New York Times Co. v. Sullivan, 376 U.S. 254 (1964).
25. Fair Housing Council of San Fernando Valley v. Roommates.com, 521 F. 3d 1157.
26. Roommates.com, 521 F.3d at 1168.
27. Id. at 1173–1175.
28. Id. at 1175.
29. Federal Trade Commission v. Accusearch, Inc., 570 F.3d 1187, 1199 (10th Cir. 2009).
30. Jane Doe No. 1 v. Backpage.com, LLC, 817 F.3d 12, 22 (1st Cir. 2016).
31. It should be noted that legislation has been passed reversing the holding in Backpage. See Allow States and Victims to Fight Online Sex Trafficking Act of 2017, Pub. L. No. 115-164, 132 Stat. 1253 (2018).
32. Roommates.com, 521 F.3d at 1174.
33. See, e.g., Jane Doe No. 1 v. Backpage.com, LLC, 817 F.3d 12, 17 (1st Cir. 2016) (CDA 230 immunity exists even when platform specifically charges for advertisements promoting prostitution).
34. See Chicago Lawyers' Committee for Civil Rights under the Law v. Craigslist, 519 F.3d 666, 672 (applying CDA 230 in part because platform did "not offer a lower price to people who include discriminatory statements in their postings"); NPS LLC v. Stub Hub, Inc., 25 Mass. L. Rptr. 478 (Super. Ct. 2009) (rejected CDA 230 immunity in part because the platform's "revenue increased in direct proportion to the price of the ticket sold," in contrast to a newspaper, which "generally charges a fixed price").
35. See, e.g., Google's "About the ad auction – AdSense Help," (https://support.google.com/ adsense/answer/160525?hl=en), which explains the Google auction system; see also Facebook's Help Center (www.facebook.com/business/help/430291176997542), which explains the Facebook auction system.
36. See Facebook's, "Welcome to News Feed," (https://newsfeed.fb.com/?lang=en), which reviews how the system curates content for users.
37. See also Tremble (2017).
38. Fair Housing Council of San Fernando Valley v. Roommates.com, 521 F. 3d 1157, 1169.
39. Id.
40. Id. 41 Id. at 1176–1189.
41. The Honest Ads Act, S. 1989, 115th Cong. (2017).

42. Id. at §8.
43. See, e.g., Mina (2017), which discusses one initiative to develop "credibility indicators."
44. See, e.g., Search King, Inc. v. Google Tech., Inc., No. 02–1457, 2003 WL 21464568, at *4 (W.D. Okla. May 27, 2003). See also Volokh and Falk (2012), which reviews these cases in the context of search results.
45. See the section "Part 1: The Disinformation Challenge" in this chapter.
46. For examples of these kinds of tactics, see Seetharaman (2017).
47. For an example of how "an understanding of the risks of machine learning (ML) drives small-c conservatism" at companies like Facebook, see Constine (2017).
48. Cf. Metz (2015), which describes the complex infrastructure for managing Google's code.
49. See Batzel v. Smith, 333 F.3d 1018 (9th Cir. 2003).
50. See Zeran v. America Online, Inc., 129 F.3d 327, 331 (4th Cir. 1997): "The amount of information communicated via interactive computer services is therefore staggering .. . It would be impossible for service providers to screen each of their millions of postings for possible problems."
51. See, e.g., Fake News Challenge (www.fakenewschallenge.org/), a competition to build machine learning models to assist in the detection of "fake news."
52. See Halfaker (2013), which describes how automation can create perverse effects that reduce volunteer contributions over time in the context of Wikipedia.
53. This is not to dispute that there are circumstances in which automation and bots can work productively with community-driven models. See Geiger (2017).
54. See Bramble (2012), pp. 359–361. However, scholars contest the notion that a "balance of power" really exists in practice; see Pasquale and Bracha (2007).
55. See generally Klein and Wueller (2017), pp. 7–9.
56. State law rights to publicity have occasionally been cast as an intellectual property claim, attempting plaintiffs to use the exception under 47 U.S.C. § 230(e)(2). See, e.g., Cross v. Facebook, CIV 537384, 2016 WL 7785723 (Cal. Super. Ct. May 31, 2016), aff'd in part and rev'd in part, No. A148623, 2017 WL 3404767 (Cal. Ct. App. Aug. 9, 2017).
57. Ashcroft v. American Civil Liberties Union, 542 U.S. 656, 660.
58. United States v. Alvarez, 567 U.S. 709.
59. See id., at 715. 61
60. id., at 719, 723.
61. id., at 727.
62. id., at 724 (citing Turner Broadcasting System, Inc. v. FCC, 512 U
63. id., at 718.
64. See, e.g., Meacham (2013), which details political lies during the 18
65. See 52 U.S.C. § 30121 and 11 C.F.R. § 110.20.

66. For an overview of some of the proposals around political advertisement micro-targeting, see Rubinstein (2014).
67. See Rubinstein (2014), pp. 919–921; see also Executive Office of the President (2014), which advocates for approaches that give individuals the ability to "participate in the use and distribution of his or her information after it is collected."
68. See Rubinstein (2014), p. 913.
69. See, e.g., Matthias Niessner's YouTube video "Face2Face: Real-time face capture and re-enactment of RGB videos (CVPR 2016 Oral)," (www.youtube.com/watch?v=ohmajJTcpNk), demonstrating the use of machine learning to create believable simulations of political leaders speaking.
70. See, e.g., Tapscott and Williams (2010), predicting the broader application of the collaborative model used by Wikipedia.

12 TRANSPARENCY IN THE DIGITAL PLATFORM ERA

A DEMOCRATIC PERSPECTIVE

INTRODUCTION: AN OVERVIEW

In the rapidly evolving landscape of the digital platform era, transparency has emerged as a cornerstone for preserving democratic values and principles. As our society becomes increasingly intertwined with digital technologies and online platforms, the need for transparency in their operations and decision-making processes is more critical than ever. This study delves into the multifaceted concept of transparency within the digital platform environment, with a specific focus on its significance in upholding democratic ideals. In an age marked by the dissemination of information, connectivity, and online engagement, understanding and promoting transparency is essential for fostering trust, accountability, and responsible governance in the realm of digital platforms. This exploration aims to provide a comprehensive analysis of the democratic implications and imperatives of transparency in the platform society, shedding light on the challenges and opportunities it presents for the future of our interconnected world.

At a time when social media and social media companies have played a complex, troubled role in recent political events, ranging from the 2016 US election and UK Brexit referendum to genocide in Myanmar, a growing chorus of scholars, policymakers, and commentators have begun proclaiming that social media – less than ten years ago cast as an emancipator "liberation technology" – may now be fomenting polarization and undermining democracy around the globe (Tucker et al. 2017). As the executives of Google, Facebook, Twitter, and other major platform companies have been called to testify before elected officials Moore and Tambini 2018), the public is increasingly demanding greater accountability from the technology companies that operate the services entrusted with their sensitive data, personal communication, and attention. In the past several years, transparency has emerged as one of the leading accountability mechanisms through which platform companies have attempted to regain the trust of the public, politicians, and regulatory authorities. Ranging from Facebook's efforts to partner with academics and create a reputable mechanism for third-party data access and independent research (King and Persily 2019) and the release of Facebook's public-facing "Community Standards" (the rules that govern what the more than 2.2 billion monthly active users of Facebook are allowed to post on the site) to the expanded advertising disclosure tools being built for elections around the world (Leerssen et al. 2019), transparency is playing a major role in current policy debates around free expression, social media, and democracy.

While transparency may seem intuitive as a high-level concept (often conceived narrowly as the disclosure of certain information that may not previously have been visible or publicly available; see Albu and Flyverbom 2016), critical scholarship has long noted that a major reason for the widespread popularity of transparency as a form of accountability in democratic governance is its flexibility and ambiguity. As the governance scholar Christopher Hood has argued, "much of the allure of transparency as a word and a doctrine may lie in its potential to appeal to those with very different, indeed contradictory, attitudes and worldviews" (Hood 2006, p. 19). Transparency in practice is deeply political, contested, and oftentimes problematic (Etzioni 2010; Ananny and Crawford 2018); and yet, it remains an important – albeit imperfect – tool that, in certain policy domains, has the potential to remedy unjust outcomes, increase the public accountability of powerful actors, and improve governance more generally (Fung, Graham, and Weil 2007; Hood and Heald 2006). As the authors of the Ranking Digital Rights Corporate Responsibility Index (an annual effort to quantify the transparency and openness of multiple major technology companies) argue, "transparency is essential in order for people to even know when users' freedom of expression or privacy rights are violated either directly by – or indirectly through – companies' platforms and services, let alone identify who should be held responsible" (Ranking Digital Rights 2018, pp. 4–5).

In recent years, a substantial literature has emerged in what might be called "digital transparency studies," much of which critiques prevailing discourses of technologically implemented transparency as a panacea for the digital age (Christensen and Cheney 2014; Flyverbom 2015; Hansen and Flyverbom 2015; Albu and Flyverbom 2016; Stohl, Stohl, and Leonardi 2016). This work has been wide-reaching, touching on the politics of whistle blowing and leaking (Hood 2011), the way that transparency can be politicized or weaponized to fulfill specific policy agendas (Levy and Johns 2016), and the way that transparency has been enabled by technological developments and encryption (Heemsbergen 2016). Yet there has been less work that surveys the scholarship on transparency more broadly (drawing on organizational studies, political science, and governance studies, law, as well as digital media and political communication research; see Flyverbom 2019) and applies it narrowly to the pressing questions around platform companies, social media, and democracy that are the focus of growing public and scholarly discussion, as well as this volume. The goal of this chapter is therefore to contextualize the recent examples of transparency as implemented by platform companies with an overview of the relevant literature on transparency in both theory and practice; consider the potential positive governance impacts of transparency as a form of accountability in the current political moment; and reflect on the shortfalls of transparency that should be considered by legislators, academics, and funders weighing the relative benefits of policy or research dealing with transparency in this area.

The chapter proceeds in three parts: We first provide a brief historical overview of transparency in democratic governance, tracing it from its origins in Enlightenment-era liberalism all the way to its widespread adoption in the twentieth and twenty-first centuries. We quickly summarize what transparency seeks to achieve in theory and how it is commonly conceptualized as furthering traditional democratic values. In the second section, we provide a necessarily not comprehensive survey of major transparency initiatives as enacted by platform companies in the social media era, with a focus on the changes that firms have made following the 2016 US election. Finally, we discuss transparency in practice, with a summary of critical insights from the "digital turn" in transparency studies, which provides ample caution against transparency as a panacea for democratic accountability and good governance.

FROM BENTHAM TO BLOCKCHAIN: THE HISTORICAL DEVELOPMENT OF THE CONCEPT OF TRANSPARENCY

Depending on how one precisely formulates what transparency is and what its key elements are, the origins of the concept can be traced back to various classical Chinese and Greek ideas about government and governance. Researchers have suggested that there are multiple, interrelated strains of pre-twentieth-century thinking that have substantially inspired the contemporary notions of transparency, including long-standing "notions of rule-governed administration, candid and open social communication, and ways of making organization and society 'knowable'" (Hood 2006, p. 5).

However, it is generally accepted that transparency as it is understood today became popularized first in the writings of certain major Enlightenment political theorists, especially Jeremy Bentham, Immanuel Kant, and Jean-Jacques Rousseau. Their notions of transparency – often posited as an antonym to secrecy – reflected their presiding views about human nature, politics, and international relations. For Kant, arguing against government secrecy about treaties in his famous essay on "Perpetual Peace," a lack of transparency could potentially worsen the effects of international anarchy and contribute to war (O'Neill 2006; Bennington 2011).

For Rousseau, transparency was primarily a way to increase the visibility of public servants, making it more difficult for them to defraud the state; he called for measures that would make it impossible for government officials to "move about incognito, so that the marks of a man's rank or position shall accompany him wherever he goes" (Rousseau 1985: p. 72 cited in Hood 2006). Bentham's even more extreme ideals about publicity and visibility, as best exemplified by his infamous "panoptic on," seem to have been fundamentally rooted in pessimistic expectations about human fallibility and the corrupting influence of power (Gaonkar and McCarthy 1994). Bentham is often identified as the forefather of modern transparency as used in the political sense (Hood 2006; Baume 2018). He famously wrote that "the more strictly we are watched, the better we behave," an edict that inspired his approach to open government, arguing that "secrecy, being an instrument of conspiracy, ought never to be the system of a regular government" (Hood 2006, p. 9).Even before Bentham's writings, however, one of the first apparent initiatives for government transparency in practice was underway in Sweden: the "Ordinance on Freedom of Writing and of the Press" (1766), proposed by the clergyman and parliamentarian Anders Chydenius (Birchall 2011; Lamble 2002), which provided citizens with statutory access to certain government documents. Chydenius, apparently inspired by the Chinese "scholar officials" of the Tang Dynasty "Imperial Censurate," who investigated government decisions and corrupt officials (Lamble 2002, p. 3), helped enact what is widely seen to be the precursor to all modern Freedom of Information Access (FOI or FOIA) legislation. While a handful of detailed historical accounts of the adoption of transparency measures as enacted by governments in specific countries exist, such as in the Netherlands (Meijer 2015), it is generally accepted that modern political transparency emerged in the United States centuries after it did in Scandinavia (Hood and Heald 2006). In the early and mid-twentieth century, a number of major American political figures, ranging from Woodrow Wilson and Louis Brandeis to Harry Truman and Lyndon Johnson, began publicly arguing that transparency was a moral good and an essential requirement for a healthy, democratic society (Hood and Heald 2006). Wilson, channeling ideas expressed by Kant more than a century earlier, blamed secret treaties for contributing to the outbreak of World War I and made diplomatic transparency a significant feature of his famous "14 points" (Hood 2006). Brandeis, a Supreme Court justice and influential political commentator, advocated for even broader forms of transparency in public affairs, famously claiming that "sunlight is said to be the best of disinfectants" (Brandeis 1913, p. 10). Brandeis's ideas would culminate decades later in what the historian Michael Schudson has called the "transparency imperative," as cultural changes and technological advances resulted in transparency becoming increasingly institutionalized in the United States across a multitude of public and private domains (Schudson 2015, p. 12).

The move toward today's much wider embrace of transparency as a facet of contemporary democratic governance in the United States began with Truman, who signed the first of a series of important administrative orders, the 1946 Administrative Procedures Act, followed notably by the 1966 Freedom of Information Act and the 1976 Government in the Sunshine Act (Fung 2013).

The 1966 legislation proved to be especially influential, with its main premise (a mechanism for citizens to request the public disclosure of certain government documents) effectively replicated by legislatures in more than ninety countries (Banisar 2006). The goal of these initiatives was to reduce corruption, increase government efficiency by holding officials accountable, and generally promote the public legitimacy of government (Grimmelikhuijsen et al. 2013; Cucciniello, Porumbescu, and Grimmelikhuijsen 2017). Through freedom of information requests – which have continued to expand in their scope since the 1960s, to the extent that "the right to know" has been postulated as a human right (see Schudson 2015) – as well as mandatory or voluntary disclosure programs, auditing regimes (Power 1997), and growing recognition of the importance of whistle blowing (Garton Ash 2016, p. 337), the concept of transparency became central to twentieth-century forms of power, visibility, and knowledge (Flyverbom 2016).

Brandeis's ideas continue to inspire transparency initiatives to this day, primarily among advocates of open government. Brandeis's famous quote even provided the name for the Sunlight Foundation, a non-governmental organization that advocates for government transparency on campaign finance, and groups such as Transparency International strive to provide access to information that can combat corruption, potentially unethical behaviour, and better document how power is exerted in a democratic society. Less widely cited, however, is Brandeis's full quote: "Sunlight is said to be the best of disinfectants; electric light the most efficient policeman. And publicity has already played an important part in the struggle against the Money Trust"(Brandeis 1913, p. 10). As Kosack and Fung (2014) note, the initial target of Brandeis's quest for transparency was not corrupt government but rather opaque corporations: the "Money Trust" of robber barons, bankers, and capitalists who were amassing great fortunes – and potentially defrauding the public – with little public accountability or oversight. In effect, Brandeis was anticipating impending corporate scandals, such as the 1929 Stock Market Crash, which led to an initial measure of corporate transparency and oversight via the formation of the US Securities and Exchange Commission, noting that the market itself provided limited information for consumers:

Then, as now, it was difficult for a grocery shopper to judge the ingredients contained in food products; this difficulty was compounded many times when an investor tried to assess the worth of more complicated products such as financial securities. Government, [Brandeis] thought, should step in to require companies such as food producers and banks to become fully transparent about their products and practices through laws and regulations. (Kosack and Fung 2014, p. 68)In particular, Brandeis broke with the Enlightenment tradition of transparency as primarily a way to hold officials to account, also arguing that it could serve as a check against private power. By doing so, he set the intellectual foundations for the corporate transparency initiatives of the twentieth century.

TRANSPARENCY AND THE CORPORATION

There has been a profound interest in transparency measures since their introduction in the United States in the 1960s (Schudson 2015), and, today, transparency measures are commonly proposed for a host of private and publicactors. Archon Fung has written extensively about the fundamental democratic ideals of transparency underlying these efforts, which he argues are based on the first principle that "information should be available to citizens so that they can protect their vital interests" (Fung 2013, p. 185). Crucially, because "democratically important kinds of information may be information about the activities of private and civic organizations rather than governments themselves" (Fung 2013, p. 188), corporations that play outsize roles in public life should also ideally be as transparent as possible. Nevertheless, corporate transparency and accountability is generally only demanded once a corporation appears to threaten citizen interests – as in the case of the powerful banks that Brandeis was concerned about or in the archetypical case of the extractive natural resource companies or petrochemical companies (Frynas2005). As multiple labour and environmental scandals across different industries emerged, transparency became increasingly packaged as part of the "Corporate Social Responsibility" movement that emerged in the 1980s and 1990s (Ruggie 2013). For instance, anticorruption activists noted that good corporate behaviour should go beyond just compliance with legal mechanisms but also involve active participation in various social responsibility initiatives and feature as much transparency as possible (Hess 2012).

Transparency was thus advocated as a core element of public accountability for business (Waddock 2004) and enthusiastically announced as a way for firms to demonstrate their social responsibility and integrity (Tapscott and Ticoll 2003). In practice, however, transparency has many important limitations. First, just like governments, corporations cannot be perfectly transparent, albeit for different reasons than governments – intellectual property is a central concern. Just as with governmental transparency, corporate transparency must achieve a compromise, which lifts "the veil of secrecy just enough to allow for some degree of democratic accountability" (Thompson 1999, p. 182). Although transparency efforts are often backed by those who oppose regulation, governance scholars have argued that "transparency is merely a form of regulation by other means" (Etzioni 2010, p. 10) and that transparency alone can be no substitute for regulation. Indeed, meaningful transparency often needs to be backed with regulatory oversight, as scholars critical about corporate transparency in practice emphasize the possible existence of "opaque" forms of transparency that do not actively make the democratically relevant information visible but rather can be used to obfuscate processes and practices beneath a veneer of respectability (Christensen and Cheney 2014; Albu and Flyverbom 2016).

Overall, the track record of corporate transparency measures for promoting good governance has been mixed. Across multiple domains, from development projects to the private sector, it has been said that "actual evidence on transparency's impacts on accountability is not as strong as one might expect" (Fox 2007, p. 664). Corporate actors do not always play along and may only do the bare minimum without fully implementing voluntary or legislatively mandated transparency measures; as a comprehensive literature review of twenty-five years of transparency research notes, "the effects of transparency are much less pronounced than conventional wisdom suggests" (Cucciniello, Porumbescu, and Grimmelikhuijsen 2017, p. 32). Empirical work into the results of transparency initiatives has shown its important limitations – for instance, a survey of mandatory disclosure programs for chemical spills in the United States suggested that the disclosures may have been up to four times lower than they should have (Fox 2007, p. 665). Measures that run the gamut from audits, inspections, and industry-wide ombudspersons to parliamentary commissions and inquiries are often formulated as mechanisms of "horizontal transparency" that strive to let outsiders (e.g., regulators, the public) see inside the corporate black box (Hansen and Flyverbom 2015). However, the effects of these efforts can vary significantly, to the extent that "it remains unclear why some transparency initiatives manage to influence the behaviour of powerful institutions, while others do not" (Fox 2007, p. 665).

The pessimism about the possibility of successful transparency efforts in both the public and the private sectors has been somewhat counterbalanced in the past two decades by increasing optimism about the possibilities of "digital transparency" or "e-transparency" (Bertot, Jaeger, and Grimes 2010). New information and communication technologies have promised to make transparency not only more effective but also more efficient by increasing the availability of relevant information (Bonsón et al. 2012). Internet utopians like Wired magazine's Kevin Kelly began arguing that the use of "digital technology in day-to-day life affords an inevitable and ultimate transparency" (Heemsbergen 2016, p. 140), and the collaborative, peer-produced "Web 2.0" seemed to provide multiple possibilities for blogs, wikis, online archives, and other tools through which interested stakeholders could access certain forms of democratically important information (Flyverbom 2016). As some hoped that information and communication technologies could start laying the foundations for "a culture of transparency" in countries without a long- standing history of democratic governance (Bertot, Jaeger, and Grimes 2010,p. 267), Heemsbergen (2016, p. 140) shows how others began proposing even more extreme forms of "radical transparency" via "networked digital methods of collecting, processing, and disclosing information" as a mechanism through which maximal social and economic growth could be achieved.

The latest technological innovations are constantly being harnessed for possible transparency initiatives – the recent spread of projects using distributed ledger systems (e.g., Blockchain) to create open registries and databases provides perhaps the best example (Underwood 2016). Bentham would likely have approved of such initiatives; with a blockchain-based registry where each change is documented and permanently encoded in the database itself, theoretical levels of perfect transparency in a specific system can be achieved. From WikiLeaks to the encrypted whistle blowing platform Secure Drop, encryption has further helped digital transparency take root, with potentially significant impacts for the redistribution of power between states, citizens, and corporations (Heemsbergen 2016; Owen 2015).

In the past decade, a new generation of technology utopians has seized the ideological foundations set by the Enlightenment thinkers, positing "openness" as an organizing principle for contemporary social life. Facebook's chief executive, Mark Zuckerberg, has preached for many years that his company's products were creating "radical transparency" at a societal level, fostering more "open and honest communities" (Heemsbergen 2016, p. 140). Zuckerberg has publicly portrayed openness and transparency as key organizing features of the digital age while running a company that made increasingly important political decisions in secret (Gillespie 2018a). However, following the multiple scandals hounding Facebook since 2016, the mantra is slowly being turned inward: Zuckerberg has claimed that he will finally bring transparency to some of the company's sensitive business dealings, most notably in the realm of political advertising (Feldman 2017). In public discourse, academics, policymakers, and civil society groups are increasingly advocating measures to look into the corporate black box of firms like Facebook and Google, positing it as a major potential governance mechanism that could rein in platform companies (Brock 2017). Yet how has transparency historically been enacted by these companies, and what are the recent measures that have been implemented in response to this public outcry?

TRANSPARENCY PRACTICES OF PLATFORM COMPANIES

A noteworthy feature of the twenty-first-century "platform society" (Van Dijck, Poell, and Waal 2018) is the relationship between, on one hand, the increasingly sophisticated socio-political and technical systems that now require transparency due to their political and democratic salience and the even more technical and complex socio-political mechanisms enacted to try and create that transparency on the other. For instance, large-scale algorithmic systems have been in the past few years roundly critiqued for their opacity (Burrell 2016), leading to a growing movement for measures that produce "Fairness, Accountability, and Transparency" in machine- learning models and data-driven systems (Barocas and Selbst 2016; Hoffmann 2019). As research in this area has shown, producing desirable forms of transparency while also preserving privacy and intellectual property in a computationally feasible manner is no easy task (Edwards and Veale 2017; Wachter, Mittelstadt, and Russell 2018). Social media platforms present a similar challenge; companies like Facebook and Google have shown themselves to be highly important venues for political speech and deliberation around the world, and their increasing role as a global channel for news and political information means that they are now clearly institutions with significant democratic implications (Garton Ash 2016; Gorwa 2019a; Van Dijck, Poell, and Waal 2018). Their apparent influence, combined with many high-profile scandals, suggests that these firms can pose a threat to the average citizen's best interests. Today, platform companies clearly meet the threshold articulated in traditional theories of democratic transparency for the types of actors that should require transparency, oversight, regulation, and accountability.

Platform companies, drawing from their ideological roots in historic countercultural and hacker movements (Turner 2009), have come to embody a very distinct favour of transparency. Internally, companies like Google and Facebook are famous for their founders' embrace of "openness," perhaps most clearly manifest in their physical workplace environments. At Facebook's offices in Menlo Park, cubicles have been eschewed in favour of one of the world's largest open-plan office spaces, meeting rooms have large glass windows or doors that allow employees to easily observe what goes on inside, and CEO Mark Zuckerberg works from the center of that open-plan office in a glass "fishbowl," visible to all (Flyverbom 2016). Google is known for its similarly designed offices and open office culture, including weekly Friday meetings where senior executives share information (oftentimes sensitive, non-public information) with effectively the entire company, engaging in an informal question-and-answer session where any employee can theoretically pose any question to higher-ups. In a 2009 blog post, a Google vice president explained that "openness" is the fundamental principle on which the company operates, ranging from their (admittedly self-serving) goal to make information "open" via their search engine and other products to their philosophy on open- source code, open protocols, and open corporate culture (Rosenberg 2009).

While platforms have this notable internal culture of transparency, they are considerably less open to the outside world. To visit Facebook or Google as an outsider (perhaps a journalist, researcher, or academic), one must make it through the reception desk and key card-entry turnstiles, usually after signing strict nondisclosure agreements. Externally, platforms are notable for their corporate secrecy – for example, it took twelve years for Facebook to release detailed information about its "Community Standards," the rules that govern speech on the site, despite long-standing civil society and academic pressure(Gillespie 2018a). As the management and organization researcher Mikkel Flyverbom has written, platforms are characterized by "strong forms of vertical transparency, where employees and employers can observe each other very easily, but also as very little horizontal transparency because outsiders have very few opportunities to scrutinize the insides of these companies" (Flyverbom2015, p. 177). This has made research into platforms difficult, especially as firms shut down the developer APIs and other tools traditionally used by researchers to access data (Hogan 2018). Much like a highly opaque bureaucracy, only a limited transparency has currently been achieved via public statements and interviews granted by their executives, as well as the occasional incident of whistle blowing and leaking. For instance, training documents issued to contractors that engage in commercial content moderation on Facebook were leaked to The Guardian, leading to significant public outcry and a better understanding of how Facebook's moderation functions (Klonick 2017). As we argue here, transparency initiatives for platforms can be classified into four camps: voluntary transparency around freedom of expression and for content takedowns; legally mandated transparency regimes; self-transparency around advertising and content moderation; and third-party tools, investigations, and audits.

VOLUNTARY TRANSPARENCY FOR CONTENT TAKEDOWNS

Virtually since their emergence in the early 2000s, platform companies have had to weigh legal requests for content takedowns from individuals and governments around the world (Goldsmith and Wu 2006). As Daphne Keller and Paddy Leerssen explain in Chapter 10 in this volume, intermediary liability laws inform online intermediaries of their legal obligations for the information posted by their users, placing platform companies in the often uncomfortable position of having to weigh content against their own guidelines, local laws, and normative goals around freedom of expression. In an effort to maintain their legitimacy (and their normative position as promoters of free expression ideologically crafted in the First Amendment tradition), platform companies have become more transparent in the past decade about these processes as they pertain to content takedowns for copyright purposes and other legal reasons. To date, the dominant mode for horizontal transparency implemented by major platform companies has been in the area of these speech and content takedown requests.

In 2008, as a component of endeavors to counteract censorship and safeguard human rights online, the Global Network Initiative (GNI) was created, with Microsoft, Yahoo, Google, and a number of civil society organizations and academic institutions as founding members (Maclay 2010). As part of a commitment to the GNI principles, Google introduced an annual "Transparency Report" in 2010, the first company to publicly release data about content takedown and account information requests filed by governments around the world, along with a "Government Requests" tool, which visualized this data and provided a FAQ of sorts for individuals interested in the government takedown process (Drummond 2010). Grandiosely citing Article 19 of the Universal Declaration of Human Rights, Google positioned itself as a defender of free expression and civil liberties violations as enacted by states (Drummond 2010). In the years to follow, these tools were expanded: In 2011, Google made the raw data underpinning the report public and, in 2012, the company added copyright takedowns under the Digital Millennium Copyright Act (DMCA) and other intermediary liability laws to the report.1 In July 2012, Twitter began publishing a biannual transparency report, which now includes information about account information requests, content-removal requests, copyright takedown notices, and requests to check content against Twitter's own terms of service.2 In January 2013, as it joined the GNI, Facebook began publishing its own bimonthly transparency report, which includes numbers about requests for user data, broken down by country, and, in July 2013, numbers about how much content was restricted based on local law.3

In July 2013, documents provided to the press by Edward Snowden documented extensive governmental systems for mass surveillance, with the disclosures suggesting that the US National Security Agency (NSA) had access to unencrypted information flowing between Google data centers (Gellman and Soltani 2013). Google disputed the extent that information was collected via PRISM and other disclosed NSA programs but expanded its transparency reporting efforts to include information about National Security Letters and Foreign Intelligence Surveillance Act (FISA) court orders.

VOLUNTARYTRANSPARENCYFORCONTENT&ADVERTISEMENTS

The significant public pressure on platform companies following the 2016 US election has led to a new series of voluntary horizontal transparency initiatives that go beyond just content takedown requests. The most notable development has been the release of an expanded, public-facing version of Facebook's"Community Standards" in April 2018. While Facebook transparency reports have since 2013 provided aggregate numbers about content that "is reported to[Facebook] as violating local law, but doesn't go against Community Standards," the details of those Community Standards were not public.4 Forinstance, the Standards stated that content that featured sexual content, graphic violence, or hate speech was prohibited but did not define any of those highly contentious categories or provide information into how they had been defined, leading civil society and academics to almost universally critique Facebook's processes as highly opaque and problematic (Myers West 2018).

Facebook's publication of more detailed "Community Standards" that have information about the policies (e.g., how hate speech is defined, how sexual content and nudity is defined) gives far more context to users and marks an important step forward. Companies are starting to also provide detail about how these policies are enforced: At the end of April 2018, Google published their first "Community Guidelines Enforcement Report," a type of transparency report that provides numbers into the amount of violating material taken down in various categories of the Community Standards and the role of automated systems in detecting content before it is reported (Google 2018). In May 2018, Facebook published a similar report, which illustrates different types of content takedowns, providing aggregate data into how much content is removed. For six parts of the Community Standards (graphic violence, adult nudity and sexual activity, terrorist content, hate speech, spam, and inauthentic accounts), Facebook provides four data points: how many Community Standards violations were found; the percentage of flagged content on which action is taken; the amount of violating content found and flagged by automated systems; and the speed at which the company's moderation infrastructure acts in each case.5

Table 12.1 Appeals data provided in Facebook's May 2019 Community Standards Enforcement Report

Policy area	Amount of content appealed	Amount of content restored after appeal
Spam	20,800,000	5,700,000
Adult Nudity and Sexual Activity	2,100,000	453,000
Hate Speech	1,100,000	130,000
Bullying and Harassment	496,000	80,200
Violence and Graphic Content	171,000	23,900
Regulated Goods – Drugs	87,400	18,100
Regulated Goods – Firearms	80,800	6,200
Terrorist Propaganda (ISIS, al- Qaeda, and affiliates)	40,100	20,300
Child Nudity and Sexual	20,600	700

Exploitation of Children

Source. Rosen (2019).

In May 2019, Facebook added multiple new categories to its Enforcement Report, including interesting data on the amount of content that is removed, appealed, and reinstated (since mid-2018, users who have content removed by Facebook's manual or automated moderation systems can have those decisions appealed). For example, the report states that from January to March 2019,19.4 million pieces of content were removed from Facebook under their policies prohibiting certain types of nudity and sexual content.6 Out of that 19.4 million, 2.1 million (approximately 10.8 percent) was appealed by users, with Facebook reversing the decision in 453,000 (approximately 21.5 percent) of those instances (Table 12.1). Given the sheer quantity of Facebook content being posted by users every day, this may not seem like an enormous number; however, consider a hypothetical situation where each one of these appeals represents a separate user (setting aside for the moment that users could have had multiple pieces of content taken down): Before Facebook began allowing appeals in 2018, more than 400,000 people around the world could have been frustrated by the wrongful takedown of their images, videos, or writing, which may have had political or artistic merit (Gillespie 2018a) or may not have been nudity at all, picked up by a faulty automated detection system, for instance.

These reports are a major step and should continue to be expanded (Garton Ash, Gorwa, and Metaxa 2019). Yet they still have notable limitations. As the Electronic Frontier Foundation's Jillian York has written, the Facebook report "deals well with how the company deals with content that violates the rules, but fails to address how the company's moderators and automated systems can get the rules wrong, taking down content that doesn't actually violate the Community Standards" (York 2018). The 2019 report focuses heavily on Facebook's increasing use of automated systems to take down hate speech; as of March 2019, 65 percent of content Facebook removes under its hate speech policies globally is automatically flagged – up from 24 percent at the end of 2017. This is presented as an un-qualified net positive, but the increasing use of automated systems in content moderation will have a number of underexplored consequences and promises to make content moderation more opaque (by adding a layer of algorithmic complexity) at a time when almost everyone is seeking greater transparency (Gorwa, Binns, and Katzenbach 2020).

In 2017 and 2018, Facebook also tested and rolled out a number of features with the stated aim to improve transparency around political advertising(especially in electoral periods). Following the discovery that Russian operatives had purchased Facebook advertisements to target American voters in the lead-up to the 2016 US election, Mark Zuckerberg issued an extended public statement in which he announced Facebook's goal to "create a new standard for transparency in online political ads" (Zuckerberg 2017). These efforts began in October 2017, when Facebook announced advertisers wishing to run election-related advertisements in the United States would have to register with Facebook and verify their identity and that these ads would be accompanied by a clickable "paid for by" disclosure (Goldman 2017). In April 2018, Facebook announced that this verification process would be expanded to all political "issue ads" (Goldman and Himel 2018). Beginning in November 2017, a feature called "view ads" was tested in Canada, where users could navigate the dropdown menu on a page to see all of the ads that it was currently running (Goldman 2017). This was expanded to the United States and Brazil in the spring of 2018 and, in June 2018, allowed users to view ads run by a page across platforms (Facebook, Instagram, and Messenger). In May 2018, Facebook launched a public political ad archive of all political ads being run; and, in August 2018, Facebook provided a political ad API that would allow researchers and journalists to access this archive (see Leathern 2018a, 2018b). Other major platform companies simultaneously rolled out similar initiatives.

In October 2017, Twitter announced a number of future advertising transparency efforts, including a "Transparency Center," which launched in June 2018 and provided users with the ability to view ads targeted to them (along with the personalized information being used to target that ad, as well as a view of all ads being run on the platform) (Falck 2017, 2018a). As well, Twitter has mandated that political "electioneering ads" are clearly distinct from other ads and has opted to provide information about the advertiser, the amount spent on the ad campaign, targeting data used, and other relevant information. These efforts remain a work in progress: In May 2018, Twitter announced their policy on political campaigning, to explain how they defined political advertising and the steps that political advertisers would have to take to register with the company; and, in August, they outlined their specific policy on issue ads (Falck 2018b). Google announced in May 2018 that it would require identification from any party seeking to run an election-related advertisement on a Google platform for a US audience and that all such ads would have a "paid for by" notice (Walker 2018). In August 2018, Google added a "political advertising" section to its transparency reports, providing a public-facing tool for users to search for certain advertisers, a district-level breakdown of political ad spending in the United States, and a searchable ad database featuring all video, text, and image advertisements about "federal candidates or current elected federal office holders."7

Mandated Transparency Regimes

Broader forms of transparency can also go beyond purely voluntary, self-regulatory processes and be mandated by either government regulation or by membership in certain organizations or institutions. Along with a commitment to public transparency via transparency reports, the GNI requires independent third-party assessments undertaken every two years to ensure compliance with the GNI principles (Maclay 2010). These assessments are performed by a series of trusted auditors, who look into processes (the policies and procedures employed by the member companies) and review specific cases, with their findings compiled into a report released by the GNI (see, e.g., GNI 2016). Under the 2011 and 2012 Federal Trade Commission (FTC) consent decrees about Google and Facebook's deceptive privacy practices, the two companies were required to subject themselves to privacy audits for twenty years (Hoofnagle 2016). As part of this regime, "compliance reports" are publicly available online at the FTC website, but the mandated third-party audits, which initially caused excitement as a possible transparency mechanism, are only published in heavily redacted and jargon-heavy form. These audits are thin on substance due to the watered-down language in the final FTC decree, making them, as one legal scholar argued, "so vague or duplicative as to be meaningless" (Gray 2018, p. 4). The German Network Enforcement Act(NetzDG), which went into force at the beginning of 2018, seems to be the first piece of legislation in the world that mandates public transparency reporting for major platforms for user-generated content. All firms defined as operating social networks with more than 2 million users in Germany (Facebook, Google, Twitter, and Change.org; the law excludes peer-to-peer messaging services like WhatsApp or Telegram) must publish biannual reports that include details about operational procedures, content removals across various sections of the German Criminal Code, and the way in which users were notified about content takedowns (Wagner et al. 2020). However, researchers have noted the limitations of the data made public in these transparency reports, which are not sufficiently granular to be empirically useful for secondary analysis (Heldt 2019), and there have been differences in how companies have implemented their complaints mechanisms, eventually leading to a 2 million Euro fine levied by the German Federal Office of Justice against Facebook due to their insufficient transparency reporting (Wagner et al. 2020).

In the past two years, a growing number of governments have pushed for platform companies to create publicly accessibly archives of political advertisements, with legislation relating to ad archiving being passed in France and Canada and being proposed and debated in the United Kingdom and the United States (Leerssen et al. 2019; McFaul 2019). The European Commission's Code of Practice on Disinformation includes a voluntary commitment from firms to develop systems for disclosing issue ads and recommends transparency without articulating specific mechanisms (Kuczerawy 2020). Ad archiving appears to be an important new frontier for transparency and disclosure, but major questions around the scope and implementation of its implementation remain (Leerssen et al. 2019).

External "Audits" and Inquiries

A final, indirect source of transparency and information about the dealings of platform companies is created by research and investigative work by third parties, such as academics and journalists. The investigative journalism non-profit Pro-Publica has conducted multiple key investigations into Facebook's advertising interfaces, successfully showing how, for example, those interfaces can be used to target anti-Semitic users or exclude certain minorities from seeing ads for housing or jobs (see Angwin, Varner, and Tobin 2017a, 2017b). This work also can rely on crowd sourcing. Before Facebook made their infrastructure for accessing advertisements through an Application Programming Interface (API) available, Pro-Publica built a browser extension that Facebook users could install to pull the ads that they saw on their Facebook, and a similar strategy was employed by the British group Who Targets Me, as well as researchers at the University of Wisconsin, who found that the majority of issue ads they studied in the lead-up to the 2016 US election did not originate from organizations registered with the Federal Election Commission (Kim et al. 2018). Although Facebook itself seems to conceptualize third-party research as a meaningful accountability mechanism (see Hegeman 2018), it has not made it easy for this work to be undertaken, which generally violates platform terms of service and puts researchers on precarious legal footing (Freelon 2018). It remains very difficult for researchers to conduct research on most platforms, with APIs having been constrained or totally discontinued by multiple companies in what some have termed an "APIcalypse" (Bruns 2019). Nevertheless, researchers and journalists have persisted in auditing and testing the systems deployed by companies, using public pressure and bad PR to mobilize incremental changes in, for example, how companies deploy their advertising tools (Sankin 2020). Since 2018, a few valiant efforts to try and provide institutionally structured and privacy-preserving data to researchers have emerged (King and Persily 2019) but have faced significant institutional, legal, and technical hurdles.

PROSPECTS FOR TRANSPARENCY IN THE PLATFORM'S FUTURE

Facebook, Google, and Twitter have made efforts to bring more transparency to political advertising and content policy. These efforts certainly demonstrate a willingness to be more transparent about processes than a decade ago but, according to many civil society organizations, still do not go far enough. Efforts to measure the transparency measures of various companies discussed, such as an annual report conducted by the Electronic Frontier Foundation (EFF), gave Facebook one out of five stars (citing a lack of meaningful notice to users who will have content taken down by a government or copyright request, as well as a lack of appeal on these decisions; see Cardozo et al. 2018). Ranking Digital Rights, a project based at the New America Foundation, which produces an annual index with scorecards for 24 technology companies, internet service providers, and other online intermediaries, gave Facebook a score of 57 out of 100 in 2019. The researchers noted that Facebook "disclos[es] less about policies affecting freedom of expression and privacy than most of its US peers" and that the company "provided users with limited options to control what information the company collects, retains, and uses, including for targeted advertising, which appears to be on by default" (Ranking Digital Rights 2018, p. 87). Google ranked first out of the companies assessed (with a score of 63 of 100), with the report noting that they now allow users to opt out of targeted advertising and make more disclosures about freedom of expression, content takedowns, and privacy than other platforms but still lack robust grievance and appeal mechanisms (Ranking Digital Rights 2018, p. 89).

The report's 2019 iteration applauded Facebook for providing more transparency and user autonomy around free expression issues (e.g., by publishing its first Content Standards Enforcement Report and beginning appeals for content takedown decisions)but noted that it still lagged behind on privacy, offering "less choice for users to control the collection, retention, and use of their information than all of its peers other than Baidu and Mail.Ru" (Ranking Digital Rights 2019, p. 20).

Transparency is important for legislators and the public to have realistic expectations about what the processes and capabilities of platform companies to make decisions and take down content are. As Daphne Keller and Paddy Leerssen discuss in Chapter 10 in this volume, without transparency, policymakers misjudge what platforms can do and draft and support poorly tailored laws as a result. Yet the existing forms of horizontal transparency as currently enacted by these companies have major limitations.

First, they are predominantly voluntary measures that have few enforcement mechanisms: The public must hope that the data provided is accurate but has little ability to verify that it is. A broader question can also be raised about the overall utility of transparency reports: While some features have clear democratic, normative importance, such as notice and appeals processes, the highly technical, aggregate statistics that are the core of most transparency reports are not necessarily useful in reducing the overall opacity of the system, where key processes, protocols, and procedures remain secret. Finally, a major limitation of the existing voluntary transparency measures, especially the advertising transparency efforts that have clearly been crafted to supplant possible regulatory regimes, is that these primarily public-facing tools may provide a rich and informative resource for students, researchers, and journalists but are notably less useful for regulators (e.g., electoral officers). Certainly, while Google's new advertising library may be useful for students trying to understand attack ads, and may yield interesting tidbits worthy of investigation for reporters, meaningful ad archives – whether fully public or only offering more sensitive information to electoral officials and trusted parties – need to permanently archives advertisements, and display meaningful and granular information about spending and targeting (Mozilla 2019).

In an important article, Mike Ananny and Kate Crawford outline ten challenges facing transparency efforts that strive to govern complex socio technical systems, such as forms of algorithmic decision-making (Ananny and Crawford 2018). The article is an important contribution to the recent literature on transparency as it pertains to technology policy issues and the digital age – a literature, one should note, that is roundly critical of the productive possibilities of transparency as a form of governing and knowing (Flyverbom 2016).

Many of Ananny and Crawford's insights (Figure 12.1) can be applied to the case of platform transparency. For example, they warn that if "transparency has no meaningful effects, then the idea of transparency can lose its purpose" and effectively backfire, as it becomes disconnected from overarching power relationships (Ananny and Crawford 2018, p. 979). If platform transparency efforts around advertising serve to make people cynical about the inevitability of poisonous attack ads or, on the other hand, ameliorate some narrow concerns about the generally problematic system of privacy-invasive advertising that funds contemporary platforms without actually making these systems more just, the efforts will fail to achieve a democratically desirable outcome (Taylor 2017). Furthermore, certain forms of transparency can "intentionally occlude" (Ananny and Crawford 2018, p. 980), burying the important insights in mounds of superfluous data or providing a distraction from the fundamental harms caused by a system. How useful are existing transparency reports, and do they distract from the end reality that some online intermediaries are making tremendously important decisions about the boundaries of acceptable political speech around the world in a fundamentally undemocratic and unaccountable manner? Do these measures provide the illusion of seeing inside a system, without providing meaningful understanding of how it really functions and operates (Ananny and Crawford 2018, p. 982)? Do existing transparency measures lend a modicum of legitimacy and due process to a host of American private companies with global reach and impact, without actually providing good governance? These are crucial questions for scholars interested in the future of social media and its relationship with democracy.

Transparency ...
can be disconnected from power can be harmful
can intentionally occlude can create false binaries
can invoke neoliberal models of agency can privilege seeing over understanding does not necessarily build trust
entails professional boundary work has technical limitations
has temporal limitations

Fig 12.1 Ten common digital transparency pitfalls

Source. Based on Ananny and Crawford (2018).

The Search for Meaningful Transparency and Oversight

As governments grapple with a host of complex policy options, transparency mechanisms seem to provide a logical path forward. Platform companies seem willing to become more transparent and are even increasingly doing so voluntarily. When compared with broad and potentially messy legislation, transparency seems a fruitful, if limited, form of accountability that has the additional benefit of yielding information that better informs the future policy climate. Legislated transparency, which comes with third-party audits and verification measures, has the potential to improve the current status quo, and policymakers in Europe are moving to include some form of mandatory disclosures and perhaps even structured access to platform data for researchers as part of the Digital Services Act discussions that began with the onset of the von Der Leyen Commission. There is a great deal that firms could do to make the data they release as part of their transparency reporting more meaningful and reproducible. Possible changes range from adding specific data points, as outlined in the Santa Clara Principles for Transparency and Accountability in Content Moderation and other civil society efforts (who have long been asking for detailed figures on false positives, the source of content flags for different forms of content – government, automated detection systems, users, etc. – and many other areas), to taking a more holistic view of how they could conduct content policy in a more transparent and community-focused manner. A Yale Law School report commissioned by Facebook to provide recommendations into how it could improve its Community Standards reporting offers a number of positive ideas, including reporting certain major changes to policy ahead of time and going beyond today's relatively ad hoc model of expert input to enact a more structured and public mechanism for stakeholder consultation (Bradford et al. 2019).

One major initiative, slated to go into effect in 2020, is the "Oversight Body" for content policy that Facebook began developing in 2019. The proposal, which built on Mark Zuckerberg's comments in 2018 about a "Supreme Court"-style mechanism for external appeals (Garton Ash, Gorwa, and Metaxa 2019), seeks to formalize a system of third-party input into Facebook's Community Standards. The initial conception of the Oversight Body focused primarily on procedural accountability, but, during a consultation process with academics and civil society groups, including the authors of this chapter, it appears to have become more broadly conceived as a mechanism "intended to provide a layer of additional transparency and fairness to Facebook's current system" (Darmé and Miller 2019). In September 2019, Facebook published a nine-page charter for the Oversight Board, which outlines how the board will be set up (via an independent trust), how members will be selected (Facebook will select an initial group, which will then select the remaining forty part-time "jurors"), and commits the company to acting on the board's binding decisions.

Much yet remains to be seen about the board's implementation and whether it truly results in a more democratically legitimate system of speech governance (Kadri and Klonick 2019; Douek 2019) for the average Facebook user – someone who is far more likely to be a non-English speaker, mobile-first, and located in Bombay or Bangkok than Boston – or if it merely becomes a new type of informal governance arrangement, with more in common with the many certification, advisory, and oversight bodies established in the natural resource extraction or manufacturing industries (Gorwa 2019b). While a group of trusted third parties publishing in-depth policy discussions of the cases they explore, if adequately publicized and implemented in a transparent manner, certainly has the potential to increase the familiarity of social media users with the difficult politics of contemporary content moderation, it may not significantly increase the transparency of Facebook's actual practices. The Oversight Board could even become a "transparency proxy" of sorts, attracting public attention while remaining little more than a translucent layer floating on top of a still highly opaque institution.

SUMMARY

Transparency should help consumers and policymakers make informed choices. As the traditional argument for democratic transparency articulates, "People need information to assess whether such organizations protect their interests or predate upon them, to choose which organizations (and so which products and services) to rely upon, to decide whether to oppose or support various organizations, and to develop and execute strategies to affect and interact with them" (Fung 2013, p. 184). Yet the contemporary "attention economy" that characterizes most digital services is profoundly opaque, and users are intentionally kept from seeing much of how their behaviour is shaped and monetized, whether by the multitude of hidden trackers and behavioural advertising pixels that follow them around the

Web or by the secret rules and processes that determine the bounds of acceptable speech and action. As citizens weigh the trade-offs inherent in their usage of social media or other services provided by companies like Facebook, Google, or Twitter, they deserve to better understand how those systems function (Suzor et al. 2019).

The companies have displayed a commendable effort in the past decade to provide some data about the way they interact with governments when it comes to freedom of expression; however, these tend to offer more insight into government behaviour rather than their own. Extracting the policies, practices, and systems through which platform companies affect free expression or other democratically essential areas such as privacy is an uphill battle, with journalists, academics, and activists painstakingly trying to obtain what they can, as if pulling teeth from an unwilling patient. Policymakers in Europe especially are starting to see the measures enacted willingly thus far by Facebook, Google, and Twitter as unlikely to result in meaningful long-term reform (Frosio 2017).

Digital transparency – whether it is enacted through technological solutions or more classical administrative and organizational means – will not on its own provide an easy solution to the challenges posed by the growing role of platforms in political and public life. More research will be required to examine how platform companies enact and perform transparency and how this transparency functions in an increasingly contested governance landscape. As Ananny and Crawford (2018, p. 983) argue, "A system needs to be understood to be governed." Transparency in key areas, such as content moderation, political advertising, and automated decision-making, should be an important first step reinforced by legislators. In the United States, the Brandeis an tradition of thinking about transparency in combating corporate power has often been neglected by the new cadre of advocates picking up the antitrust banner. While it is important to reflect critically on the pitfalls and shortcomings of transparency initiatives, a significant amount of robust transparency, legislatively mandated where necessary, would certainly contribute to the public understanding of the digital challenges facing democracies around the world.

REFERENCES

Albu, O.B., & Flyverbom, M. (2019). Organizational transparency: Conceptualizations, conditions, and consequences. Business & Society, 58(2), 268–297. https://doi.org/ 10.1177/0007650316659851

Ananny, M., & Crawford, K. (2018). Seeing without knowing: Limitations of the transparency ideal and its application to algorithmic accountability. New Media& Society, 20(3), 973–989.

Angwin, J., Varner, M., & Tobin, A. (2017a). Facebook enabled advertisers to reach "Jew haters." ProPublica, September 14. www.propublica.org/article/facebook- enabled-advertisers-to-reach-jew-haters

(2017b). Facebook (still) letting housing advertisers exclude users by race. ProPublica, November 21. www.propublica.org/article/facebook-advertising-discrimination- housing-race-sex-national-origin

Banisar, D. (2006). Freedom of Information around the World 2006: A Global Survey of Access to Government Information Laws. London: Privacy International.

Barocas, S., & Selbst, A. (2016). Big data's disparate impact. California Law Review,104(3), 671–732. https://doi.org/10.15779/Z38BG31

Baume, S. (2018). Publicity and transparency: The itinerary of a subtle distinction. In E. Alloa & D. Thomä (Eds.), Transparency, Society and Subjectivity (pp. 203–224). Cham: Springer. http://link.springer.com/10.1007/978-3-319-77161-8_10

Bennington, G. (2011). Kant's open secret. Theory, Culture & Society, 28(7–8), 26–40. Bertot, J. C., Jaeger, P. T., & Grimes, J. M. (2010). Using ICTs to create a culture of transparency: E-government and social media as openness and anti-corruption tools for societies. Government Information Quarterly, 27(3), 264–271.

Birchall, C. (2011). Introduction to "secrecy and transparency": The politics of opacity and openness. Theory, Culture & Society, 28(7–8), 7–25.

(2014). Radical transparency? Cultural Studies? Critical Methodologies, 14(1),77–88.

Bonsón, E., Torres, L., Royo, S., & Flores, F. (2012). Local e-government 2.0: Social media and corporate transparency in municipalities. Government Information Quarterly, 29(2), 123–132.

Bradford, B., Grisel, F., Meares, T. L. et al. (2019). Report Of The Facebook Data Transparency Advisory Group. The Justice Collaboratory, Yale Law School. https:// law.yale.edu/system/files/area/center/justice/document/dtag_report_5.22.2019.pdf

Brandeis, L. D. (1913). What publicity can do. Harper's Weekly, December 20.

Brock, G. (2017). How to regulate Facebook and the Online Giants in One Word: Transparency. The Conversation, October 16. http://theconversation.com/how- to-regulate-facebook-and-the-online-giants-in-one-word-transparency-85765

Bruns, A. (2019). After the "APIcalypse": Social media platforms and their fight against critical scholarly research. Information, Communication & Society, 22(11), 1544– 1566. https://doi.org/10.1080/1369118X.2019.1637447

Burrell, J. (2016). How the machine "thinks": Understanding opacity in machine learning algorithms. Big Data & Society, 3(1). https://doi.org/10.1177/ 2053951715622512

Cardozo, N., Crocker, A., Gebhart, G., Lynch, J., Opsahl, K., & York, J. C. (2018). Who Has Your Back? Censorship Edition 2018. Electronic Frontier Foundation report. www.eff.org/who-has-your-back-2018

Christensen, L. T., & Cheney, G. (2014). Peering into transparency: Challenging ideals, proxies, and organizational practices. Communication Theory, 25(1), 70–90.

Cucciniello, M., Porumbescu, G. A., & Grimmelikhuijsen, S. (2017). 25 years of transparency research: Evidence and future directions. Public Administration Review, 77(1), 32–44.

Darmé, Z. M., & Miller, M. (2019). Global Feedback & Input on the Facebook Oversight Board for Content Decisions. Facebook report. https://fbnewsroomus.files.wordpress.com/2019/06/oversight-board-consultation-report-1.pdf

Douek, E. (2019). Facebook's Oversight Board: Move fast with stable infrastructure and humility. North Carolina Journal of Law and Technology, 21(1), 1–78.

Drummond, D. (2010). Greater transparency around government requests. Google (blog), April 20. https://googleblog.blogspot.com/2010/04/greater-transparency-around-government.html

Edwards, L., & Veale, M. (2017). Slave to the algorithm: Why a right to an explanation is probably not the remedy you are looking for. Duke Law & Technology Review, 16(1), 18–84.

Etzioni, A. (2010). Is transparency the best disinfectant? Journal of Political Philosophy,18(4), 389–404.

Falck, B. (2017). New transparency for ads on Twitter. Twitter (official blog), October 24. https://blog.twitter.com/official/en_us/topics/product/2017/New-Transparency-For-Ads-on-Twitter.html

(2018a). Providing more transparency around advertising on Twitter. Twitter (official blog), June 28. https://blog.twitter.com/official/en_us/topics/company/2018/ Providing-More-Transparency-Around-Advertising-on-Twitter.html

(2018b). Increasing transparency for political campaigning ads on Twitter. Twitter (official blog), May 24. https://blog.twitter.com/official/en_us/topics/company/ 2018/Increasing-Transparency-for-Political-Campaigning-Ads-on-Twitter.html

Feldman, B. (2017). Facebook hands over data to Congress and promises transparency on political ads. New York Magazine, September 21. http://nymag.com/selectall/ 2017/09/facebook-promises-transparency-on-political-ads.html

Flyverbom, M. (2015). Sunlight in cyberspace? On transparency as a form of ordering. European Journal of Social Theory, 18(2), 168–184.

(2016). Transparency: Mediation and the management of visibilities. International Journal of Communication, 10(5), 110–122.

(2019). The Digital Prism: Transparency and Managed Visibilities in a Datafied World. Cambridge: Cambridge University Press.

Fox, J. (2007). The uncertain relationship between transparency and accountability. Development in Practice, 17(4–5), 663–671.

Freelon, D. (2018). Computational research in the post-API age. Political Communication, 35(4), 665–668. https://doi.org/10.1080/10584609.2018.1477506

Frosio, G. F. (2017). Reforming intermediary liability in the platform economy: A European digital single market strategy. North-western University Law Review, 112, 19–46.

Frynas, J. G. (2005). The false developmental promise of corporate social responsibility: Evidence from multinational oil companies. International Affairs, 81(3), 581–598. Fung, A. (2013). Infotopia: Unleashing the democratic power of transparency. Politics &Society, 41(2), 183–212.

Fung, A., Graham, M., & Weil, D. (2007). Full Disclosure: The Perils and Promise of Transparency. Cambridge: Cambridge University Press.

Gaonkar, D. P., & McCarthy, R. J. Jr. (1994). Panopticism and publicity: Bentham's quest for transparency. Public Culture, 6(3), 547–575.

Garton Ash, T. (2016). Free Speech: Ten Principles for a Connected World. New Haven,CT: Yale University Press.

Garton Ash, T., Gorwa, R., & Metaxa, D. (2019). Glasnost! Nine Ways Facebook Can Make Itself a Better Forum for Free Speech and Democracy. Reuters Institute. https:// reutersinstitute.politics.ox.ac.uk/our-research/glasnost-nine-ways-facebook-can-make- itself-better-forum-free-speech-and-democracy

Gellman, B., & Soltani, A. (2013). NSA infiltrates links to Yahoo, Google data centers worldwide, Snowden documents say. Washington Post, October 30. www.washingtonpost.com/world/national-security/nsa-infiltrates-links-to-yahoo-google- data-centers-worldwide-snowden-documents-say/2013/10/30/e51d661e-4166-11e3- 8b74-d89d714ca4dd_story.html

Gillespie, T. (2018a). Custodians of the Internet: Platforms, Content Moderation, and the Hidden Decisions That Shape Social Media. New Haven, CT: Yale University Press.

(2018b). Regulation of and by platforms. In J. Burgess, A. Marwick, & T. Poell (Eds.),The SAGE Handbook of Social Media (pp. 254–278). London: SAGE.

GNI (Global Network Initiative). (2016). Public Report on the 2015/2016 Independent CompanyAssessments. https://globalnetworkinitiative.org/gin_tnetnoc/uploads/ 2018/02/Public-Report-2015-16-Independent-Company-Assessments.pdf

Goldman, R. (2017). Update on our advertising transparency and authenticity efforts.

Facebook Newsroom, October 27. https://newsroom.fb.com/news/2017/10/update-on-our-advertising-transparency-and-authenticity-efforts/

Goldman, R., & Himel, A. (2018). Making ads and pages more transparent. Facebook Newsroom, April 6. https://newsroom.fb.com/news/2018/04/transparent-ads-and- pages/

Goldsmith, J. L., & Wu, T. (2006). Who Controls the Internet? Illusions of a Borderless World. New York: Oxford University Press.

Google. (2018). More information, faster removals, more people: An update on what we're doing to enforce YouTube's Community Guidelines. Google (official blog), April 23. https://youtube.googleblog.com/2018/04/more-information-faster-removals-more.html

Gorwa, R. (2019a). What is platform governance? Information, Communication & Society, 22(6), 854–871.

(2019b). The platform governance triangle: Conceptualising the informal regulation of online content. Internet Policy Review, 8(2), 1–22. https://doi.org/10.14763/ 2019.2.1407

Gorwa, R., Binns, R., & Katzenbach, C. (2020). Algorithmic content moderation: Technicalandpoliticalchallengesintheautomationofplatformgovernance. Big Data & Society, 7(1). https://doi.org/10.1177/2053951719897945

Gray, M. (2018). Understanding and improving privacy "audits" under FTC orders. Stanford CIS White Paper. https://cyberlaw.stanford.edu/blog/2018/04/understanding-improving-privacy-audits-under-ftc-orders

Grimmelikhuijsen, S., Porumbescu, G., Hong, B., & Im, T. (2013). The effect of transparency on trust in government: A cross-national comparative experiment. Public Administration Review, 73(4), 575–586.

Hansen, H. K., & Flyverbom, M. (2015). The politics of transparency and the calibration of knowledge in the digital age. Organization, 22(6), 872–889.

Heemsbergen, L. (2016). From radical transparency to radical disclosure: Reconfiguring (in) voluntary transparency through the management of visibilities. International Journal of Communication, 10(5), 138–151.

Hegeman, J. (2018). Facing facts: Facebook's fight against misinformation. Facebook Newsroom, May 23. https://newsroom.fb.com/news/2018/05/facing-facts-facebooks-fight-against-misinformation/

Heldt, A. (2019). Reading between the lines and the numbers: An analysis of the first NetzDG reports. Internet Policy Review, 8(2). https://doi.org/10.14763/ 2019.2.1398

Hess, D. (2012). Combating corruption through corporate transparency: Using enforcement discretion to improve disclosure. Minnesota Journal of International Law, 21, 42–74.

Hoffmann, A. L. (2019). Where fairness fails: Data, algorithms, and the limits ofantidiscrimination discourse. Information, Communication & Society, 22(7),900–915. https://doi.org/10.1080/1369118X.2019.1573912

Hogan, B. (2018). Social media giveth, Social media taketh away: Facebook, friendships, and APIs. International Journal of Communication, 12(5), 592–611. https://ijoc.org/index.php/ijoc/article/view/6724

Hood, C. (2006). Transparency in historical perspective. In C. Hood & D. Heald (Eds.), Transparency: The Key to Better Governance? (pp. 3–24). Oxford: Oxford University Press.

(2011). From FOI world to WikiLeaks world: A new chapter in the transparency story? Governance, 24(4), 635–638.

Hood, C., & Heald, D. (Eds.) (2006). Transparency: The Key to Better Governance? Oxford: Oxford University Press.

Hoofnagle, C. J. (2016). Assessing the Federal Trade Commission's privacy assessments.IEEE Security & Privacy, 14(2), 58–64.

Kadri, T., & Klonick, K. (2019). Facebook v. Sullivan: Building constitutional law for online speech. Southern California Law Review, 93(1), 37–99.

Kim, Y. M., Hsu, J., Neiman, D. et al. (2018). The stealth media? Groups and targets behind divisive issue campaigns on Facebook. Political Communication, 35(4), 515–541. https://doi.org/10.1080/10584609.2018.1476425

King, G., & Persily, N. (2019). A new model for industry–academic partnerships. PS: Political Science & Politics, 1–7. https://doi.org/10.1017/S1049096519001021

Klonick, K. (2017). The new governors: The people, rules, and processes governing online speech. Harvard Law Review, 131(6), 1598–1670.

Kosack, S., & Fung, A. (2014). Does transparency improve governance? Annual Review of Political Science, 17, 65–87.

Kroll, J. A. et al. (2016). Accountable algorithms. University of Pennsylvania Law Review, 165, 633.

Kuczerawy, A. (2020). Fighting Online Disinformation: Did the EU Code of Practice Forget about Freedom of Expression? In G. Terzis, D. Kloza, E. Kuzelewska, &D. Trottier (Eds.), Disinformation and Digital Media as a Challenge for Democracy(pp. 291–308). Cambridge: Intersentia.

Lamble, S. G. (2002). Freedom of information: A Finnish clergyman's gift to democracy.Freedom of Information Review, 97, 2–8.

Leathern, R. (2018a). Shining a light on ads with political content. Facebook Newsroom,May 24. https://newsroom.fb.com/news/2018/05/ads-with-political-content/ (2018b). Introducing the ad archive API. Facebook Newsroom, August 22. https://newsroom.fb.com/news/2018/08/introducing-the-ad-archive-api/

Leerssen, P., Ausloos, J., Zarouali, B., Helberger, N., & de Vreese, C. H. (2019).Platform ad archives: Promises and pitfalls. Internet Policy Review, 8(4), 1–21.

Levy, K. E. C., & Johns, D. M. (2016). When open data is a Trojan horse: The weaponization of transparency in science and governance. Big Data & Society, 3 (1). https://doi.org/10.1177/2053951715621568

Maclay, C. M. (2010). Protecting privacy and expression online: Can the Global Network Initiative embrace the character of the net. In R. J. Deibert, J. Palfrey, R. Rohozinski, & J. Zittrain (Eds.), Access Controlled: The Shaping of Power, Rights, and Rule in Cyberspace (pp. 87–108). Cambridge, MA: MIT Press.

McFaul, M. (Ed.) (2019). Securing American Elections: Prescriptions for Enhancing the Integrity and Independence of the 2020 U.S. Presidential Election and Beyond. PaloAlto, CA: Stanford Cyber Policy Center.

Meijer, A. (2015). Government transparency in historical perspective: From the ancient regime to open data in the Netherlands. International Journal of Public Administration, 38(3), 189–199.

Moore, M., & Tambini, D. (Eds.) (2018). Digital Dominance: The Power of Google, Amazon, Facebook, and Apple. Oxford: Oxford University Press.

Mozilla. (2019). Facebook and Google: This is what an effective ad archive API lookslike. Mozilla (official blog), March 27. https://blog.mozilla.org/blog/2019/03/27/ facebook-and-google-this-is-what-an-effective-ad-archive-api-looks-like

Myers West, S. (2018). Censored, suspended, shadowbanned: User interpretations ofcontent moderation on social media platforms. New Media & Society,1461444818773059.

O'Neill, O. (2006). Transparency and the ethics of communication. In C. Hood & D. Heald (Eds.), Transparency: The Key to Better Governance? (pp. 75–90). Oxford: Oxford University Press.

Owen, T. (2015). Disruptive Power: The Crisis of the State in the Digital Age. Oxford: Oxford University Press.

Power, M. (1997). The Audit Society: Rituals of Verification. Oxford: Oxford University Press.

Ranking Digital Rights. (2018). 2018 Corporate Accountability Index. New AmericaFoundation, Washington, DC.

(2019). 2019 Corporate Accountability Index. New America Foundation, Washington, DC.Rosen, G. (2019). An update on how we are doing at enforcing our communitystandards. Facebook Newsroom, May 23. https://newsroom.fb.com/news/2019/05/enforcing-our-community-standards-3/

Rosenberg, J. (2009). The meaning of "open." Google (blog), December 21. https://googleblog.blogspot.com/2009/12/meaning-of-open.html

Ruggie, J. G. (2013). Just Business: Multinational Corporations and Human Rights.New York: W. W. Norton & Company.

Schudson, M. (2015). The Rise of the Right to Know: Politics and the Culture of Transparency, 1945–1975. Cambridge, MA: Harvard University Press.

Stohl, C., Stohl, M., & Leonardi, P. M. (2016). Managing opacity: Information visibility and the paradox of transparency in the digital age. International Journal of Communication, 10(5), 123–137.

Suzor, N. P., West, S. M., Quodling, A., & York, J. (2019). What do we mean when we talk about transparency? Toward meaningful transparency in commercial content moderation. International Journal of Communication, 13, 1526–1543.

Tapscott, D., & Ticoll, D. (2003). The Naked Corporation: How the Age of Transparency Will Revolutionize Business. New York: Simon & Schuster.

Taylor, L. (2017). What is data justice? The case for connecting digital rights and freedoms globally. Big Data & Society, 4(2), 2053951717736335.

Thompson, D. F. (1999). Democratic secrecy. Political Science Quarterly, 114(2),181–193.

Tucker, J. A., Theocharis, Y., Roberts, M. E., & Barberá, P. (2017). From liberation to turmoil: Social media and democracy. Journal of Democracy, 28(4), 46–59.

Turner, F. (2009). Burning Man at Google: A cultural infrastructure for new media production. New Media & Society, 11(1–2), 73–94.

Underwood, S. (2016). Blockchain beyond Bitcoin. Communications of the ACM, 59(11), 15–17.

Van Dijck, J., Poell, T., & de Waal, M. (2018). The Platform Society: Public Values in a Connective World. New York: Oxford University Press.

Wachter, S., Mittelstadt, B., & Russell, C. (2018). Counterfactual explanations without opening the black box: Automated decisions and the GDPR. Harvard Journal of Law and Technology, 31(2), 841–887.

Waddock, S. (2004). Creating corporate accountability: Foundational principles to make corporate citizenship real. Journal of Business Ethics, 50(4), 313–327.

Wagner, B., Rozgonyi, K., Sekwenz, M.-T., Cobbe, J., & Singh, J. (2020).

Regulating transparency? Facebook, Twitter and the German Network Enforcement Act. Paper presented at the ACM Conference on Fairness, Accountability, and Transparency in Machine Learning (FAT*). January 27– 30, Barcelona, Spain.

Walker, K. (2018). Supporting election integrity through greater advertising transparency. Google (official blog), May 4. www.blog.google/outreach-initiatives/public-policy/supporting-election-integrity-through-greater-advertising-transparency/

Warofka, A. (2018). An independent assessment of the human rights impact of Facebook in Myanmar. Facebook Newsroom, November 5. https://newsroom.fb.com/news/ 2018/11/myanmar-hria/

York, J. C. (2018). Facebook releases first-ever Community Standards Enforcement Report. Electronic Frontier Foundation, May 16. www.eff.org/sv/deeplinks/2018/ 05/facebook-releases-first-ever-community-standards-enforcement-report

Zuckerberg, M. (2017). Facebook post, September 12. www.facebook.com/zuck/posts/10104052907253171

FOOTNOTE

1. This paragraph draws on a timeline of Google's transparency reporting efforts; see Google's Transparency Report (https://transparencyreport.google.com/about).
2. See Twitter's Transparency Report (https://transparency.twitter.com/).
3. See Facebook's report Government Requests for User Data (https://transparency.facebook.com/ government-data-requests/jan-jun-2013) and Content Restrictions Based on Local Law (https:// transparency.facebook.com/content-restrictions/jul-dec-2013).

4. Facebook's report Content Restrictions Based on Local Law (https://transparency.facebook .com/content-restrictions), n.p.
5. See Facebook's Community Standards Enforcement Report (https://transparency.facebook.com/ community-standards-enforcement).
6. See ibid.
7. Google's Transparency Report. https://transparencyreport.google.com/political-ads/library.

13 THE CHALLENGES AND OPPORTUNITIES FOR SOCIAL MEDIA RESEARCH

INTRODUCTION: AN OVERVIEW

Social media has become an integral part of our daily lives, revolutionizing the way we connect, communicate, and share information. As a result, it has also emerged as a dynamic and multifaceted field of research, offering both exciting opportunities and daunting challenges to scholars and practitioners alike. In this rapidly evolving landscape, understanding the intricate interplay of technology, human behaviour, and societal impact is of paramount importance. This brief overview aims to provide a glimpse into the diverse challenges and opportunities that confront researchers in the realm of social media, shedding light on the potential for transformative insights and the complexities that lie ahead.

We began this volume by noting the relationship between basic research on the impact of social media and politics and the open policy questions concerning social media regulation. The preceding chapters have demonstrated that scholars have learned a great deal in a relatively short period of time about social media's impact on political communication and elite and mass political behaviour. It is equally clear that many, many important questions remain to be answered in the coming years.[1] Moreover, as we hope this volume has demonstrated, the answers to these questions are desperately needed to inform major decisions regarding public policy around the world. Responding to an environment of panic surrounding social media's impact on democracy that may very well be amplified by the Covid-19 pandemic, regulators and other political actors are rushing to fill the policy void with proposals based on anecdote and folk wisdom emerging from whatever is the most recent scandal. The need for real-time production of rigorous, policy-relevant scientific research on the effects of new technology on political communication has never been more urgent.

In this concluding chapter, we turn to a different aspect of the link between research and social media policy: the need for new policies to guarantee the continued production of high-quality research to ensure society has answers to the many crucial questions concerning the relationship between social media and democracy. We begin by laying out the many serious challenges facing the field in terms of access to the necessary data to conduct this research, including political, legal, and logistical factors. We then provide what we hope will serve as a set of key principles that can underline arguments regarding the importance of data access for research and a framework for thinking about how such access can be provided moving forward. We close with an assessment of where we are now and some recommendations for how to get to where we need to be.

OBSTACLES IN INVESTIGATING THE INTERSECTION OF SOCIAL MEDIA AND DEMOCRACY

To some extent, it has been the best of times and the worst of times when it comes to social media research. As the first half of this book reveals, we are beginning to gain important insights into the dynamics of the communication revolution underway. However, despite these achievements and the widely recognized importance of this research, unique constraints have hindered the necessary concerted academic effort to answer the most important empirical questions. The key social media datasets to answer these important questions are not as readily available as were politically relevant datasets of years past. Moreover, unique legal barriers prevent analysis of such data, and related ethical and privacy concerns have arisen that have chilled academic inquiry.

First, the difficulties in obtaining access to the relevant data cannot be overstated. Unlike most politically relevant datasets, the data necessary for social media research are largely controlled and "owned" by private companies. Whereas most political science data analysis, until recently, has utilized administrative data produced by the public sector, such as election returns and census data, or data produced by researchers themselves, such as surveys or experiments, a large portion of the data necessary to investigate the Internet's effect on democracy and elections is locked inside firms, such as Facebook and Google. Although different platforms have exerted different levels of effort to make data available for outside research, it remains the case that making data accessible for outside research has not been – and is highly unlikely to be in the future – part of the core mission of these companies. Indeed, it can often get in the way of a platform's profit-making mission, especially (as has often been the case of late) if outside researchers discover problems with the product or identify potential damage it may cause to society.

As a result, the research agenda for studying the effect of social media on democracy – as well as the scientific insights produced from such research – run the risk of being biased by the kind of data platforms make available to researchers. For example, the vast majority of the research studies on which we report in this volume are analyses of Twitter data; clearly, this is not because there is a consensus that Twitter is the most politically consequential social media platform. Although Twitter is certainly important for politics in many countries, this imbalance in research occurs because Twitter data have historically been among the most easily accessible for outside research, especially compared to Facebook data.

Twitter pays a price for this openness, however. Officials at Twitter are quick to recount how journalists and scholars can paint a misleading picture of what happens on the platform by merely reporting the volume of problematic content without giving context as to the share of user Twitter feeds in which the content appears. However, moving beyond counts of phenomena to more valuable measures, such as ratios (i.e., measuring the denominator in addition to the numerator), exposure, and longitudinal trends, requires time- and cost- intensive data-gathering strategies. These are often hampered by the platform's own terms of service, to say nothing of policies that remove the activities of malicious actors (such as foreign influence campaigns) or whole classes of data (such as exposure or recommendation) from outside access.2 The most influential analyses of Facebook data, by contrast, have largely been written by Facebook researchers themselves or by academics working through special arrangements with Facebook, often requiring prepublication approval from the company.

In the summer of 2018, Facebook initiated a data-sharing initiative with Social Science One, an academic effort seeking to make Facebook and other industry data available to the larger scientific community (King and Persily 2019).3 Through the Commission created by Social Science One, which was funded not by Facebook but by a set of non-profit foundations, academics have gained access to some Facebook datasets. Working with Facebook, Social Science One issued a Request for Proposals (RFP) for analysis of a specific dataset, beginning in July 2018. Scholars who seek access to the data must have projects approved by their universities' Institutional Review Board and undergo a separate evaluation for legal and ethical compliance; their universities must then sign a research data agreement that ensures protection against unauthorized disclosure. It took almost twenty months for Facebook to produce a dataset similar to the one promised in the original RFP – a dataset of almost 38 million links comprised of several trillion cell entries delineating the numbers and types of people who saw and engaged with the URLs, but with statistical noise added to the data to protect users' privacy. The dataset also contained information about the URL, such as whether it was fact-checked or labelled hate speech, but was limited only to URLs that were shared publicly approximately 100 times or more (a serious limitation to the data). The fact that it took ten times longer than expected for anything close to the original dataset to become available for analysis illustrates the fundamental challenges facing large internet companies in finding a way to make their data available for outside research. Indeed, the now-released URLs dataset was supposed to be the less interesting, "easy" dataset for Social Science One, as it did not contain data at the individual level. Even this "easy" limited dataset turned out to be incredibly challenging to produce, however, given the privacy-related challenges and data infrastructure requirements for such a broad and inclusive research effort.

Moreover, Facebook's cooperation with Social Science One stands as an exception to the general rule of tech corporations denying access to user data. In general, these companies view themselves as having much more to lose from sharing data than they have to gain. On top of potential reputational and financial damage caused by findings that put the firm in a bad light, the firms are reluctant to risk the possibility of unauthorized disclosure and breaches of privacy. Today, academic requests for access to these kinds of data are seen in the light of the now-infamous Cambridge Analytica scandal. As is now well known, in 2014 a researcher at Cambridge University, acting in his personal capacity, placed a psychological questionnaire on Facebook's platform. Users who took the survey consented to deliver data about their profile and activity on Facebook and that of their friends (who never consented to the survey). That researcher transferred the data to Cambridge Analytica, a political consulting firm that was working with, among many others, the campaign for then-candidate Donald Trump. As a result, some data of at least 50 million Facebook users were delivered to a political consulting company that said it had developed and employed new methods of psychographic profiling that could be used for political advertising and other forms of campaign targeting.

Cambridge Analytica was a political and corporate scandal, but it was an academic scandal as well. An academic misused the Facebook data of tens of millions of Facebook users. (Whether the researcher actually violated Facebook's terms of service remains an object of debate, but, regardless, the violation of un-consenting friends' privacy highlighted a problem with making the Facebook social graph data accessible under those circumstances.) Even if he was acting in his personal, rather than academic, capacity, his misdeeds have had a chilling effect on academic (and other) access to the critical stores of data social media firms possess on politically relevant questions. Often invoked in policy discussions, the scandal has lived on beyond its particular facts to embody a larger controversy regarding firms' misuse of users' private data, which can be exploited for political, economic, or other purposes. In the wake of Cambridge Analytica and other data privacy scandals, the platforms have reevaluated their data accessibility protocols for researchers and all other users and in the process reduced or shut down altogether pre-existing access to APIs.4

In the midst of all this, regulators around the world have, predictably, flexed their muscles to constrain the platforms' ability to make private data accessible to anyone outside the firm and, in some cases, to prevent collection of certain data by the firm itself. Since 2011, Facebook had been under a consent decree with the US Federal Trade Commission (FTC). That decree, which arose out of Facebook's failure to comply with its articulated privacy policies, constrains all kinds of potential data access for academics and others. It also places Facebook under intense and continuous oversight by a federal agency. Based on its perceived breach of the consent decree in the Cambridge Analytica scandal, the FTC entered into a new settlement and decree with Facebook, which involved a $5 billion fine and additional future oversight of Facebook procedures (FTC 2019).5

The most influential law governing researchers' (and any outsiders') access to social media data, however, is the European Union's General Data Protection Regulation (GDPR). That law has presented new and somewhat indiscernible constraints on the use and release of social media data for research. GDPR contains exceptions for certain types of research (Article 89), but both the rule itself and, in particular, the member states' divergent implementation of it have been less than clear as to the boundaries of this exception. Confusion revolves around the required procedures to minimize risks to privacy, as well as the degree of anonymization (or pseudonymization) required for social media data. Although individual names and identifying information can be removed from social media datasets, doing so might not be sufficient to pass the legal bar of anonymization given the richness of those datasets and the outside chance that researchers might theoretically be able to reidentify people if they were committed to combining multiple datasets from other sources.

To be sure, arguments about GDPR and other privacy laws sometimes appear as pretexts from one or another platform to justify restricting outside access to data. However, in this environment of legal uncertainty, the platforms have taken (understandably, from their standpoint, but frustrating from the research community's perspective) a very restrictive view in terms of sharing individual-level data, often regardless of whether the data are anonymized or could lead to reidentification. Moreover, Facebook has said that it will apply GDPR worldwide, in part because many other governments have either passed or are considering similar legislation. To address widespread misperceptions about the chilling effect of GDPR on research, the European Data Protection Supervisor issued in January 2020 "A Preliminary Opinion on data protection and scientific research" (European Data Protection Supervisor 2020). The guidance also attempts to reinforce the message of the importance of research and its consistency with the goals of GDPR. Nevertheless, even given this further guidance, lawyers at the platforms remain very conservative in their interpretation of when, what, and how data can be made accessible to researchers.

Given this impasse, the research community needs more than a mere clarification of GDPR. It needs a clearly defined safe harbor or a research pathway sanctioned by the European Commission. This could involve the designation of secure facilities and computers to analyze data, government vetting of researchers requesting data access, surveillance and recording of researchers while they analyze data, auditing of research results to ensure privacy is protected, pre-review of publications to ensure no privacy leakage, and significant penalties for any researcher who seeks to re-identify individuals in the dataset provided. (Such procedures, while seemingly draconian, are already in place for other sensitive datasets involving census, tax, or health data.) What would make the harbor safe, however, is that, in exchange for delivering data under these conditions, the platforms would receive complete legal immunity for granting data access to researchers. Indeed, given the value of research access to society for a whole host of reasons, not only should the platforms be immunized when they are willing to provide data; they should be legally compelled to do so. Governments need to spell out the legally safe pathway for granting researcher access, and then they need to require that the platforms follow it. Only then will lawyers inside the platforms recalibrate their legal risk assessments so as not to overcorrect on GDPR. Indeed, the Kofi Annan Commission on Elections and Democracy in the Digital Age (2020)recommended this specific proposal of legally compelled researcher access to platforms' privacy-protected data in a recent report on how to address the challenges that new technologies pose for democracy. (Disclosure: Persily was a commissioner on the Kofi Annan Commission that issued the report.)

The privacy-related obstacles to research access are not limited to those legislated by governments, however. In the wake of Cambridge Analytica, other privacy scandals, and governments' regulatory responses, a powerful privacy movement has arisen in civil society. The privacy policies of the platforms themselves, as well as surveillance by governments, are the main targets of this movement. The movement is both necessary and salutary given the real dangers to privacy that the evolving digital environment portends. Academic research, however, has become collateral damage in this battle between privacy advocates and the platforms. At one end of the divide are those who argue that individuals who provide data to social media platforms do not do so with the intent that these data will be used for purposes beyond simply sharing their posts with the intended audiences, and therefore outside academic research should not be permitted. These "other purposes," of course, include the bread and butter of social media platforms' business models – targeting ads – but also potential uses of digital trace data for social good, including but not limited to scholarly research in the public domain. From this perspective, academics should be permitted to analyze only data that the user has expressly made public or has been specifically designated for academic analysis (e.g., through a survey instrument designed to gain consent for research).

At the other end of the spectrum are those who consider social media data as akin to "administrative data." Administrative data are generally defined in the research community as data that are produced for one reason (e.g., giving students grades in a class to illustrate their competency in a subject area) but can be analyzed for another purpose (e.g., to discern the most efficient way to spend tax dollars on education). Political scientists have long analyzed administrative data at both the aggregate level (e.g., election results, protest participation, unemployment rates) and the micro level (e.g., voter registration data, census data) without assuming that the analysis of such data requires individuals to have consented to be considered as subjects in a research study. For administrative data, therefore, it is unnecessary for those individuals to provide explicit consent in order for the data to be analyzed. Requiring explicit consent for research on administrative data would prohibit, for example, any study of election results or employment rates.

Of course, to describe social media data as administrative data has the potential to diminish its sensitive personal nature. Although some social media data seem "administrative" (e.g., number of friends, popularity of URLs, whether one has posted using a mobile or desktop device, time zone, etc.), other data appear qualitatively different in that they do not contain records of behaviour so much as the personal thoughts and observations of individuals. However, some forms of administrative data, such as those involved with medical treatment and health statistics, are equally sensitive – perhaps even more so – than social media data. Yet, we may be moving toward a data access regime in which personal medical data may be more accessible to researchers than what users share or read on Facebook.

A privacy paradigm that requires explicit user consent for social media research will prevent scholars from answering some of the most important questions surrounding social media's impact on democracy. The most basic questions, such as how much disinformation the average user sees in a newsfeed or which categories of users see questionable or polarized sources, will not be answerable from data available only from a statistically biased set of users willing to provide it. For example, as recounted earlier in this volume, researchers have begun to find evidence that consumption and forwarding of disinformation, at least in the United States, is concentrated among older people. To be confident in this conclusion, though, researchers must be able to analyze – in the aggregate – exposure to different media sources conditional on the age of the user. However, many people do not publicly reveal their age on Facebook or other platforms. Although preventing researchers from deliberately uncovering a particular individual's age without user consent seems a perfectly reasonable barrier to protect privacy, preventing aggregate analysis of different age cohorts of users on the same basis would necessarily prevent us from understanding how social media exposure varies based on age.

A research paradigm based on consent as the touchstone would prevent both kinds of inquiries.

The Necessity of Adopting a Fresh Approach to Data Sharing

As we think through possible data-sharing paradigms, it is important to begin with an understanding of the fact that prohibiting the sharing of social media data for analysis by the scholarly community – or any researchers who are committed to sharing findings in the public domain – does *not* mean that social media data are not being mined for insights. Rather, it means that *employees of the platforms will be the only ones* analyzing the data and learning the answers to the most pressing questions as to social media's impact on democracy and other social phenomena.[6] Insights and expertise will therefore flow solely to a small number of very large (and politically influential) corporations, which can then pick and choose on their own which questions to ask and what conclusions to share with the public at large. Recognizing this inconvenient truth, the question as to research access and privacy is not whether user data should be analyzed for insights, but whether the platforms should have a monopoly on such access or inquiry.

Commentators often describe Google and Facebook as information monopolies. Usually, this accusation provides fodder for arguments about antitrust and competition law – such as whether the companies should be broken up into their constituent parts or regulated as public utilities (Stigler Center 2019). However, they are also information monopolies in a more literal sense – the firms control the information necessary to understand basic facts about contemporary society. As dangerous as these information monopolies may be for purposes of economic competition, such dangers are compounded when only those who work for the firms and share in their corporate missions are able to gain social insights from the data they possess. Social media companies control both the information valuable to their competitors and the personal data valuable to their users. More importantly for academics and those hoping to use rigorous scientific research to inform policymaking, though, the platforms control the information that most richly describes politics and society and therefore the data necessary to make sound judgments across virtually all major policy domains.

A recent decision of the US Court of Appeals for the Ninth Circuit appears to recognize the pervasive impact of platform control of information. In hiQ v. LinkedIn, No. 17-16783 (9th Cir. 2019), the Court protected a company's right to scrape user-provided data on LinkedIn. As the Court explained, "giving companies like LinkedIn free rein to decide, on any basis, who can collect and use data – data that the companies do not own, that they otherwise make publicly available to viewers, and that the companies themselves collect and use – risks the possible creation of information monopolies that would disserve the public interest." Admittedly, the Court's decision arose in the special context of the Computer Fraud and Abuse Act's potential prevention of scraping of publicly available data by a private company, but the parties in the case, as well as the opinion itself, noted that academic researchers often must resort to scraping to get the information under platform control. The decision echoes arguments that academic researchers have themselves made about the need, and perhaps even the right, to scrape social media data, when doing so is in the public interest but against the terms of service of a given platform (see Freelon 2020).

The platforms' monopoly control over relevant social scientific data, which admittedly derives from their users' private communication and behaviour, requires a reframing of the debate around access to social media data.7 We need to move beyond the normatively pleasing paradigm of "should the platforms respect the privacy concerns of their users?" – with which, of course, everyone agrees in the abstract – to one that fully embraces the trade- offs inherent in making data accessible to outside researchers. Such a framework might be oriented around several key principles:

Social media platforms' business models are entirely dependent on insights gained from analyzing data provided by their users;

There are legitimate privacy (and legal) concerns when the platforms grant access to social media data to third parties for research purposes; but There are real differences between private actors who analyze these data in order to support for-profit businesses with no obligation to release findings to the public (and indeed may even have obligations to shareholders not to do so) and other actors in society whose goals are to analyze these data in order to advance scientific knowledge and share their findings in the public domain, or to build tools for (nonprofit) social good; There are real gains – economic, political, and social – that can result from the public sharing of insights from analyzing social media data. These benefits run the gamut from medical discoveries to disaster prevention to identifying and preventing foreign interference with elections. There are also dangers when public policy is made without the advantage of the insights that can be gained through analysis of social media data.

Thus, the question of whether social media data ought to be shared more or less widely than they currently are is not merely a question of how platforms can better respect the privacy concerns of their users. Rather, policymakers and advocates need to consider the trade-offs between a world in which data are shared less frequently but gains from analysis accrue only to large for-profit companies and a world in which data are shared more frequently but gains from analysis can accrue to the public at large. Under the former, privacy can (usually) be better protected but net social gains are likely to be smaller; under the latter, privacy would be more at risk without the appropriate safeguards but the opportunities for social gain are larger as well.

One could go even farther than acknowledging the trade-off between privacy concerns and the benefits accrued by research in the public domain to raise the question of whether it is even appropriate to think of social media platforms "owning" the data provided by users of the platform, with a concomitant right to be the only entity allowed to accrue knowledge from analysis of the user-provided data. Such an argument could start from acknowledging the role that the major digital platforms play in contemporary society: They are not merely places people visit online but rather central nodes of our social, economic, and political lives.8 Thus, social media – much like jobs reports, election results, or even census data – are a crucial component of our understanding of contemporary social, economic, and political systems. However, unlike traditional sources of administrative data, digital platforms are distinguished by the fact that they are both wholly privately owned and highly concentrated. Thus, society has a special claim on these data precisely because (1) they will not otherwise be made available in the public domain (the way, for example, census or election data will be) and (2) these companies provide not a single service (like airline or automotive companies) but rather a collection of services that inextricably link these platforms to society's social, economic, and political life.

Taken together, these arguments suggest that, although such data are currently considered a private good owned by the corporations, they ought to be considered a public good.

Therefore, we may need to begin thinking about updating our concept of the public's right to data in the context of these information monopolies. This right should supersede the proprietary right of companies to enjoy exclusive access to the digital trace data created by users of their products at some point when those data are necessary for a complete understanding of the basic social, economic, and political functions of society. Of course, it would be folly to suggest that the builders of the platforms would not have access to the data they are collecting, but ought they be the only ones allowed to do so? Perhaps these firms are better conceptualized as "data stewards" (or "information fiduciaries" to use the term coined by Yale Law Professor Jack Balkin; see Balkin 2016) entrusted with managing the data that they have acquired for the good of their users and society at large, in addition to their shareholders. From this perspective, providing access to data for public-facing research would be considered an obligation for data stewards above a particular size.

We can consider two even more radical arguments in this regard. One would be to shift the policy focus from who "owns" the data – for example, as long as Facebook or Google "owns" their data, they can do what they want with it but cannot be permitted to transfer the data to other actors – toward a "use" approach to privacy rights.9 For example, companies that collect data could be entitled to use the digital trace data collected from their users' behaviour to maximize profits but not to actively support particular political actors in domestic political competitions. Similarly, scholars could be permitted to use these data for the purpose of scientific research but not to re-identify any individual users.

Another idea that involves a more radical rethinking of existing policy is to introduce the concept of a "data tax" on the platforms to be paid back to society. By this we mean not a traditional monetary tax that would be assessed based on how much data a company holds but literally a tax "paid" by the contribution of some proportion of user-provided data into a repository for independent analyses, the results from which would need to be put into the public domain to inform citizens and policymakers alike. Companies can be compelled, of course, to surrender a portion of their earnings to fund the state that provides the infrastructure (e.g., courts, roads, security, etc.) that allow those companies to conduct business. Why not similarly require provision of a portion of their data, as well, to be returned to the public as a way of contributing to the society in which their users reside? Such an argument would potentially be even more compelling if the data were being used in a manner to address potential problems caused by the platforms themselves, such as in the case for research addressing the impact of the platforms on elections and democracy.

We would also suggest that the scholarly community plays an especially important role in leveraging the gains that accrue to the public at large. To be sure, academics and other researchers can engage in malfeasance, conduct unethical research, pursue narrow "academic" questions, or publish erroneous results. However, scholars are incentivized to release the results of their research publicly. Indeed, the currency of academia is publications, with an emphasis on the public part of that word: we get paid to publish, and we get rewarded when people reference our research. Although other non-profit efforts have made great use of social media data in a range of domains including public health, election protection, disaster preparedness, and consumer welfare, their incentives do not always run in the direction of publication of research results, whatever the conclusions.

Furthermore, there are peculiar features of social media data that make time- consuming and methodologically complex academic research particularly important. Namely, it is exceedingly easy (and often misleading) to find cursory evidence of anything on social media because there is so much of it and, by dint of being digital trace data, it is almost by definition optimized for search. Thus, if pundits and journalists want to find evidence of some particular phenomenon, they can probably find a Facebook group, a YouTube channel, or some choice Tweets to illustrate that the phenomenon exists. Even simple counts over time (such as a Google trends timeline) are easy enough to produce. Indeed, a search for any particular type of pathological content can often return millions of results – which appears overwhelming but may be misleading unless one knows the share of total content that is problematic or the likelihood that any given person may have been exposed to it (see, e.g., Siegel, Chapter 4, this volume). The more important questions, such as the relative prevalence of a phenomenon, trends over time, or assessments of causal relationships, however, require much more complex research designs, sustained research efforts, and (often) sophisticated methodological tools. This is where the public-facing research community, and especially academic researchers, have a crucial role to play.

It is worth acknowledging that the social media platforms can, of course, choose to release the results of their own internal research. Indeed, many seminal papers using Facebook data referenced throughout this volume were written or co-authored by internal Facebook researchers. The concern here is that, to the extent that we are reliant on employees of the platforms for research, we have to wrestle with the implications of firms reserving the right to approve papers written by their employees before they are submitted for peer-review. This is a version of what is known in academia as "the file drawer problem," a term used to refer to a concern that positive results are more likely to be published than negative results due to journals' preferences for positive findings, thus presenting a skewed overall view of what we know about a particular topic (Franco, Malhotra, and Simonovits 2014). However, the problem can be even more pernicious when we consider for-profit companies playing the role of gatekeeper, where the assumption would be that research making the company look bad would be more likely to be withheld. To be sure, there are important works that have been published by data scientists working for the platforms that have less than flattering implications for the firms themselves and have contributed significantly to our understanding of how these platforms work. However, if a key goal for the public and policymakers is to learn the impact of a particular new technology/platform/product on relevant outcomes in society (e.g., political polarization), then having access only to published research that has survived vetting from that company is deeply problematic. Imagine letting tobacco companies vet research on the effect of smoking on health, for example.

Moreover, we believe that, in the long term, solving this file drawer problem would benefit the platforms as well. Today, if a firm releases studies that show positive societal benefits from usage of its platform, how can policymakers know if there were fifty other studies the company had run that showed the opposite effect? Thus, as long as the company only selectively releases research, the results from any studies released publicly that paint the company in a positive light are likely to be greeted with skepticism. Conversely, if public-facing researchers have access to data to confirm results published by internal researchers, the public is more likely to trust the firm's research, in general.

A closely related question is whether studies funded by one of the platforms, but not carried out by researchers who are employees of the platforms, would suffer from the same concerns. Clearly, if funding from a platform came with a right of prepublication approval by the platform (or any funder for that matter), it would raise the same type of file drawer problem. Under such conditions, one might also worry that, even if a funder did not have the right of refusal on research publications, the lure of potential future funding might be sufficient to cause researchers to be selective about what they choose to publish. Further, this problem could be equally serious if the platform was providing access to normally inaccessible data. This is similar to the type of problems that can arise in the context of medical research if researchers tailor their work in an effort to make it more likely that a drug manufacturer will fund further research.

One potential way out of this problem would be to establish a rule or norm prohibiting academic researchers from accepting funding from the platforms. However, there are costs to this approach as well – namely, funding for social media research is quite scarce and the platforms have money. Moreover, it is a legitimate question to ask whether, if research is necessary to understand the impact the platforms are having on the world, the platforms ought to be footing the bill for some of this research. (Indeed, the fact that the platforms now hire away a considerable number of graduate students who otherwise might join the academic ranks also begs the question whether they owe some compensation for the university-paid training provided to their employees.) The trade-off is perhaps even starker when considering the question of data access. When money is the barrier to research, it is always hypothetically possible that someone else could supply funding. If data access is the primary barrier to research, then the cost of not cooperating with a platform in some cases will be that the research simply will not take place or, alternatively, that the research will be carried out by employees of the platform.

However tricky these questions are, some common-sense guidelines seem like they would go a long way in addressing this particular challenge:

Academic researchers studying social media or utilizing social media data should not accept funding from the platforms when a condition of the funding is that the platform has the right to approve papers before they are submitted for publication.10

Academic researchers who receive funding from social media platforms should be transparent regarding (i.e., disclose) all funding as part of all relevant publications. (This should also apply to any paid consulting relationships.) Academic researchers who are involved in data-sharing partnerships directly with platforms should be transparent regarding (i.e., disclose)these partnerships (and their conditions, if any) as part of all relevant publications.11

The question of how scholars navigate the issue of accepting funding from the platforms to conduct social media-oriented research will continue to be an important one because this type of research is expensive. Funding for necessary research comes from a limited range of sources – individuals, foundations, corporations, or governments – each with its own set of risks and limitations. (We should take this occasion to reiterate our thanks to the John S. and James L. Knight Foundation for funding this volume.) While we are extremely encouraged by the provision of nontrivial amounts of funding from foundations in recent years in this space and we remain hopeful that governments around the world will prioritize the study of social media and politics for public funding, the question of the extent to which the platforms themselves fund this type of research is not going to disappear. Ideally, independent institutions dedicated to social media research could form a trust that can serve as a repository for funds from these different actors. Doing so might assist in creating financial distance between any funder (corporate or otherwise) and the researcher to prevent both the reality and the appearance of funder control of the research. Moreover, if a diverse group of corporate, foundation, individual, and government funders participate, no single contributor could be said to be sponsoring the research. One promising way to seed such a trust would be with a portion of the recent $5 billion FTC fine levelled against Facebook.

What the future holds

We had hoped to write in this conclusion that the future of social media research is not only certain but bright. Yet we remain quite unsure how the tensions we have identified here will be resolved. Indeed, we see cause for optimism and concern.

Optimists might point, for example, to the development of new technologies of differential privacy that might help us out of the privacy versus access trade- off. These new methods, which have met with mixed success as part of the research effort of Social Science One, usually add statistical noise to datasets in such a way that one could prove mathematically that no particular individual in the dataset can be identified. For some, such methods will not resolve the question about consent for research subjects – that is, those who see a personal dignity interest in data might not be assuaged by the analysis of that data, even when users cannot be re-identified. Others will consider these new datasets to be truly "synthetic" – that is, not composed of real data and therefore not actually requiring the consent of anyone for analysis. Yet, if a platform can demonstrate mathematically that there is little risk of re-identification, many of the concerns about user privacy will be alleviated. The US Census Bureau has adopted this approach and has promised to protect user data in the 2020 Census through a system of differential privacy.[12]

At the same time as researchers are developing ways to protect user privacy in social media datasets, the platforms themselves are moving in directions that might make collection of most user data impossible. After Mark Zuckerberg declared in early 2019 that "the future is private," Facebook announced its plan to tie together several of its products (Instagram, Messenger, and WhatsApp) into a suite of encrypted communications. Given concerns about privacy, doing so is understandable and even desirable from the users' standpoint. However, once the platforms move toward widespread encryption, outside analysis will become particularly difficult. As difficult as it is to conduct social media research on platforms already skittish about sharing data, it becomes even more difficult when the platforms do not have access to the communication itself.

At least for now, encryption makes it theoretically impossible for the platforms themselves to see any of the text of communications, let alone for scholars to get access to these data.13 To be clear, this does not mean that no "data" can be analyzed; it is still possible, for example, to see how often an account is sending out messages and therefore, for example, to make assessments as to whether the account is more likely to be controlled by a human or an algorithm (or even whether a set of accounts appears to be operated by the same actor). Nevertheless, if one wanted to explore whether actors were spreading misinformation or, potentially more worrisome, calls for violence, the platforms would be unable to do so. Members of an encrypted chat group would still have access to the text of messages, though, raising the temptation for analysts to join groups for research purposes.

Indeed, social media researchers, particularly in the developing world, are already confronting difficult ethical questions as to when and how they can participate and observe communication occurring on encrypted platforms such as WhatsApp. Researchers in Africa, Latin America, and South Asia, where WhatsApp has become a dominant social media platform, are adopting the techniques of anthropologists by embedding themselves in the communities they study. Yet, unlike the anthropologists who became part of the communities they studied, social media researchers can lurk on WhatsApp groups outside of view. Even if they announce themselves when they first join, as ethical guidelines require, groups will change over time and participants are unlikely to be aware that their communications are being surveilled. However, to the extent that invitations to join political WhatsApp (or Telegram, Signal, or other encrypted messaging apps) groups are posted publicly,14 there is a legitimate question as to whether people who join such groups should have a reasonable expectation of privacy or not. Herein lies the ethical rub: If such groups are having an important political impact – and misinformation spread on WhatsApp groups has been blamed for interethnic violence in many countries (McLaughlin 2018; Arun 2019) – then scholars are going to want to understand that impact and policymakers are going to need the results of such research to inform public policy. Yet, as long as the data remain encrypted, these types of ethically challenging strategies to recover the content of such conversation will be the easiest – and perhaps only – option available.

In addition to the technological challenges and opportunities posed by developments such as differential privacy and encryption, the field will also continue to wrestle with the policy debates surrounding privacy and access. Indeed, we hope that one contribution of this volume is to help us better understand the parameters of the trade-offs between limiting the spread of users' data out of concern for user-privacy versus the potential scientific progress that can be made when digital trace data are made available for scholarly analysis. On the one hand, the preceding chapters have presented a large amount of knowledge that has entered into the public domain due to the fact that scholars have managed – through a variety of suboptimal processes – to secure access to some social media data during the first decade of the Web 2.0 era (as well as to come up with many creative research designs that do not rely on access to social media data but speak to the political phenomena related to social media). These lessons, insights, and discoveries are testament to the remarkable potential of social media data to drive the accumulation of knowledge and, in particular, knowledge about the effects of the platforms themselves. At the same time, the volume also highlights the costs of restricting access to data: Time and time again, chapters have referred to what we do not yet know. Of course, there are always remaining questions to be asked in social science research, but it is notable how often the authors in this volume cite limitations in access to social media data as an important cause of these research gaps.

Most "state-of-the-field" edited volumes end with a list of important next steps. These often include research questions and aspirations for new types of data collection. For research on the study of social media and democracy, we find ourselves in a somewhat unusual position. The data we need to conduct our research are plentiful – indeed, the amount of data out there is far beyond our wildest dreams as compared to even a decade ago. Even if one is concerned about the generally observational nature of social media data, the opportunities for experiments abound. Although we cannot prove it – which is sort of the point – we are quite confident that there were more experiments on behavioural outcomes carried out by Facebook and Google this year than the sum total of those carried out by members of the American Political Science Association's Experimental Political Science section.

Yet we also live in a time when a whole host of factors outside of the academy can have huge effects on the degree to which scholars can access these data. These factors include, but are not limited to, policy decisions by government authorities such as the US FTC and the European Data Protection Board and internal business-related choices by platforms to restrict access to APIs. We are truly at the mercy of outside forces that do not often elevate the importance of academic research in their decision- making processes.

Taken together, we would like to suggest, then, that there are essentially three paths to ensuring and expanding the continued production of the type of research featured in this volume. The first is to work with the platforms, through efforts like Social Science One, other forms of research partnerships, or by directly lobbying for APIs that are optimized for academic research. The second option is to work independently of the platforms, to try to come up with creative ways to collect social media data that are not dependent on platform cooperation; this could include, for example, deprivation studies (where people agree to go off the platforms for a period of time and then agree to be surveyed by researchers), "citizen science" efforts (where citizens are encouraged to download their own data from the platforms and donate them to academic research), or traditional off-platform survey efforts. Finally, researchers can work with governments to ensure that data access for outside research is properly valued and considered a crucial component of any attempt to regulate social media platforms.15 Owing to the many obstacles facing each of these strategies, our best path forward is to pursue all of them at once.

With these goals in mind, we hope that this volume can alert all the relevant private and public players as to the value of research using social media and digital trace data. At the same time, this book represents a clarion call for making social media data available for research, with results concomitantly released in the public domain, even while recognizing the importance of users' privacy concerns and the legal and business interests of the firms. If we want the public to know more about hate speech online, the relationship between digital media and political polarization, and the pathways of misinformation through modern communication networks, then we need to ensure that scholars who publish in the public domain have access to the data necessary to carry out these studies. Moreover, if we want policymakers to make informed choices in setting policies regarding digital advertising, regulating new media, and addressing harmful content online, they need to be able to draw on rigorous scientific research conducted with the appropriate data. So much of the research reviewed in this volume concerns topics we might not even have imagined fifteen years ago; it is literally cutting-edge research. Yet it is also research that informs crucial questions of public policy, meaning that the failure to move this research agenda forward will have consequences that reverberate far beyond academia. We hope this concluding chapter, as well as the entire volume, represents a first step on the path toward a future of greater understanding of the challenges social media presents for democracy and, by consequence, a future with better informed policies to address those challenges.

REFERENCES

Arun, C. (2019). On WhatsApp, rumours, and lynchings. Economic & Political Weekly,54(6), 30–35.

Balkin, J. (2016). Information fiduciaries and the First Amendment. U.C. Davis Law Review, 49, 1183–1284.

The Economist. (2020). Special report: Are data more like oil or sunlight? The Economist, February 20. www.economist.com/special-report/2020/02/20/are-data-more-like-oil-or-sunlight

European Data Protection Supervisor. (2020). A Preliminary Opinion on Data Protection and Scientific Research. https://edps.europa.eu/sites/edp/files/publication/20-01- 06_opinion_research_en.pdf

Evans, G., & King, G. (2019). Statistically valid inferences from differentially private data releases. Working paper. http://j.mp/38NrmRW

FTC (Federal Trade Commission). (2019). FTC imposes $5 billion penalty andsweeping new privacy restrictions on Facebook. Federal Trade Commission press release, July 24. www.ftc.gov/news-events/press-releases/2019/07/ftc-imposes-5-billion-penalty-sweeping-new-privacy-restrictions

Franco, A., Malhotra, N., & Simonovits, G. (2014). Publication bias in the social sciences: Unlocking the file drawer. Science, 345(6203), 1502–1505.

Freelon, D. (2020). Computational research in the post-API age. Political Communication. Gidney, C., & Ekera, M. (2019). How to factor 2048 bit RSA integers in 8 hours using20 million noisy qubits. arXiv.org. https://arxiv.org/abs/1905.09749

King, G., & Persily, N. (2019). A new model for industry–academic partnerships. PS: Political Science & Politics, 1–7. https://doi.org/10.1017/S1049096519001021

Kofi Annan Commission on Elections and Democracy in the Digital Age. (2020). Protecting Electoral Integrity in the Digital Age. Report. www.kofiannanfoundation.org/app/ uploads/2020/01/f035dd8e-kaf_kacedda_report_2019_web.pdf

McLaughlin, T. (2018). How WhatsApp fuels fake news and violence in India. Wired, December 12. www.wired.com/story/how-whatsapp-fuels-fake-news-and-violence- in-india/

Munger, K. (2019). Temporal validity. OSF, September 2. osf.io/3mnzu

Narayanan, D., & Ananth, V. (2018). How the mobile phone is shaping to be BJP's most important weapon in elections. Economic Times, August 23. https://economictimes.indiatimes.com/news/politics-and-nation/how-the-mobile-phone- is-shaping-to-be-bjps-most-important-weapon-in-elections/articleshow/65508743.cms

PTI. (2019). 2019 polls: BJP to form chain of WhatsApp groups to strengthen communication between party workers. Economic Times, December 23. https:// economictimes.indiatimes.com/news/politics-and-nation/2019-polls-bjp-to-form- chain-of-whatsapp-groups-to-strengthen-communication-between-party-workers/articleshow/67219816.cms

Stigler Center. (2019). Digital Platforms and Concentration. Stigler Center for the Study of the Economy and the State. https://promarket.org/wp-content/uploads/2018/04/ Digital-Platforms-and-Concentration.pdf

Warren Democrats. (2020). Fighting Digital Disinformation. Plan. Warren Democratswebsite. https://elizabethwarren.com/plans/fighting-digital-disinformation

FOOTNOTE

1. Indeed, Kevin Munger has argued that, because of the speed at which the underlying architecture of major social media platforms and networks change, we should – in addition to tackling new unanswered questions – be revisiting questions that we think have already been answered in order to ensure the temporal validity of the original findings (Munger 2019).
2. Twitter does deserve praise for its recent efforts to make data produced by foreign influence campaigns available for scholarly research after having removed these posts from the platform; see "Information Operations" in the Twitter Transparency Report. https://transparency.twitter .com/en/information-operations.html.

3. Disclosure: Social Science One is co-chaired by Gary King and one of us (Persily); the other one of us (Tucker) chairs an advisory committee on disinformation and election integrity, and several of the authors appearing in this volume are also involved with the effort.
4. APIs, or Application Programming Interfaces, are tools by which data produced online can be directly delivered to external (or, for that matter, internal) researchers without, for example, having to actually render a web page. They offer much greater speed than the alternative means of collecting social media data – which is scraping the web page directly – and provide the platforms with a degree of control over what can and cannot be downloaded, as well as how much data can be collected within a given time period. Of course, platforms can also choose to charge for access to APIs, as well as to make scraping information from web pages directly against its terms of service.
5. One potentially valuable use for a portion of this and similar fines would be to support indepen- dent research on the impact of the platforms on society.
6. Moreover, such questions will be studied only if the platforms choose to devote corporate resources to trying to answer these sorts of questions in the first place. In most cases, these data will not be analyzed to answer questions to advance scientific knowledge but rather to bolster efforts to maximize profits. To be clear, we do not and should not expect the platforms to substitute a public mission for their economic interests. Instead, we seek to point out that the use of these data for societal good – such as understanding the impact of social media on democracy, the goal of this volume – by necessity requires those outside the platforms to have access to these data.
7. Indeed, a recent issue of The Economist features an entire special report on the new data-driven economy, with a section of the report devoted to questions around data access (see The Economist 2020).
8. We thank Sam Gill of the Knight Foundation for suggesting this line of reasoning in response to having read an earlier draft of this chapter.
9. Again, we thank Sam Gill for suggesting this point.
10. To be clear, we are referring to unconstrained rights of refusal to allow publication. We are not suggesting, for example, that platforms that have provided data to researchers under particular conditions (e.g., that publications only release aggregated as opposed to individual-level data) do not have the right to ensure compliance with terms of data-use agreements.
11. We are grateful to the Knight Foundation and the Social Science Research Council (SSRC) for convening a meeting in the fall of 2018 – in which one of us (Tucker) served as a co-convener and the other (Persily) was a participant – where these questions and potential guidelines were explicitly discussed.
12. Many questions remain to be answered as to the appropriateness of existing statistical methods for analyzing differentially private data, as well as how fast new methods for doing can be developed and validated. See, for example, Evans and

King (2019), as well as accompanying software available at https://github.com/georgieevans/PrivacyUnbiased.

13. We say "at least for now" because the rise of quantum computers may challenge conventional understanding of the impenetrability of encrypted data; see Gidney and Ekera (2019).
14. See, e.g., Narayanan and Ananth (2018); PTI (2019).
15. We are encouraged by the fact that some policymakers are beginning to recognize the importance of data access for independent research. Indeed, in Elizabeth Warren's "Fighting Digital Disinformation" plan, she included the following component: "Open up data for research: Research by academics and watchdog organizations has provided the public with important insights into how disinformation spreads online, but these efforts are greatly limited by social media platforms' unwillingness to share data. Platforms like Facebook currently provide only limited and inconsistent access. Research can help evaluate the extent of, and patterns within, disinformation on social media platforms. It can also offer the public an objective evaluation of how the features that platforms offer, including those that allow for rapid dissemination of content, contribute to disinformation. Social media companies must provide an open and consistent application programming interface (API) to researchers" (Warren Democrats 2020).

INDEX

www.ingramcontent.com/pod-product-compliance
Lightning Source LLC
LaVergne TN
LVHW062111200926
848484LV00007B/1642